DAVID FELLMA[N]
Vilas Professor of Political
University of Wiscon[sin]
ADVISORY EDITOR TO DODD, MEA[D]

Ideologies and
Modern Politics

Ideologies
and
Modern
Politics

Reo M. Christenson
Alan S. Engel
Dan N. Jacobs
Mostafa Rejai
Herbert Waltzer

ALL OF MIAMI UNIVERSITY
OXFORD, OHIO

Dodd, Mead & Company
NEW YORK   1971   TORONTO

ISBN   0–396–06311–X
Library of Congress Catalog Card Number: 79–143291

Printed in the United States of America

Preface

Ideologies and Modern Politics is designed as a supplementary book for introductory courses in political science (or in American government, a course title that may mislead a bit), as well as courses in modern political ideologies.

We have sought to cover not only the conventional ideological themes—descriptions of traditional democratic and totalitarian ideologies—but have also dealt with related areas usually overlooked by authors in this field. Thus, we have included a chapter on ideology as a general political phenomenon, another on guerrilla communism, and still another on extremism of the right and left. A concluding chapter presents contrasting views on the "end of ideology" debate which has roiled the academic waters in recent years. Hopefully, then, the major facets of the current ideological landscape have come in for recognition.

Ideologies originate and develop in response to unique political, economic, and social circumstances. Thus, it seemed fitting to incorporate considerable historical background into this book, believing that such information would illuminate particular ideologies in an essential way. We were also interested in pursuing the concrete impact of ideologies in various political states—some of us wrestling with that perennial question, does ideology shape events or vice versa? A brief book covering such a vast subject could not purport to deal exhaustively with its themes. Rather, we have sketched some broad outlines, filled in some significant details, and left ample opportunity for the classroom instructor to add his expertise to our skeletal structure. We have sought to combine contemporaneity, readability, insight, and objectivity, while aware that subjective preferences are never entirely absent from any book which treats the ideas men live by.

Each of our five authors has written specific portions of the book. Herbert Waltzer, the chapters on Political Ideology and Democracy; Mostafa Rejai, the chapter on Guerrilla Communism; Alan Engel, the chapters on

Totalitarian Ideologies, and Fascism and Naziism, as well as the section on the Radical Right; Dan Jacobs, the chapter on Soviet Communism and the section on the New Left; Reo Christenson, the chapters on Democratic Capitalism and Democratic Socialism. Professors Rejai and Waltzer, in that order, shared authorship of the last chapter. While each author received useful comments and criticisms from his coauthors, each assumes full responsibility for his chapters and his alone. As befits normally contentious academics, we disagreed vigorously (but amiably) from time to time, sometimes taking comfort from the fact that the benighted author who rejected our cogent views must ultimately face his critics alone.

As will be readily apparent to the reader, five authors possess five quite different writing styles. Reo Christenson attempted to exercise general editorial oversight (as well as raising substantive questions from time to time) but did not undertake the futile task of establishing a common literary style. "The style is the man" and it is hoped that the readers will find the stylistic variations to be refreshing.

To our wives and children, we are only moderately indebted, since writing a few chapters was not that disruptive of our households. To our former chairman, James R. Woodworth, we hope his cooperation with the process of academic gestation has mysteriously proved rewarding. To Jean West and her daughter Joanne, our appreciation for work well and promptly done. To Virginia Hans, for a superior job of editing. Finally, we are individually responsible for any errors of fact or judgment appearing in our respective chapters.

REO M. CHRISTENSON
ALAN S. ENGEL
DAN N. JACOBS
MOSTAFA REJAI
HERBERT WALTZER

Contents

Chapter 1

Political Ideology: Belief and Action in the Arenas of Politics

This book examines the major political ideologies of our time—their origins and development, doctrines and institutional patterns, consequences and prospects for the future. Since the purpose, necessarily, is simply to whet the appetite—to provide a foundation for thought and discussion—more questions, perhaps, will be raised than answered. What, indeed, is the role of ideology—religious, scientific, political—in the life of man? What is the origin of ideology? What is its nature?

Man has the need and ability to respond innovatively to his environment. For his survival and well-being in a hostile natural environment, he requires material satisfactions and social fellowship, security and self-respect in a world that is reasonably orderly and predictable. To satisfy these requirements, he has sought to understand, organize, and control his physical and societal worlds. Thus, he has provided himself with tools and weapons, extracted from his physical environment the commodities of necessity and luxury, built cities as refuge-fortresses against nature and man, formed human societies, produced a science and technology to probe and master nature. He has, in brief, created *ideas, inventions,* and *institutions* to groom the earth and make it habitable.

The level and complexity of man's intellectual-emotional structure uniquely qualify him to understand and order his natural and societal universe. He gathers information which he systematically organizes and stores. He thinks logically and generalizes—that is, abstracts and conceptualizes. He invents complex languages and communicates with his fellows.

1

He is purposive and adaptive, establishing goals for himself and devising means for their attainment. These purposes are complex, varied, of broad scope, and durable—extending beyond the lifetime of generations. Man discovers, innovates, and invents in the political as well as the other aspects of his life. He chooses how his life and society will be ordered, and he manufactures the means to achieve that order.

Man, however, is entrapped as well as freed by his nature and his creations. He is dependent upon the science and technology that have liberated him from nature's harsh constraints. He is enmeshed in the complex relationships of power and dependence that exist in the society that has freed him from mere solitary grubbing for existence. Finally, he is unable intellectually and emotionally to manage the ambiguities and tensions of life in a universe not yet rendered intelligible, predictable, purposeful, and hopeful by his systems of religious, scientific, and political beliefs.

Focusing on the particular concern of this book, what ideas and beliefs are to be found in the arenas of politics? Society is a distributive system for the allocation of scarce resources—wealth, status, and power—and these resources, except in the yet unfulfilled promises of utopians, are distributed unequally. In every society and time, there are the rich and the poor, the privileged and the underprivileged, the powerful and the less powerful. Consequently, man seeks an explanation of his lot, a guide to his conduct, a basis of self-identification, and the promise of a better life through political ideologies, which explain and justify existing or proposed allocation systems for society.

Indeed, since the end of the eighteenth century political ideologies have been classified from "left" to "right" by their distributive formulas—their advocacy of societal orders that are egalitarian or elitist in their allocations of wealth, status, and power. (The terms "left" and "right" appear to have originated during the First French Republic, when—in the summer of 1789 —the National Assembly met in Paris. Three political groupings were represented—conservatives opposed to change and any diminution of the powers of the monarchy or privileges of the nobility, liberals favoring representative government, and radicals advocating equality and liberty. In the horseshoe shaped amphitheater in which the Assembly convened, the conservatives sat to the right of the speaker, the radicals to the left, and the liberals in the center.) [1]

Political ideology is a fundamental of politics; it is a guiding, supporting, and restraining factor in the political behavior of individuals, groups, and

[1] For a discussion of the inadequacy of these terms to describe contemporary political ideologies and movements, see Kenneth K. Krogh, "Needed: New Political Labels," *Saturday Review,* XLIII (December 3, 1960), 17–19, 63–64.

nations. "Prior to politics, beneath it, enveloping it, restricting it, conditioning it . . . is ideology." [2] To some degree we are all ideologues, consciously or unconsciously. We must and do choose among ideologies, and our political behavior is influenced by them. As David Riesman says, "Rejecting ideology, like rejecting abstraction or being sincere and natural, is more easily said than done. There is always a tacit ideology." [3] In providing this ideology, the political ideologist plays a role not unlike that of the novelist, "paint[ing] pictures in words of a political life that we might choose, or that we are now leading but do not fully comprehend. He records his reflections upon politics to help us to decide how we are to live. As Plato observed, that task is no mean one." [4]

Ideology: the Meaning of a Word

In our quest to understand the major ideologies that vie in our time for the allegiance of men, we must agree on the meaning of *ideology*. This task is more difficult than it may seem because the word has become an epithet. The concept behind the word is a complex one, and there is considerable controversy among scholars as to what ideology is—and is not. While the major theories of ideology are treated in a subsequent section of this chapter, it would be useful at this juncture to examine some of the problems that obstruct agreement on the meaning of "ideology," to state our definition of the word, and to distinguish ideology from other forms of political thought.

Ideology as Epithet

A bad odor surrounds the word *ideology*. It suffers from ill-repute, and, to some, is identified with hated totalitarian beliefs and is characterized as false, delusory, and "highfalutin propaganda." The origins of this anti-ideology syndrome run deep in history.[5] The word *"idéologie"* was coined by the French philosopher Antoine Destutt de Tracy during the French

[2] Robert A. Dahl, *A Preface to Democratic Theory* (Chicago: University of Chicago Press, 1956), p. 132.

[3] David Riesman, "Intellectuals and Discontented Classes," *The Radical Right*, ed. Daniel Bell (Garden City, New York: Doubleday Anchor, 1964), p. 156, n. 15.

[4] David G. Smith, "Political Science and Political Theory," *American Political Science Review*, LI (September, 1957), 746.

[5] For discussion of the history of the term "ideology" see: George Lichtheim, *The Concept of Ideology and Other Essays* (New York: Random House, 1967), pp. 3–46; Joseph S. Roucek, "A History of the Concept of Ideology," *Journal of the History of Ideas*, V (October, 1944), 479–488; J. W. Stern, "Beginning Ideology," *South Atlantic Quarterly*, LV (April, 1956), 163–170.

Revolution; and its original meaning, "science of ideas" (the study of the origins, evolution, and nature of ideas), remains today as one of the common dictionary definitions of ideology. A pejorative connotation, however, quickly attached to the word in the early years of the nineteenth century, when Napoleon used it as a derogative. He denounced as *"idéologues"* the liberal intellectuals of the Institut de France, who previously had promoted his rise to power but whose republican and antireligious ideas he now regarded as a threat to his church-supported absolutism. Fearful of their challenge to the authorities of church and state and of their advocacy of radical reforms, he forbade the teaching of moral and political science at the Institut and, in a famous speech in December, 1812, decried their ideas as abstract, false, and irresponsible speculation—as "the dark metaphysics" of ideology which compares poorly with "the knowledge of the heart and lessons of history." [6] This negative connotation of ideology as abstract, utopian, and factitious—not derived from the human spirit or experience—also has persisted as a dictionary meaning of "ideology."

Wide circulation has also been given to the definitions of the word offered by Karl Marx and by the sociologist Karl Mannheim (whose theories of ideology will be discussed later). Marx viewed ideology as the ideas of the ruling (capitalist) class, seeking to rationalize and justify the prevailing order (capitalism) and their privileged position in it. Mannheim, in a similar view, labeled as "ideology" the conservative, interest-based and biased ideas of the dominant class in society. This notion of ideology as a self-serving set of ideas designed to promote the interests of an advantaged or ruling class continues to have major currency.

Finally, however, in our own time—in which the political potentialities of ideology have been most fully recognized and exploited—establishment of the individious connotation of the word owes much to Hitler and his propaganda minister Goebbels, to Stalin and his "agitprop," and later to Mao Tse-tung and his "cultural revolution."

Difficulties in reaching agreement on the meaning of "ideology" also stem from people's tendency to approach the concept from a "we-they," "cops and robbers" dichotomy: we have a political philosophy, they have an ideology; we have cherished values, they have dogma; we have founding fathers and leaders, they have false prophets and tyrants; we are steadfast and true to our principles, they are fanatics. Within this frame of reference, "ideology" is defined as "a system of ideas that is empirically false and morally wrong; designed to delude, corrupt, and enslave." In this sense, ideology is to philosophy what superstition is to religion. The odium of

[6] Maurice Cranston and Sanford A. Lakoff, eds., *A Glossary of Political Ideas* (New York: Basic Books, 1969), p. 315.

ideology thus derives from the tendency to selective perception and self-protective interpretation: to see and portray *ourselves* as guided by knowledge and reason, and motivated by the highest idealism; and to see and portray *others*—especially those we label as "enemies"—as misguided by error and emotion, driven by base self-interest and power-lust.

This penchant for labeling ideology as "evil" is prevalent in the United States. Americans see themselves as enjoying a political system called by the friendly name "democracy"—not one based on an ideology characterized by the sinister hissing sound of "ism." They have an economic system they call "free enterprise" (or at worst "a capitalist system," but rarely "capitalism"), and respond negatively to the name (but not some of the programs) of that "ism" called "socialism." Americans thus tend to believe that democracy is not an ideology, and that ideological allegiance is unbecoming to free men. The rulers of Nazi Germany, and of Communist Russia and China, have distrusted ideologically uncommitted men, and have sought to eliminate ideological heresy by purge and terror. Ought not we, then, to be wary of ideological commitment? The pragmatic, piecemeal, problem-solving, reformist approach—not one dependent on doctrinaire ideological considerations—is the American approach to political issues. American self-perception is that of intellectually free men who see the world realistically through eyes undistorted by ideological prisms, of politically free men who do not sell their political souls for a dish of ideological pottage—who choose leaders and face specific issues, who vote for the man and the program. They see their opponents, on the other hand, as intellectual prisoners of ideologies that falsify the human condition and seduce with promises of millennia that are always around another corner, as faceless political *castrati* who trade their freedom for the security of ideological belief—whose only political right is the duty to fill arenas and squares and punctuate the speeches of their false prophets with "Sieg Heil" and "Du-ce, Du-ce, Du-ce."

To so define ideology, while perhaps psychically satisfying, serves no purpose useful to scholarship and understanding. If one man's philosophy is another man's ideology, and vice versa—if to a democrat communism is a political ideology and democracy a political philosophy, and vice versa—then definition and understanding of ideology are impossible.

Political Ideology: A Working Definition

Political ideology is a belief system that explains and justifies a preferred political order for society, either existing or proposed, and offers a strategy (processes, institutional arrangements, programs) for its attainment. It is "a verbal image of the good society and the chief means of constructing such a society." [7] It offers "a reasonably coherent body of ideas concerning practical means of how to change, reform (or maintain) a political order. . . ." [8] Thus, political ideology includes a set of basic assumptions, both normative and empirical, about the nature and purposes of man and society which serve to explain and judge the human condition, and to guide the development of or preserve a preferred political order.

The creators and advocates of political ideology, most importantly, seek belief and action. They seek commitment to the ideology and its consequences: followers who identify their lives with it, accept its tenets, and work loyally for it. Ideology usually exercises a strong emotional appeal (or repulsion) for those who accept (or oppose) it. The power of an ideology derives "from the feeling it arouses or action it incites" [9]—from the human energies it unleashes. Political ideology, therefore, is aimed at directly influencing political behavior. A system of ideas "ceases to be an intellectual abstraction and becomes an active social agent, or an ideology, when it is applied to concrete situations and becomes a guide to action." [10] As ideas-in-action political ideologies are attached to corporate political bodies— organized movements, groups, parties. They are doctrines espoused to win belief and bring men to accept or reject their political lot, to man the palace steps in defense of the existing order or march in revolution against it.

How do we distinguish political ideology from other forms of political thought? From creeds, doctrines, programs, and platforms and the other words commonly used to denote political ideas active in the arenas of politics? [11] Indeed, several factors differentiate political ideology as a variant form of political thought: its greater comprehensiveness of scope, its explicit formulation of basic premises, its more systematic integration around one or a few preeminent beliefs (e.g., equality, ethnic purity and superiority), its greater insistence upon active commitment and consensus of belief, and its association with an organization intended to realize the ideology.

It was observed that the terms "political philosophy" and "political

[7] Anthony Downs, *An Economic Theory of Democracy* (New York: Harper, 1957), p. 96.

[8] Carl J. Friedrich, *Man and His Government: An Empirical Theory of Politics* (New York: McGraw-Hill, 1963), p. 90.

[9] Harold D. Lasswell and Abraham Kaplan, *Power and Society: A Framework for Political Inquiry,* paperbound ed. (New Haven: Yale University Press, 1950), p. 104.

[10] Zbigniew K. Brzezinski, *Ideology and Power in Soviet Politics,* paperbound ed. (New York: Frederick A. Praeger, 1962), p. 97.

[11] For an interesting attempt to make these distinctions see Edward Shils, "The Concept of Ideology," in *The International Encyclopedia of the Social Sciences,* ed. David L. Sills (New York: Macmillan and Free Press, 1968), VII, pp. 66–76.

ideology" are used as value antonyms. In a contradictory manner they also —with another related term, "political theory"—are used interchangeably as synonyms. With easy and often unconscious frequency, in order to avoid the monotony of word repetition, one is substituted for another as an equivalent word symbol. For example, the phrases "communist philosophy," "communist theory," "communist ideology," and "communism" are employed interchangeably. While these terms belong to the same *genre* of political thought, however, they have quite separate meanings and represent different kinds of political idea systems. Brief definitions in more precise language of "political philosophy" and "political theory" might help clarify the distinctions.

Political philosophy has been defined as a "disinterested search for the principles of the good state and the good society." [12] The political philosopher seeks to identify the nature and scope of things political, and to find ultimate explanation for political man and his political society. At its core, political philosophy seeks to answer the question: What is the best form of government? It seeks to clarify and prescribe the politico-ethical values having the greatest moral validity. The political philosopher is not so much interested in explaining how men *do* behave in politics as he is in recommending how they *ought* to behave. The political philosopher relies primarily on deduction; his primary appeal is to reason. His conclusions about the ideal political system and right political conduct are logically derived from basic politico-ethical value premises which cannot be empirically proven true or false. The political philosopher seeks "to mould the totality of political phenomena to accord with some vision of Good that lies outside the political order." [13]

Political theory, on the other hand, has been defined as a "disinterested search for knowledge of political and social reality." [14] Taking this definition a step further, a "political theory," as the term is currently employed by political scientists, then, is a set of empirically validated, logically ordered, and functionally related propositions about the actual political behavior of men and societies. The political theorist develops generalizations about the existential political world that are testable and verifiable through observable data. He is not primarily concerned with questions of political morality and an ideal political order. He is interested in actual political behavior and in developing generalizations (theory) that are increasingly more com-

[12] Andrew Hacker, *Political Theory: Philosophy, Ideology, Science* (New York: Macmillan, 1961), p. 5.
[13] Sheldon S. Wolin, *Politics and Vision: Continuity and Innovation in Western Political Thought* (Boston: Little, Brown, 1960), p. 19.
[14] Hacker, *op. cit.,* p. 5.

prehensive in their explanatory powers and, therefore, increasingly more powerful in enabling men to understand, predict, and control political behavior. Some scholars refer to political philosophy as "normative or prescriptive" theory, and to political theory as "empirical or descriptive" theory. For clarity, and to reserve the word "theory" for empirically based generalizations about political reality, the more distinctive terms "political philosophy" and "political theory" are used in this discussion.

This is not to suggest that the distinctions among philosophy, theory, and ideology are absolute. Indeed, quite the contrary is true. Political philosophy includes the empirical propositions common to political theory, and the ideas of political philosophers (Hegel, Nietzsche) have served as the foundations of political ideologies (German National Socialism). Political theory requires inquiry into and understanding of the ideologies and other political ideas men hold that guide their behavior, while theorists draw upon the insights and observations of philosophers and ideologists. Finally, political ideology contains both normative and empirical propositions from political philosophy and political theory.

Questions of definition are often difficult, and the term "ideology" poses added problems both because of the loose use of the word and the connotations that have adhered to it. The extended description offered by the political scientist Carl J. Friedrich therefore is a useful orientation to the study of the major contemporary political ideologies.

Ideologies are action-related systems of ideas. They typically contain a program and a strategy for its realization, and their essential function is to unite organizations which are built around them. It is confusing and fails to provide the opportunity for political analysis, to call any system of ideas an ideology, such as the philosophy of Aristotle or the theology of the Old Testament. Such systems of ideas *may* provide the *basis* for an ideology, but only after being related to action in a specific sense and for a specific situation. Ideologies are sets of ideas related to the existing political and social order and intended either to change it or to defend it . . . what makes them (*ideas*) "ideology" is their function in the body politic. The ideology is a set of ideas which unites a party or other group for effective participation in political life.[15]

Ideology: Characteristics and Functions

As significant factors influencing the behavior of political systems, regimes, and men, political ideologies have substantive characteristics which contribute to their political functions. However, in examining the characteristics of ideology, it should be remembered that while they are typical,

[15] Friedrich, *op. cit.* (above, n. 8), p. 89.

they are not necessarily manifested uniformly in all political ideologies. Each ideology is unique in its "mix." Similarly, ideologies typically perform certain functions but not in precisely the same way, or with the same priorities for all categories of persons in all political contexts. The functioning of a particular ideology varies in terms of the ideology itself, the political system, the societal environment, the groups of primary appeal, and the issues and circumstances of the time. Nevertheless, the general characteristics and functions of political ideology can be catalogued. The political scientist David Easton offers a good introductory and summary description:

> [*Ideologies are*] articulated sets of ideals, ends, and purposes, which help members of the system to interpret the past, explain the present, and offer a vision for the future. Thereby they describe the aims for which some members feel political power ought to be used and its limits. They may be deceptive myths about political life; they may be realistic appraisals and sincere aspirations. But they have the potential, because they are articulated as a set of ethically infused ideals, to capture the imagination. From a manipulative or instrumental point of view they may be interpreted as categories of thought to corral the energies of men; from an expressive point of view we may see them as ideals capable of rousing and inspiring men to action thought to be related to their achievement. Values of this kind, consisting of articulated ethical interpretations and principles that set forth the purposes, organization, and boundaries of political life, I shall describe by their usual name, *ideologies*.[16]

The Characteristics of Ideology

"*Ideologies arise in conditions of crisis* and in sections of society to whom the hitherto prevailing outlook has become unacceptable." [17] The human disposition to ideological construction and belief surfaces when people strongly perceive and feel that they are being neglected or exploited under the existing order, or threatened in their status by fundamental changes occurring in society. When their felt needs and purposes are not being satisfied under the existing order, they find the dominant (or emerging) ideology inadequate to explain their experiences, justify their condition, or guide their conduct. In short, they do not accept it as authoritative in defining what is tolerable and possible in their lives. During these periods of intense social strain those disgruntled by the past or fearful of the future turn to emergent or resurgent ideologies, in which they find the vision of a better life— whether in a liberal call for progressive reform or a conservative defense of a traditional order, in a revolutionary manifesto of radical transformation or a reactionary yearning to return to a "golden" past.

[16] *A Systems Analysis of Political Life* (New York: John Wiley, 1965), p. 290.
[17] Shils, *op. cit.* (above, n. 11), p. 69, *italics mine.*

Ideology has a broad but varying scope. It ranges, in its horizontal dimension, from partial explanations to comprehensive "world-views" (*weltanschauung*). In part, the comprehensiveness of an ideology depends upon its proposed scope of power. A totalitarian ideology, for example, which calls for public authority to regulate virtually all significant aspects of life, will be more comprehensive than a democratic ideology.

In its vertical dimension, *ideology includes several strata of thought and belief,* ranging from sophisticated complexes of ideas to simplified slogans and symbols that express these ideas in forms suitable for mass communication and understanding. Ideology, in other words, exists on varying bases and produces varying degrees of understanding and acceptance. Attachments to ideological movements may be based on intellectual, emotional, or interest-serving attractions; or opportunities for personal ambition or social fellowship; or on the magnetism of a charismatic leader. Ideologues have militant and doctrinaire fanatics, faithful and active supporters, and passive acquiescents. There are conscious and articulate ideologies, plus much more numerous ones whose ideological beliefs are vague, rudimentary, below the level of consciousness, or nonexistent.

In discussing the bases of voting behavior, the political scientist V. O. Key, Jr., observed, "Ideology, in the sense of a systematic ordering of specific issues in terms of general beliefs, seems to be limited to a small fraction of the electorate." [18] However, while the explicit ideology is propagated by an influential and critical minority, the political behavior of people is still to some degree guided by ideologically based or derived attitudes and habits of response. Robert Lane, another student of political behavior, after probing to discover the ideology of the "ordinary" American, concluded that "the common man has a set of emotionally charged political beliefs. . . . Of course, there are differences between the articulated, differentiated, well-developed political arguments put forward by informed and conscious Marxists or Fascists or liberal democrats on the one hand, and the loosely structured, unreflective statements of the common man . . . [and] occasionally it is useful to distinguish between these two varieties. In these few cases I distinguish between the 'forensic' ideologies of the conscious ideologist and the 'latent' ideologies of the common man." [19]

While mass publics may lack articulated ideologies, be unable to grasp the abstractions of ideologies or relate specific events to ideological principles, they nevertheless are linked to ideology through ideological *carriers*

[18] *Public Opinion and American Democracy* (New York: Alfred A. Knopf, 1961), p. 49.
[19] *Political Ideology: Why the Common Man Believes What He Does* (New York: Free Press, 1962), pp. 15–16.

—political elites (in political parties, interest groups, education, communications media)—from whom mass publics accept leadership and guidance, and from whom they take their ideological cues. These carriers, in turn, use the simplified principles, slogans, and symbols of ideology to mobilize and manipulate mass publics. Finally, it should be remembered that the manifest "ideological-ness" of people is variable, not constant; people become more ideological when there are public or private crises, and when they perceive as intolerable the substantial gaps between the reality and the possibility of their condition. Ideology, therefore, is a political resource by which men exercise power over men.

Ideology is a systematic pattern of political thought. An ideology is huckstered in the market of politics, not as haphazard and scattered ideas, but as an ordered arrangement of pertinent and logically related ideas offering an explanation and vision of human destiny. Moreover, an *ideology is self-contained and self-sufficient.* It is a pattern of ideas integrated around one or a few basic premises, containing its own (often self-fulfilling) rules of change and development. Though it often offers a simple picture of consistency and order nowhere present in complex reality, it may not be internally consistent—frequently embodying contradictory and incompatible propositions, reflecting the ambivalence of human nature and the capacity of men to compartmentalize their thinking and engage in what George Orwell called "doublethink." Following in part from this simplicity, *ideology is abstract*—not a picture of reality but a model derived from perceptions of reality. It isolates certain features of political life as salient and crucial, and applies a few ideas to explain and prescribe political behavior, subsuming the details under them. In general, therefore, *ideology tends to be reductionist,* offering general and simple explanations and recommendations that are rather easily grasped.

Ideology includes both empirical and normative elements—empirical assertions that certain conditions exist, and normative assertions that a certain political order is to be preferred. It is a variable blend of fact and value, diagnosis and prescription. In an ideology, "belief in the set of values is associated with the acceptance of certain descriptive propositions of an explanatory or causal sort." [20] These ideas about what is and what ought to be in politics are related and mutually reinforcing.

Ideology tends to be exclusive, absolute, and universal. Each ideology, in terms of its own logic and evidence, claims to embody, exclusively, the "true" principles of progress and justice. Thus, ideology is not subject to bargain or compromise; its rules and standards of conduct are not negoti-

[20] Vernon Van Dyke, *Political Science: A Philosophical Analysis* (Stanford, Calif.: Stanford University Press, 1960), p. 173.

able. Ideology tends, rather, to present a dichotomy of friendly and hostile forces, permitting a ready discrimination between friends and foes. Finally, although ideology emerges from and is applied to specific and unique political contexts, it nevertheless is framed in universal terms. In part, this is a result of ideology objectifying personal, group, and national interests and goals, legitimizing them as being "good and true" for all men. The corps of believers speak and act on behalf of the much larger social stratum, society, or species. Ideology, therefore, regardless of its content and program of implementation, assumes a humanitarian posture. Robert Michels observed that no ideological movement "fails before starting its march for the conquest of power, to declare solemnly to the world that its aim is to redeem, not so much itself as the whole of humanity, from the yoke of a tyrannical minority, and to substitute for the old and inequitable regime a new reign of justice." [21]

Ideology is a persuasive argument designed normally to motivate active involvement. It is intended not merely to inform but to persuade and to generate emotion. Ideologists seek the commitment that transforms the life of the individual, group, and society—and as a consequence transforms the lives of the individuals, groups, and societies around them. The ultimate power of an ideology lies not in its empirical or logical proofs but in its ability to inspire and sustain belief and action. (However, ideologies vary from those that are psychologically possessive and exhausting, demanding total passion and engagement, to those that, by recognizing private spheres of thought and action, are less demanding.) *Ideology is millennial,* transcending the present reality and offering the promise of the best (or, if more modest, best possible) world. Machiavelli warned his prince, "Great expenditures must be compensated not only by great reward but by the certainty of reward." [22] Because of its polemic and inspirational attributes, *ideology tends to be excessive.* It is predestined not fully to succeed; like More's *Utopia,* it is something we "wish rather than expect to see followed." Perhaps it is our vision not of the "probable" but of the "not impossible." The Italian political scientist Giovanni Sartori has said that ideology as an *"ought* is not meant to take the place of *is.* It is meant to be a counterweight, which' is a completely different matter. The *ought* is always excessive, it smacks of *hubris* . . . ideals are not made to be converted into facts, but to challenge them." [23]

Ideology is personalized and scripturalized, having its heroes (founding fathers and great interpreters, charismatic leaders and martyrs), sacred

[21] *Political Parties* (New York: Hearst's International Library, 1915), p. 15.
[22] *The Discourses,* I.
[23] *Democratic Theory* (New York: Frederick A. Praeger, 1965), pp. 64–65.

documents (manifestos, declarations, constitutions), and rituals (pledges, anthems, salutes, holidays). *Ideology is programmatic,* involving strategies which, if carried out, would alter (purportedly) the goals and ordering of society.

Ideology undergoes development but is resistant to fundamental change. Initially, one powerful and creative mind (Marx) may lay the foundations of an ideology, but others (Lenin, Trotsky, Stalin, Mao) add to and interpret it. Ideologists offer their wares as complete and authoritative; they resist explicit revision of their handiwork. Changes in ideology, therefore, tend to come slowly and painfully; and ideology, depending upon the relative closedness or openness of its structure, either exhibits immobility or lags behind changes in societal conditions. Thus, while ideologies may change in content and application, they often are subject to intense conflicts (orthodoxy vs. revisionism) over the propriety of and need for change, as well as to tortuous interpretations by those claiming to interpret correctly and adhere most closely to the revered original formulation (and formulator) of the ideology.

However resistant to innovation, all ideologies undergo development, as the evolutions of the specific ideologies discussed will reveal. Political ideologies, like all systems of belief (scientific and nonscientific), are never wholly congruent with reality or completely adequate to explain experience. Ideologies have ambiguities, inconsistencies, and gaps which generate attempts at clarification. Moreover, although ideologies include plans to reconstruct man and society, the realities of human nature and social orders being somewhat intractable, often it is simpler and more economical to adapt the ideology to reality, than vice versa. Circumstances arise which create the pragmatic necessity to alter the ideology. Ideologies may also need to change to rationalize their failures and, ironically, to adapt to their successes. As the programs of the ideology are implemented, the resulting changes in society—both foreseen and unforeseen—require changes in the ideology to make it more consistent with the new reality. Furthermore, ideologies are born in crises, and when the social and personal tensions of those crises abate, there is an accompanying diminution of ideological commitment, which in turn produces revision of the belief system to account for the inability to remake man and society. Often the zeal for radical and complete transformation wanes when primary grievances are ameliorated. Since the ideology must adapt to the goals and interests of subsequent generations which have different experiences and perceptions, time takes its toll of ideology. Intergenerational relations produce ideological conflict and change. Ideologies, in sum, must develop or adapt to survive.

Finally, *ideology is entwined in political movements.* As a body of ideas-in-action, ideology requires organization; it is through organization that ideologies are disseminated and implemented. Conflicts of ideology are not merely conflicts of ideas, they are conflicts of ambitions and organizations. In order to achieve power, men must couple ideology to political organization.

The Functions of Ideology

Men employ belief systems to help them understand and live in their natural and societal environments. Thomas Carlyle saw the human need for "myths," and urged that their creators be worshipped as "heroes" for aiding men "to know what they were to believe about this universe, what course they were to steer in it, what in this mysterious Life of theirs, they had to hope and to fear, to do and to forbear doing." [24] Robert MacIver, the distinguished political sociologist, noted, "Wherever he goes, whatever he encounters, man spins around him his web of myth, as a caterpillar spins its cocoon. Every individual spins his own variant within the greater web of the whole group. The myth mediates between man and nature. From the shelter of his myth he perceives and experiences the world. Inside his myth he is at home in his world." [25]

The construction of and faith in political ideology are not only a means by which individual men formulate and face the business of living, ideology serves similar and related functions for men in community. Societal life requires that members be joined; and ideology—providing a common way of looking at themselves, at their society, and at others—helps to join them. As such, ideology performs important instrumental functions for the society founded upon it, and it performs similar functions for political movements seeking to change the societal order.

First, as a political belief system, ideology provides a cognitive structure —a formula of ideas through which the universe is perceived, understood, and interpreted. The vast and complex reality of nature and human community is rendered more intelligible, hospitable, and meaningful by ideology —"man's way of apprehending things, his way of coming to terms with his world." [26] It provides a vocabulary to communicate about politics. Meta-phorically speaking, it serves both as map and compass with which to orient oneself in politics. It is an economy, reducing the intellectual and emotional strain on men by providing a simple, coherent, and rather comprehensive framework into which they can fit their observations and experiences, and grapple with a complicated and demanding world. It is a lens

---

[24] *On Heroes and Hero-Worship* (New York: Doubleday Dolphin, n.d.), p. 14.
[25] *The Web of Government* (New York: Macmillan, 1947), p. 5.
[26] MacIver, *ibid.,* p. 4.

through which men put their world into focus, providing them, as Hannah Arendt put it, with a "sixth sense." [27]

The cognitive orientations of political ideology help men to avoid ambiguity in their lives, and provide a sense of certainty and security. If men see powerful and unpredictable forces around them, ideological faith becomes a sanctuary. It permits them to believe in something outside and beyond themselves, and in ideas and prospects derived from a higher power —religious, moral, historical, scientific. Ideology thereby makes the future more predictable and certain. The potency of this human need, and its fulfillment by ideology, is indicated by men's tendency to think in black-and-white stereotypes and simplified either-or dichotomies, and to overlook apparent contradictions and incongruities in their ideologies. Men "see" selectively through their ideologies—ignoring that which contradicts their beliefs or perceiving it in such a way as to render it congruent with their beliefs. Ideology's role as a refuge against uncertainty varies with personality, group, and context, and is generally more prevalent among those frustrated by their condition and during times of crisis or social change. On a community scale, political ideology provides an ordering for society. It supplies a constitution for society, a higher law, with major and articulated premises for organizing society.

The second function of ideology is to provide a prescriptive formula—a guide to individual and collective action and judgment. It is a set of rules regulating how one may act in politics, specifying the goals which may be pursued and the means used to pursue them. It defines permitted and prescribed outlets for personal and collective ambitions; stipulates rights, privileges, and obligations; and sets the parameters of expectations. Ideology also defines powers and the limits of power, and the purposes and organization of political life.

Ideology not only affords standards of judgment to choose among alternative courses of political action, but also provides a sense of self-justification, a means to evaluate the political conduct of others, and a basis for political legitimacy. It explains and justifies (or denounces) society's allocation of scarce resources. Consequently, one can accept and defend (or oppose) one's long or short rations as appropriate and deserved. Through ideology, personal and collective ambitions and behavior are identified with human destiny, and tied less exclusively to selfish motives.

Ideology provides criteria for evaluating the beliefs, goals, and conduct of other individuals, groups, and nations. A major basis of support for a regime, for example, is the conformity of its conduct with the accepted

[27] *The Origins of Totalitarianism* (New York: Meridian, 1958), p. 471.

ideology. As a consequence, ideology both captures and is captured by leaders who must meet its expectations and, in turn, justify their actions in its terms. Ideology, therefore, is a standard of conduct and judgment for individuals and groups, and for organization, policy, and leadership in politics.

By explaining and justifying the societal order—its distribution and inequalities of wealth, status, and power—an ideology causes believers to accept it as legitimate, as necessary, desirable, and morally binding. The political order and particular regimes cannot long rest on naked power but must be clothed in the mantle of ideological legitimacy. Ideology explains and justifies the way in which power is organized, distributed, used, and limited, thereby converting power into its most highly durable, reliable, and effective form—authority. An ideology adopted by a citizen or subject becomes his "ethical predisposition to accept the actions of authorities within recognized or determinable limits." [28] As such, it builds a "reservoir of freely available support" [29] and voluntary compliance—so long as authority is exercised in the manner understood and expected by those sharing the ideology. Lacking the support of ideology, political power becomes "naked power"; this may require the obligation not to obey but to resist.

Third, ideology functions as a tool of conflict management and integration. At the personal level, ideology functions to help the individual cope with the conflicts within himself and with others, giving wholeness to his life by integrating the various aspects (roles) of individual life. In societies (and groups), ideology eliminates some conflicts, and routinizes others along channels of nondisruptive competition. "The existence of a common ideology tends to minimize behavior differences due to different wants of different members. A common ideology does this by creating a core of *common wants* among members and by inducing a *common method of expressing different wants.*" [30] Furthermore, for the sake of continuity and concerted effort, societies (and groups) require not only conflict control but also political integration of their members. Every society is invaded from within by successive waves of barbarians—new generations who must be taught appropriate social behavior. It is through ideology that new members are instilled with the ideas and ideals that define permitted and prohibited goals and expectations, that create feelings of common identification and allegiance, that anchor members in the social order, and that build and sustain

[28] Easton, *op. cit.* (above, n. 16), p. 290.
[29] Easton, *ibid.,* p. 289.
[30] David Krech *et al., The Individual and Society* (New York: McGraw-Hill, 1962), p. 402.

a nation. Ideology, then, is the code of induction into society, with socialization as the means of induction.

Fourth, self-identification is defined through ideology. Ideology is not only a lens through which men see their world, but is also a looking glass in which they see themselves and a window through which others see them. Ideology is the way men and nations define and see themselves, and hope others see them and interpret their actions in its light. In an important sense, ideology is a personal, group, or societal impressionistic self-portrait. Ideology defines the *being* of men and communities, and foreshadows their *becoming.* By helping answer the question, who am I? ideology is an especially important instrument for self-identification for young people (and nations). For in seeking to find themselves, they are drawn to ideologies, sometimes to those which reject the existing order and appeal to youth as "the wave of a new future." [31]

Ideology contributes to a sense of belonging in that through it, one's life is not isolated but knit into the fabric of the corporate group or society and its history—linked to the past and directed to the future. As an instrument of national identification, ideology is more than a society's wishful vision of itself because ". . . if there did not exist in the minds of all of us an overall operative idea of our country, no matter how diffused, variegated, or inarticulated it may often—even usually—be, our country, as a coherent social entity, would not exist. It would merely be a random aggregation of individuals living in proximity but unable to converse and act together." [32]

The final function of ideology is to serve as a dynamic force in individual and collective life, providing a sense of mission and purpose, and a resulting commitment to action. The prescriptions of ideology are not only standards of conduct and appraisal but also goals to be pursued. Every ideology holds the promises of the good life and the good society. As Dostoevsky observed, "The Golden Age is the most unlikely of all dreams that have been, but for it men have given up all their life and strength. . . . Without it the people will not live and cannot die." At the level of groups and societies, ideology helps galvanize masses into cohesive and committed wholes, and moves those wholes to action. "Ideology is the conversion of ideas into social levers." [33] It moves people to work, to serve, to sacrifice. Ideology can bring the members of a society to populate a wilderness, contribute to national

[31] See Erik H. Erikson, *Childhood and Society* (New York: W. W. Norton, 1960); and *Young Man Luther* (New York: W. W. Norton, 1958).

[32] H. Mark Roelofs, *The Language of Modern Politics: An Introduction to the Study of Government* (Homewood, Ill.: Dorsey, 1967), p. 54.

[33] Daniel Bell, "On the Exhaustion of Political Ideas in the Fifties," *The End of Ideology,* ed. Daniel Bell (New York: Free Press, 1960), p. 370.

economic development, defend their homelands, build an empire, or battle to defend or overthrow the political order.

Ideology: A Political Phenomenon in Search of a Theory

There are several and often conflicting theories of political ideology. Each offers a definition, and an explanation of how and why ideology exists as a part of political life. Each assigns to it a role in politics—ranging all the way from a role of primary, creative determinant of political history and behavior, to one of mere *post facto* rationalization of a societal order promoting the values and interests of certain groups.

The Rule of Reason: Idealist Theories of Ideology

Idealists assert that man reasons about his life, and that his behavior and institutions are largely products of his reason. Political behavior and institutions are, therefore, shaped and guided by how and what men think about politics. According to this theory, political ideology is a causal link in politics between reason and action. If one is interested in understanding, influencing, or predicting political behavior, it is to political ideology that one must look. The most influential expression of the idealistic approach has been that of the German philosopher Hegel. To the question: What is the engine of history?—Hegel replied that history is propelled on its course by the inexorable process of the conflict of ideas. This conflict or dialectic of ideas—of thesis and antithesis—ultimately destroys the sources of the conflict through the formation of a synthesis or new idea, which in turn becomes a thesis to be challenged by a new antithesis. This spiraling path of history leads inevitably to a final synthesis—an unchallengeable ultimate idea which, for Hegel, was the idea of the state.

Few social scientists matriculate in the idealist school today. Objections to the theory of the primacy of ideas include the counterassertion that reason alone (or mainly) has not brought common ideologies and, therefore, common political institutions and behavior. Second, it seems to critics a strong—and suspicious—coincidence that the ideologies advocated and adopted by men are rather consistently attuned to their interests. Third, ideologies often are too vague and open to a wide range of formulations and interpretations, to serve as the key guides to political action. Fourth, ideological situations and conditions vary. The tide of ideological belief ebbs and flows, making it difficult for political ideology to be accepted as the consistently basic determinant of political behavior. Fifth, men don't reason in a vacuum—political ideologies are not spontaneously generated *ex nihilo*. Men reason not only about politics but in politics, and political ideology not only shapes political behavior but is itself shaped by it. Men live in and adapt to a political environment, and their ideologies reflect this. Finally, attitudinal and opinion research seem clearly to indicate that most people do not articulate an elaborate conscious ideology, and that their responses to political issues are only slightly related to and influenced by ideological considerations.[34] Even the acts of political leaders (elites), who often do articulate sophisticated ideologies, cannot be assumed to be governed by ideological considerations. Do not personal political ambitions and interests often displace ideology in shaping the political attitudes and actions of elites? Do not socioeconomic interests often displace (or coincide with) ideology among socioeconomic classes and groups? Do not national and global ambitions and interests supersede ideology in shaping the behavior of nations? In short, political interests and actions are not mere reflections of political ideology and belief. But is the reverse true?

The Rule of Realism: Materialist Theories of Ideology

Materialist—or, more broadly, realist—theories of political ideology assert that ideas and ideologies are determined by the interests and actions of men rather than vice versa. If men are rational, the materialists say, their rationality manifests itself in a conscious and calculating pursuit of self-interest. They seek the social and economic resources of status and wealth. These resources are scarce, however, and competition over them is keen.

---

[34] Surveys made in 1956 and 1960 by the Survey Research Center, University of Michigan, to probe the level of ideological thinking of American voters, revealed that, according to the criteria of the Center, only 2½% of the total sample could be classified as "ideologues," and 9% could be classified as "near-ideologues." In their responses to political issues, 42% replied in terms of "group interest," 24% in terms of the "nature of the time," and 22½% exhibited "no issue content" in their responses. Angus Campbell *et al., The American Voter* (New York: John Wiley, 1960), Chap. 10; and, Philip E. Converse, "The Nature of Belief Systems in Mass Publics," *Ideology and Discontent,* ed. David E. Apter (New York: Free Press, 1964), pp. 206–261.

However, two other researchers, using Survey Research Center data for the 1964 as well as the 1956 and 1960 elections, offer evidence that casts doubt on the conclusion in *The American Voter* that the limited amount of ideological thinking in the electorate occurs at a fairly constant rate because it is a product of the "cognitive limitations" of the voters. They found that in the context of the 1964 election, with the rather clear identification of "Goldwater conservatism" as a campaign issue, the percentage of "ideologues" rose to 35%. While this represents just one-third of the electorate responding in ideological terms, it does involve a noticeable increase and does suggest that ideological thinking is influenced by the characteristics of the political environment as well as those of the voters. See John O. Field and Ronald E. Anderson, "Ideology in the Public's Conceptions of the 1964 Election," *Public Opinion Quarterly,* XXXIII (Fall, 1969), 380–398. For another interesting approach to the issue see William H. Form and Joan Rytina, "Ideological Beliefs on the Distribution of Power in the United States," *American Sociological Review,* XXXIV (February, 1969), 19–31.

Moreover, social and economic institutions allocate these resources, and the allocation is always unequal. Those men with the greatest resources have larger amounts of power for protecting and improving their positions. They develop and defend political institutions for strengthening their status, wealth, and power. They also develop an ideology that both justifies their favored socioeconomic position and political rule, and explains the plight of the less favored. On the other hand, those disadvantaged by this system may aspire to effect a new distribution of resources, a new set of political institutions to enforce it, and a counterideology to justify the overthrow of the existing order.

Thus, ideology is largely a rationalization of material and derivative political interests, tending to be either a defense of the status quo or a clarion call for change. And, as a practical matter, neither the "ins" nor the "outs" have much difficulty in engaging intellectual-rhetoricians—men of words and ideas who will "perform the grand task of designing a suitable ideology." [35]

The materialist explanation of political ideology has been advanced ever since man began to think about politics. Plato in *The Republic* attributes this view to Thrasymachus, who asserted that man's nature is ruled by egoism and that justice is merely the "interest of the stronger." Aristotle in *The Politics* observed that men rationalize their class interests, and that these interests motivate efforts to retain or change the order of society. The framers of the American Constitution, John Adams and James Madison in particular, also saw politics as largely determined by economics. Indeed, victims of those who shared their own views, they were torn from their pedestals as men of noble ideas and ideals when the economic determinists of the Progressive Era, led by Charles A. Beard, interpreted their ideas and acts as reflections of their propertied class interests.

The interpretation of the materialist theory of ideology that has had the most dramatic impact, however, is that of Karl Marx and Friedrich Engels [36] who, in the matter of ultimate causality, claimed to have "stood Hegel on his feet." To Hegel, man's history and existence were determined by ideas, and the struggles of men were manifestations of the conflict or dialectic of ideas. To Marx, on the contrary, man's material existence determined his ideas, and the basis of this conflict was material rather than ideal —to be found in the economic modes of production and the resulting class system which produced economic class warfare. According to this view, the dialectic of materialism irresistibly shapes human history.

[35] Robert A. Dahl, *Modern Political Analysis* (Englewood Cliffs, N.J.: Prentice-Hall, 1963), p. 108.
[36] For brevity, subsequent reference will be made just to Marx.

But what of ideology? In Marxian analysis the substructure of society is its system of economic relationships; the superstructure, its political institutions and ideology. All aspects of human behavior are conditioned by the material base, and changes in the base make changes in the superstructure inevitable. Thus, in the Introduction to *Critique of Political Economy,* Marx wrote:

> The mode of production of the material means of existence conditions the whole process of social, political, and intellectual life. It is not the consciousness of men which determines their existence, but on the contrary it is their social existence which determines their consciousness. . . . Life is not determined by consciousness, but consciousness by life.

According to Marx, each economic mode has its privileged class which controls the prevailing means of production and dominates society. The privileged seek to maintain this class structure by creating political institutions and utilizing their coercive powers, as well as by creating and inculcating political ideologies to justify and support their privilege and power. The class that is the ruling material power in society is its ruling intellectual power. As stated in *The Communist Manifesto,* "The ruling ideas of each age have ever been the ideas of its ruling class."

Thus, to the Marxist, ideology is merely the rationalization of the class interests and political power of the dominant class. It is camouflage to mask the bare and brute facts of economic controls, and a cosmetic to disguise the ugly facts of privilege, exploitation, and oppression. All the spiritual and intellectual efforts and values of men—all religion, philosophy, ethics, law, literature, art—dissolve into ideology, maidservant to the power and privilege of the dominant class. According to this construction, ideology is doubly false. As an intellectual rationalization of prior economic interests, ideology has no independent validity. As a tool used by the dominant class to try to create a protective web of beliefs against change, it is a delusion. Nothing, certainly not the tinsel of ideology, can alter the historic inevitability of changes in the modes of production, and the resultant class struggle, leading ultimately to the classless society. Ideology, therefore, is a false promise and a false hope. However, Marx in his *Manifesto* was not unduly harsh with the capitalists.

> The selfish misconceptions that induce you to transform into eternal laws of nature and of reason the social forms springing from your present mode of production and form of property—historical relations that rise and disappear in the progress of production—this misconception you share with every ruling class that has preceded you.

Marx challenged the great Western tradition of rationalism that dated to the early Greeks; and the systems of thought that were part of that tradition became for him "claptrap"—ideology. Indeed, pre-Marxist and non-Marxist socialisms were sneeringly labeled by Marx as "utopian" (unscientific). Marx looked upon his own system of ideas, on the other hand, as scientific and positive, as a unique and unprecedented insight into the course of historical development, not as ideology but as a science of history. It is a supreme irony that Marxism, which views ideology so negatively, should produce political systems with such intense concern for it—and in which so much energy is expended to inculcate and enforce loyalty to it. The doctrine that ideology is but a weapon of the capitalist ruling class has resulted in the most intense ideological production the world has ever known.

The materialist Marxist theory of ideology was planted firmly in modern social science by Karl Mannheim. Like Marx, Mannheim viewed beliefs as related to the situation of the individual, and determined by his socioeconomic interests and experience. Thus, according to Mannheim, ideologies emerge from interests and life experiences and are not to be regarded as intrinsically true. To Mannheim, a *particular ideology* is a reflection of the special interests of competitive groups in society. It is a "more or less conscious disguise of the real nature of the situation," a distortion which ranges "all the way from conscious lies to half-conscious and unwitting disguise." Regarding the ideologies of one's opponents to be merely reflections of their interests, one next becomes aware that all beliefs are conditioned and colored by the interests and social situations of their believers. From this one develops a *total ideology* or *sociology of knowledge:* "an all-inclusive principle according to which the thought of every group is seen arising out of its life conditions." [37] Mannheim saw a new era—in which a "sociocracy" would be ruled by an intellectual elite trained in the sociology of knowledge, and thus able to transcend the biases of particular ideologies and to rule rationally.

A major point regarding materialist theories is that they strip ideology of independent meaning or consequence, except as a *post facto* rhetorical effort to dress up prior material interests. The attraction of this approach, which has been powerful, is that it seemingly is hardheaded and unsentimental, apparently based on common sense and experience. It appears congenial to the pragmatic, critical, skeptical, perhaps cynical, mind. The ways men earn bread and prestige shape their politics, and create political ideologies of self-justification. Here is a no-nonsense perspective that is not hatched in some ivory tower but rooted in realism.

[37] *Ideology and Utopia: An Introduction to the Sociology of Knowledge,* trans. Louis Wirth and Edward Shils (New York: Harcourt, Brace, 1936), pp. 55–56, 49.

However, materialist theories of ideology, like their idealist opposites, suffer from oversimplification. The economic interests of men do not always control their political actions and ideas. People with the same class interests often differ politically. Conversely, people with different class interests often hold similar political beliefs and act similarly in politics. This "deviant" behavior cannot be shrugged off by protesting that such people are "traitors to their class" or "misguided." If traitors, what brought this treachery? If misguided, what led them astray? If it is that they reason knavishly or foolishly about politics, then ideology is readmitted, although by the back door, as an active agent in the process by which people make political choices.

Furthermore, so simplistic a concept of material interest—food, shelter, clothing, wealth—does not accord with the complex and relatively open nature of human wants. The status, wealth, and power which men seek have various components, and no fixed hierarchy. Some men prefer income to status, others status to income, and others power to both. Others may pursue still different values.

Finally, materialist theories suffer from the same ills of overemphasis which their advocates diagnosed in the idealist theories. It seems safe to suggest, for instance, that ideology is more than a reflex. It has a creative impact and is a formative force, shaping and molding what it touches. Even Marxists like George V. Plekhanov, Lenin's teacher, admit that ideas, although manifestations of anterior economic forces, can and do exercise a reciprocal and significant influence on these forces. Mannheim, too, conceded that even though the intellectual may serve only as an apologist for class interest and party activity, he leaves a meaningful imprint on them. The ideology of man "is not automatically produced by the times. It results from [man's] efforts at understanding the times." [38]

The materialists succeeded in focusing attention upon socioeconomic interests and conditions as factors in politics. Their critics, on the other hand, without necessarily adopting or endorsing idealism, concede that ideology influences and is influenced by politics. The relationship of political ideology to interests and conditions is not a simple one of dependent and independent variables, but a complex and as yet not fully fathomed one of interaction and interdependence. Each plays a role—along with such factors as technology and experience—in shaping political behavior and institutions. There is no persuasive evidence that human history is a *process* subject to an automatically operating law of nature or history. Rather, it is *development* to some degree malleable by human will and desire. As an

[38] William Y. Elliott, *The Pragmatic Revolt In Politics* (New York: Macmillan, 1928), p. 74.

empirical matter, ideology has a creative impact on politics and is a significant datum of politics. One need not lose sight of reality to explore the structure of ideology as well as of material interest, and the linkages between belief and behavior in politics.

The Status Quo and Change: Positional Theories of Ideology

Positional theories of ideology derive from the materialist (realist) approach, specifically from Marx's use of "ideology" as an epithet for the capitalist's rationalization of the status quo. (Marx also employed the term "utopia" to characterize the "fuzzy hopes" of the non-Marxist species of socialist "dreamers.") The critics of Marxism charge that it is no less ideological than capitalism, that it is no less an expression of the class consciousness and interests of the workers than capitalism is of the class consciousness and interests of the bourgeoisie. When Marxists come to power, as in Russia, Marxism also becomes a justification of the power of the ruling group—the Communist party. Marxist analysis of ideology, they argue, is itself an ideology.

Karl Mannheim attempted to save Marxism from the gap in logic just outlined by recasting the image of utopia, and dividing political thought into *Ideology and Utopia.* Here Mannheim defined "ideology" solely in terms of its conservative function as the outlook of the dominant class intent on preserving the established order, and "utopia" solely in terms of its revolutionary function as the belief of aspiring classes seeking to overthrow the prevailing order of society, and their vision of a new order. In the Mannheim tradition, Harold D. Lasswell and Abraham Kaplan state, "The *ideology* is the political myth functioning to preserve the social structure; the *utopia* to supplant it." [39]

There is an opposite trend to define ideology as an instrument of social change, which seems to be a product of the emergence of totalitarian ideologies and the efforts of totalitarian regimes to remold their societies in the images of their ideologies; and the emergence of newly independent nations in which ideology is seen as playing a role in quests for national independence, identity, and modernity. For example, Carl J. Friedrich and Zbigniew Brzezinski define ideology as "a reasonably coherent body of ideas concerning practical means of how to change and reform a society, based upon a more or less elaborate criticism of what is wrong with the existing, or antecedent, society." Ideology, therefore, is critique plus blueprint for change; and a totalitarian ideology is unique only in its concern with "total de-

[39] Lasswell and Kaplan, *op. cit.* (above, n. 9), p. 123.

struction and total reconstruction, involving typically an ideological acceptance of violence as the only practical means for such total destruction." [40]
In a similar vein, Chalmers Johnson in a study of revolutionary change re-
serves the word "ideology" for an *alternative* value system, as opposed to
the *prevailing* value structure of a society. As such, ideology emerges under
conditions of distress and deprivation; it is always a challenger, "an alternative paradigm of values." [41]

These opposing perspectives on ideology, which define and explain
"ideology" in terms of purpose, either as supportive of the status quo or
of change, seem indefensible. Even their advocates evidence uneasiness
about them. Mannheim was uncomfortable with his distinction between
"ideology" and "utopia," noting that "it is possible that the utopias of today
may become the realities of tomorrow; utopias are often premature
truths." [42] Lasswell and Kaplan, having made their distinction between the
two terms, admit, "Symbols functioning at one time as utopias may at another serve as ideology, as indeed usually happens in the case of successful
revolution—utopian symbols are retained regardless of their increasing divergence from the power facts." In a footnote on the same page they state,
"A less misleading term might be *counter-myth;* we retain utopia, however,
because of its familiarity in technical contexts in its present sense." [43] To
define "ideology" solely in its revolutionary aspect poses parallel problems.
If the terms of "myth" and "counter-myth" are less misleading, perhaps
they should be used.

It is here assumed that ideology is a political belief system seeking commitment either to sustain, modify, or overthrow the order of society. In
different times or contexts a particular political ideology may be *reigning
ideology,* justifying an existing order, or a *counterideology,* calling for the
overthrow of a system and its replacement. As the sociologist Talcott Parsons has noted, an ideology is a "system of beliefs, held in common by the
members of a collectivity, i.e., a society, or sub-collectivity of one—including a movement deviant from the main culture of the society. . . ." [44]

The Human Ego and Social Stability: Functional Theories of Ideology

The tradition of looking at ideology as caused rather than causal, as a
reflection of things external to the belief system, has had a deep impact on

[40] Carl J. Friedrich and Zbigniew K. Brzezinski, *Totalitarian Dictatorship and
Autocracy,* paperbound ed. (New York: Praeger, 1961), p. 74.
[41] *Revolutionary Change* (Boston: Little, Brown, 1966), p. 82.
[42] Mannheim, *op. cit.* (above, n. 36), p. 183.
[43] Lasswell and Kaplan, *op. cit.* (above, n. 9), p. 123.
[44] *The Social System* (New York: Free Press, 1951), p. 349.

the study of ideology. It has led social and behavioral scientists to look for their data and clues to political behavior, not in the contents of ideologies, but in the functions that ideology performs. These functional theories of ideology deal—at the micro-level of political man—with the psychological factors that create a need for political belief and lead men to propagate, live under, and die for, ideologies; and—at the macro-level of political society —with the role of ideology in producing political stability or change, maintaining or destroying the social fabric and the legitimacy of rule.

PSYCHOLOGICAL FUNCTIONS OF IDEOLOGY. Implicit in the studies of Sigmund Freud is the conclusion that political ideology stems from intrapsychic forces, and is to be explained in psychological terms.[45] In studying human behavior, especially neurotic behavior, Freud focused upon the process of socialization, by which society imparts its values and norms. During the socialization process, the individual's psychological desires are restrained but not eliminated. They become suppressed—that is, so internalized that he ceases to be conscious of them even though they remain in his unconscious and influence his behavior. Psychoanalysis enabled Freud to delve into the unconscious realm of suppressed desires which bring men to depart from the rules of acceptable conduct. In the unconscious, according to Freud, men were driven by the conflicting but intense impulses to love and life (Eros), and death and destruction (Thanatos).

Freud postulated three mechanisms by which the unconscious influences behavior: (1) rationalization—the process by which an individual finds socially acceptable reasons for justifying his behavior, when in reality he is prompted to act by socially unacceptable and unconscious desires; (2) displacement—the process by which an individual deflects, or redirects along another channel or at another target, an activity which he finds socially impossible or imprudent to release along a "natural" channel or at a "natural" target; and, (3) projection—the process by which an individual psychologically rids himself of guilt for socially unacceptable (evil) thoughts and deeds by attributing these to others. Freud observed that it is in the political realm more than any other that the unconscious manifests itself. According to Freud, in politics men rarely admit to selfish motives but elaborate ideologies to objectify and rationalize those motives; frequently create scapegoats to permit the release of aggressive impulses, with ideologies devised to justify the cruelty; and project guilt onto others, developing ideologies that attribute their misfortune to oppression and that justify their actions as "righting" injustice. Thus, to understand and predict political be-

[45] See Paul Roazen, *Freud: Political and Social Thought* (New York: Alfred A. Knopf, 1968).

havior, attention must center not on the substance of ideology but on the psychological causes or motives behind it.[46]

Psychologists like Erich Fromm [47] see modern man possessed by feelings of inferiority, insecurity, impotence, loneliness, humiliation, and insignificance. Consequently, he is driven to seek superiority, security, power, belongingness, status, and glory in the political arena, especially through totalitarian ideologies and movements. In complex urban and industrial society man confronts bigness, impersonal forces, and complex issues that challenge his understanding, belittle his powers of control, and make him feel isolated and powerless. Unable to face this, he flees from freedom into the arms of totalitarian ideologies which provide gratifying explanations for his plight, and all-encompassing yet simple answers to his problems. Modern man flees from the self-government and responsibility of freedom to the security of freedom from responsibility. Exchanging his painful doubts of a free mind and the troublesome obligations of self-government for the dogma of a total creed and for total conformity, he is molded into a social whole and becomes part of an historic cause. As Eric Hoffer noted, totalitarian ideologies and movements offer a refuge "from the anxieties, barrenness and meaninglessness of an individual existence." They free men "from their ineffectual selves . . . by enfolding and absorbing them into a closely knit and exultant corporate whole." [48]

Finally, there is a psychological approach that finds the key to understanding ideology in the behavioral tendencies common to the human species. Abraham Maslow,[49] for example, sets forth a system of basic human needs which are arrayed hierarchically—that is, some are primary and must be satisfied before the others emerge. First, man needs to exist and survive, and these needs must be relatively satisfied (food, water, shelter, clothing,

---

[46] For an application of Freudian theory in political science see Harold D. Lasswell, *Power and Personality* (New York: W. W. Norton, 1948); and *Psychopathology and Politics* (New York: Viking Compass, 1960).

[47] *Escape from Freedom* (New York: Farrar and Rinehart, 1941). Cf. Karen Horney, *Neurosis and Human Growth* (New York: W. W. Norton, 1950); Alfred Adler, *The Practice and Theory of Individual Psychology* (New York: Harcourt, Brace, 1929); Theodore W. Adorno *et al., The Authoritarian Personality* (New York: Harper & Row, 1950); Gabriel Almond, *The Appeals of Communism* (Princeton, N.J.: Princeton University Press, 1954); Carl J. Friedrich, ed., *Totalitarianism* (Cambridge, Mass.: Harvard University Press, 1954); David Riesman, *The Lonely Crowd* (New Haven, Conn.: Yale University Press, 1950); and Milton Rokeach, *The Open and Closed Mind* (New York: Basic Books, 1960).

[48] *The True Believer* (New York: Harper, 1951), p. 39.

[49] "A Theory of Human Motivation," *Psychological Review,* L (1943), 370–396. An interesting discussion of psychological theories and their relationships to political behavior is offered by James C. Davies, *Human Nature in Politics: The Dynamics of Political Behavior* (New York: John Wiley, 1963).

health, safety from bodily harm, sex) before other needs become insistent. Second, man needs security. He requires that his environment, physical and societal, be reasonably safe, orderly, and predictable. Until man attains these, his other needs are muted. Third, man needs community—to live together with his fellows in affectionate relationships. Man needs to belong, to be respected, to love and be loved. Fourth, man needs self-esteem. While, on the other hand, man seeks to identify with a community, on the other hand, he seeks separate identity and dignity. He seeks individuality as well as membership, to be apart from as well as a part of society. Moreover, man has a derivative need for equality. To be sure, man seems impelled to deny equality to others and reject objective equality of worldly goods, responsibility, and power. However, he seeks subjective equality, that is, to be regarded, in his own eyes or those of others, as equal to others in worth, dignity, and opportunity. Equality, according to Maslow's theory, is not only a moral value but an inherent need of man. Fifth, man needs self-actualization, that is, to pursue happiness through inherently satisfying activity. Therefore, seeking to order their society and lives to fulfill these needs, men will create and adopt ideologies to help achieve that end.

SOCIAL FUNCTIONS OF IDEOLOGY. To Marx, society and its political institutions rested primarily on the possession and exercise of coercive power by the ruling class through its control of the state. But can the stability of a social order rest exclusively, or even primarily, on force? So blunt an exponent of the force theory as Hobbes admitted, "Even the tyrant must sleep." As Rousseau warned, "The strongest man is never strong enough to be always master, unless he transforms his power into right and obedience into duty." To survive and function, the order of society must rest on a base other than force, and the reigning ideology supporting that order cannot merely be the belief system accepted by the ruling class. Ideology is not just a rationalization for privilege and power; it is also an active component of the social system, contributing to or detracting from its stability and operation. Social stability, in other words, is usually a product of faith in the system, not merely fear of it; and power in society, therefore, must be *legitimate*—accepted by members as morally binding—if stability is to be assured.

The sociologists Max Weber and Emile Durkheim recognized class structure but rejected the Marxian view that this was maintained largely by coercion. Instead, they stressed society as a collectivity of people sharing an ideology which legitimizes inequalities and causes people to accept them as "just." Talcott Parsons similarly rejects the force theory, asserting that

society is not possible unless it is integrated by "common value patterns" [50]
—that is, unless the adult members of the society jointly adhere to some
principles, some ideology, that renders the division of labors and rewards
intelligible and tolerable. The Italian political sociologist Gaetano Mosca
also expresses this view in *The Ruling Class,* writing that there is a universal
human need "of governing and knowing that one is governed not on the
basis of mere material or intellectual force, but on the basis of a moral principle, . . ." He continues:

> . . . ruling classes do not justify their power exclusively by de facto posses-
> sion of it, but try to find a moral and legal basis for it, representing it as the
> logical and necessary consequence of doctrines and beliefs that are generally
> recognized and accepted. . . . The majority of a people consents to a given
> governmental system solely because the system is based upon religious or phi-
> losophical beliefs that are universally accepted by them . . . the amount of
> consent depends upon the extent to which, and the ardor with which, the class
> that is ruled believes in the political formula by which the ruling class justifies
> its rule.[51]

Robert MacIver in *The Web of Government* further observes that it is the
"myth-complex" (ideology) of society, not force, that "links the governors
and the governed," and brings "to government a ratification without which
no prince or parliament, no tyrant or dictator, could ever rule a people." [52]
As the political scientist Charles E. Merriam has said, ". . . the might that
makes right must be a might different from that of the right arm." [53]

   In sum, a body of social science theory holds that a minimum level of
ideological consensus is required for the stability and survival of society
and its political order. In the absence of this consensus, support for a system would require more costly methods of material rewards or force; and
in the long run these are weak and perhaps impossible bases for society.
Ideological agreement does not eliminate conflict, but it does reduce it and
channel it along less disruptive lines. Belief in an ideology causes individuals and classes more readily to accept their shares and those of others as
"fair."

   Functionalists view political ideology as an integral part of the social
system, operating to meet certain needs that must be satisfied if the system

   [50] Parsons, *op. cit.* (above, n. 44), p. 42. A useful summary statement is made by
D. F. Aberle *et al.,* "The Functional Prerequisites of a Society," *Ethics,* LX (January,
1950), 100–111.
   [51] Trans. Hannah D. Kahn, intro. Arthur Livingston (New York: McGraw-Hill,
1939), pp. 71, 70, 97.
   [52] MacIver, *op. cit.* (above, n. 25), 17
   [53] *Political Power* (New York: McGraw-Hill, 1934), p. 102.

is to continue to exist. They do not see ideology functioning independently and in isolation to produce stability. Instead, they see it operating at a given time in relation to the resources, technology, institutions, and processes of society. Ideology, to serve as a stabilizing force, must be reasonably well synchronized with the actual order and conditions of society so that the experiences men have will be in accord with their expectations.

A society cannot function without an ideology, or function well at cross-purposes with its ideology. If the ideology does not change with technological innovation or institutional practice, for instance, it may ultimately find itself challenged by a counterideology. Similarly, lack of synchronization may be a product of change in the ideology without parallel change in the social environment, as when an ideology is imported into a society without regard to cultural differences. When ideology bears, or is perceived to bear, little relation to actual conditions, social disorder threatens. If stability, then, is dependent upon the congruence of ideology and socioeconomic and political conditions, the key to social-science analysis is in the study of the substance of ideology and its relationship to reality.

The Study of Ideology: to Understand, to Reflect, and Choose

The nature of political ideology has been examined to provide a platform for the understanding and analysis of the major political ideologies that men currently live under or wish to live under, that hold and are competing to hold the political allegiances of men. The more practical tasks remain to suggest the utilities of the study of political ideologies, some tools of analysis, and some common pitfalls to avoid in evaluating ideologies.

Why Study Ideologies?

Political ideologies reveal important data about the people who create and believe in them: how they see themselves and their political world; what they want (or think they want), why they want it, and how they hope to get it; and the consequences of their vision. As tools for understanding and predicting political events and behavior, ideologies permit the study of whole systems, eras, and movements. In sum, the study of political ideologies is useful and important because the latter "are variables in the explanation of political behavior. Whether they 'cause' behavior we may never be able to know for certain, but they are unmistakable links in the chain of political phenomena at the level of the individual, the level of the group, and the level of society." [54] Indeed, the study of political ideologies and

[54] David W. Minar, *Ideas and Politics: The American Experience* (Homewood, Ill.: Dorsey, 1964), p. 4.

their consequences should provide some clues as to whether and how ideology influences political behavior, as well as clues to the nature, conditions, and effects of that influence.

The study of political ideologies provides a base for political evaluation and judgment. Hopefully this book will offer some synthesis and clarity of understanding and thought amid the clamor and confusion of the claims and counterclaims, charges and countercharges, of a political arena crowded with ideologies. Politics cannot be contemplated without making decisions —including decisions about ideology. A knowledge of man's more recent ideological experiences, and of the conditions which led to those experiences, provides an essential background for understanding, reflecting, and choosing an ideology.

The Tools of Analysis

Political ideologies vary in their susceptibility to systematic analysis; their empirical and normative propositions may be close to or far removed from the referents of political life, and therefore may be subject to greater or lesser empirical verification, and logical and rational analysis. However, the following broadly defined tests can be used in the analysis of ideology.

THE TEST OF LOGIC. Logical analysis identifies the component elements of an ideology, unearths frequently hidden premises, traces out remote implications of assumptions, makes explicit the implicit structure of ideas, evaluates the connecting links among propositions, and determines whether the ideology is compatible with its premises. But logic, while a useful and powerful tool, is also a tricky and dangerous one. Logically deduced "truths" are absolute (irrefutable) in the sense that once you accept the premises you cannot refuse to accept the conclusions that follow from them. However, it must be understood that a premise is a proposition that precedes the logical process and its truth cannot be established. Therefore, while logic is an important tool in unraveling an ideology, it doesn't establish the empirical truth or falsity of the propositions of an ideology. To make the easy surrender to logic is to commit yourself to an apparently logical ideology that includes premises and derivative conclusions which may or may not be factually true or valid.

THE TEST OF REALITY. Political ideologies contain empirical and normative propositions. While the value components are beyond empirical testing, the fact assertions are testable by empirical-scientific investigation to examine the truth or falsity of their descriptions of political reality, and the reliability of their predictions (and promises) of a future political reality. Thus, the record of history can be examined to discover whether in fact men have behaved in politics as an ideology contends, what have been the

consequences of the ideology, what kinds of political systems it has produced, and whether the political systems built upon it have corresponded
with what was prescribed or predicted by the ideology. Social-science
knowledge can be used to determine the feasibility of the ideology—to
determine the conditions necessary for its implementation, the probability
that people can behave as it requires, and the probability that the means
proposed will achieve the ends promised. In sum, it can help us discover if
some of the ideology's claim to truth is true.

To be sure, choice among political ideologies is a value judgment. "Science can only tell us *how* to achieve goals, it can never tell us *what* goals
should be sought." [55] However, the test of reality is an important base for
evaluating and choosing among ideologies. We cannot decide wisely without
knowing what means are available to attain promised values, and what have
been and are likely to be their consequences.

THE TEST OF VALUES. Ideologies define values for men and societies,
and institutions are means to achieve and enforce values. At the same time,
political values are neither true nor false empirically but are only preferences to be accepted or denied. There are, however, scholars who hold that
there are values common to man. Giovanni Sartori writes, ". . . there is
ample evidence from the very beginning of time that once men have begun
to enjoy the values of respect for human life and for the dignity of the individual person, their relation has always been the same, namely, to prize
these values." [56] The dimensions of the empirical issue of whether there are
values common or potentially common to man are beyond the scope of this
book.[57] In any case, one need not conclude that because values are preference choices and their relative merits cannot be scientifically ascertained,
one must opt for either nihilism or moral absolutism. Rather, one can make
a thoughtful comparative appraisal of competing values—and hope the
choice was wise.

Some Caveats in the Study of Ideology

The path of analysis of political ideology is difficult and full of pitfalls.
First, there is the fallacy of ideological reification—of forgetting that an
ideology is an abstraction and not reality itself. This fallacy confuses the
simple, tidy, and pleasing model of an ideology with the complex, turbulent,
and hard world of politics. Ideology consists of word-symbols men devise
in part to explain the real world. They are not labels which nature put on

[55] William J. Goode and Paul K. Holt, *Methods in Social Research* (New York:
McGraw-Hill, 1952), p. 2.
[56] Sartori, *op. cit.* (above, n. 23), p. 172.
[57] For a provocative positive response to this issue see Reo M. Christenson, "The
Moral Imperative in Politics," *Polity,* I (Winter, 1968), 179–190.

real things. Ideologies seek to create (and we must avoid being entrapped by) the illusion of being reality. Second, there is the fallacy of logic—of assuming because something is consistent it is true; because something is inconsistent it is false; and because something appears evil its opposite is good. It is necessary to evaluate carefully the premises of an ideology, and to relate its propositions to reality. Third, there is the fallacy of history—of concluding that because something once has worked it will work again, because something has not worked it will not work again, or because something has existed and worked it is automatically to be preferred over something yet untried. Our conclusions ought not to be limited by our historical memories alone. Fontenella's rose knowingly nodded its head and solemnly proclaimed that all gardeners are immortal because no gardener had ever died within the memory of a rose.

Fourth, there is the fallacy of values defined as facts. Ideologies frequently dress their values in the garb of facts. A value so misrepresented "[gains] force from its pseudo-scientific character," but such misrepresentation is "at best a mistake and at worst a lie because it consists in getting someone to alter his valuation under the false impression that he is . . . correcting his knowledge of the facts." [58] Falling prey to this fallacy is not an uncommon occurrence. Indeed, *The Declaration of Independence* proclaims, "We hold these truths to be self-evident . . . ," not "We hold these values to be preferred. . . ." While it is reassuring to see one's values proclaimed as facts—self-evident truths—it is not prudent judgment to accept values as definitions that purport to be statements of facts.

Fifth, there is the fallacy of certitude: scientific and moral. Absolute certainty of political wisdom or morality is unattainable. Man is doomed to decide and act on the basis of inadequate evidence and a fallible intellect. To wait for all the evidence is to let others decide. Political certainty is to be found only in deceptive simplicities or resounding generalities through which a kernel of truth (Jews occupy powerful positions in our society) is inflated into a falsehood (theories of Zionist conspiracies to world domination, and resulting antisemitic ideologies). The choice is not between complete certainty or complete doubt, between smug absolutism or total skepticism. Neither the absolutist nor the skeptic has much fun: the absolutist, embalmed in the certainty that he has *the* truth, has no basis for a friendly argument; and, the skeptic, sterilized by his conviction that there are no meaningful truths or values, logically has no argument with anyone. Decisions about political choices, moreover, need not be irrevocable. Decision and commitment can occur without closing the mind to further evi-

[58] Joan Robinson, *Economic Philosophy* (London: Watts, 1962), pp. 167, 170.

dence or argument. One benefit—perhaps the most significant one—of the study of political ideologies is what we learn about ourselves, through reflecting upon our choices.

Bibliography

Adorno, Theodore W., *et al. The Authoritarian Personality.* New York: Harper & Row, 1950.

Almond, Gabriel A. *The Appeals of Communism.* Princeton, N.J.: Princeton University Press, 1954.

Apter, David E., ed. *Ideology and Discontent.* New York: Free Press, 1964.

Arendt, Hannah, *The Origins of Totalitarianism.* New York: Harcourt, Brace, 1951.

———. *The Human Condition.* Chicago: University of Chicago Press, 1958.

Aron, Raymond. *The Opium of the Intellectuals.* New York: W. W. Norton, 1962.

Barnes, Samuel H. "Ideology and the Organization of Conflict." *Journal of Politics,* XXVIII (August, 1966), 513–530.

Bell, David, ed. *The End of Ideology.* New York: Free Press, 1960.

Bergman, Gustav. "Ideology." In *The Metaphysics of Logical Positivism.* New York: Longmans, Green, 1954. Pp. 300–325.

Brecht, Arnold. *Political Theory: The Foundations of Twentieth-Century Political Thought.* Princeton, N.J.: Princeton University Press, 1959.

Burns, James MacGregor. "Political Ideology." *A Guide to the Social Sciences.* Ed. Norman MacKensie. New York: New American Library, 1966. Pp. 205–224.

Cobban, Alfred. "The Decline of Political Theory." *Political Science Quarterly,* LXVIII (September, 1953), 321–337.

Dahl, Robert A. *Modern Political Analysis.* Englewood Cliffs, N.J.: Prentice-Hall, 1963.

Field, John O., and Ronald E. Anderson. "Ideology in the Public's Conception of the 1964 Election." *Public Opinion Quarterly,* XXXIII (Fall, 1969), 380–398.

Form, William H., and Joan Rytina. "Ideological Beliefs on the Distribution of Power in the United States." *American Sociological Review,* XXXIV (February, 1969), 19–30.

Friedrich, Carl J., ed. *Totalitarianism.* Cambridge, Mass.: Harvard University Press, 1954.

——— and Zbigniew Brzezinski. *Totalitarian Dictatorship and Autocracy.* New York: Frederick A. Praeger, 1961.

Fromm, Erich. *Escape from Freedom.* New York: Farrar & Rinehart, 1941.

Hoffer, Eric. *The True Believer.* New York: Harper, 1951.

Jenkin, Thomas P. *The Study of Political Theory.* New York: Random House, 1955.

Johnson, Harry M. "Ideology and the Social System." In *International En-*

cyclopedia of the Social Sciences. Ed. David L. Sills. New York: Macmillan and Free Press, 1968. Vol. VII, pp. 76–85.

Lane, Robert E. *Political Ideology: Why the Common Man Believes What He Does.* New York: Free Press, 1962.

LaPalombara, Joseph. "Decline of Ideology: A Dissent and an Interpretation." *American Political Science Review,* LX (March, 1966), 5–16.

Lasswell, Harold D. *Power and Personality.* New York: Norton, 1948.

———. *Psychopathology and Politics.* New York: Viking, 1960.

——— and Abraham Kaplan. *Power and Society: A Framework for Political Inquiry.* New Haven, Conn.: Yale University Press, 1950.

Lichtheim, George. *The Concept of Ideology and Other Essays.* New York: Random House, 1967.

Lipset, Seymour M. *Political Man: The Social Bases of Politics.* New York: Doubleday, 1960.

McCloskey, Robert G. "The American Ideology." In *Continuing Crisis in American Politics.* Ed. Marian D. Irish. Englewood Cliffs, N.J.: Prentice-Hall, 1965. Pp. 10–25.

McClosky, Herbert. "Consensus and Ideology in American Politics." *American Political Science Review,* LVIII (June, 1964), 361–382.

MacIver, Robert M. *The Web of Government.* New York: Macmillan, 1947.

Mannheim, Karl. *Ideology and Utopia: An Introduction to the Sociology of Knowledge.* Trans. Louis Wirth and Edward Shils. New York: Harcourt, Brace, 1936.

Merelman, Richard M. "The Development of Political Ideology: A Framework for the Analysis of Political Socialization." *American Political Science Review,* LXIII (September, 1969), 750–767.

Minar, David W. *Ideas and Politics: The American Experience.* Homewood, Ill.: Dorsey, 1964.

———. "Ideology and Political Behavior." *Midwest Journal of Political Science,* IV (November, 1961), 317–331.

Pye, Lucien W. "Personality Identity and Political Ideology." *Political Decision-Makers.* Ed. Dwaine Marvick. New York: Free Press, 1961. Pp. 290–313.

Riesman, David. *The Lonely Crowd.* New Haven, Conn.: Yale University Press, 1950.

Rokeach, Milton. *The Open and Closed Mind.* New York: Basic Books, 1960.

Shils, Edward. "The Concept and Function of Ideology." In *International Encyclopedia of the Social Sciences.* Ed. by David L. Sills. New York: Macmillan and Free Press, 1968. Vol. VII, pp. 66–76.

Shklar, Judith. *After Utopia: The Decline of Political Faith.* Princeton: N.J.: Princeton University Press, 1957.

Talmon, J. L. *The Origins of Totalitarian Democracy.* New York: Frederick A. Praeger, 1960.

Watkins, Frederick M. *The Age of Ideology—Political Thought, 1750 to the Present.* Englewood Cliffs, N.J.: Prentice-Hall, 1965.

Waxman, Chaim, ed. *The End of Ideology Debate.* New York: Funk and Wagnalls, 1968.

Chapter 2

Totalitarian Ideologies

Fifty years ago the word "totalitarian" was not a part of our vocabulary. With the emergence of Stalinist Russia, however, totalitarianism—in this case, of the left—became a major political reality. The appearance of Hitler and Mussolini signaled the onset of a comparable political system—totalitarianism of the right. Today, of course, totalitarianism of the right is confined to relatively small states, but totalitarianism of the left is firmly established in two leading nations—Russia and China—as well as in a number of lesser states. Furthermore, the threat of new right-wing totalitarian regimes is always present, particularly during periods of great social upheaval. Totalitarianism has thus earned its place in the study of political ideologies. And it commands our interest no less for what it may tell us about the interaction between ideology and political behavior.

As a starting point, this section seeks the distinctive common denominators associated with the variant forms of totalitarian ideologies. The questions leading to these common denominators are simple, the answers more complex. What is totalitarianism? How did it originate and what facilitated its development? Moving to the specifics of totalitarian variety and experience—most notably Italian fascism, German Naziism, Soviet and Chinese communism—we ask more pointed questions. How well does each fit the model of totalitarianism? Are there properties unique to each system and irreconcilable with the others? How close a kin is practice to theory? Equally important, how relevant is totalitarianism to our day and to the future?

The Totalitarian Concept

"The Fascist conception of the State," wrote Benito Mussolini, "is all-embracing; outside of it no human or spiritual values can exist, much less have value. Thus understood, Fascism is totalitarian, and the Fascist State —a synthesis and a unit inclusive of all values—interprets, develops, and potentiates the whole life of a people." [1] Mussolini had "christened" an ideology, and with it a new era. "A party governing a nation 'totalitarianly' is a new departure in history," he continued, and "we are free to believe that this is the century of authority, a century tending to the 'right,' a Fascist century." [2] While neither the communists nor the Nazis displayed much affection for the totalitarian label, they both shared Mussolini's conviction that a new political age was dawning in the image of their respective ideologies. "We have created a new kind of state" was the claim attributed to Lenin,[3] and matched by Hitler in references to a "new state conception . . . a new world conception." [4]

Mussolini's assertion that totalitarianism is something new under the sun may occasion some skepticism. Indeed, the lexicon of political science was already replete with such familiar antidemocratic terms as absolutism, authoritarianism, autocracy, despotism, dictatorship, and tyranny. Given our acquaintance with nondemocratic regimes of the past, would it be more accurate to dismiss totalitarianism as simply another kind of dictatorship in semantically pretentious clothing?

While there is no denying a number of obvious parallels between totalitarianism and the conventional dictatorship, the differences are even more considerable. At the top of the list stands the dimension of control.[5] Where dictatorships have customarily concentrated the exercise of power in the political sphere, totalitarianism reaches *all* categories of behavior. Mussolini's language, in the passage just cited, is particularly instructive in his use of the term "all-embracing" to describe the fascist version of totalitarianism. The very word which he appropriates as a name for the system

---

[1] Benito Mussolini, "Fascism: Doctrine and Institutions," *Enciclopedia Italiana,* XIV (1932).

[2] *Ibid.*

[3] As quoted in Carl J. Friedrich and Zbigniew K. Brzezinski, *Totalitarian Dictatorship and Autocracy,* 2nd ed. (New York: Frederick A. Praeger, 1965), p. 3.

[4] Adolf Hitler, *Mein Kampf* (trans.) (Boston: Houghton Mifflin, 1962), p. 378.

[5] Friedrich and Brzezinski, *op. cit.,* pp. 3f. See also Else Frenkel-Brunswik, "Environmental Controls and the Impoverishment of Thought," in Carl J. Friedrich, ed., *Totalitarianism* (New York: Grosset & Dunlap, 1964), pp. 172f. But not all would agree that totalitarianism is totally unique: cf. N. S. Timasheff, "Totalitarianism, Despotism, Dictatorship," in *ibid.,* pp. 39f.

—*total*itarian—underlines the point. Hence, totalitarianism may lay claim to uniqueness by virtue of its extensive concern for politics *plus* social and economic behavior.

Two postscripts might well be added to this point. The first is that the totalitarian involvement with extrapolitical matters is significantly related to the objective of restructuring man and society.[6] This involvement too would seem to distinguish totalitarianism from traditional dictatorships in that the latter usually had no such missionary aims, far more frequently devoting themselves to maintaining the status quo. In short, where the control of behavior has generally sufficed for dictatorship, the control of behavior *and* values is consistently identified with totalitarianism. Second, it is precisely this inclusive pattern of control which suggests that totalitarianism is a distinctively twentieth-century phenomenon.[7] The more pervasive the control objectives, the more sophisticated the apparatus to achieve that end. Hence it appears entirely reasonable to observe that a system which aspires to control the beliefs of men must possess a technical competence— for example, in communications and education—capable of supporting the effort. Since these are among the resources of industrialized systems, the special link to the twentieth century is entirely plausible.

The thesis that totalitarianism is no mere carbon copy of dictatorship does not rest on the matter of control alone, however. What also gives it uniqueness is its designation as a mass movement,[8] especially in the demonstrative sense. Mussolini, again, gives insight to this feature of totalitarianism in his writings: "Fascism desires the State to be strong and organic, based on broad foundations of popular support." And he adds: "A State based on millions of individuals who recognise its authority, feel its action, and are ready to serve its ends is not the tyrannical state of a mediaeval lordling. It has nothing in common with the despotic States existing prior to or subsequent to 1789. Far from crushing the individual, the Fascist State multiplies his energies, just as in a regiment a soldier is not diminished but multiplied by the number of his fellow soldiers." [9]

The classic model of dictatorship would seem to have a much different set of priorities. Far from seeking an active popular reinforcement, such regimes usually have preferred disengaging the masses from politics. Following the strategy that it is easier to rule when left alone to do so, the ideal more likely is an apathetic and uninvolved population. In contrast, it was

---

[6] Friedrich and Brzezinski, *op. cit.*, p. 16.

[7] *Ibid.*, p. 17. See also George F. Kennan, "Totalitarianism," in Friedrich, *op. cit.* (above, n. 5), p. 20; and Carl J. Friedrich, "The Unique Character of Totalitarian Society," in *ibid.*, p. 56.

[8] *Ibid.*, p. 57. But cf. Kennan, *ibid.*, p. 23.

[9] Mussolini, *op. cit.* (above, n. 1).

not mere acquiescence which Mussolini made the norm: it was the mobilization of the masses in active support of values and policies.

What emerges then is a weighty claim—based at the very least on the components of control and mass—as to the distinctiveness of totalitarianism. Other reasons, too, have been advanced: totalitarianism is unique because it is unrivaled in its possession of irresponsible and unaccountable power; because of its concentration of power in the hands of an elite; because of its homogeneous and antipluralistic posture; because of its revolutionary overtones; or because of its unprecedented party organization.[10] Some have even hypothesized that the pseudoreligious flavor of totalitarianism sets it apart.[11] It is not altogether clear, however, that these are properties peculiar only to totalitarianism; they might be characteristics shared by dictatorships as well. Moreover, in at least some cases these would be considered part and parcel of the mass-control framework. One thing is clear, however; totalitarianism is indeed a new breed of ideology, a new species of politics.

Building upon these preliminary observations, we can better confront the question: what is totalitarianism—its nature and characteristics? Beyond the more original aspects of totalitarianism are still other factors which play a vital part in the system. Here it is useful to arrange these factors under two headings: first, there is need to consider the values (beliefs and attitudes) of the totalitarian system; second, the organization (institutions and structural arrangements) of such a system.

If there is any single first premise to totalitarian doctrine, a good case could be made for identifying it as the idea of conflict and struggle. The clashing of men, groups, and nations are all part of the natural order of things. Moreover, the basic inequality between men (or classes or nations) dictates that only the fittest—or best—are to survive. All political systems must therefore contend with continuing problems of conflict; but where democratic systems have sought to ameliorate conflict, or to peacefully accommodate it, totalitarianism seems to accept it as both inevitable and uniquely constructive. Similarly, democratic philosophies have usually been quite pointed in their professions of equalitarianism, while most totalitarian systems see positive merit in a universe of unequals. Undoubtedly, the most familiar manifestation of this latter idea is that associated with the fascists and Nazis, whose language has been explicit on the subject. Less

[10] See, for example, Hannah Arendt, *The Origins of Totalitarianism* (New York: Harcourt, Brace, 1951), p. 364.

[11] This provocative approach is taken by Waldemar Gurian, "Totalitarianism as Political Religion," in Friedrich, *op. cit.* (above, n. 5), p. 122. See also Frenkel-Brunswik, in *ibid.*, p. 173. Related material may also be found in Seymour Lipset, *Political Man* (Garden City, N.Y.: Doubleday, 1963), pp. 97–100.

obvious, but still relevant, is the communist view concerning the inevitability of intranational conflict, and—to a degree—the companion attitude toward differing economic classes, economic systems, and the like. From this basic belief in the inevitability and virtue of conflict-among-unequals, then, a number of important totalitarian ideas flow.

For one thing, the totalitarian is led to conclude that life is sharply dichotomized, the world a study in contrasts. The strong, the fittest, the best, survive; the meek do not inherit the earth—nature leaves little room for weakness in the inescapable pattern of conflict. Thus the universe divides into the strong and weak, the fit and the unfit, winners and losers, the good and the bad, friends and enemies. The totalitarian tendency to categorize in either/or terms, and the absence of shades between black-and-white in its system, have been commented upon widely. Some have described totalitarianism as oversimplified; others have associated it with stereotyped reasoning.[12]

Given the polarized outlook of totalitarianism, a world in which men (or systems) are either good or bad, what should be the attitude of nature's favorites toward nature's hindmost? Regarding this question, the totalitarian is no mere neutral, content to let nature take its course and confident that the survival-of-the-fittest theory will prove to his advantage; rather, the equation of survival with virtue (and weakness with evil) now transforms the conflict into a quasi-religious cause, and prompts him to a more active role. The question is rephrased: Can God coexist with the devil? Convinced that the highest ethic (the divine equivalent) is with him, and that the lowest ethic (the devil incarnate) is against him, the totalitarian sees no alternative but to strike down evil where he finds it—to hasten the inevitable.

In this context, finally, it is clear enough to comprehend the crucial role of "the enemy" in totalitarian thought. Deeply embedded in the concept of the enemy are the ideas of the struggle for existence, the dichotomous view of life, and the imperative to purge evil. The totalitarian is also prone to attach an absolute responsibility to the enemy for all misfortunes. Why did Germany lose the war? Because of the Jews! Why did Germany suffer depression? Because of the Jews! Why must the Berlin Wall be built? Because of capitalist spies and agents provocateurs. Why must Czechoslovakia be invaded? Because capitalist and imperialist elements have wormed their way into positions of power. And so forth, *ad infinitum*. What is at work here is a "devil-theory" of politics, which provides a useful insight into the phenomenon of scapegoating so characteristic of totalitarian society. Thus the concept of the enemy looms large in the totalitarian system, taking on all

[12] See Frenkel-Brunswik, *op. cit.* (above, n. 5), p. 186.

the earmarks of an obsessive paranoia. It is no mere coincidence, in this light, that fascists, Nazis, and communists alike have singled out their targets for hostility. As one political scientist puts it: "A man may be known by his friends, but in politics a movement may be understood by its enemies." [13] In the concept of the enemy we see important links to what is often termed the "fanatic-irrationality" of totalitarianism, as well as to its violence and its antipluralism.[14] In this concept—the first major component of the totalitarian doctrine—we have, in sum, an important key to the understanding of totalitarianism.

The second major component of totalitarian doctrine—also derived from the premise of conflict-among-unequals—is the authoritarian principle. Since among nations and parties there is a natural inequality, it follows that one party (group) must necessarily be superior to other parties, or that one leader (man) must likewise be superior to all others. Hence we derive the elitist overtone of totalitarianism. Call it minority rule, the one-party state, or the leadership principle, it expresses the totalitarian rationale for the disposition of power.[15] Thus the concept of an inherently superior party (an elite) accords with the basic totalitarian view of life (inequality) and is legitimized thereby. Moreover, it logically follows that this elite should possess a commensurate amount of authority. As a consequence of the premised monopoly of political wisdom and virtue, there is also premised a monopoly of political power and authority. It is thus characteristic of totalitarian thought that one party alone lays claim to truth and virtue; hence competition is both unnecessary and undesirable; and hence there can be no sharing or division of political power. To do otherwise would seem to imply the fallibility of the elite, and negate the premise.

The direct corollary to this concept of an omnipotent elite is to be found in the relative position of the nonelite, and in the relationship between the two. It follows, obviously, that those outside the inner circle of superiority must be relegated to an inferior and subservient role. And, predictably, the structuring of society into a superior-inferior hierarchy also finds expression in the political roles which are assigned. The obligation of the superior is to decide—the obligation of the inferior is to follow and obey. To the extent that authoritarianism can permeate the entire fabric of a society, and can gain popular adherence, it is linked to earlier considerations of total control and mass reinforcement. Equally important, the authoritarian

[13] Gilbert Abcarian, in "Radical Right and New Left: Commitment and Estrangement in Mass Society." An unpublished paper presented to the Midwest Conference of Political Scientists (Purdue University, April 29, 1967), p. 16.

[14] On the subject of fanaticism see Arendt, *op. cit.* (above, n. 10), p. 174, and Friedrich and Brzezinski, *op. cit.* (above, n. 3), p. 26.

[15] *Ibid.,* pp. 21f.

framework of totalitarianism makes sharper still the conflict of values with democratic systems.

Finally, we may round out this picture of totalitarianism by consideration of a third major component of totalitarian doctrine—violence—again, one suggested by the primary doctrine of conflict among unequals. Does it not follow that those who perceive the world in terms of struggle between the strong and the weak (or the historically destined and the historically damned) will naturally seek appropriate expressions of power? One totalitarian view is well expressed by Mussolini in the context of his writings on fascism:

. . . Fascism does not, generally speaking, believe in the possibility or utility of perpetual peace. It therefore discards pacifism as a cloak for cowardly supine renunciation in contra-distinction to self-sacrifice. War alone keys up all human energies to their maximum tension and sets the seal of nobility on those peoples who have the courage to face it. . . .[16]

If at one time it might have been believed that violence had only a chance connection to totalitarianism, that is no longer the case. The consistent pattern of war, revolution, purges, and concentration camps suggests strongly that violence is indeed an integral feature of the totalitarian system. This has, of course, been commented upon widely and in a variety of ways. Hannah Arendt, for example, expresses the generally shared view: "Terror, in the form of the concentration camp, is more essential than any other institution to the preservation of the regime's power. It accomplishes the complete domination of the ruled, and sustains the belief of the rulers." [17] Violence is thus understandable not only as a concomitant of basic totalitarian premises, it is linked as well to the concept of total control and to the reinforcement of the superior-inferior structure of society. Since violence also complements the enemy-oriented and antipluralistic attitudes of totalitarianism, we are now better positioned to see how the different components interrelate to form a common ideological bond.

To canvass the beliefs and values of totalitarianism, as we have attempted, should substantially help us to understand its nature and char-

[16] Mussolini, *op. cit.* (above, n. 1). Communism does not exalt violence or war per se, however.

[17] Arendt, *op. cit.* (above, n. 10), p. 456. See also Alex Inkeles, "The Totalitarian Mystique: Some Impressions of the Dynamics of Totalitarian Society," in Friedrich, *op. cit.* (above, n. 5), pp. 89 and 106. (Whether a totalitarian system can eventually become so firmly established, by means of propaganda, familiarity, and economic success, that an excessive reliance on force is unnecessary, remains to be seen. Soviet communism has this objective, of course; whether it can succeed largely depends on the vitality of the Russian people's urge toward freedom despite prolonged conditioning by coercive institutions and totalitarian propaganda.)

acteristics. As has already been suggested, the answer may be made still more meaningful and complete by focusing on some of the more outstanding organizational features of totalitarian society. We should anticipate, of course, that the way in which a totalitarian system is structured will also reflect the ideas and attitudes previously surveyed.

Perhaps the most sophisticated and useful inventory of structural components—one which we will follow in exploring the organizational features of totalitarianism—is that suggested by Friedrich and Brzezinski.[18] Of particular interest in their inventory is the identification of a ruling elite, police terror, a monopoly of weapons, a monopoly of communications, and a controlled economy.[19]

First on the list as a structural feature in the organization of totalitarian society is the familiar pattern of elitist rule. Friedrich and Brzezinski have further refined this point in observing that this elite typically consists of a single leader at the head of a one-party state—the party comprised of "hard core" adherents and representing no more than ten percent of the total population.[20] One does not have to reach far to find conspicuous examples across the board of totalitarian regimes: Mussolini and the *Fasci Italiani di Combattimento* (Fascist Party), Hitler and the *National Sozialistische Deutsche Arbeiter Partei* (Nazi Party), or Brehnev and the *Kommunistscheskoi Partii Sovetskovo Soyuza* (Communist Party).[21] In each of these cases we have dramatic evidence of a concentration of power arranged hierarchically between leader and party, and inhospitable to rival interests. Moreover, the consistent appearance of this pattern has prompted the conclusion that there is a necessary kind of interdependence between the strong leader and the single party. The party is the vehicle by which the leader gains access to power and through which, once in power, he can rule and maintain his position. Conversely, the leader may be perceived as a convenient, useful, and potentially rewarding focal point of the party members' goals. Thus understood, the pattern may also help explain why such leaders are frequently described as charismatic (here the magnetic embodiment of a cause), why the party takes on the trappings of a restricted, semisecret, and militant society (functional for both the acquisition and safeguarding of power), and why a complex bureaucratic system tends to evolve in the

[18] Friedrich and Brzezinski, *op. cit.* (above, n. 3).
[19] *Ibid.*, pp. 21ff. Omitted from the original inventory is the item "ideology," which has been separated out for purposes of this analysis.
[20] *Ibid.*, p. 22.
[21] Friedrich and Brzezinski reckon both the Fascist and Communist parties at about five percent of their respective populations. The Nazis permitted a larger membership, but there is evidence to indicate that this was offset by the formation of a new elite (the SS) within the old. See *ibid.*, pp. 56ff.

wake of this organization (as an aid to the exercise of total power by the leader and party).[22]

How well do such developments coincide with the core values and beliefs of totalitarianism? Rather well, if we cast back briefly to the totalitarian image of natural inequality and its derivative notions of elitism and antipluralism. The concept of an elite, we noted earlier, finds considerable support in the basic totalitarian view of life as a conflict among unequals. It follows therefore that the state ought to be organized around those—the one man and the one party—who are superior. And, finally, we are again reminded that the totalitarian looks intolerantly at those who stand apart—considering them in fact as adversaries. Antipluralism, in sum, contributes significantly to the organizational characteristic of one-man and one-party rule.

Second among the recurrent structural features of totalitarian organization is that of police terror. Whatever the specific apparatus may be called —the *Squadrista* and OVRA in Italy, the SS in Germany, or the MVD and KGB in the Soviet Union—such institutional machinery appears to be one of the conspicuous characteristics of totalitarian operation.[23] In one form or another the totalitarian elite has available an agency possessed of extraordinary powers and capable of applying extensive force (both physical and psychological) throughout the system. In short, the ever-present threat of police terror tends to function as an important institutional mechanism for securing conformity.

How shall we account for the persistent phenomenon of police terror in totalitarianism? One readily available explanation might well be found in the positive value attached to violence (or the readiness to resort to it) by the totalitarian. Certainly the attachment to a terroristic police would seem

---

[22] *Ibid.,* Chaps. 3, 4, and 16.

[23] In Italy the *Squadrista* served as the party's secret police, while the OVRA (*Opera Volontaria per la Repressione Antifascista*) was the equivalent for the state. In Germany the secret police arrangements were far more complicated. Originally it was the SA (*Sturmabteilung* or stormtroopers) brownshirts which functioned in this capacity. The SA was in turn superseded by the Gestapo (*Geheime Staatspolizei* or Secret State Police) and the SS (*Schutzstaffeln* or Elite Guards). The SS eventually absorbed the Gestapo, and both became part of a larger complex called the RSHA (*Reichssicherheitshauptamt,* or Reich Control Security Office). Yet another echelon was added, the SD (*Sicherheitspolizei* or Security Police), which may have constituted an elite arm of the SS and RSHA. Similar complexities seem to have surrounded the secret police organization in the U.S.S.R. Beginning with the Cheka, which was superseded by the GPU (State Political Administration) and OGPU (Unified Government Political Administration), we can trace the development of the secret police to the NKVD (People's Commissariat of Internal Affairs), which in turn was supplanted by the MGB (Ministry of State Security) and MVD (Ministry of Internal Affairs). The present apparatus couples the MVD with a KGB (Committee for State Security). *Ibid.,* Chaps. 13 and 14.

to be entirely consistent with the Nazi-fascist belief system, which associates power with nobility and weakness with inferiority. It has also been suggested that the emphasis on violence is directly related to the companion values of total control and antipluralism. With respect to the idea of total control, Friedrich and Brzezinski have particularly emphasized the cause-and-effect relationship between the desire to dominate all aspects of society and the kind of machinery (police terror) necessary for the accomplishment of that objective.[24] In a sense it is the very magnitude of the totalitarian goal which compels equally extreme measures to reach it. Again, the corollary to total control is the unqualified rejection of a pluralistic society —hence the premium on unanimity. Here the role of police terror has relevance not only for the kind of conformity it engenders amongst a fearful population at large, but also for the like effect which it comes to have within the leadership circle itself. Thus police terror also serves to reinforce the elite's claim to power, particularly that of the leader. Perhaps this obsessiveness with conformity, and the sense of security which the leader finds in it, may also help to explain why the pattern of police terror tends to persist even in the more matured totalitarian systems.

The third structural feature suggested by the Friedrich and Brzezinski analysis relates to the monopoly of weapons.[25] There is, of course, an obvious parallel between this characteristic of totalitarian organization and the preceding discussion of police terror. It seems safe to conclude at least that exclusive control over the means of force should serve much the same function as do the various enforcement agencies. One aspect of this topic does, however, warrant further comment at this point—the significant role of the military. Here again the most casual survey of totalitarian regimes offers convincing evidence to suggest that a highly developed military establishment is native to all such systems. Yet there is also reason to believe that the armed forces occupy an especially delicate institutional position. On the one hand, of course, there should be little doubt that a powerful military resource would be compatible with the postulates of totalitarian ideology. A heavily armed capability augurs the extinction of the enemy: it can function to preserve the homogeneous complexion of society; it affords additional leverage in the accomplishment of total control; and it may serve to symbolize the vitality of violence. Since totalitarian systems have also generally aspired to a more universalistic influence, there is an imperialistic

[24] *Ibid.* The suggestion has also been made that the kind of police terror required for the ambitious aims of totalitarianism is such that only a technologically sophisticated society could provide it. This idea would agree with the earlier observation that totalitarianism is truly a modern-day phenomenon, requiring an advanced development.

[25] *Ibid.*, p. 22; related material is contained in Chap. 26.

thrust to the movement which again underscores the importance of the military establishment.

In spite of this, however, and contrary to the popular assumption of a "perfect" marriage between the leader and the military, the romance has its problems. Friedrich and Brzezinski make the point, first of all, that there is not quite the same kind of initial attachment between the military and the leader in the coming-to-power of totalitarianism as there is in a more conventional dictatorship.[26] It is in the case of the latter that the military coup more regularly coincides, not infrequently elevating one of its own to supreme power. The early history of the communists, fascists, and Nazis, by comparison, was much more independent of the military. This is not to say that the armed forces were hostile; indeed, there is reason to believe that they contributed to the totalitarian cause if only through their crucial acquiescence to the new regime. In any event, though, the totalitarian leader would seem to be identified more closely with an active party than with a passive and more distant military. More important still may be the recognition of the potential threat to the position of the elite which the military represents. A strong armed force may well constitute an independent interest group, violating the ideal of total control and homogeneity, and providing a realistic base of operation for the overthrow of the regime.

Thus the military poses a dilemma for totalitarianism in the sense that it is both an indispensable and a threatening institution within the system. Of course totalitarian ideology strongly suggests that the leader cannot passively accept the possibility of a rival allegiance within the system (especially if the rival has a monopoly of weapons). To maximize the usefulness of the military, while minimizing its danger, the elite is impelled to undertake measures which will make the armed forces politically secure. The intrusion of party influence within the military is indeed one of the observable characteristics in the history of the major totalitarian regimes. Although such efforts have met with varying degrees of success, they testify well to the pervasiveness of the total-control norm.

We come now to the fourth structural feature of totalitarian organization, the monopoly of communications. The control of all media of expression—including access to information—is one of the consistent characteristics of the system.[27] The monopoly of communications bears an important relationship to the realization of at least two other earmarks of totalitarian structure: an extensive propaganda effort, and a systematic arrangement for the ideological indoctrination of children.

For example, Hitler's awareness of the utility of propaganda, and the

[26] *Ibid.*
[27] *Ibid.*, Chap. 11.

resulting apparatus under the highly centralized control of Dr. Joseph Goebbels, has its parallels in totalitarian systems generally. The reasons, of course, are by now familiar: propaganda offers potential reinforcement for the infallibility of the leader, obedience to elite control, and hostility to the "enemy." Moreover, it may serve to make the formation of opposition more difficult, and it is a vital element in the successful prosecution of a military effort. In sum, propaganda may be an important vehicle in the building of mass solidarity.[28]

The monopoly of communications also facilitates the political "education" of the mass, reaching with equal vigor toward the youngest generational levels. It is a striking and significant fact that totalitarian leaders have uniformly expressed a high priority interest in the political potential of youth. If the system is going to endure, if the ideology is to be carried forward, the leaders must look to the generation from which tomorrow's elite will be drawn and from which the new followers are also to come. It follows, therefore, that the totalitarian regime would have a vested interest in institutionalizing and controlling the education of the young. And so it is that we find exactly such programs in the forms of the ONB (*Balilla*) under Italian fascism, the *Hitlerjugend* under German National Socialism, and the Young Communist League (*Komsomol*) in Soviet communism.[29]

The monopoly of communications, propaganda, and the directed effort at early political indoctrination thus make sense in the totalitarian context of maintaining total control. And yet it might seem as if such measures would have a lower priority—perhaps even be superfluous—in light of the more compelling techniques (e.g., police terror) available to reinforce the system. Perhaps the answer lies not simply in the specific content of the ideology, but in the role which the ideology performs. The point is well expressed by Robert Dahl: "One reason why leaders develop an ideology is

---

[28] On the other hand, as Friedrich and Brzezinski note, the system may also find itself confronted with new problems as a result of propaganda saturation: one is that propaganda eventually breeds a kind of cynicism which manifests itself in an increasing reliance on rumor as an alternative to the "official" source of information. Secondly, it is quite possible for propaganda to become so well integrated into the system that the system echoes a like propaganda back to the top. As a result, the elite is increasingly isolated from an accurate reading of their followers. *Ibid.*

[29] The Soviet arrangement actually divides into three age levels: children under 10 years belong to the Octobrists, between 10 and 14 to the Young Pioneers, and over 14 to *Komsomol.* Such programs are intended to supplement the related ideological program of the school system. In content they appear heavily oriented toward the cultivation of militancy, discipline, and obedience—both ideologically and physically. This content also mirrors the general totalitarian fetish for physical accomplishment, and its persistent strain of anti-intellectualism. Moreover, youth groups again seem to reflect the adult totalitarian world in their own development of an elite, as illustrated in the case of the *Stamm-HJ* within the *Hitlerjugend. Ibid.*, Chap. 12.

obvious: to endow their leadership with legitimacy—to convert their political influence into authority. And it is far more economical to rule by means of authority than by means of coercion." [30] Since popular acceptance of the regime is both a more dependable and less costly operation than the alternative of terror, the monopoly of communications assumes a still more basic function in the totalitarian system.

Finally, a few brief comments on the subject of the fifth structural feature of totalitarian organization, the controlled economy. In view of the pattern which has begun to crystallize, we should not be surprised to find that the economic sector has a well-defined role to play in the overall structure of totalitarian society. More explicitly, this means that all of the basic components of production—employers, labor force, and farmers—are to be brought into line. Such control, of course, invites two further expectations about the nature of totalitarian organization: first, since the regulation of the economy is purposeful, some kind of apparatus must perform a planning function; and, second, the accomplishment of planning would seem to necessitate the development of a vast hierarchic bureaucracy. Indeed, these are precisely the conditions encountered in our experience with fascism, Naziism, and communism, albeit in different form and degrees. Although the communists have provided a more dramatic example of the managed economy—in the form of state ownership, management, and a long succession of five-year plans—the fascists and Nazis appear to have travelled a similar road, if only a bit more circuitous, in their reliance on state control of private cartels. [31] In all, however, the basic subservience of economy to the interests of the regime was the net result.

This feature of totalitarian organization bears in some respects an interesting likeness to the position of the military. Earlier we had occasion to note that totalitarian policy toward the armed forces was as much dictated by the fear of an independent power within its midst, as it was by the way it could usefully serve the interests of the regime. A like observation might well apply here. It is not difficult to perceive that the various interest groupings of industrialists, labor unions, etc., represent a potential impediment if left to their own devices. The alternative of integrating them within the system may have its risks, but the advantage is no less than the

[30] Robert Dahl, *Modern Political Analysis,* 2nd ed. (Englewood, N.J.: Prentice-Hall, 1970), p. 42.

[31] The Italian system of the corporative state is particularly interesting. The economy was organized into industry-wide corporations, each composed of syndicates for workers, employers, and professionals. The Fascist party then dominated the corporation, guarantying full control. The Nazis also had a type of corporate state, but of a different order, more like a military command. See Friedrich and Brzezinski, *op. cit.* (above, n. 3), part V.

perpetuation of the entire ideology. Hence control over the economic sector finds its place in the totalitarian concept of total control over the society.

Totalitarian Origins

To ask "how did totalitarianism originate?" would seem to pose a simple historical question, requiring only a simple historical answer. Yet the problem is more complicated—not alone because historical questions are rarely simple—but also because the meaning of "origin" has broad implications. In the sense that our objective is to understand the factors out of which totalitarianism developed, we must add both a philosophical and a socio-economic approach to the basic historical one. Within these three frameworks, considered below, are to be found the prevailing theories as to the "origins" of totalitarian ideology.

Since a more elaborate account of the early history of the various totalitarian systems follows this chapter, we shall confine ourselves here to a somewhat more general view of the subject. One very basic impression, of course, already exists: that is, that totalitarianism is essentially a twentieth-century phenomenon. As a matter of pure chronology it was the communist revolution in Russia (1917) which marked the earliest appearance of a totalitarian state. Italian fascism was not far behind (1922), after which came German National Socialism (1933). Of the major totalitarian regimes under consideration here, Chinese communism was the last to be established (1949).

Although in long-range terms this chronology may be reason enough to fix totalitarianism as a by-product of the age, in shorter-range terms it would seem to offer a bewildering sequence of events. Does there exist some kind of historical common denominator which is at root here?

The consensus on this point seems to have centered about a "crisis-theory" as a viable explanation for the emergence of totalitarianism.[32] In essence this theory holds that conditions of acute distress—e.g., war, economic disaster, and so forth—can precipitate an intense reaction among a people in the form of insecurity, frustration, and resentment. And in the wake of such anxieties the people may despair of the system which "failed" them and look for a more drastic alternative solution. Thus, the appeal of totalitarianism—as a way out, replete with the "security" of a father-like leader and the promise of good triumphant over evil.

There is, indeed, much to be said for this theory. Totalitarianism came to

[32] See, for example, Arendt, *op. cit.* (above, n. 10), pp. 315, 331; Kennan, *op. cit.* (above, n. 7), p. 26; Frenkel-Brunswik, *op. cit.* (above, n. 5), p. 177; and Friedrich and Brzezinski, *op. cit.* (above, n. 3), p. 17.

Russia at a time of aggravated discontent over social, economic, and military problems; at a time when ". . . Russian political life was in a state of hopeless chaos. . . ." [33] It came to Italy ". . . when social and economic unrest was pushing the nation to the brink of civil war" [34]—at a time, too, when Italians felt deprived of their share of the fruits of war. Totalitarianism came to Germany in the midst of social, economic, and political crisis, and on the heels of its humiliation in World War I. It was a time, as one writer puts it, when ". . . discontent and bitterness mounted to menacing proportions." [35] And, finally, totalitarianism came to China under like circumstances of economic, social, and political instability, generated by years of fighting and years of neglect. [36]

Crisis would thus appear to be at the very heart of the matter from the standpoint of a historical analysis. Yet it seems unlikely that this condition alone can suffice. For the obvious question remains: Since crisis surely is not the exclusive property of the twentieth century, why have past crises not also generated totalitarian responses?

One highly provocative, although perhaps problematic, answer to this question suggests that the crisis must be coupled with a kind of social climate conducive to a totalitarian result. [37] In other words, in some cases the traditions are strong enough to weather the storm of crisis, while in others the immunity to totalitarianism is much more fragile. This is, perhaps, a variation of a "national character" approach, and is closely akin to such popular expressions as "a Hitler was possible in Germany only because of the basic authoritarian and militaristic character of the German people." While the factor of tradition cannot be discounted, it courts some difficulty in its resemblance to a kind of "bad-blood" theory. Moreover, it begins to assume a tautological dimension insofar as it seems to argue that some systems tend to be totalitarian because they tend to be totalitarian!

Perhaps a more promising answer turns on the nature of the crisis itself. Today's world, today's society, and today's problems—all are different from their counterparts in the past. Twentieth-century man confronts a bigger and more complex environment, and carries with him an equally changed set of anxieties. Relative to the specific occurrence of totalitarianism in the twentieth century, we can hypothesize that in such factors as in-

[33] Dan N. Jacobs, *The Masks of Communism* (New York: Harper & Row, 1963), p. 41.

[34] S. William Halperin, *Mussolini and Italian Fascism* (New York: D. Van Nostrand, 1964), p. 32.

[35] Theodore Abel, *The Nazi Movement: Why Hitler Came to Power* (New York: Atherton, 1966), p. 121.

[36] Jacobs, *op. cit.* (above, n. 30), p. 191.

[37] William M. McGovern, *From Luther to Hitler* (Boston: Houghton Mifflin, 1941), p. 6. Frenkel-Brunswik, *op. cit.* (above, n, 5), p. 171.

dustrialization and mass society are to be found unprecedented crises and unprecedented political behavior. Thus the increasing theme: that one of the seemingly unavoidable costs of a modern society is the blurring of individual identity.[38] In sum, perhaps totalitarianism is of recent vintage because the problems are of recent vintage.

There are problems with this answer too. It is probably no exaggeration to assume that every age has regarded its crises as uniquely severe. Moreover, some societies have—even in the twentieth century—faced problems not unlike those of the totalitarian nations without going the totalitarian way. At best, then, there seems to be no conclusive or definitive answer to the question of origins, at least from the standpoint of history.

Our second approach to the problem lies in the area of political philosophy. While it is unlikely that this approach alone can tell us why totalitarian ideology finds sympathetic reception in some quarters but not in others, it can nonetheless contribute to our understanding of how such ideas take shape. The task, indeed, is not an easy one. Not because totalitarianism—as a new breed of ideology—has no debts to the past; quite the contrary, it is complicated because it has borrowed as widely as most other ideologies have. Thus the late Professor William McGovern made an arguable case for tracing fascist origins back to the sixteenth century (with the inception of the nation-state), while acknowledging that a more distant cousin could be found in the writings of Plato (in the concept of elite rule over a collectivity).[39] This less ambitious discussion is confined to a rather select group of philosophical progenitors—and the discussion of their influence confined largely to the fascists and the Nazis since the ideological influence of Hegel, Marx, and Engels is considered in a later section, on communism (see pp. 96 ff.).

Side by side with the introduction of Marxist philosophy in the nineteenth century came two other currents which figured significantly in the development of totalitarian ideology. One of these was Social Darwinism, a political version of the famous biological theory, and one with which Darwin himself was not involved. This school of thought, typified by the writings of Walter Bagehot and Ludwig Gumplowicz, attempted to take up where Darwin left off by postulating an evolutionary theory for political and social institutions.[40] Thus they argued that incessant struggle for survival is the natural

[38] Erich Fromm, *Escape from Freedom* (New York: Farrar and Rinehart, 1941). Also William H. Whyte, *The Organization Man* (Garden City, N.Y.: Doubleday, 1956). Both are classic expressions of this problem.

[39] McGovern, *op. cit.* (above, n. 34), p. 21.

[40] Social Darwinism also found another disciple in Herbert Spencer, but with somewhat different results. Spencer was a champion of individualism and laissez-faire theory. *Ibid.*, Chap. 10.

order of life in politics as much as in biology. And within such conflict it is the fittest which survive and succeed. Of course being fittest requires being strong, and so certain measures are now mandatory. As Bagehot observes:

Unless you can make a strong co-operative bond, your society will be conquered and killed out by some other society which has such a bond. . . . The members of such a group should be similar enough to one another to co-operate easily and readily together. The co-operation in all such cases depends on a felt union of heart and spirit; and this is felt only where there is a great degree of real likeness in mind and feeling, however that likeness may have been attained.[41]

Not only homogeneity is required, but also an elite to insure the kind of conformity which will keep the state strong. Gumplowicz puts the matter thus:

The rulership of a majority over a minority is as unthinkable as it is absurd. It lies in the nature of things that a pyramid must rest on a broad basis, becoming smaller and smaller as it rises to the top. It is impossible to place a pyramid upside down, with its broad base suspended in the air. In like manner it lies in the nature of rulership that it can only exist in the domination of the minority over the majority.[42]

Finally, as the Social Darwinists see it, survival of the fittest brings evolution—and progress—to the world of politics no less than to the world of biology. Going beyond Darwin, therefore, they hold the principle of survival of the fittest to be not only inevitable, but also desirable.

It is not at all difficult to match the concept of Social Darwinism with the composite picture of totalitarianism presented earlier. Not only did the Darwinists provide an explicit rationale for the conflict-among-unequals orientation, but they also lent philosophic support to the derivative ideas about the enemy, the elite, and violence.

Moreover, Social Darwinists such as Bagehot and Gumplowicz were relatively tame compared to others who attached themselves to this school. One group of disciples, for example, went much further in defining the fit and the unfit along racial, religious, and ethnic lines. Comte Arthur de Gobineau, as a case in point, was one of the extreme exponents of this idea, stressing the "natural" and "inherent" superiority of white over yellow skin, and yellow over black. Within the white elite, moreover, he found yet another pecking order: Slavs over Semites, and Aryans over all.[43] Gobineau

---

[41] Walter Bagehot, *Physics and Politics, Works,* VIII, p. 138; quoted in *ibid.,* p. 467.

[42] Ludwig Gumplowicz, *Rassenkampf,* p. 220; quoted in McGovern, *op. cit.* (above, n. 34), p. 484.

[43] Gobineau's use of the term "Aryan" referred to the original Germanic tribes, but also to an aristocratic element in France and England during his own time. McGovern, *op. cit.* (above, n. 34), p. 503.

thus set the stage for much of the racist thinking in German National Socialism, but it was Houston Stewart Chamberlain—another member of the school—who put the finishing touches on it. While Gobineau had found it possible to tolerate some "racial impurity" in the form of intermarriage, Chamberlain would have none of it. Indeed, even social contact with the non-Aryan was dangerous: "Often it needs only to have frequent intercourse with Jews, to read Jewish newspapers, to accustom oneself to Jewish philosophy, literature and art" to infect the Aryan.[44] Chamberlain therefore recommended the deportation of all Jews from Europe. And finally, he made clear that it was Germany and the "Germanic peoples" which represent the true embodiment of Aryanism, and to whom fate had entrusted the responsibility for preventing racial decay.

Beside Social Darwinism there was a second contributing group of philosophers, the "Irrationalists," who figured significantly in the development of totalitarian ideology, finding particular favor with Mussolini. Among them, Friedrich Nietzsche was perhaps the best known.[45] While Nietzsche retained some of the flavor of Social Darwinism, he did so with an added twist. In his image of the world the one preeminent motivating force is the blind struggling "will"—a kind of unconscious impulse or drive. But Nietzsche's will is not simply a compulsion to survive, it is a will to control and dominate all others: it is a "will to power." In a world of this order, Nietzsche finds no rationality (hence the label), no absolute truth or morality—only the inexorable struggle of wills. Nor does he despair at this state of affairs; quite the contrary, he appears to endorse the kind of positive fulfillment enjoyed by those who embrace it. What Nietzsche finally derives from this view is a concept of a divided universe: one part strong-willed, a "race" of "supermen" who rule by a morality based on the nobility of strength; the other part weak-willed, to be ruled by a different morality—dedicated to serving their superiors.

With the Irrationalists, then, the doctrine of conflict and inequality occurs again. But the example of Nietzsche discloses still more: the basic anti-intellectualism found in totalitarian ideology, the idealization of the elite, and the virtuousness of violence. Understanding these philosophical views, we can better understand the source of totalitarian ideas about the exalted place of violence and aggressiveness.

Putting aside history and philosophy, there is yet a third and much different way in which it is possible to speak of the sources of totalitarian-

[44] Houston Stewart Chamberlain, *The Foundations of the Nineteenth Century*, I, p. 491, quoted in McGovern, *op. cit.* (above, n. 34), p. 508.

[45] Nietzsche was heir apparent to the philosopher Arthur Schopenhauer, and the views of irrationalism are also passed along in the writings of Georges Sorel and Vilfredo Pareto.

ism. A more eclectic approach to the problem takes shape in the form of social scientists' efforts to find meaning in the socio-economic and psychological bases of totalitarianism. In a very figurative sense, the emphasis here turns from the question "what" to the question "who."

It is, of course, the basic inseparability of politics from society—and from groups within the society—which prompts the hypothesis that political behavior (and political ideas) may be the product of differing socio-economic classes. The proposition is empirical enough: Is there any evidence to support the notion that totalitarianism is indigenous to some particular stratum of society? The research of Seymour Martin Lipset [46] is highly instructive on this point, and deserving of serious consideration.

Professor Lipset does indeed find a link between totalitarianism and social class, but the pattern requires further differentiation. Not only is there no *one* class with ties to totalitarianism, but any given class can yield either a democratic or nondemocratic response. In this sense there is no single predictive instrument. But what Lipset does find is that among the major types of totalitarianism, each has its own distinctive socioeconomic base of support. Thus the communist version of totalitarianism finds its primary following among the lower classes, while the fascist (and Nazi) appeal can be identified with the middle class.

This finding warrants some explanation, especially in light of the popular belief in the liberalism of the lower classes, and the equally familiar assumption of fascism as an upperclass phenomenon.

In the lower classes Lipset has identified, first, a basic predisposition toward authoritarianism—a kind of latent congeniality toward totalitarian values. To be sure, the lower classes are not completely devoid of all liberalism, but closer inspection reveals that such liberalism is primarily *economic,* while the concerns of civil liberties command very little support.[47] There is, in fact, a rather marked intolerance about lower-class perspectives, which can be explained in a number of ways. For one thing the lack of educational attainment which typifies lower-class standing means an outlook of narrow dimensions (thinking in "either-or" terms), a preference for "action" rather than "verbalization," and a general inclination toward the uncomplicated answer. Low income, as another factor, means a condition of persistent discontent which makes attractive the excuse of the scapegoat and the emphasis on instant-cure programs. Moreover, economic insecurity tends to foster the primacy of short-range plan-

[46] Lipset, *op. cit.* (above, n. 11), Chaps. 4 and 5.
[47] The illusion of lower-class affection for civil liberties is explained by Lipset as a historical phase during which the working classes found it expedient to champion such rights for economic reasons. *Ibid.,* p. 122.

ning as opposed to the long-range planning of the middle class. (It is considerably easier to be future-oriented when the next meal is not in doubt, and when the paycheck leaves something for savings!) It has also been argued that this predisposition toward authoritarianism is further reinforced by the family life-style of the lower class: in a home environment characterized by constant frustration and friction, interpersonal relations tend to be more "authoritarian" and intemperate. The net effect of this entire configuration is a general climate of intolerance, a relative paucity of conditions usually regarded as requisite for a democratic political system, and a substantial vulnerability to totalitarian appeal. The point is not that totalitarianism is an inevitable result; indeed, more often than not the likely consequence is that lower class individuals are discouraged from political involvement and withdraw in the form of nonvoting, etc. But the basic predisposition towards authoritarianism of which Lipset speaks, suggests that only some circumstance of extreme stress may be necessary to activate the latent tendencies. In that event the economic interests of the lower class might easily find expression in a totalitarianism of the "left."

At first blush the circumstances of middle-class life seem so conspicuously different from the impoverishment of lower class education and economics that a parallel link with totalitarianism would appear a bit remote. And yet the data are impressive: it was the middle class which carried Hitler and the National Socialists to power in Germany, while—contrary to common opinion—the upper classes remained at arm's length until Naziism was a *fait accompli*.[48] Indeed, Lipset has provided us with a composite picture of the "average" follower of Hitler: "The ideal-typical Nazi voter in 1932 was a middle-class self-employed Protestant who lived either on a farm or in a small community, and who had previously voted for a centrist or regionalist political party strongly opposed to the power and influence of big business and big labor."[49] Within this description we have an important clue to an understanding of the socio-economic bases of support for both fascism and National Socialism. If we take our lead from the finding that the middle-class totalitarian was psychologically at war with the interests of *both* unions *and* corporate industry, then we can properly speak of a middle class threatened from both above and below, a class which perceives itself "caught" in the middle. It seems to be precisely this kind of psychological "squeeze" which begins to explain the resultant political behavior. Coupled with this was the fact that the middle class—once the power which shook the older order—now found its political and social fortunes in a declining state. In sum, the crisis of the middle class can be

[48] *Ibid.*, pp. 138 ff.
[49] *Ibid.*, p. 148.

described as its increasing isolation and insecurity in the face of new rivals. And out of this anxiety comes the quest for some political program which promises the restoration of lost or losing glories. It was this development, in large measure, which sealed the bargain between the middle classes and noncommunist totalitarianism.

Throughout the preceding discussion of the socio-economic bases of totalitarianism there has threaded a recurrent reference to a psychological component, about which something more needs to be said. As evidenced by the recognition already given to family influences on political attitudes, there has been growing interest among students of political behavior as to the crucial role of socialization and the early formation of political attitudes. Is there a psychological syndrome—a personality type—which may be more susceptible than other types to the values of totalitarianism?

Psychological research has marshaled some impressive evidence on this subject, at the center of which stands the work of T. W. Adorno and associates, in *The Authoritarian Personality*.[50] The thrust of their thesis is that a basically authoritarian parent-child relationship tends to produce a personality type with marked authoritarian attitudes. Such individuals are, in a manner of speaking, psychologically scarred, and they are unable to manage the hostility which such relationships engender toward their parents and toward themselves. As a result, their "adjustment" takes the form of transferring—or displacing—their bitterness towards others. Ironically, they end by emulating the very same type of authoritarian relationship as that which precipitated the problem. What, then, are the manifestations of such a relationship? The Adorno study answers:

> The most crucial result . . . is the demonstration of close correspondence in the type of approach and outlook a subject is likely to have in a great variety of areas, ranging from the most intimate features of family and sex adjustment through relationships to other people in general, to religion and to social and political philosophy. Thus a basically hierarchical, authoritarian, exploitive parent-child relationship is apt to carry over into a power-oriented, exploitively dependent attitude towards one's sex partner and one's God and may well culminate in a political philosophy and social outlook which has no room for anything but a desperate clinging to what appears to be strong and disdainful rejection of whatever is relegated to the bottom.[51]

Attitudes of rigidity and hostility, then, are central to the concept of the authoritarian personality. Rigidity expresses itself in terms of a highly con-

---

[50] (New York: Harper, 1950). See especially pp. 228 ff. More recent refinements are contained in Richard Christie and Peggy Cook, "A Guide to Published Literature Relating to the Authoritarian Personality through 1956," *Journal of Psychology*, XLV (April, 1958), 171–199; and Milton Rokeach, *The Open and Closed Mind* (New York: Basic Books, 1960).

[51] Adorno, *op. cit.*, p. 971.

ventionalized system of values—unbending, uncritical, and stereotyped. Such individuals, in a political sense, would exhibit the behavior of the rabid party-liner, with a penchant for simplistic slogans and superficial explanations. Moreover, the concept of rigidity would also have its effect in terms of a slavish obedience to these values.

Hostility may also be seen in several ways: in cynicism, in disdain for weakness and idealization of power and strength, and in a fixation for the punitive. Hence the politically hostile individual is one likely to mistrust the regular political process, even to the point of a paranoid suspiciousness which sees conspiracies and treachery everywhere. Betrayal, of course, is regarded as the child of weakness: there would be no evil if only men were strong enough to resist the hostile forces which threaten from all sides. And what better personification of this idea than the heroic leader who promises to restore strength and pride to all who would follow him? This means, too, that in the ultimate confrontation between the good (strong) and the evil (weak) there will be an end to compromise and talk. There will be instead the long-awaited men of action, and swift, sure judgment for all opposition.

There is much to be said for the utility of the authoritarian personality thesis, though it is by no means without its critics. One major reservation concerns its almost exclusive preoccupation with the psychology of the individual, and its failure to give sufficient attention to situational or group influences. Some would argue that authoritarianism requires an understanding of the cultural dynamics and specifically the subcultures of a given society, for both contribute to the experiences of an individual, and to the shaping of his political responses. It may well be that much of what passes for personality factors according to the authoritarian thesis are in reality the result of group influences and environment.[52]

Nonetheless, research on the authoritarian personality is an important contribution to the study of totalitarianism. The search for a possible cluster of psychological attitudes has generated widespread interest, and it may well prove to be one of the most useful and sophisticated tools for analysis and understanding of the problem.

Totalitarianism versus Totalitarianism

Having examined certain generalities about totalitarianism, it should be possible now to comprehend the kind of ideological kinship which brings communism, fascism, and Naziism under one label. And yet it is not only

---

[52] See Richard Christie and Marie Jahoda, eds., *Studies in the Scope and Method of "The Authoritarian Personality,"* (Glencoe: Free Press, 1954); and Don Stewart and Thomas Hoult, "A Social-Psychological Theory of the Authoritarian Personality," *American Journal of Sociology,* LXV (November, 1959), 274–279.

the points of convergence which command attention, but also the points of divergence. What meaningful differences exist between the various types of totalitarianism?

A partial answer to this question is contained within some of the previous material. It was noted earlier, for instance, that the socio-economic base of support is considerably different for the communists as opposed to the fascists and Nazis. The differential association of the lower classes with the communists and the middle classes with the fascists and Nazis has given rise to speculation about the possibility of communism being linked to the poorer and pre-industrialized nations, while fascists and National Socialists are linked to the wealthier and post-industrialized states. Furthermore, we can be quite certain that just as the fascists and Nazis distinguished themselves from the communists in their explicit anti-Marxism, so the communists set themselves apart from Nazi-fascism, regarding the latter as a terminal phase of capitalism.

There may be other critical differences as well. In terms of totalitarian involvement in the planning and management of the economic sector, it has been suggested that the communists may well differ from noncommunists in degree; and there is evidence also to suspect that a similar distinction exists between fascists and Nazis. Communist practice, not surprisingly, involves much greater control of light industry and small business than Nazi-fascism.

The basic orientation, furthermore, seems considerably different between communists and noncommunists. Where class struggle seems to dominate the former, it is the concept of race and nation which appears uppermost to the fascists and Nazis. In addition, the communists do not exalt violence for its own sake (however readily they may resort to it in attaining or perpetuating power). Nor do they extol the irrational and the mystical; every effort is made to reduce communist ideology to a science. While Nazi-fascist ideology is formally built around the leader principle, communist ideology is not (even though Maoist, Stalinist, Ho Chi Minh, and Castroite communism turned out in practice to be leader-obsessed).

Even this abbreviated list—which is intended to be suggestive rather than exhaustive—points toward the need for a much more detailed exploration of the various subsystems of totalitarianism. Only through a case-by-case analysis of fascism, Naziism, and communism can we precisely define their parallels and singularities. That is the task to which we now turn.

Bibliography

Adorno, Theodore W., et al. *The Authoritarian Personality*. New York: Harper, 1950.

Arendt, Hannah. *The Origins of Totalitarianism*. New York: Harcourt, Brace, 1951.

Bell, Daniel, ed. *The Radical Right*. Garden City: Doubleday, 1963.

Blanksten, George I. *Peron's Argentina*. Chicago: University of Chicago Press, 1953.

Edinger, Lewis J. *Politics in Germany*. Boston: Little, Brown, 1968.

Friedrich, Carl J. *Totalitarianism*. Cambridge, Mass.: Harvard University Press, 1954.

————, and Brzezinski, Zbigniew K. *Totalitarian Dictatorship and Autocracy*. 2d ed. New York: Frederick A. Praeger, 1965.

Fromm, Erich. *Escape From Freedom*. New York: Holt, 1941.

Lipset, Seymour. *Political Man*. Garden City: Doubleday, 1960.

Macridis, Roy C., and Ward, Robert E. *Modern Political Systems: Europe*. Englewood, N.J.: Prentice-Hall, 1963.

McGovern, William M. *From Luther to Hitler*. Boston: Houghton Mifflin, 1941.

Newman, Edwin S. *The Hate Reader*. Dobbs Ferry, N.Y.: Oceana, 1964.

Rokeach, Milton. *The Open and Closed Mind*. New York: Basic Books, 1960.

Spitz, David. *Patterns of Anti-Democratic Thought*. New York: Macmillan, 1949.

Chapter 3

Fascism and Naziism

Fascism

What many have suspected about totalitarianism in general, and about fascism in particular, was confirmed by Mussolini near the very end of his career: "Fascism is Mussolinism . . . what would Fascism be, if I had not been?" [1] Megalomania aside, Mussolini's reflection underscores the crucial role of the leader and the elite in totalitarian systems; and whether or not it is literally true that the system *is* the leader, few would dissent from the proposition that leader and system are inextricably bound together. If, however, the leader does indeed leave an indelible mark in shaping the character of the system, there is good reason to turn first in his direction.

The man who brought fascism to Italy has been called many things—opportunist, extremist, cynic, rebel, demagogue, egotist, bellicose, cunning—and perhaps he was all of these if not more. Altogether, Benito Mussolini was a complex study in contradictions, much like the system he fostered. The son of a blacksmith and schoolteacher, he was born in 1883 in a rural Italian village. From his mother, a highly devout Catholic, he drew encouragement to train as a teacher, and for a few brief years he made the classroom his vocation. But it was from his father, socialist and anti-cleric, that the young Mussolini seems to have drawn his politics and his activism.

The Italy in which Mussolini came to maturity was not a very happy one. Along with the vast majority of his countrymen he experienced firsthand the meaning of poverty and all that went with it. For the peasants especially the situation was acute; and there was little consolation to be had

[1] Herman Finer, *Mussolini's Italy* (New York: Grosset & Dunlap, 1965), as quoted in the section, "From Mussolini's Italy to Italy's Italy."

from the Government, which discredited itself at the local level by its corruption and unconcern. Indeed, if anything, the Government seemed to have allied itself with the wealthy interests, on whose side it intervened in the sporadic clashes between the classes.

If government at the local level did not inspire confidence, the condition of national politics was not much better. True, there was a united Italy under a constitutional monarchy—and a parliamentary system somewhat akin to the British. But it was far from having the substance to go with the form. Its principal defect, as Professor Herman Finer so shrewdly put it, was that "Italy from 1870 to 1922 had a Parliament but no parliamentarianism." [2] The most conspicuous symptom of Italy's political plight was its extremely fragmented party system. The socialists were a crucial element, but even they could not command a majority: their competition divided among Liberals, Radicals, Republicans, Christian Democrats, and Nationalists, etc. There was a grand total of at least ten parties, each seeking political control, and none able to attain it. [3] The government of Italy was thus a series of highly tenuous coalitions, changing every year-and-a-half on an average, lacking in program and responsibility, and most of all lacking in popular support. [4] To fill this vacuum, Italian politics turned increasingly to a more highly personalized style of leadership—to dominant premiers such as Crispi and Giolitti. Where political stability and confidence were concerned, Italy was still adrift.

It was against this background that Mussolini made his way onto the stage of Italian politics. His labors on behalf of the Socialist party had earned him a party office, at age twenty-six, and with it the editorship of a Socialist newspaper, *Il Popolo*. [5] For the next few years he continued to work for the party and edited another paper, *La Lotta di Classe*. [6] For Mussolini this was an important period in at least two respects: his views on socialism seem to have crystallized in the direction of the more extreme revolutionary wing of the party, and his reach into national politics began.

By the eve of World War I, Mussolini had won his place in the upper echelons of the Italian Socialist Party, and had been named editor of the official party organ, *Avanti!* [7] It was the war, however, which brought an abrupt end to all this, and which seems to have been the turning point in his life. Mussolini, like the Italian nation itself, was apparently torn between the role of neutral and belligerent. The Socialist party maintained its

[2] *Ibid.*, p. 62.
[3] *Ibid.*, p. 63.
[4] *Ibid.*, p. 82.
[5] The People.
[6] The Class Struggle.
[7] Forward!

ideological opposition to war, and thereby supported the Government's announced policy of neutrality. So too did Mussolini—at first. But by late autumn of 1914, he had fully reversed himself and taken up the cause of an Anglo-Italian alliance with a vengeance.[8] Excommunicated by the party for his stand, thereafter he surrounded himself with like-minded interventionists and became involved with a new paper, *Popolo d'Italia.*[9] The war Mussolini continued to agitate for came to Italy in May, 1915. Six months later he was in uniform, serving until 1917, when he was mustered out on account of wounds.

Postwar Italy was a bitter pill for many Italians, Mussolini not excepted. Far from enjoying a reinvigorated government, Italian politics seemed more impotent than ever to cope with the problems that confronted the nation: acute inflation, severe unemployment, and the kind of general social dislocation which comes in the wake of war. Furthermore, where was Italy's share—as co-victor—of the spoils of war? What Mussolini mirrored, as he returned to his columns in *Popolo d'Italia,* was a widespread mood of disillusionment, discontent, and hostility.

The years 1919 to 1922 were critical for Italian politics. Unrest boiled over in the form of strikes and violence; this was a great boon to the Socialist party, which prospered as never before in numbers and power. But for Mussolini, whom the party regarded as a heretic, the political left was increasingly a lost cause. Neither could he cast his lot with the also powerful Catholic party—*Partito Popolare.* Increasingly independent, Mussolini struck out in a new direction with his founding of the *Fasci di Combattimento,* a veterans' organization with political overtones. In its first test of power, however, the fascists never got off the ground: an estimated 17,000 adherents failed to capture a single seat in the Chamber of Deputies election of 1919, and Mussolini polled an unflattering 1½ percent of the vote in Milan.[10]

It was a strange twist of fate which rescued Mussolini and his fascists from their rather inauspicious beginning. Ironically, it was the Socialist party which paved the way. The mood of the left had worsened and spilled more frequently into the streets; and further adding to the volatility of the situation was a strike, late in 1920, in which factories were actually seized by the workers. Such events were sufficient to excite the worst fears of the propertied upper and middle classes about the menace of socialism— thoroughly confused with bolshevism as anxieties intensified. And to make matters worse, the Government's response to the crisis had been weak.

[8] See Finer, *op. cit.* (above, n, 1), pp. 100 ff.
[9] People of Italy.
[10] Finer, *op. cit.* (above, n. 1), pp. 121 ff.

These facts were apparently not lost on Mussolini. Acting in the capacity of self-appointed vigilantes to defend against the "Red Menace," Mussolini's fascist squads—the Black Shirts—moved swiftly and violently to put down the demonstrations of socialists (and others not-so-socialist). The new wave of fascist intimidation and brutality—with its shootings, beatings, and castor oil treatments—proved to be far from unpopular in some quarters of the community. Among the propertied upper and middle classes in the throes of hysteria, Mussolini gained favor as a welcome relief from an impotent government. And while the Government was less than happy with the leader of the fascists, he was after all extremely useful. Far from discouraging Mussolini's activities, therefore, the police reacted favorably or not at all.

The message was now plain: an anti-Red crusade pays big dividends, and violence is no disqualifier. As evidence of this, fascist popularity rose to new heights with a following of more than 100,000 persons, and 35 seats in the national legislature, by the year 1921.[11] Mussolini was on the road to power.

In the fateful year which followed, violence bred yet more violence. There were by now some voices of alarm at the continued tactics of the Black Shirts—even amongst those who had earlier applauded Mussolini's tough line against the left. Mussolini himself seems to have recoiled at some of the violence, perhaps fearing that some of his support would come to see the remedy as worse than the disease. But his admonitions—and the temporary truce which followed—were short-lived among the local fascist organizations. Violence returned, and it is hard to say whether Mussolini could have any longer contained it. And if Mussolini could not, who could? The socialist forces were already in disarray, both inside the legislature and without. Only the Government remained as a force to contain the rising fascist tide. As Finer observes, "Even now a whiff of grapeshot would have saved constitutional liberties." [12] But as usual it was not forthcoming.

In the absence of any effective opposition by the Government, the fascist leadership grew bolder still. There was now talk of a fascist march on Rome to take the Government by force. Although Mussolini toyed with the idea of a possible "deal" by which the fascists might yet legally come into a coalition government, he was increasingly brought over to the more militant position favored by his lieutenants. Thus, by early fall of 1922 he declared his position to a fascist rally in Naples:

The moment has arrived, in fact, when the arrow must leave the bow, or the cord, too far stretched, will break. . . . We Fascisti do not intend to arrive at government by the window; we do not intend to give up this magnificent spiri-

[11] *Ibid.*, pp. 131, 135.
[12] *Ibid.*, p. 156.

tual birthright for a miserable mess of ministerial pottage. . . . As a matter of fact, at turning-points of history, force always decides when it is a question of opposing interests and ideas. This is why we have gathered, firmly organized and strongly disciplined our legions, because thus, if the question must be settled by a recourse to force we shall win. . . .[13]

Thus Mussolini mobilized his forces for a march on Rome.

The coup commenced on October 27, 1922. Fascists seized control of local communities, utilities, and various government installations; and an estimated 26,000 militants moved on Rome in three columns.[14] At last the Government seemed to grasp the gravity of the situation and prepared to announce a state of siege—which would have likely resulted in a complete rout at the hands of the army. What snatched victory out of defeat for the fascists, however, was the timidity of King Victor Emmanuel, who refused to sign the orders which would have activated the army in defense of Rome. Apparently having miscalculated the strength of his own position, and now fearing for his throne, he accepted the uprising as a *fait accompli*. By the 29th of October it was all over, and Mussolini was on his way to Rome to organize a fascist government.

At its inception the new fascist regime was much less than a full-blown totalitarian state. It was in fact a rather strange admixture of carrots and sticks which Mussolini served up. Addressing the legislature for the first time, for example, the new Prime Minister set the tone:

What I am doing in this hall today is to perform an act of formal courtesy . . . for which I ask no mark of special gratitude. . . .

Although I could have abused my victory, I refused to do so. . . . I could have transformed this drab, silent hall into a bivouac. . . . I could have nailed up the doors of parliament and formed a government consisting exclusively of Fascists. . . .[15]

In a gesture of accommodation, the fascists found room for their opposition (socialists and communists excluded of course) in the Government; the opposition was reminded at the same time that the fascists had it within their power to close the Parliament down altogether. Not surprisingly, Mussolini received an overwhelming vote of confidence—the facade of legality —and along with it he obtained a legislative grant of temporary dictatorial powers.

What followed from this rather modest foothold of power was simply a gradual but persistent erosion of the last remaining vestiges of constitutional

[13] Quoted in *ibid.,* p. 155.

[14] S. William Halperin, *Mussolini and Italian Fascism* (Princeton, N.J.: D. Van Nostrand, 1964), p. 37. Mussolini remained prudently in Milan.

[15] Speech of November 16, 1922, quoted in *ibid.,* pp. 107 ff.

government. In a very broad sense this was accomplished in two phases: first, in the period 1922–26, the emphasis seemed to be one of consolidating power within the existing framework, largely by a series of maneuvers which harassed and ultimately emasculated the opposition. From that point on, even the framework became fair game.

In the context of the first period, Mussolini's opponents found themselves increasingly pushed to the sidelines as fascist appointees displaced them in the Cabinet and Senate. Still more damaging was the 1923 Acerbo Election Law, which guaranteed that a party winning by plurality (read fascist) would be awarded two-thirds of the seats in the legislature. As if this was insufficient to foreclose any effective opposition, the fascists also resorted to the use of stronger medicine, reminiscent of their earlier tactics. The Black Shirts now had the cloak of law [16] and they had a heavy hand in the violence which scandalized the elections of 1924.

The new wave of fascist violence was indeed highly effective—almost too effective, in fact—and aroused a new round of public criticism. Once again Mussolini was forced to disassociate himself from the excesses of his own party, and might have tripped over his own mistakes—had it not been for the ineptitude of his opponents. Not only were the antifascist forces unable to lay aside their internal differences for the sake of joining hands in a united front, they bolted the legislature [17] and took their grievances—of all places—to the King. To make matters worse, there were several abortive assassination attempts made on Mussolini's life at the time, and these played directly into his hands, providing ample warrant for him to retaliate with even more repressive measures against the opposition. Thus ensued, in the years 1925–26, a series of highly restrictive and punitive enactments: speech and press came under strict censorship, criticism of the Government (including symbols like the flag) was a punishable offense, due process fled the courts, and the death penalty reached a new class of political crimes. It only remained for the fascists to outlaw the opposition directly; and, predictably, that was followed by a ban on the socialists and then another against the remaining parties.

From 1926 on, there was little left to the Italian parliamentary system except the illusion; and even that gave way to a more transparent form of fascist political organization. Until then at least a formal distinction be-

[16] As of 1922 they acquired official status as the MVSN (*Milizia Volontaria per la Sicurezza Nazionale*), with primary responsibility to Mussolini. The institutionalization of terror was further aided by the establishment of the OVRA (*Opera Volontaria Repressione Antifascista*) in 1926.

[17] The so-called Aventine Secession of 1924. The event was triggered particularly by the assassination of Giacomo Matteotti, socialist leader, who had threatened to expose the fascist election rigging.

tween party and state had persisted; but the law which elevated the Fascist Grand Council to authority in 1928 changed all that. Hitherto, the Fascist Grand Council had had no official standing beyond its role as party policy maker; but now it was vested with important powers to influence the choice of successor for both king and prime minister, and to oversee the government. More crucial still, the Grand Council bore a new legal relationship to the legislature—one which virtually put the Chamber of Deputies in its pocket. Henceforth the Council would select a list of four hundred candidates (from a list of one thousand names submitted to it), and this entire legislative slate would then be presented to the electorate on an all-or-none approval basis. The Grand Council thus emerged as the very heart of the new political system, which in turn meant undisputed control for Mussolini —who by law was recognized as president of the thirty-man Council.

At about the same time that the fascists were welding together a one-party-government amalgam, they were also transforming the system in another quite fundamental way. Mussolini's concept of the "corporative state" has often been singled out as perhaps the most novel feature of fascism. Although primarily tied to the economic organization of the state, its implications for the political system make it relevant for consideration here. Simply put, the corporative state was an institutional arrangement which effectively guaranteed political control over the economic sector. Superficially it resembled capitalism—with all of the customary trappings such as private property, employers, and employees; but from the very beginning the fascists aired their distaste for all the standard economic brands, and flirted with the idea that the state should master the forces of the economy no less than the forces of politics.[18] It was not until the year 1926, however, that the plan for the corporative state began to crystallize. Under the terms of the new Rocco Labor Law, strikes and lockouts were officially prohibited.[19] With the aid of subsequent enactments,[20] the law virtually preempted control over all economic associations and labor-management relations. Specifically, it provided for an elaborate apparatus by which all economic activity was divided into seven fields (e.g., industry, agriculture) or "corporations." The corporations in turn consisted of two associations or "syndicates"—one for the employers and the other for the employees.[21] Since each one of these syndicates was legally recognized as the *sole* bar-

[18] Early fascist leanings were much influenced by the syndicalists and contemplated associations composed of employers and employees working in cooperation with each other.

[19] Article 18, Law of April 3, 1926.

[20] Decree on Corporations, July 1, 1926; and the Charter of Labor, April 21, 1927.

[21] A total of thirteen in all. The lone exception was the one undivided corporation for intellectuals.

gaining agent for all workers or employers within a given corporation, the whole corporate structure assumed vital importance as the framework within which economic policy was to be set. The fascists, however, chose not to leave crucial economic decisions to the unfettered and chance discretion of the syndicates. Accordingly they arranged for the new laws to insure fascist control in two ways: first they made it a legal certainty that only fascist syndicates could secure membership in the corporations; and, second, they superimposed a governmental Ministry of Corporations (with Mussolini at its head), declaring the corporations to be agencies of the state.

There were further refinements. In 1930 the Ministry of Corporations was replaced by a National Council of Corporations; and in 1934 the number of corporations was expanded from the original seven to a new total of twenty-two. By this time there could be no misreading of the corporative state concept: it vested the fascists with full control over production, prices, wages, and labor disputes—in sum, with the same monopoly of power which they enjoyed politically. Yet one of the most interesting and unique aspects of the system—the fusion of party, government, and corporations into an integrated whole—was still to come. In a sense the stage had already been set for this eventuality, in the form of the political remodeling which occurred in 1928. It will be recalled that the much revised Chamber of Deputies was to draw its membership from those candidates who were among the list of one thousand nominees submitted to the Fascist Grand Council, and who subsequently were approved by both Council and electorate.[22] What gave added significance to this arrangement, and which now affords insight into the developing links between government and economy, was the mechanism which the fascists provided for the purpose of gathering up the initial list of the thousand eligible candidates. Eight hundred of the nominees were picked by the executive councils of the syndicates.[23] Thus the fascists could count it a foregone conclusion that the Chamber of Deputies would be manned by loyal party followers, drawn overwhelmingly from loyal party corporations. From this *de facto* merger of politics and economics, it remained only to apply the finishing touches, already prophesied by Mussolini: ". . . some have already spoken of the end of the present Chamber of Deputies . . . a time will come when a National Corporative . . . (Assembly) may replace *in toto* the present Chamber. . . ."[24] The finishing touches were indeed applied in 1938, when the so-called Suicide Chamber obligingly abolished itself to make way, in

[22] See p. 66.

[23] With this innovation the legislature ceased to have a conventional population or geographic base of representation, and instead was declared to rest on a *functional* pattern which was supposed to reflect various economic interests.

[24] As quoted in Halperin, *op. cit.* (above, n. 14), pp. 56 f.

1939, for the more appropriately named Chamber of Fasces and Corporations. In this final form were joined seven hundred members representing party, government, and corporations—all appointed by Mussolini, and embodying that kind of homogeneity for which the fascists had long labored.

Such were the events and currents which brought Mussolini to power, accomplishing in Italy the first experimental venture into fascist political organization. At the same time that this particular history chronicles the complex interrelationship between leader and movement, it also serves to document many of the ideas advanced in the preceding chapter concerning the genesis and operational characteristics of a totalitarian state. It offers in sum a vital background for an understanding of the system. Yet an important question remains: To what extent did the emergent pattern fit the theory of fascism?

Because fascism did not offer itself, initially at least, as a systematic body of thought or even as a well-integrated program, it is not easy to compare the ideology to the practice. Disclaimers concerning ideology seemed, in fact, a matter of pride with Mussolini:

. . . We have torn to pieces all the revealed truths, we have spat upon all the dogmas, we have rejected the paradises, scoffed at all the charlatans, white, red and black, who market miraculous drugs to give happiness to mankind. We do not believe in programmes, in schemes, in saints, in apostles; we do not, above all, believe in happiness, in salvation, in the promised land. . . .[25]

And again:

We do not believe in dogmatic programmes, in that kind of rigid frame which is supposed to contain and sacrifice the changeable, changing, and complex reality. We permit ourselves the luxury of bringing together and conciliating and surmounting in ourselves those antitheses in which others stupefy themselves, which are fossilized in a monosyllable of affirmation or negation. We permit ourselves the luxury of being aristocrats and democrats, conservatives and progressives, reactionaries and revolutionaries, legalitarians and illegalitarians, according to circumstances of time, place and environment—in a word of the history in which we are constrained to live and act.[26]

As these and previous references suggest, it is far easier to say what fascism was against, than what it was for. Still, we are not left totally without a guide; for in 1932 Mussolini set down what has since been regarded as

---

[25] Article of 1919–20, as quoted in Finer, *op. cit.* (above, n. 1), p. 123.

[26] *Ibid.,* pp. 17 f. Also to the point: "Our programme is simple: we wish to govern Italy. They ask us for programmes, but there are already too many. It is not programmes that are wanting for the salvation of Italy, but men and will power." *Ibid.,* p. 151.

the closest approximation to a definitive statement of fascist ideology. His statement, "The Doctrine of Fascism," [27] has been abstracted here as a highly useful framework within which to proceed.

To begin with, the premises on which Mussolini builds his ideological structure are plainly articulated: fascism disdains liberalism, socialism, and democracy. Predicated as they are on sterile ideas of sentimentalism and visions of individual satisfactions, such systems are anachronistic. The monumental error of such regimes was their utopian exaltation of the individual, and their passivity; conversely, they depreciated the value of the state and the need for action. In a word, they were unrealistic.

Fascism denies the possibilities of the materialistic concept of "happiness"— it leaves that to the economists of the first half of the Seventeenth Century; that is, it denies the equation "well-being happiness," which reduces man to the state of the animals, mindful of only one thing—that of being fed and fattened; reduced, in fact, to a pure and simple vegetative existence.

Hence, it is as a reaction to outmoded forces that fascism emerges as a new and historically relevant concept. A new age has called forth a new dimension in ideology.

Mussolini's view of man, and the world in which he lives, is of course much different from that of the forces which he disdains. The fascist realistically sees life as a struggle, but one in which the man of action—the man of discipline—can will himself to master all. Yet the crucial point appears to be that man cannot realize his full potentiality if simply left to his own devices. What is required for this purpose is a state, one which is attuned to the active spirit of man, and one which itself embodies the highest and most noble values.

It is thus the concept of the state, the *fascist* state, which is at the very heart of the ideology. Mussolini conceives of the state as a kind of living organism which embodies the quintessence of all that is good. Thus:

The capital point of the Fascist doctrine is the conception of the State, its essence, the work to be accomplished, its final aims. In the conception of Fascism, the State is an absolute before which individuals and groups are relative. Individuals and groups are "conceivable" inasmuch as they are in the State. The Liberal State does not direct the movement and the material and spiritual evolution of collectivity, but limits itself to recording the results; the Fascist State has its conscious conviction, a will of its own, and for this reason it is called an "ethical" State.

[27] *Enciclopedia Italiana*, Vol. XIV (1932). The essay was in two parts: the first, entitled "Fundamental Ideas," was actually authored by Giovanni Gentile, a leading fascist writer, but Mussolini was still agreeable to having it published under his own name; the second part is labeled "Political and Social Doctrines." Unless otherwise noted, all quoted material hereafter is from the *Enciclopedia* article.

The state, as Mussolini sees it, is something more than mere policeman or philanthropist: it is much more akin to a spiritual or mystical incarnation. And only in the state can man find his true identity.

What is this state, which Mussolini credits as being ethically ideal? It is first of all to be understood as oriented toward a community of power and activism. The model is dynamic, revolutionary, energetic, and bold. Indeed, Mussolini gives clear and unmistakable expression to the aggressive bent of the fascist state:

. . . Fascism above all does not believe either in the possibility or utility of universal peace. It therefore rejects the pacifism which masks surrender and cowardice. War alone brings all human energies to their highest tension and sets a seal of nobility on the peoples who have the virtue to face it. . . .

Fascism also transports this anti-pacifist spirit into the life of individuals. The proud *squadrista* motto *"me ne frego"* [28] scrawled on the bandages of the wounded is an act of philosophy—not only stoic. It is a summary of a doctrine not only political: it is an education in strife and an acceptance of the risks which it carried: it is a new style of Italian life. It is thus that the Fascist loves and accepts life, ignores and disdains suicide; understands life as a duty, a lifting up, a conquest. . . .

And while he disclaims that belief in this doctrine necessarily obliges territorial conquest, he concludes:

. . . For Fascism, the tendency to empire, that is to say the expansion of nations, is a manifestation of vitality, its contrary is a sign of decadence. Peoples who rise, or who suddenly flourish again, are imperialistic; peoples who die are peoples who abdicate. . . .

It is veneration of the state as force and power which leads Mussolini to a companion view, the state as disciplinarian. The strong state (in which the individual finds his only identity) demands self-sacrifice, discipline, and obedience. The state asserts the right to restructure society—"rebuilding" man on the one hand, and forewarning harsher consequences for those less educable.

Finally, Mussolini adds a third dimension to his conception of the state, the notion of "unity" or, less euphemistically, *totality*. Simply put, the state is everything—political, economic, and moral. It demands the complete individual and his entire loyalty; and it is equally unambiguous as to the impossibility of tolerating internal opposition. Mussolini puts the matter squarely:

. . . for the Fascist, all is comprised in the State and nothing spiritual or human exists—much less has any value—outside the State. In this respect Fascism is a

[28] "I don't give a damn!"

totalising concept, and the Fascist State—the unification and synthesis of every value—interprets, develops and potentiates the whole life of the people.

No individuals nor groups (political parties, associations, labour unions, classes) [exist] outside the State. . . .

To summarize, fascist ideology is born out of hostility to more liberal regimes which it sees as ill-suited to a world of conflict and struggle; its touchstone is the state, an ethical organism of force and discipline, all-encompassing: The theory does indeed approximate the practice.

In retrospect it is all too obvious that the negativism of fascist ideology towards its competitors was evident from its earliest dealings with the socialists, and was so still more dramatically in the 1926 law which prohibited all political opposition. Neither is it difficult to find in the record an ample showing of the primacy which attached to the state—witness the preeminent position of the government in economics through the corporative-state structure—matching again the ideological line.

Much has already been made of the violence which marked the fascist coming-to-power, and of its continuation in subsequent elections. The case concerning fascist emphasis on force and discipline is considerably broader than this, however. Among other things, an analysis of fascist propaganda —with mottoes and slogans such as the oft-quoted one, "Believe! Obey! Fight!"—gives some indication of applied doctrine. So do the activities of youth organizations, which were geared explicitly to premilitary training and discipline. Yet what testifies all the more clearly and impressively to the kinship of fascist theory and practice is the role of force as the mainstay of Mussolini's foreign policy. Beginning with an assault on Ethiopia in 1935, the quest for a Mediterranean Empire led Italy to military intervention in Spain, to the armed conquest of Albania, and ultimately, of course, into the ill-fated partnership with Germany in World War II.

Rounding out the picture of theory vs. practice, finally, there is the matter of the ideological claim to totality. Here too the evidence would seem to argue that the practice corresponded positively to the expressed values of the system. Socially, as well as politically and economically, the state achieved primacy under the fascists.

It has already been observed that in the field of communications the fascists had maintained a strict political censorship. More specifically, this meant governmental control over all media—publications, radio, as well as the performing arts. Moreover, the fascists seem to have employed an exceedingly generous definition of the "political" in terms of their overall sensitivities. That is suggested, at least, by their eventual reach into literature, art, music, and even architecture. The concept of a fascist culture, in other words, was a real and operational one. In a second and related area, education, a similar pattern was followed. Here the state was in direct control over the curriculum, choice of textbooks, and personnel. As a dramatic case in point, a law of 1931 required of all professors a qualifying Fascist Loyalty Oath. In brief, the entire educational machinery of the state was well integrated into the political design of the society.

That these were not isolated examples of totalitarianism operating in the social sphere is suggested also by a third point, one concerning private associations. It was earlier made plain that the fascist state had little room for political and economic groupings other than those officially sanctioned; and there is a strong suggestion that life was similarly uncomfortable for those social organizations which were not squarely in the fascist ranks. This is to be seen—in a rather interesting application—in the relations of church and state. For reasons of expediency on both sides, Mussolini and Pius XI managed to come to terms in 1929, with the result that the fascists could depend upon political cooperation from the Catholic Church in return for fascist recognition of Catholicism as the established religion.[29] Even this quasi-state monopoly did not go far enough to please the fascists, apparently, since their interest in education put them in fundamental opposition to the Church in this sphere. As a result, even the Catholics found themselves the target of fascist harassment, much as any other group which had its differences with the state. To put it bluntly, as Mussolini did, the state ". . . is Catholic, to be sure, but it is above all Fascist—exclusively, essentially Fascist." [30]

The fascist involvement in thought, speech, education, culture, and associations by no means exhausts the list. What Mussolini made of his notion about social unity is also to be seen in the state's programs for organized recreation and sports,[31] and in extensive efforts to engineer a higher birth rate. In sum, the totality of which he spoke was translated into real-life terms, and into an unprecedented reach of the state over virtually all dimensions of human activity. It is this fact which warrants the conclusion that fascist ideology did indeed find expression in practice, and that it quite accurately fits the model of totalitarianism.

Naziism

Between Mussolini's fascism and Adolf Hitler's National Socialism there is a certain family resemblance, an historic and ideological twinship. And

[29] The Lateran Accords.

[30] *Opera Omnia di Benito Mussolini,* eds. Edoardo and Duilio Susmel (Florence: La Fenice, 1951–62), XXIV, 75–76, 89; as quoted in Halperin, *op. cit.* (above, n. 14), p. 70.

[31] The *Dopolavoro.*

yet the likeness has its limits: at the most, these were fraternal rather than identical twins. Unlike the Italian *Duce,* the German *Fuehrer* was no almost-socialist; where Mussolini made his way to power by coup, Adolf Hitler found much greater profit at the polls; what World War I contributed to the fascists was the frustration of paradise lost, whereas to the Nazis it was a national humiliation demanding satisfaction; and while it required but a scant three years for an obscure totalitarian party to win power in Italy, the gestation period for German National Socialism was more than four times as long.

All of these were obvious points of difference and yet two other factors even more clearly sharpen the contrast. There is, first, the crucial distinction between fascist and Nazi ideologies—and their subsequent practices—with respect to "race." To be sure, Mussolini found it useful to play with his myths about a superior fascist type, and there are in his writings the related allusions to a modern-day resurrection of the Roman Empire man. But for all the fascist genuflecting in the direction of an Italian racism—including even a belated declaration of antisemitism—such images were more adornments than a vital part of the system. With Hitler, however, it was quite another story. The myth of a super race, magically embodied in the pure German Aryan, translated into a pathological compulsion to eradicate its opposite number. There is in Italian racism, in other words, simply no equivalent to the Nazis' consuming hatred of the Jews, the resultant persecution, concentration camps, and ultimate attempts at genocide. In a word, it was Auschwitz (or Dachau or Buchenwald or any of the other centers where an estimated six million persons were exterminated) which made the difference.

Apart from this stands a second major distinction between the two systems: whatever the nature of their aspirations, Mussolini's "Empire" was at best a poor imitation of Hitler's Third Reich where territorial conquests were concerned. Fascism was simply not in the same league with the kind of Nazi expansionism which overran Austria, Czechoslovakia, Poland, Norway, Denmark, France, Luxembourg, Belgium, the Netherlands, Romania, Bulgaria, Yugoslavia, Greece, and Russia to the door of Moscow. By the measure of its aggressiveness, therefore, Hitler's version of totalitarian politics proved far more threatening than Mussolini's in terms both of its potential and its actuality.

Still, a superficial likeness may be found between the two regimes, notwithstanding the fact that the extremes of Naziism are not duplicated in fascism. There is a kind of crude similarity in the tortuous path which both traveled to power: both drawing capital from charismatic rhetoric; both carried to power with the aid of an extremist following, intimidation, and a talent for manipulating; both unswerving in their determination to stand atop the very pinnacle of the state, there to reconstruct it in the image of a totalitarian ideal.

Another similarity deserving of special attention is the almost carbon-copy quality of the circumstantial opportunity which paved the way to power. Hitler and Mussolini alike exploited conditions of acute national distress—postwar crises which rent the political, economic, and social order—together with moods of widespread despair and frustration. Such events were tailor-made to the aims and stratagems of a radical politics. Not only were such events a fertile breeding ground for the cult of fascist and Nazi militants, but they also provoked a reinvigorated challenge from the socialist and communist left; and it was the latter—with its specter of a proletarian revolution—which both Hitler and Mussolini seized upon as a highly useful and convenient target. The rising tides of bolshevism and the impending Red Menace were the fears on which they fed, the tickets which would take them to power. Finally, there was the conspicuous absence of an effective resistance to either fascists or Nazis. For Hitler, no less than for Mussolini, the outcome might have been considerably different had it not been for an impotent and acquiescent government. Similarly, each found little to fear from a highly fragmented and unstable multiparty system, in which the opposing forces were hopelessly disarrayed and irreconcilable. This sums up, perhaps, in the familiar observation that Hitler and Mussolini happened along at similarly propitious times and places of history.

Adolf Hitler's early and formative years need detain us far more briefly than Mussolini's. For Hitler there was no pre-World War I political activism. The pertinent background may be summarized as follows: he was born in 1889 to parents of lower middle-class circumstances and Austrian nationality. Despite his father's apparent desire that he should follow in his footsteps and become a civil servant, young Hitler set his course for a career in art. The aspiration took him, at age twenty, to Vienna, and, as it turned out, to four years of personal disaster. Failing as an artist, he fell on unhappy and impecunious days.

What Hitler took from Vienna, upon his departure in 1913, was something more than a taste of frustration and suffering. He carried with him two ideas, if not near-fixations: first, he came away a confirmed Pan-German nationalist, unalterably wedded to the vision of a German hegemony, a German Austria, and an end to the crumbling Hapsburg conglomerate. At the very least, this was his first conscious expression of the claim to empire. Equally important was the second idea he acquired: an unequivocal and intense hatred of the Jews. Later, he wrote:

. . . since I had begun to concern myself with this question and to take cognizance of the Jews, Vienna appeared to me in a different light than before. Wherever I went, I began to see Jews, and the more I saw, the more sharply they became distinguished in my eyes from the rest of humanity. . . .

Was there any form of filth or profligacy, particularly in cultural life, without at least one Jew involved in it?

If you cut even cautiously into such an abscess, you found, like a maggot in a rotting body, often dazzled by the sudden light—a kike! [32]

At age twenty-four he came to Munich—a much more hospitable center for a person of Hitler's political persuasion. A poverty-stricken year later he volunteered for military service with a Bavarian regiment at the outbreak of World War I. In 1918, he returned—an ex-lance corporal, recipient of the Iron Cross, having been wounded and gassed—consumed with the humiliation of Germany's defeat. It was then that Hitler found himself and his new life in politics.

If Hitler's turn to politics was purposeful, his beginning association with the Nazi-party-to-be was a bit by accident. Still on the army payroll from 1919–20, he found employment as a kind of military propagandist and undercover agent, assigned in part to investigate the activities of the radical left organizations which were multiplying everywhere. Thus it was that he was routinely sent to infiltrate and report on a suspicious sounding band, the German Workers' Party. What he found was something altogether different from a Marxist plot. It was in fact a kind of chauvinistic group which espoused many ideas paralleling his own. Attracted by its infancy, and by the opportunity to be among its charter members, Hitler became the seventh member of the party.

The German Workers' Party with which Hitler cast his lot was hardly a political oddity. Such groups—ranging from extremists of the right to revolutionaries of the left—were legion throughout postwar Germany. In a very real sense they symbolized the festering condition of national politics, the brooding forces that would eventually reveal the basic fragility of the government. At the root of the problem, of course, was the stinging impact of Germany's defeat, a lingering wound which was perpetuated by persistent complaints that an impending military victory had been undermined by traitors back home.[33] To make matters worse, there was also the painful

[32] Adolf Hitler, *Mein Kampf* (trans.) (Boston: Houghton Mifflin, 1962), pp. 56 f. First published in Berlin: Verlag Frz. Eher Nachf., G.M.B.H., 1925.

[33] Hitler traded on the idea that the "November criminals"—civilian slackers, traitors, Marxists, and Jews—had "stabbed" the Army in the back. In fact, however, it appears to have been General Erich Ludendorff and Field Marshal Paul von Hindenburg, of the Army High Command, who took the initiative and persuaded the civilian authorities to sue for peace. See William L. Shirer, *The Rise and Fall of the Third Reich* (New York: Simon & Schuster, 1960), pp. 31 f.

reckoning of accounts at Versailles, where Germany was stripped of such prized possessions as Alsace-Lorraine, the Saar, Upper Silesia, Danzig, "The Polish Corridor," [34] and all colonies—a net loss of about one-eighth of her European territory, with a population of six and a half million. Besides having to forfeit most of the Bismarck Empire, Germany was given the bill for all damages,[35] forced to disarm her military forces to token strength, and declared open to Allied occupation. The final blow to national pride was the required confession of war guilt,[36] and the public indictment of Kaiser Wilhelm II, et al., as war criminals. The victors were not about to forgive, and Germany was not about to forget. Once again, therefore, frustration called forth the familiar theme: the same treacherous groups which had betrayed Germany in the field had also sold out at the peace table.

Those who took refuge in transferring the blame for Germany's misfortunes found their principal scapegoat in the postwar government of the Weimar Republic. It was the Weimar Republic, of course, which had agreed to the Armistice. And it was the Weimar Republic which had put its hand to the fateful Diktat at Versailles. From its very beginning, therefore, the Republic was destined to bear the onus for Germany's fall, and the fatal political burden that went with it. The new government, with its socialist and centrist elements, was caught in a cross fire of nationalists, Nazis, and communists—an estimated total of thirty to forty percent opposition [37]— leaving the Republic in a continuing crisis of confidence. That, however, was but the first of its troubles. In the chaos which followed the war, extremists of both left and right had attempted to seize the government by force. Thus the Republic came increasingly (and precariously) to rely on the army for support. It was a dubious alliance, however, for power was bestowed upon a group whose basic loyalty the Republic could not command. Within the civil bureaucracy the problem was much the same:

[34] The "Polish Corridor" is a narrow band of 80 miles width and 260 miles length extending from Poland to the Baltic and providing the only Polish access to the sea. It also assumes critical importance because it stands between Germany and Prussia.

[35] Reparations began with a "down payment" of five billion dollars. Later, the total bill was officially set at $32,000,000,000—a figure which represented about twice the available supply of gold in the world! Although the Allies later softened the repayment terms, the reparations question was to prove a continuing source of abrasion.

[36] The now famous Article 231 of the Versailles Treaty reads: "The Allied and Associated Governments affirm and Germany accepts the responsibility of Germany and her allies for causing all the loss and damage to which the Allied and Associated Governments and their nationals have been subjected as a consequence of the war imposed upon them by the aggression of Germany and her allies."

[37] See Karl W. Deutsch and Rupert Breitling, "The German Federal Republic," in Roy C. Macridis and Robert E. Ward, eds., Modern Political Systems: Europe (Englewood Cliffs, N.J.: Prentice-Hall, 1963), p. 284.

stability and reinforcement, which the government expected to draw from the established court system, was not forthcoming. The Republic found few friends among the judges, while the courts provided a public platform for those bent on bringing down the government.

Finally, the economic afflictions which beset Germany, and the imprudent policies which dealt with them, brought the Weimar regime one step closer to the grave. Beginning with the breadlines, mass unemployment, and poverty which gripped Germany in 1919, there followed a runaway inflation. Despite the havoc which this brought to lower- and middle-class income groups, both the industrial sector and the government appear to have found common cause in an inflationary trend which more easily relieved them of their war debts. Hence, it has been estimated that by November of 1923, one dollar equaled 4,000,000,000 marks.[38] Inevitably, therefore, the Republic bore the stigma for a wide variety of follies, some deserved and some not. To sum it all up, while the Weimar Republic ". . . was, on paper, the most liberal and democratic document of its kind the twentieth century had seen, mechanically well-nigh perfect, full of ingenious and admirable devices which seemed to guarantee the working of an almost flawless democracy," [39] it was also politically moribund.

Such was the precarious situation which confronted Germany in the early twenties—a situation which bred groups like the German Workers' Party, and radicals like Adolf Hitler. Still, the ultimate success of the party depended upon more than opportunity, and this extra Hitler contributed with his unparalleled skill for pressing every advantage. Having resigned his post with the army in 1920, he put his entire energies to the goal of transforming an obscure political organization into a movement of massive power. As the party's propaganda head, Hitler proved an electrifying and charismatic orator, a master at the craft of sensing and manipulating public opinion. And so the party prospered in numbers: possessing an estimated 3,000 members by 1921, 6,000 a year later, and 55,000 by the end of 1923.[40] More than elisting new recruits, Hitler also gave the party a brand-new image: a change of name to the National Socialist German Workers' Party (*National Sozialistische Deutsche Arbeiter Partei,* or N.S.D.A.P., from which the term "Nazi" is derived); a symbol (the *"Hakenkreuz"* or swastika); and a uniformed identity. Equally important, the party acquired its own newspaper, *Völkischer Beobachter* (National Observer), and a strong-arm band of Brown Shirts—the *Sturmabteilung* [41]—a fair equivalent of

[38] Shirer, *op. cit.* (above, n. 33), p. 61.
[39] *Ibid.,* p. 56.
[40] Theodore Abel, *The Nazi Movement: Why Hitler Came to Power* (New York: Atherton, 1966), p. 311.
[41] The S.A. or Stormtroopers.

Mussolini's Black Shirts. From these efforts Hitler was able to extract, after a brief intraparty fight in 1921, undisputed power as leader.

This first phase of the Nazi party development, including its reach for power and crusade against the Republic, culminated with a dramatic and near-disastrous confrontation with the government toward the end of 1923. As the economic situation continued to deteriorate, and as grievances continued to mount against the Republic, the antigovernment forces seemed to be multiplying everywhere. In Bavaria, especially, revolutionary sentiment ran high—a prime example being the National Socialists, who had made the capital city of Munich their home. Allied with other insurgent groups of a similar bent, in an organization called the *Deutscher Kampfbund* (German Fighting Union), it appeared to the Nazis that the government was at last ripe for the taking. A variety of factors urged them on. There was real apprehension among the ardent nationalists in the group that unless their brand of strong central government came to power, the alternative might well be a disastrous breaking apart of the individual states; surely, they thought, the government could hardly depend upon the army to block the revolution, since the sympathies of the military were increasingly on the side of the nationalists. Then there was the question of whether the pressures building within the insurgent groups themselves could long contain the more aggressive members of the party, who thirsted for action; and finally, there was the example of Mussolini and his march on Rome, proof that revolution could be successful!

Hitler's plan was two-phased. First, he would move boldly to force the Bavarian authorities to cast their lot with him. Then, having a more powerful army at his command, he would carry the revolution *"Auf nach Berlin."* On November 8, 1923, Hitler literally fired the opening shot of the uprising, better known as the "Beer Hall Putsch." [42] It was an ill-fated effort, however, which met its end the following day, and which saw Hitler in custody by November 11.

Never had the future looked so unpromising for Hitler and his followers. The party stood in ignominious defeat, and Hitler would have considerable

---

[42] So-called because the attempted coup commenced with the capture of the Hofbräuhaus, a Munich meeting hall, where the top officials of Bavaria were assembled. With Stormtroopers surrounding the building, Hitler made a dramatic entrance by leaping to the top of a table, and firing a shot into the ceiling to command attention. He proclaimed the revolution to be under way, and sought to bluff his listeners into believing that the government had toppled. He then took the Bavarian commissioners hostage, extracting promises of cooperation from them. But the hostages managed to slip through his fingers, and quickly turned against him. Undaunted, Hitler tried to salvage his revolution the next day by an armed march to take over the heart of the city. When the police opened fire on the Nazis, and Hitler hastily fled, the putsch was broken. See Shirer, *op. cit.* (above, n. 33), pp. 68 ff.

difficulty in holding it together from the jail cell he so likely faced. These were the prospects as he went to trial for treason early in 1924.

In fact, however, Hitler's trial proved to be much more of an advantage to him than a disaster. A not unfriendly court permitted him to air his political views generously; and an interested press brought Hitler and the gospel of national socialism to a hitherto oblivious national and international audience. Hitler made the most of this opportunity, with the ironic result that the government lost more than Hitler gained. So it appeared, at least, from the final disposition of the case: a charitable sentence of five years, of which Hitler would serve less than one.

If ten months' confinement in the Landsberg Fortress Prison was supposed to show Hitler the error of his ways, it did so in only one respect—experience persuaded him that the road to power was paved with ballots rather than bullets. As he put it to one of his confederates:

When I resume active work it will be necessary to pursue a new policy. Instead of working to achieve power by armed coup, we shall have to hold our noses and enter the Reichstag against the Catholic and Marxist deputies. If outvoting them takes longer than outshooting them, at least the result will be guaranteed by their own constitution. Any lawful process is slow. . . . Sooner or later we shall have a majority—and after that, Germany.[43]

Otherwise his mission remained unchanged, and even within his cell he was far from idle. There was, of course, the problem of the party (torn and bleeding after the putsch, and now under official ban), as well as the security of his position as its leader. Still, Hitler found it possible to intrigue his way around the latter difficulty—mainly by a strategic undermining of any effective effort to rebuild the party during his absence, thus guaranteeing that no one else should fill his shoes.

Finally, the period of Hitler's imprisonment was to find repayment in another, more eventful, way. "I decided to set forth the aims of our movement, and also to draw a picture of its development." [44] Thus, the imprisoned leader of the Nazi Party undertook to set down in writing the ideology of the national socialist movement. What he produced was a much more elaborate image of Naziism than that of fascism in Mussolini's celebrated essay. Hitler intended his book, he tells us, for the enlightenment of his followers; and it did indeed become a kind of Bible among the party faithful. Its significance, however, goes well beyond this: *Mein Kampf*

[43] As quoted in *ibid.*, p. 119, from Kurt Ludecke, *I Knew Hitler* (London: 1938), at pp. 217 ff.

[44] Hitler, *Mein Kampf, op. cit.* (above, n. 32), p. vii. The title translates to "My Struggle." Two volumes comprise the work, the first published in 1925, and the second in 1926.

openly predicted the direction of future events in Germany, as well as sharpening our picture of both the man and the ideology.

The general tone of Hitler's writing and outlook is revealed in the title he first proposed to give his book: *A Four and One-Half Year Struggle Against Lies, Stupidity, and Cowardice: Settling Accounts with the Destroyers of the Nationalist Socialist Movement.* While the title was finally softened, the contents remained vitriolic, intemperate, and impassioned. Essentially it speaks the language of militant nationalism in its more extreme form, the quintessence of chauvinism.

The core of Hitler's political ideology is to be found in a very special construction of German nationalism—the "Folkish State." Simply put, the concept of the Folkish State translates into an image of a homogeneous national community, based on primitive bonds of blood and race. Hence the motto, "One blood demands one Reich" as *Mein Kampf* opens; and a like refrain at its conclusion: "A state which in this age of racial poisoning dedicates itself to the care of its best racial elements must some day become lord of the earth." [45] Hitler's ideas on this subject appear to have been derived in much the same way as Mussolini's theories about the natural validity of the fascist state. Hitler, too, sees the natural order of things as an incessant struggle between the strong and the weak. Neither would he disagree with Mussolini as to the contrast between the virtues of the powerful state and the inevitable undoing of the weak and sentimental democracies. But for Hitler the intrinsic difference between the strong and weak turns on other ground—a world of superior and inferior races. "All who are not of good race in this world are chaff." [46]

In this scheme of things a romantic notion of Nature's favored people—the Aryan race—begins to emerge. Hitler writes:

All the human culture, all the results of art, science, and technology that we see before us today, are almost exclusively the creative product of the Aryan. This very fact admits of the not unfounded inference that he alone was the founder of all higher humanity, therefore representing the prototype of all that we understand by the word "man." He is the Prometheus of mankind from whose bright forehead the divine spark of genius has sprung at all times. . . .[47]

It is not entirely clear, however, who the Aryans are. Hitler's most frequent reference, of course, is to a "Germanic element"; and it is plain that he considers Germany to be the direct repository of the Aryan bloodline. Beyond this there are only vague hints that the phenotype may be some sort of blond and fair-skinned Nordic breed.

[45] *Ibid.,* p. 688.
[46] *Ibid.,* p. 296.
[47] *Ibid.,* p. 290.

As to who he means by "chaff," Hitler is much less elusive. It is the Jews whom he singles out as his prime example of an inferior "race." "The mightiest counterpart to the Aryan," Hitler writes, "is represented by the Jew." [48] In the language of *Mein Kampf* the sins of the Jew are unending: he is a "parasite" who robs the host culture of its riches, and he is without scruple: ". . . he stops at nothing, and in his vileness he becomes so gigantic that no one need be surprised if among our people the personification of the devil as the symbol of all evil assumes the living shape of the Jew." [49] But worst of all, in Hitler's eyes, is the damage which the Jew inflicts to the purity of the Aryan race:

With satanic joy in his face, the black-haired Jewish youth lurks in wait for the unsuspecting girl whom he defiles with his blood, thus stealing her from her people. With every means he tries to destroy the racial foundations of the people he has set out to subjugate. Just as he himself systematically ruins women and girls, he does not shrink back from pulling down the blood barriers for others, even on a large scale. It was and it is Jews who bring the Negroes into the Rhineland, always with the same secret thought and clear aim of ruining the hated white race by the necessarily resulting bastardization, throwing it down from its cultural and political height, and himself rising to be its master.[50]

The net result is:

Culturally he contaminates art, literature, the theater, makes a mockery of natural feeling, overthrows all concepts of beauty and sublimity, of the noble and the good, and instead drags men down into the sphere of his own base nature.[51]

For Hitler, the issue is well joined. Nature has set two races loose upon the earth, one strong and the other weak; Nature has put the two in unavoidable conflict with each other; and Nature demands that the nobler of the two should triumph. But how? It is Hitler's answer to this question which brings us precisely to the heart of his concept of the Folkish State:

. . . the folkish philosophy finds the importance of mankind in its basic racial elements. In the state it sees on principle only a means to an end and construes its end as the preservation of the racial existence of man. Thus, it by no means believes in an equality of the races, but along with their difference it recognizes their higher or lesser value and feels itself obligated, through this knowledge, to promote the victory of the better and stronger, and demand the subordination of the inferior and weaker in accordance with the eternal will

[48] *Ibid.,* p. 300.
[49] *Ibid.,* p. 324.
[50] *Ibid.,* p. 325.
[51] *Ibid.,* p. 326.

that dominates this universe. Thus, in principle, it serves the basic aristocratic idea of Nature. . . .[52]

All of this Hitler sees as the primary, indeed the sacred, duty of the state. Failing this, civilization will fall; accomplishing it assures a higher culture, presided over by a master Aryan race.

Understanding the Folkish State is thus of paramount importance for understanding Hitler and the Nazi movement—all the more for its obvious implications with respect to the shape of the political system to come. *Mein Kampf* makes plain its rejection of equalitarianism, majority rule, and minority rights—in sum, anything remotely resembling a democracy. In contrast it postulates a political design which all but labels itself "totalitarian." For Hitler, the call to racial purity finds its meaning in the homogeneous state—one which eschews pluralism or opposition. For the Jews, therefore, the Folkish State bodes ill. "There is no making pacts with Jews," Hitler warns, "there can only be the hard: either—or." [53] Lest there be any doubt about what this augurs for the future, it is well clarified by the end of *Mein Kampf,* in language more direct and prophetic:

If at the beginning of the War and during the War twelve or fifteen thousand of these Hebrew corrupters of the people had been held under poison gas, as happened to hundreds of thousands of our very best German workers in the field, the sacrifice of millions at the front would not have been in vain. . . .

. . . And in my opinion, it was then the very first task of a truly national government to seek and find the forces which were resolved to declare a war of annihilation on Marxism, and then to give these forces a free road; it was their duty not to worship the idiocy of "law and order" at a moment when the enemy without was administering the most annihilating blow to the fatherland and at home treason lurked on every street corner. . . .[54]

What Hitler envisioned as his ideal state does not end here, however. For one thing, his preoccupation with racial purity also spilled over into the more elaborate role he had in mind for the government. To preclude any further dilution of the precious Aryan blood, the state must strictly regulate all human propagation; and at great length Hitler urges that "most ruthless decisions" must be applied to defectives, the incurably sick, prostitutes, and syphilitics. Moreover,

This cleansing of our culture must be extended to nearly all fields. Theater, art, literature, cinema, press, posters, and window displays must be cleansed of all manifestations of our rotting world and placed in the service of a moral, po-

[52] *Ibid.,* p. 383.
[53] *Ibid.,* p. 206.
[54] *Ibid.,* pp. 679 f.

litical and cultural idea. . . . The right of personal freedom recedes before the duty to preserve the race.[55]

Hence, it is a pattern of total control which Hitler espouses.

A state of this description would require a compatible style of political organization, and *Mein Kampf* presumes to have found it. As suggested earlier, Hitler had only contempt for parliamentary democracy—typified by his epithet that it was a " 'monstrosity of excrement and fire. . . .' " [56] Instead, the Folkish State would look for its leader among those who

> . . . bear in their hearts fanatical faith in the victory of a movement, but also . . . indomitable energy and will, and if necessary . . . brutal ruthlessness, to sweep aside any obstacles which might stand in the path of the rising new idea. For this only beings were fitted in whom spirit and body had acquired those military virtues which can perhaps best be described as follows: swift as greyhounds, tough as leather, and hard as Krupp steel.[57]

These are the elite who will stand at the forefront of the Nazi movement and state; yet even here Hitler is persuaded that only *one* man is to stand astride the whole political structure, and he alone will make the ultimate decisions.

> There must be no majority decisions, but only responsible persons, and the word "council" must be restored to its original meaning. Surely every man will have advisers by his side, but *the decision will be made by one man.*
>
> The principle which made the Prussian army in its time into the most wonderful instrument of the German people must some day, in a transferred sense, become the principle of the construction of our whole state conception: *authority of every leader downward and responsibility upward.*
>
> Even then it will not be possible to dispense with those corporations which today we designate as parliaments. But their councillors will then actually give counsel; responsibility, however, can and may be borne only by *one* man, and therefore only he alone may possess the authority and right to command.[58]

With this statement Hitler has contributed a basically authoritarian framework—the *"Fuehrerprinzip"* or leader principle—to the concept of the Folkish State.

In sum, these were the major tenets of the ideology set forth in *Mein Kampf*—the measure of things past, present, and future. To Hitler they provided ample explanation for Germany's recent fall from power, and the current inability to put the pieces back together. More important still was

[55] *Ibid.*, p. 255.
[56] *Ibid.*, p. 78.
[57] *Ibid.*, p. 356.
[58] *Ibid.*, pp. 449 ff.

the consequence of his reasoning applied to the years ahead. The more Hitler thought about the great destiny which awaited the Folkish State, the more was he convinced that Germany must expand territorially. That Germany had lost ground as a result of the war was bad enough; but surely a vigorous and triumphant race of Aryans would require much, much more territory in the future. To the concept of the Folkish State, therefore, Hitler applied a new keyword—*"Lebensraum"*—the need for living space:

And so we National Socialists consciously draw a line beneath the foreign policy tendency of our pre-War period. We take up where we broke off six hundred years ago. We stop the endless German movement to the south and west, and turn our gaze toward the land in the east. At long last we break off the colonial and commercial policy of the pre-War period and shift to the soil policy of the future.[59]

Of course Hitler was well aware that German expansion would not go unchallenged. The opposition, however, would not prevail. Furthermore, he plainly asserts that virtually any means—from agreement of expediency to the outright use of force—is justifiable if it serves the interests of the Folkish State. He concludes: *"We must clearly recognize the fact that the recovery of the lost territories is not won through solemn appeals to the Lord or through pious hopes in a League of Nations, but only by FORCE OF ARMS."* [60]

Such were the main articles of faith which Adolf Hitler proclaimed on behalf of the German National Socialists.

It was, of course, one thing for Hitler to beckon Germany toward the Third Reich on paper, quite another to actually sell his ideas in the political marketplace. From all outward appearances, as he looked to 1925 and parole, it seemed as if the nation was not buying. More precisely, the Nazi party had come to near extinction: not only was the Republic able to fend off its opponents by means of a very timely economic recovery, but as an added precaution the N.S.D.A.P. had been outlawed and Hitler barred from speaking. National socialism thus seemed an improbable threat.

Hitler was not so easily dissuaded, however. It proved relatively easy to convince the authorities to soften their hard line, and that was all that was needed for Hitler to apply himself with new dedication to the task of reconstructing the party. As for the upsurge of prosperity in Germany, there was little that he could do—except wait. Meanwhile, his efforts met with

[59] *Ibid.*, p. 654. At this very early stage of the game, Hitler had already established his priorities: Germany would first "settle accounts" with France, after which he nominated Russia and the Slavic states as the next target. Curiously, he toyed with the idea that England might be a partner in this venture.

[60] *Ibid.*, p. 627.

some success: a smoother and more elaborate organization, and a steadily growing membership—27,000 members in 1925; 178,000, in 1929.[61]

Then came the Great Depression. In the economic catastrophe which engulfed Germany, Hitler found the opportunity that he so badly needed and confidently expected. For four years the Weimar Republic had maintained an economic recovery with borrowed American dollars. When this money evaporated, and foreign markets folded, the German collapse followed: falling production, a deluge of bankruptcies, unemployment of epidemic proportions, a nightmare of shattered finances and personal hardship. It was all reminiscent of the chaos and suffering which had first plagued Germany at the conclusion of the war; now all of these grievances converged in a rising tide of bitterness, frustration, and open hostility toward the Republic. The elections tell the story: preceding the crash, in 1928, the Nazis had polled about 800,000 votes, and claimed only a dozen seats in the national legislature; by 1930, their popular vote had swollen to roughly 6,500,-000, and their 107 seats in the Reichstag made them Germany's second largest political party. The Depression thus signaled a changing of the political guard in Germany—for the Weimar government it was one handicap too many, and for the national socialists it provided the momentum needed to carry them to the top.

After the Nazis' windfall in the 1930 elections, it took Hitler only two more years to parlay his growing popularity to the point of crowning success. Although he failed to unseat the incumbent old warhorse and patriarch, President Paul von Hindenburg, in 1932, the Nazis could draw consolation from the Reichstag elections later the same year: doubling the previous totals, they amassed upwards of 13,000,000 votes and won 230 seats in the 608-member legislature. National socialism was still shy a majority, but it now stood first among the parties. It was this fact which provided Hitler with the final leverage to power. As the crucial year of 1932 ran its course, President von Hindenburg appointed one chancellor after another—each with the vain hope that he could somehow bring the Nazis into a working coalition, but without conceding any substantial power to Hitler. For the Nazis, however, cooperation had a much higher price tag —either they would lead the government (with Hitler as chancellor) or else they would defeat any effort to secure the backing of the legislature. One by one, Hindenburg's chancellors confronted the Nazi impasse, and one by one they fell before it. At the very last, the eighty-five-year-old President was persuaded that there was no alternative but to deal with Hitler. And so, on January 30, 1933, the Nazis officially came to power, and Adolf Hitler to the office of chancellor.

[61] Abel, *op. cit.* (above, n. 40), p. 311.

Where Hitler now stood was not unlike the position of Mussolini a decade earlier. The party had reached the point of authority, but its share was far from absolute. Indeed, Hitler was obliged to settle for a somewhat diluted chancellery, resting on a very brittle coalition of Nazis and conservative nationalists. It remains, then, to account for the final phase of Germany's conversion to a totalitarian state.

At what precise point the process was completed would be hard to say, but it was well on its way by 1936. The key to it all, of course, was in a plan of Hitler's: supreme power would be his as soon as the legislature (by two-thirds vote) granted the chancellor extraordinary decree-making authority, thus elevating him to the equivalent of a "legal" dictator. In essence, this was the same game that Mussolini had played. Hitler therefore proceeded to call for new elections to the Reichstag, and with the added resources of the government now at his command, to seek the seats needed to assure his supreme authority. The Nazis waged a vigorous campaign in their quest for votes, particularly against the communists and the social democrats, who were the targets of Stormtrooper raids. Matters reached something of a climax about one week before the elections, when the Reichstag was destroyed by arson. Although it seems to have been the Nazis who put the torch to the legislature, they successfully pinned the blame on the communists, contributing to a rising tide of Red hysteria. The elections of March, 1933, however, still failed to give Hitler what he wanted: the Nazi vote of 17,000,000 (44 percent of the total) yielded 288 Reichstag seats, well below the crucial two-thirds majority.

This vote was a disappointment to Hitler, but hardly a deterrent. He could, after all, still pressure the legislature to grant him unlimited power. The battle was waged on all fronts: besides his own sizable following, the nationalists and Catholic centrists were brought into line with bargains and promises; while the less cooperative legislators (communists and social democrats) were harassed, even arrested, in an effort to keep them from voting. When the final vote was tallied on March 23, 1933—amid the threats of Stormtroopers from without—the Reichstag had come over to Hitler. By 441 to 84, the legislature had capitulated in the form of a new law ". . . for Removing the Distress of People and Reich," otherwise known as the Enabling Act.[62] For all practical purposes it amounted to a gift of absolute power.

Needless to say, Hitler made the utmost use of his newfound prerogatives. Within a year's time he had succeeded in decreeing away all rival political

---

[62] *Gesetz zur Behebung der Not von Volk u. Reich.* Shirer, *op. cit.* (above, n. 33), pp. 198 ff.

parties, leaving the N.S.D.A.P. with an exclusive claim to legality.[63] Furthermore, he made short shrift of Germany's federal system by centralizing all power into a unitary design. Even these moves—offering all the advantages of a legal political monopoly—did not entirely placate Hitler. Thus, it was by wholesale murder and violence that Hitler "settled accounts" on June 30, 1934, with those associates whose loyalty to the Nazi party was in doubt.

For all intents and purposes, Hitler was now the state—minus only one final formality. To bring the constitutional farce to its logical conclusion, the Nazis could not very well tolerate a situation in which a Von Hindenburg could stand as President above Hitler as chancellor. As it turned out, the Nazis did not have long to wait to tidy up the matter, for Von Hindenburg died in August, 1934. Now Hitler moved swiftly, and with the use of his emergency powers he dissolved the office of President, while transferring its authority to a new and virtually omnipotent chancellery. Henceforth it was to be Adolf Hitler, Fuehrer and Reich Chancellor. Moreover, his expanded office also carried with it the title of Commander-in-Chief of the Armed Forces, and perhaps more important still, an oath of *personal* allegiance from the military.[64] Thus did supreme power—over party, government, and the instruments of force—synthesize into a full-blown dictatorship. And lest there be any lingering doubts as to the "legality" of the political New Order, Hitler went the added length of soliciting a national plebiscite. Aided by Von Hindenburg's last will and testament, which paid considerable tribute to Hitler (and which "conveniently" turned up just before the election), the outcome was never in doubt. What may well have been the last exercise of *pro forma* German democracy was the orderly process by which more than 38,000,000 voters, representing ninety percent of the electorate, signified their agreement.

Hitler was now in full possession of the power necessary for the accomplishment of a totalitarian society. And, as detailed previously, *Mein Kampf* made no secret of Hitler's ideological intentions to accomplish precisely that result. Indeed, it has already been observed that the first moves in the direction of total control had come to pass in the form of one-party politics. But what of the other social and economic components of the Nazi to-

[63] Law of July 14, 1933.

[64] "I swear by God this sacred oath, that I will render unconditional obedience to Adolf Hitler, the Fuehrer of the German Reich and people, Supreme Commander of the Armed Forces, and will be ready as a brave soldier to risk my life at any time for this oath." As quoted from Shirer, *op. cit.* (above, n. 33), p. 227. The army was in a position to have blocked Hitler, but he had already taken care to trade promises of mutual cooperation with the generals.

talitarian system? And inseparably related to this question is another: What of Hitler's most central thesis, the Folkish State?

With respect to the social sector, Hitler made good his promise to purge the culture of its pre-Nazi inclinations and to reorder society in the image of national socialist ideology. The process of nazification meant that the social organization of the nation was invested with political and ideological significance, to be reflected in a system of extensive controls and in the general subordination of individual freedom to the interests of the state. Here, it should suffice to cite but a few well-placed examples out of the endless inventory available.

Like Mussolini, Hitler would not share power over the communications media—written, spoken, or artistic—with any competing group. As early as the Reichstag fire, in fact, he had initiated a decree suspending rights of expression, publication, assembly, and association. From there it was only a matter of months until the Nazis possessed an effective monopoly of the entire field. As a case in point, the press was restricted by law [65] to delete

. . . anything which in any manner is misleading to the public, mixes selfish aims with community aims, tends to weaken the strength of the German Reich, outwardly or inwardly, the common will of the German people, the defense of Germany, its culture and economy . . . or offends the honor and dignity of Germany.

Censorship was also coupled with a further regulation which excluded Jews and "other non-Aryans" from editorships. To oversee these policies, the Reich Propaganda Ministry, headed by Hitler's close associate, Dr. Paul Goebbels, was created. Meanwhile, the Reich Chamber of Culture proceeded to organize and direct the creative professions according to the national socialist interpretation of culture.

Hitler had long emphasized the political potential of an ideologically indoctrinated youth, and to this end the Nazis responded with an elaborate and tightly controlled program. In the more formal aspects of education, the entire system was coordinated by a Reich minister, and this effectively insured the nazification of curriculum and teachers. But the training of youth was by no means confined to the schoolroom. In the extracurricular realm the party offered (on a mandatory basis!) the Hitler Youth program, a combination of ideological and paramilitary preparation, and a preliminary testing ground for the recruitment of potential elites.

Such was the pattern of social control which intruded into virtually all aspects of the private sector—associations, recreation, religion, population policy, *ad infinitum*. It was a pattern of control more far-reaching than that

[65] Reich Press Law, October 4, 1933.

of the fascists. And it did provide, as Hitler pledged, the "most ruthless decisions" in the interests of a new and homogeneous social order.

If there was any one prime moving force behind Hitler's brand of economics, it was undoubtedly related to the expansionist aims of the Third Reich. Reduced to its simplest form, the concept of *Lebensraum* committed Germany to the inevitability of war, and that, in turn, argued the necessity of an economy equal to the task. From the earliest days of Hitler's regime, therefore, the operational objective was a totally self-sufficient system, and one which would not falter in the face of economic blockade. In a word, the aim was autarky; and to achieve it, controls were needed.

Hence, the Nazis viewed economics primarily as an instrument for political purposes, the practical consequence being an institutional arrangement to insure the dominance of party policy. As usual it was a hierarchical structure, headed in this case by the Reich Ministry of Economics, and modeled along the lines of Hitler's *Fuehrerprinzip*.

The process of converting to a guns-over-butter economy left few groups untouched. Cartels made the adjustment more easily than small business. Beginning in 1934, Hitler reorganized the independent labor unions into the state's equivalent of a "company union," the Labor Front. Labor was divested of all effective bargaining power (including the right to strike), and the worker's position was somewhat akin to that of the medieval serf: security at the price of a Spartan existence. So too was the farmer's. By law the small farm owner was protected against the loss of his land, but the same law barred him from leaving it. Like industrial wages and prices, the entire agricultural marketplace finally was brought under unified command —in this case that of the Reich Minister of Food and Agriculture. The economy thus had been well harnessed to serve the interests of national socialist politics.

Putting together all that has been said of the political, social, and economic components of Naziism yields a picture of an ideologically integrated and extensively engineered totalitarian state. By the same token, it provides at least part of the answer to the question: How well did Nazi practice fit the theory of the Folkish State? It should be unnecessary at this point to detail any further the consequences of Hitler's program for remodeling the culture, or for reordering the state along authoritarian lines, all of which were part of the same syndrome. Neither is it the purpose here to belabor the well-recorded and widely familiar facts of Nazi expansionism, with more than a dozen conquests testifying to the applied realities of a *Lebensraum* theory. Certainly these are reasons sufficient to argue, in the case of the Folkish State, an identity of theory and practice.

Yet, there is another measure of the Folkish State theory—in many respects far more critical and far more telling. At bottom, it is simply not possible to unravel the ideology of Hitler without focusing on the core concept of "race" (or more accurately stated, of the Jews). The very heart of the Folkish State, it will be recalled, was precisely the idea that all turned on blood purity—threatened by the non-Aryan Jew—and that preservation of the race was the fundamental mission and organizing principle of the state.

It would be difficult indeed to find a more dramatic and convincing proof of ideology converted to practice—or, for that matter, of the intensity with which totalitarianism can be made operative—than in the history of the Nazi state regarding the Jews. In its "mildest" form, immediately after Hitler took power, the persecution of the Jews involved exclusion from a wide variety of employment fields—coupled with a generous dose of Nazi terror. By 1935, the efforts at "racial purification" found expression in the Nuremburg Laws which prohibited the intermarriage of Jews and non-Jews, and also denied German citizenship to all Jews. Nonetheless, such measures were relatively tame compared to the unrestrained violence which was directed at the Jews (and various ethnic groups which were also regarded as inferior) beginning about 1941. Concentration camps, ghettos, and the like, had already made their appearance several years before; but it was not until 1941 that the order went down for the "Final Solution"—the systematic and purposefully calculated effort to exterminate *every* Jew. On the question of theory and practice, then, the record is here very clear. *Mein Kampf* had come full circle in a system which attempted the practice of genocide, which methodically eradicated six million Jews, and which came finally to speak the language of Rudolf Hoess:

. . . when I set up the extermination building at Auschwitz, I used Zyklon B, which was a crystallized prussic acid which we dropped into the death chamber from a small opening. It took from three to fifteen minutes to kill the people in the death chamber, depending upon climatic conditions.

We knew when the people were dead because their screaming stopped. We usually waited about a half hour before we opened the doors and removed the bodies. After the bodies were removed our special commandos took off the rings and extracted the gold from the teeth of the corpses.

Another improvement we made over Treblinka was that we built our gas chambers to accommodate 2,000 people at one time, whereas at Treblinka their ten gas chambers only accommodated 200 people each.[66]

---

[66] Quoted in Shirer, *op. cit.* (above, n. 33), p. 968, from the deposition of Hoess—one-time commandant and S.S. leader at Auschwitz—recorded at the Nuremburg trials.

Totalitarianism Revisited

In Hitler and Mussolini, it seemed to many, the totalitarian ideology had found its ultimate personification. Thus it was not uncommon to believe that the war which put an end to Hitler and Mussolini would also bury totalitarian ideology. In this, the final confrontation between ideological systems, the destruction of fascism and Naziism would symbolize the unconditional surrender of an *idea,* and the ultimate vindication of democracy.

Such was the illusion. It was quickly shattered, of course, in the face of the communist challenge which continued. The lesson was plain: neither Hitler nor Mussolini had any *exclusive* claim to totalitarianism. Indeed, a totalitarianism of the left is every bit as credible as a totalitarianism of the right or center. Moreover, the broad-scale following of communism has called further into question the erstwhile comfortable assumption that totalitarian ideology is an unmarketable commodity, against which all men will naturally gravitate toward the intrinsic superiority of the democratic ideal. To argue that force and terror *alone* can account for the thirty-eight million voters who gave Hitler their blessings, or that intimidation *alone* is responsible for maintaining the Soviet or Chinese systems, simply will not do.

In one respect, at least, the lesson has not been missed: totalitarianism is clearly recognizable in the form of communist politics, notwithstanding its lip service to democracy. The lesson has been learned so well in fact, that communist totalitarianism now preoccupies our attention in much the same way that Naziism and fascism formerly did. Of course communism *is* the principal challenge to democracy in terms of present world tensions. And yet, the attitude still seems to persist that it is the *exclusive* threat, that there is little likelihood of another Hitler, and that there is little to be feared from anything less than left of center. In that respect the lesson has not been so well learned.

Briefly put, the point is that totalitarianism not only survived Hitler in the shape of communism, but also in an undying succession of neo-Nazi and neofascist revival efforts. Admittedly the noncommunist variety of totalitarianism is a lightweight compared to its opposite number, and it certainly possesses no powerful homeland as it once did in Germany and Italy. Neither is there much point to overinflating its present position by means of some highly imaginative conspiratorial theory which sees neo-Nazis lurking in the shadows. But to say that the totalitarian center of gravity is presently on the left is not to say that the Nazi-fascist variety is void of all potential. Indeed, our thesis is that the kind of conditions which facilitated the acceptance of Hitler and Mussolini are still extant, and unlikely to abate in the foreseeable future; that the capacity of men to respond to crisis is still such that authoritarian attitudes—now latent—may again be activated; and finally that the neo-Nazi-fascist may be aided and abetted by the politics of a society in which the measure of all things is communism vs. *anything* anticommunist.

By no means is this thesis entirely a matter of conjecture, though we are far from having any exact index as to the prevalence of noncommunist totalitarianism. One example of the hard data which is available, and which may help to throw some light on the subject, focuses attention on Germany in an effort to assess the residual sympathies for Naziism—particularly after the efforts at democratization. What it revealed, ten years after the war was over, was that nearly fifty percent of the young men sampled thought national socialism was a "good idea," and that forty-two percent agreed that "Hitler without the war would have been one of the greatest statesmen." [67] A more recent survey shows some weakening in the respondents' esteem for Hitler, but still leaves the figure at one out of every three persons interviewed.[68] Such findings are not confined to Germany alone, of course. Much closer to home, in fact, there is also reason to believe that totalitarianism of the right and center in the United States has sympathizers and potential supporters in greater numbers than those who parade under the banner of the American Nazi Party. In some quarters, at least, there is a good deal of significance attached to the recent surfacing of groups like the John Birch Society, Minutemen, and similar organizations.

If totalitarianism, *both* right and center as well as left, is still a force to be reckoned with, as contended here, how are we to account for this? The answer to this question is implicit in the case studies in this text of communism, fascism, and Naziism; and it brings into focus some of the preliminary observations concerning the nature and origins of totalitarianism. Two points particularly warrant recapitulating.

It is worth reemphasizing, first, that totalitarianism appears to be inseparably related to situational factors of a crisis nature. Economic catastrophe, national humiliation, social disorganization—these are the breeding grounds for such radical and revolutionary movements, for desperate men seeking desperate remedies. In such circumstances, the existing regime is put severely to the test. And where the government itself is both a

[67] Based on the research of Elisabeth Noelle Neumann and Erich Peter Neumann, *Jahrbuch der öffentlichen Meinung*, II (1957), 149; as reported in Deutsch and Breitling, *op. cit.* (above, n. 37), p. 290. The poll was based on a sample of one thousand men, born during the years 1929–39.

[68] According to a 1964 study reported by Lewis J. Edinger, *Politics in Germany* (Boston: Little, Brown, 1968), p. 76.

contributing cause and effect of the crisis, totalitarianism becomes all the more an attractive alternative. If the old order cannot adequately cope with the forces that threaten and disrupt the community, then the old order will have to give way to the promise of new and aggressive leadership. Hence the irresistible attraction of the strong man and the strong party.

Crisis is not simply an objectified condition of the economy, or of regime stability, and the like. In a sense it is much more than that: it is as much a state of mind, a psychological response. In these terms the condition of crisis may relate to such anxieties and frustrations as attend the growth and increasing complexity of society. The modern, industrial, urbanized society —for all its benefits—is also impersonal, confusing, ambiguous, and not infrequently difficult to cope with. And for many it is psychologically impenetrable, and deeply alienating. Again, therefore, many are driven by it to seek refuge in a safer, more secure arrangement.

In a large sense the problem may well be that described by Erich Fromm, in his insightful work *Escape from Freedom*.[69] It is, according to Fromm, the problem of many who are chronological adults, but who are political children in the sense that they recoil from the hard choices and responsibilities which freedom imposes. What they yearn for most is the comfort and security of the all-wise father figure who will give order and direction to their lives, and rescue them from drift, helplessness, and uncertainty.

The second point is, then, that the chaos and upheaval of a crisis society, and the personal turmoil of the individual, coordinate perfectly under totalitarianism with the man and the ideology. The man is dynamic, charismatic, strong, and commanding. He promises simple answers to long-standing and complex problems; he promises well-delineated standards of right and wrong, of good and evil; and he promises a political rebirth to all who would follow him. So, too, the ideology. It defines the enemy and the source of all suffering; it speaks of new strength where weakness prevailed; and it conjures up images of glories unequaled.

From such components, totalitarianism derives its character, its appeal, and its following. What it persuades us to believe is that its fortunes are intimately tied to many of the conditions and much of the psychology of modern societies. It did not go to the grave with Hitler and Mussolini, nor will it likely go with a communist equivalent because its lure transcends any given regime. So long as severe crises go unresolved—which seems the ever-present problem of twentieth-century society—we shall also have to confront the possibility of a totalitarian response.

[69] *Escape from Freedom* (New York: Rinehart, 1941).

Bibliography

Abel, Theodore. *The Nazi Movement: Why Hitler Came to Power.* New York: Atherton, 1965.

Adorno, Theodore W., *et al. The Authoritarian Personality.* New York: Harper, 1960.

Bullock, Allan. *Hitler: A Study in Tyranny.* New York: Bantam Books, 1958.

Edinger, Lewis J. *Politics in Germany.* Boston: Little, Brown, 1968.

Finer, Herman. *Mussolini's Italy.* New York: Grosset & Dunlap, 1965. First published in London: Victor Gollancz, 1935.

Halperin, S. William. *Mussolini and Italian Fascism.* Princeton, N.J.: D. Van Nostrand, 1964.

Hitler, Adolf. *Mein Kampf.* Boston: Houghton Mifflin, 1962. First published in Berlin: Verlag Frz. Eher Nachf., G.M.B.H., 1925.

Kogon, Eugen. *The Theory and Practice of Hell.* New York: Berkley Publishing Co., 1950.

Laqueur, Walter, and Mosse, George. *International Fascism.* New York: Harper, 1966.

McRandle, James H. *The Track of the Wolf: Essays on National Socialism and its Leader, Adolf Hitler.* Evanston, Ill.: Northwestern University Press, 1965.

Mosse, George L. *Nazi Culture.* New York: Grosset & Dunlap, 1966.

———. *The Crisis of German Ideology: Intellectual Origins of the Third Reich.* New York: Grosset & Dunlap, 1964.

Shirer, William L. *The Rise and Fall of the Third Reich.* New York: Simon & Schuster, 1960.

Snell, John. *The Nazi Revolution.* Lexington, Mass.: D. C. Heath, 1959.

Sterm, Fritz, ed. *The Paths to Dictatorship.* New York: Frederick A. Praeger, 1967.

Chapter 4

Soviet Communism

There is not *a* communist ideology. There are communist ideolog*ies*. There is the philosophic communism of Marx; there is a Marxist-Leninist ideology; there are also Marxist-Leninist-Stalinist, Marxist-Leninist-Stalinist-Khrushchevite, Marxist-Leninist-Maoist, and Marxist-Leninist-Titoist ideologies. And even these do not exhaust the list of defunct, moribund, or still-evolving varieties. Towards the end of his life, Marx wrote "Of one thing I am certain; I am no Marxist." [1] Even then so many psuedo-Marxist doctrines were being paraded that Marx had to protest his innocence.

The proliferation of socialist dreams has continued since the earliest visions of an egalitarian society. In the days of Jesus of Nazareth a number of contemplative sects were based on the principle of equal shares—and portions of the New Testament suggest the desirability and righteousness of such an arrangement.

In the more immediate past, beginning with the second half of the eighteenth century, there were numerous schemes for reconstituting society on a more egalitarian basis. Mably, Morelley, Meslier, Saint-Simon, Fourier, Owens, Blanqui, Babeuf, are but some of the better known publicists, theoreticians, and radical political actors of the time who blamed the evils of the period upon private property and sought to ameliorate suffering by advocating the equalization of wealth or opportunity. [2]

Their grievances were serious ones. Undermined by the Industrial Revolution, the long-standing feudal structure was being destroyed as destitute

---

[1] Cited in various biographies, e.g., Isaiah Berlin, 2nd ed. *Karl Marx* (New York: Oxford University Press, 1948), p. 258.

[2] These precursors of Marx are well treated in detail in Edmund Wilson's *To the Finland Station* (New York: Harcourt, Brace, 1940).

peasants were swept into cities and factories.[3] Some critics spoke out against the disintegration of feudal morality; more were shocked by the conditions of the urban centers. Unprepared and unwilling to cope with the flood of immigrants thrust upon them, the town and city fathers largely looked the other way as overcrowding became severe, as water sources became fouled and sewers clogged, as unemployment forced thousands into the streets and forced others—including women and children—to work under less-than-humane-and-safe conditions at less-than-living wages. Famine, disease, poverty, and rats stalked the cities. Some men profited, but vastly greater numbers were victimized by the industrial and social transformation.[4]

Thus many men before and during Marx's time deplored the evils precipitated by the Industrial Revolution—and prescribed social remedies. Marx sought to refute them all, challenging their diagnoses in some causes and their prescriptions in others. A good many socialists were dismissed as "utopian" for believing that reason and altruism would create the good society, for ignoring the role of class conflict and the impossibility of eliminating social ills unless the downtrodden class—the workers, the proletarians—overthrew by revolution the prevailing ruling class—the bourgeoisie. According to Marx, the bourgeoisie had risen to wealth and then to power and then to more wealth on the backs of the proletariat. The cruel, decadent, and demoralizing society that existed was a bourgeois society. Life for the multitudes would not improve until it had been replaced by a proletarian society; this could be accomplished only by a widespread recognition of the problem and, probably, by violence.

The Marxist Foundation

Karl Marx was a hardheaded observer of his times. At his desk in the British Museum, where he spent most of his later years, he studied books, newspapers, and private reports that convinced him of the intolerable inequities of society as well as of their cause. Men's conditions and beliefs, he thought, were largely determined by economic relationships. All other relationships rested on an economic base. In every society, those who possess property—thereby controlling the *means of production*—determine the course of that society; those who lack property have their fate determined by others—and so it has been since man first said "this is mine," asserting the private right to property. Marx further believed that property ownership patterns revealed the most significant elements about society and

---

[3] Cf. Chap. 7.
[4] Richard Pipes (and others) have sometimes contended that the alleged suffering caused by the Industrial Revolution has been overdrawn. The author disagrees.

its social structure.[5] Thus, until property was possessed by all, it would continue to enslave the majority. As Proudhon, a contemporary of Marx, put it: "Property is the principle of evil."

With the very considerable assistance of Friedrich Engels,[6] Marx traced the development of property and property relationships through the various stages into which he divided history. But his chief interest was in the arrangement of the productive forces in his own age. In capitalist society, wrote Marx, the proletariat is the source of its own suffering, for it provides the labor which produces the wealth which results in its own enslavement.[7] Labor, according to Marx, is the only commodity which in being consumed creates new values. Essentially, the cost of a product consists of the cost of the raw material plus the cost of the machinery employed, plus the cost of labor. But the selling price is greater than the cost. The difference between the selling price and the cost Marx calls *surplus value*—belonging only to those actively engaged in the act of production. It does not belong to the man who owns or operates the factory, nor to the man who advances the capital to purchase raw materials, pay wages, etc., nor to the man who has used his ingenuity in inventing or promoting the product. The only real source of value is that physical labor involved in the productive process, and this is provided by the worker alone. He alone creates new value— and he alone *should* enjoy it.[8] Under capitalism, however, the one who profits from the production process is the entrepreneur, who pays only for the costs of production, but gets the surplus value *free of charge,* since, by Marx's definition, he has expended no labor in creating the new value.

Marx's concentration on the economic element makes up the materialistic component of Marx's dialectical materialism. This dialectic further demonstrates that social change is constant, that it comes about through struggle, that in the capitalist stage the struggle is between the bourgeoisie and the proletariat, that the ultimate defeat of the bourgeoisie and the victory of the proletariat is assured and inevitable.

As with most components of Marx's philosophy, the dialectic is not original with him, nor did he claim it as such except in its application. It was, in fact, the concept of G. W. F. Hegel, the Prussian philosopher, to whose

[5] *Poverty of Philosophy.*

[6] Engels is often overlooked. *Das Kapital* is much more a work of collaboration than is usually believed. At least part of this misassessment is attributable to Engels' self-effacing personality, and Marx's will to dominate.

[7] There are many texts that explain the Marxist hypothesis. One of the best and most readable is Alfred Meyer, *Marxism* (Cambridge: Harvard University Press, 1954).

[8] Marx's definition of "value" is not always consistent. Whereas labor is always prominent in the definition—at times land, capital, and resources are also included, as in Vols. II and III of *Das Kapital.*

ideas Marx was attracted for a time. Hegel held that all of life is in constant flux and that the moment of creation begins a process terminating in dissolution and death. Every idea (thesis) is inevitably opposed by a contrary concept (antithesis) and out of their struggle emerges synthesis. At the moment of its emergence, synthesis becomes thesis, renewing the cycle again. The thesis-antithesis-synthesis trio is known as the *triad;* the process through which the triad is realized is the *dialectic;* and the *dialectic,* according to Hegel, is the way life proceeds and will continue to proceed.

For Marx, what is most essential in the dialectic is the presence of struggle and the element of inevitability. The struggle in every stage of development is between the old and the new—and the.new inevitably triumphs. Feudalism overcomes slavery; capitalism, feudalism; and, in the inexorable course of history, socialism will replace capitalism. Events can temporarily alter the process, and delay the timetable, but the dialectic will not be thwarted.

The dialectic gives Marxism its assurance concerning the future. From his long years of research, Marx concluded that man's history had been determined by the principles of dialectical materialism; the same was true of the current epoch, and would be, inevitably, the future, as well. "Scientific socialism," then, was grounded in extensive research, based on "history" and historical inevitability, on travail and struggle rather than on "utopian" concepts of the "reasonableness" of man and the triumph of noble ideas.

In accordance with the ground rules drawn up by Marx himself, the correctness of his analysis must, in large part, be judged by the accuracy of his forecasts. The bourgeoisie must be destroyed, capitalism must be toppled and the proletariat, now encompassing all of society, must be deposited on the felicitous shores of communism.[9]

But if capitalism is not tottering and the bourgeoisie is not collapsing, the spuriousness of the Marxist doctrine is suggested or, at least, the presence of error that must be explained away. Many disciples of Marx, including Lenin, have undertaken the latter task during the one hundred years since the publication of *Das Kapital.*

The birth of capitalism, according to Marx, was to be found in the tiny shop operated by an individual or a family. Such a shop would have only one rather primitive machine. But the owner, assisted by his family, would

---

[9] Any discussion of the differences between socialism and communism is likely to be unsatisfactory, because of their myriad interpretations. To Marx they were often indistinguishable; to Lenin, socialism is stage one of communism, though he, too, often confused the two. To Lenin's Russian successors, socialism is also an earlier stage—achieved by 1936 in the Soviet Union. Communism, then, is the fulfillment of the socialist struggle. Moreover, it must be kept in mind that in non-Marxist circles, socialism has often had connotations in conflict with communism.

work long hours, produce salable goods, live frugally, and be able to save. These savings (later dubbed "primitive capital accumulation"), laboriously accumulated over many years of hard work, ultimately would provide the small craftsman who owned and operated the shop with the means to purchase a second machine. In theory, what he could save from each day's operations would then double, until he could purchase a third machine, a fourth, and so on. Along the way, the owner would become an entrepreneur and his small shop, a factory. He would rely no longer only upon the family, but would hire outside workers and deprive them of the surplus value that was rightfully theirs, since he had done nothing to create that value.

In such a society, said Marx, not only is the workman deprived of his economic rights, but he is completely at the mercy of the entrepreneur. The bourgeoisie inevitably acts as the agent of the system, whose every institution is established for the advantage of the owning class. The state, therefore, is the handmaiden of the bourgeoisie; it is, in every stage of development, the tool of the ruling class, the means of enforcing its will upon the ruled.

While the working class is the victim of the system, the bourgeois capitalist does not lead a completely "free" life either. He is inexorably moved to maximize surplus value. He cannot forswear the compulsion, even though some capitalists may comprehend the destructiveness of such compulsion.

Since the capitalist must seek to maximize surplus value, he must minimize his costs. And it is the worker who bears the brunt of this effort. The capitalist as entrepreneur induces the worker to produce more in a shorter time, or work longer hours for the same or less pay, and so forth. Thus, the capitalist accelerates the rate of exploitation and, as he does so, his capital resources grow. With his additional funds, he purchases more and usually superior machinery, which requires still less labor to produce still greater quantities of goods. He now has additional goods to put on the market, but unfortunately for him the capacity of society to consume these goods has not risen as rapidly as its ability to produce them. A backlog develops in the entrepreneur's warehouses—and in hundreds of other warehouses. Workmen must be laid off. And thus the capacity of society to consume is reduced still more.

The entrepreneur may try a number of devices to improve his position. He may lower prices or try in other ways to stimulate trade. But not enough consumers can buy even at reduced prices. To lower the price of his goods, he may lower wages—since there are ample numbers of increasingly desperate unemployed willing to work for almost any wage—but this only further reduces the capacity to buy. Depression sets in.

In the early stages of its development, a robust capitalism is able to work its way out of such crises. It is vigorous and soon regains its equilibrium. But such crises come with increasing frequency, each deeper than the one before, each taking a longer period for recovery, and each bringing inevitably closer the collapse of the capitalist system.

In the process of the decline and disintegration of capitalism, society is marked by a more and more clear-cut distinction between proletariat and bourgeoisie. The contacts between the two become embittered. Class war sharpens. The suffering of the proletariat deepens. Those with a foot in both camps are ruined and fall into the ranks of the proletariat. As for the bourgeoisie itself, its numbers are depleted. Through such devices as monopolies, the capitalists, ever seeking greater surplus value, try to strengthen their hand. Instead of ten producers of an item, there is finally only one. The other nine have either been forced out of business or bought out. In the latter instance the capitalist may attempt to invest what he has received for his plant, but the opportunities for profitable investment are few. He must live off his capital. Soon he—certainly his progeny—is ruined. The entire family joins the rapidly swelling proletariat.

The ruined capitalist is not alone in his decline. Professional men, hitherto largely dependent upon the bourgeoisie (which alone can now afford the luxury of medical or legal service) have a decreasing clientele. The decreasing ranks of the bourgeoisie require fewer physicians and fewer lawyers and fewer professors. Those displaced also become proletarians.

But these members of the *intelligentsia* function within the proletariat in a particular capacity—as the *class-conscious* element of the proletariat. The proletariat, in general—made up of the uneducated masses—knows that it is suffering, but doesn't know why. The class-conscious segment of the proletariat, however, composed both of displaced intelligentsia and workers educated by the bourgeoisie to operate its increasingly sophisticated plants and businesses, understands what is happening, comprehends what must be done, and can organize the masses to act.

Ultimately, capitalism will become so demoralized and its structure so weakened that the "next" economic crisis will present a revolutionary situation. It is possible that by this time the reduced and distintegrating bourgeoisie will simply melt away and that the entire productive apparatus of society, as well as its institutions, will fall, like overripe plums, into the hands of the proletariat. Much more likely, however, the bourgeoisie, as with every ruling class in history, will fight to maintain its possessions and power. A determined bourgeoisie may, even under desperate circumstances, attempt to hold on. But if the class-conscious members of the proletariat have done their job, they have organized the proletarians to seize what is rightfully theirs. The final struggle between the bourgeoisie and its successor will bring violence, but the former is so weakened that the struggle will be brief. The revolution will have been achieved. The proletariat will have become the master of its own fate.

At the point of capitalism's demise, Marx combines voluntarism with inevitability. Although the collapse of capitalism is inevitable, the class-conscious elements of the proletariat—by recognizing the nature of the struggle and by organizing and planning for revolution—can speed the process of dissolution, and bring about an earlier rather than a later revolution.

Where will the revolution occur? Marx is, in a sense, quite specific. It will occur in the country having the greatest contradictions of capital, where —at the same time—productive capacity is most highly developed, the disintegration of the capitalist class is most advanced, and the suffering of the proletariat is most acute. It may take place in Great Britain, France, or Germany but it is most likely to break out first in Germany.[10] From Germany it will spread to other highly industrialized states, and from there to less highly industrialized ones. Every country will have to undergo the process of transition from feudalism to capitalism and endure the pains of industrial growth [11]—but the fact that the revolution has been successfully carried out in one country will facilitate its realization elsewhere. Each successful revolution brings the next one nearer and makes it easier.

As has been noted above, Marx's chief interest is in capitalism: its inception, maturation, and decay. He is exhaustive in its treatment. His description of the march to revolution is detailed. But as to the new order, he is considerably less specific. Perhaps this is understandable, since in the former instance Marx merely reports the scene unfolding before him, while in the latter he is asked to prognosticate. Nevertheless, if he is forecasting and urging the destruction of the present, he must have the future society in mind. To a limited degree, Marx does.

Immediately after the revolution, the dictatorship of the proletariat will be established. In all probability, neither the capitalists nor their institutions will have been completely eliminated by the revolution. Both will have to be controlled. The possibility of counterrevolution is not to be discounted. Thus the defunct dictatorship of the capitalists will be replaced by the dictatorship of the proletariat; whereas previously the small minority ruled over the overwhelming majority, positions are now reversed. But the dic-

[10] See Bertram Wolfe, *Marxism: One Hundred Years in the Life of a Doctrine* (New York: Dial, 1965), which deals at length with Marx's German orientation and expectations.

[11] Karl Marx, preface to Vera Zasulich's translation of the *Communist Manifesto*.

tatorship of the proletariat will be of short duration. The power and habits of the *ancien regime* will soon be swept away and the classless society ushered in.

If the chief purpose of the state and government is to enable the ruling class to control institutionally the exploited, as Marx holds, then with the passing of exploitation in a classless society, state and government will become unnecessary. They will "wither away." As Engels put it: "The state will be placed into the museum of antiquities, next to the spinning wheel and the bronze ax." [12]

If the state and its coercive apparatus pass away, however, how can society control man's acts of violence: robberies, assaults, murders? These, held Marx, are almost exclusively the products of capitalist society. Violence grows out of economic deprivation. Give men sufficient food, clothing, and shelter, and the necessity for force will recede, until, as Lenin suggested, the only coercion necessary will be exerted by white-coated men in hospitals.[13]

When the classless society has been achieved, not only will class differences disappear, but national differences as well. The latter are largely, according to Marx, concomitants of capitalist society developed by the bourgeoisie to lead the proletariat of one nation to fight the proletariat of another for markets and colonies, while simultaneously diverting the attention of the proletarians from their *true* class enemies, the bourgeoisie. Thus, to protect themselves, the French bourgeoisie encourage the French proletariat to hate Germans and the German bourgeoisie encourage its proletariat to hate the French. National differences thus are rooted in capitalism. With capitalism's destruction they will disappear and all men will live as brothers in Marx's scientific, nonutopian Utopia.

On the specific details of the communist state, Marx is yet more vague. Of course, the principle of equality of distribution will be adhered to strictly. The guidepost of communist justice will be "from each according to his ability, to each according to his needs." Marx is not concerned that the ready availability of ample food and shelter will cause some members of society to stint their labor. Each *will* give according to his ability, because in the new society he will *want* to do so.

As for the distribution of production, this will be carried out through gigantic warehouses. At first, it is quite true, women may make a run on the shoe warehouse, for instance. If shoes are free each may want a dozen pairs. But soon it is discovered that the supply of shoes is not going to run

[12] Friedrich Engels, *The Origin of the Family, Private Property and the State,* Chapter IX.
[13] Concluding paragraph of Chapter V of *State and Revolution.*

out; more are available as needed; and it *is* a burden to find storage room for a dozen pairs of shoes. In Marx's scheme, production is not the problem; the problem is overproduction. There is more than enough for all— as there was before the revolution. Capitalism flounders because it cannot get the available production into the hands of the consumers; this, communism accomplishes.

Marx is concerned about a variety of aspects of the individual's work role in the new society. He anticipates that physical labor, already stultifying in its boredom, will be further automated and routinized. Jobs will become readily interchangeable; the man pushing one set of buttons this month will push another set next month. In the increasingly mechanized factory, there will be fewer and fewer hours of toil per week. Marx briefly recognizes the problem of greater leisure time, but assumes that the cultivation of hobbies, such as fishing (one of Marx's favorites) and other avocations hitherto denied the proletariat by the demands of capitalism, will provide a ready solution. According to Marx, man is dominated by the compulsion to create, to produce. Hitherto his creative drive has been shackled by the structures of the economic system. But once released, he will contribute according to his abilities, because it is his nature to do so.[14]

In the assignment of jobs, Marx asserts that the supervisory function will be as routinized as any other. Today's bench hand will be tomorrow's foreman, supervisor, and general manager. For Marx, administrative skills are easily come by. Marx is forced into this position because he argues that capitalist management makes no contribution to the productive process and therefore is entitled to no share of surplus value. The belief that administration requires sophisticated and essential skills is a capitalist fiction designed to protect the economic privileges of the entrepreneurial class. The consequences of such an assertion for the followers of Marx-come-to-power has been considerable. The ideological necessity and predisposition to downgrade management skills at a time when technological development has placed greatly increased reliance upon them has severely handicapped the efficient management of industry in countries influenced by the Marxist word.[15]

The attractiveness of the Marxist ideology is apparent. To the dissatis-

[14] Karl Marx, *Economic and Philosophical Manuscripts.* Also see Robert C. Tucker, *Philosophy and Myth in Karl Marx* (Cambridge: Cambridge University Press, 1961).

[15] In the 1960's there were still no schools of administration in the Soviet Union. In a few schools there has been a trend towards offering a course or two, but not under the name of administration. The clearest indication that the Soviets were at last beginning to recognize the existence of a "science" of administration was their request to send Russian students to American schools of administration under the American-Soviet academic exchange program.

fied, the malcontent, the powerless, the suffering, it offers hope. It offers a pinpointed explanation of what is wrong with modern society. It assigns blame. It provides a plan for action. It assures the victory of justice and international brotherhood *even if nothing is done*. Indeed, it offers a heaven on earth to all who will but believe—and its interpretations and prophecies are based not on "utopian" idealism, but on "science."

When he penned the *Communist Manifesto* with Engels in 1848, Marx, it has often been said, expressed his prejudices. He then spent the next twenty years trying to document them in *Das Kapital*. Long before the first volume of *Das Kapital* was published in September, 1867, however, contemporaries began to criticize his positions. But with the publication of *Das Kapital,* the so-called Bible of socialism, a broader, more visible target was presented. Just as *Das Kapital* established the reputation of Marx as the "father" of socialism, it also concentrated the fire of opposition upon him and his work.

Though the attack upon classical Marxism has come from every possible direction, the critics have four basic arguments focusing, respectively, upon the dialectic, the labor theory of value, Marx's psychology, and his forecasts.

In taking up the first argument, critics have suggested that while the dialectic may be an ambitious attempt to place all history in the framework of thesis-antithesis-synthesis, such an attempt is no more than an intellectual exercise. Generation and death are the way of life. All things come to an end. The new is not always, or even usually, victorious. The persistence of the old, even if in slightly modified form, is the norm. But it need not even be shown that the persistence of the old institution occurs more often than its replacement by a new one. To challenge the meaningfulness of the dialectic, it is enough to show that the old sometimes survives the assault of the new.

Marx's assertion that it is only or chiefly physical labor that imparts "surplus value" to any manufactured item is also subject to question. Marx holds that neither managerial skill nor creative capacity nor the risk of capital legitimately participate in the creation of surplus value. Opponents argue that this is a highly arbitrary expression of Marx's prejudices. The experience of even the socialist countries provides abundant evidence that creativity and management skills, not to mention capital, are indispensable to the productive process; [16] the latter cannot be successfully or optimally maintained without them.

[16] Beginning in the early 1960's many excellent articles on this subject have appeared: for example, Marshall Goldman's "Economic Revolution in the Soviet Union," *Foreign Affairs,* Vol. 45, no. 2 (January, 1967), 319–331, and H. G. Shaeffer's article on the Czech economy in the *Journal of Industrial Economy,* Vol. 15 (November, 1966), 44–53.

The third basic fault often attributed to Marx is his simplistic view of human nature. Marx, it is argued (particularly by those who tend to disregard his early, more humanistic, views), sees man as essentially governed by his material needs. According to this view, man resorts to evil only because he is physically deprived. Marx is probably correct in contending that man's hostility and aggressions are based on deprivation, but there are deprivations other than physical. The need for love, prestige, and self-respect are commonly recognized today. And the acts of violence committed by man are frequently attributable to spiritual, as opposed to physical, deprivations. While we still do not comprehend all of the sources of adult human aggressions, some antisocial behavior appears to stem from physiological causes as well as material ones.

Ultimately, though, as pointed out earlier, the Marxist analysis must largely stand on the correctness of its forecasts. While the preceding arguments *contra* Marx are cogent, there are counterarguments for them. No one would care much whether history revealed that the dialectic or the labor theory of value was valid, and so forth, *if* Marx's prognostications had been verified by events; *if* the size of the proletariat had greatly expanded and its plight had become agonizingly desperate; *if* the advance of capitalism and industrialization had further exacerbated the workers' condition; *if* depressions had accelerated in frequency and duration; and *if* the leading industrial nations had experienced the revolution. But history appears to have run in other directions.

The fact is that the plight of the working class in those countries where Marx forecast revolution has not deteriorated; indeed, in the traditionally industrialized countries, the working class has prospered. Instead of the bourgeoisie falling into the proletariat, many of the latter's sons and daughters have moved up the economic and social ladder. Capitalism is not inexorably borne along either by the necessity to constantly maximize surplus value. Through the development of trade unions and a growth of understanding, most employers—and societies—perceive that the welfare of their own enterprises is dependent upon the welfare of the employees: economic life for the bourgeoisie cannot flourish when workmen are in penury. Contrary to Marx's prognosis, threfore, business has shown that it can forego immediate profits for other values, if necessary. Finally, economic science has indicated that it can limit and even prevent depression. True, as it has adjusted to meet its challenges, capitalism has changed fundamentally from the doomed monster which Marx described. But the point is, Marx was sure it could not change.

The Leninist Actualization

Today a Marxist-type revolution is a negligible threat in those countries where Marx prophesied revolution. In the wake of war or depression, the prospects for such a revolution were once greater,[17] but in modern times they have never been less promising than in the 1970's.

Yet today nearly half of the world lives under regimes that call themselves Marxist and which, despite evidence to the contrary, continue to anticipate the imminent decline of capitalism. Furthermore, most of those regimes exist in countries that are (or were when they started out on the Marxist path) economically backward and underdeveloped—not producers of economic surplus whose chief problems were overproduction and maldistribution. How has this shift, which belies the very foundation of Marxism, been accomplished? The answer is to be found in Marx's brilliant Russian disciple, Vladimir Ilyich Lenin.

When Lenin arrived upon the political scene in the 1890's, Marx had already been dead ten years. But even before his death, the failure of some of his forecasts was apparent. Even his sympathizers often felt it necessary to revise his estimates. Marx himself had not tolerated such "revisionism" and indeed reserved his most pointed barbs for "enemies" with similar ideologies who sought to modify his theories. As Marx's disciple, however, Lenin could not be oblivious to the serious criticisms of Marxism that were being made. He railed against such revisionist purveyors of "anti-Marxist" calumnies as the German Social Democrats, Eduard Bernstein and Karl Kautsky. But castigation alone was not enough; Lenin had to meet argument with counter-argument. In so doing, he revised Marxism far more basically than did some of the revisionists he had attacked.

Lenin was faced with the fact that Marx's forecasts concerning the proletariat had not materialized. Its condition was not deteriorating—on the contrary, it seemed to be significantly improving—and its class consciousness differed little from that of a half century earlier. Why hadn't the revolution occurred, or at least come significantly closer to realization?

Lenin's answer [18] was that there had been a new development in capitalism: its highest and therefore final stage prior to collapse, namely, imperialism. The race for colonies in the latter half of the nineteenth century had provided the developed nations with cheap raw materials and labor; with markets for disposing of their surplus production; and, most importantly,

17 After World War II there was a widespread fear in the West that the inability of war-ravaged countries to get on their feet might make them susceptible to communist revolutions. The Marshall Plan adopted by the United States in the late 1940's was the American response to the threat.

18 Cf. *Imperialism as the Highest Stage of Capitalism.*

according to Lenin, with areas in which to invest their surplus profits. As a result of the advent of imperialism, capitalism had been able to ease its contradictions. The position of the working class in the developed countries had been improved; but only temporarily and at the expense of the international working class, which was now caught in the clutches of capitalism.

The supply of colonies was, however, limited. When it was exhausted, the contradictions of capitalism would again be sharpened, as worker competed with worker for the dwindling supply of jobs. Moreover, at this stage, the developed countries, each trying to survive a deepening economic predicament, would turn against one another; in the resulting wars, the crisis of capitalism would be further sharpened.

Thus, while the demise of capitalism had been postponed by imperialism and, to a degree, by the development of monopolies which brought increased order to a kaleidoscopic situation, the prospects of revolution on a world-wide basis—for capitalism had spread the contradictions of capitalism to the corners of the globe—were inevitably bright. The revolution would occur.

If the changes Lenin made in Marxism are to be more fully grasped, though, it is necessary to go beyond a statement of doctrinal shortcomings and the means that Lenin used to come to grips with them. It is necessary to be aware of the great personal determination which moved Lenin to make revolution.

Lenin was *going* to have a revolution—and it was going to be *his* revolution. He was going to shape it, develop it, lead it. In contrast to Marx, who was—in large part—satisfied to write about revolution, secure in his conviction of inevitability, Lenin wanted the revolution to come while he was still alive to enjoy it. Lenin wrote constantly, the latest Russian edition of his works running to fifty-five volumes. But as he was to confide shortly after the Revolution of 1917, "it is much better to live revolution than to write about it." [19]

If Marx knew that revolution would occur, Lenin "knew" he was always right about the steps necessary to bring the revolution to pass. If others disagreed with him, they must either become converted or leave "his" movement. Lenin never feared fractionalization. There was only one truth: his truth. This did not mean that Lenin could not compromise; but it would be his compromise, worked out by him, according to his reading of the objective situation. [20]

[19] Postscript to First Edition of *State and Revolution*.

[20] Lenin became angry at those who forgot that Marx and Engels had declared that their theory was not a "dogma" but a "guide to action." Short-term compromise, under conditions determined by Lenin, was acceptable to obtain long-term goals. Cf. Lenin, *"Left Wing" Communism: an Infantile Disorder*, in *Selected Works* (New York: International Publishers, 1943), pp. 112–114.

Lenin's interest, then, was primarily organizing to speed the revolution. Marx, in his more mature years, thought of the party as a mass organization encompassing hundreds of thousands, perhaps millions, of the proletariat. But Lenin saw little chance of recruiting millions, particularly in Russia. He designed a small, tightly knit group of experienced, full-time revolutionaries devoting all of their attentions and energies to only one aim—the overthrow of the Tsarist regime in Russia.[21] It was in his drive to actualize the revolution that Lenin made his first fundamental modification of the Marxist program.

Lenin's Russian-centeredness ultimately led to other far-reaching consequences for Marxism. As previously pointed out, it was inextricably linked with the Marxian hypothesis that the revolution would occur in a country suffering the pangs of overproduction, a country where the contradictions of capitalism were the greatest. But Russia was not such a country. It was scarcely embarked upon capitalism; much of it still languished in feudalism. Its proletariat composed not the overwhelming proportion of the population, but less than fifteen percent. Production was not overdeveloped. But Lenin wanted revolution there. At first he was convinced it could occur in Russia only after it had broken out elsewhere. But a disastrous war threatened the established order in Russia with dissolution. Russia succumbed to revolution in February, 1917—and Lenin made that revolution his own in October, 1917.[22] Even before, doctrine was changed to revolution occurring in the "weakest link" of capitalism, which, by Leninist definition, was Russia.

But once the revolution had occurred in Russia, Lenin feared it could not succeed unless it spread rapidly to the more highly developed capitalist states. The existing capitalist governments, he was convinced, would not permit the revolution to remain in power in Russia. At the first possible moment they would intervene to smash the Bolsheviks,[23] as Lenin's group was called, unless they too were unseated. Lenin therefore marked the days

21 Lenin writes on organization in *What Is to Be Done?*
22 Studies of the Bolshevik take-over are legion. A vivid, highly pro-revolution account appears in John Reed's *Ten Days That Shook the World* (New York: Vintage Books, 1960). N. Sukhanov's much more extensive eyewitness account (*The Russian Revolution,* 1917 [London: Oxford University Press, 1955]) is more balanced, though Sukhanov also had axes to grind. Among the histories written by nonparticipants, Robert V. Daniel's *Red October: the Bolshevik Revolution* (New York: Charles Scribner's Sons, 1967) is recent and good.
23 The name Bolshevik or "majorityite" was attached to Lenin's fraction of the Russian Social Democratic Labor Party as the result of an incident at the second party congress in 1903. Lenin's group was a minority of the congress, but at one point, when other elements walked out, his position became the majority. From that time on, the Lenin group was known as the Bolsheviks, and the chief opposition within the RSDLP—in practice the majority—as the Mensheviks or "minorityites."

of his revolution off on the calendar in his Kremlin office awaiting the outbreak of revolution in the West and hoping that his revolution would at least outlive the seventy-one days allotted its predecessor, the Paris Commune of 1871.[24]

Gradually, however, it became apparent that Britain, France, Germany, and the United States—at first engaged in World War I and then too exhausted and indecisive to act—would not commit sufficient strength to overthrow the revolution in Russia. Just as previously Lenin was dominated by the determination to make the revolution come alive in Russia—his concern now focused on *maintaining* the revolution in Russia. The welfare of the revolutionary movement throughout the world, he now decided, depended upon the welfare of the new Soviet [25] Republic in Russia. If the Republic fell, the revolution throughout the world would suffer a disastrous setback. Consequently, in the form that the argument eventually was to take, the cause of the Russian revolution must take precedence over all other revolutionary causes. Other movements must suffer if necessary in order to preserve the Russian movement. The most extreme form of the concept, termed "Socialism in One Country," was developed by Joseph Stalin, Lenin's successor; but its outlines were clearly laid down by Lenin before his death.

The emphasis upon the role of the Soviet Union in the world movement not only worked against the basic concept of internationalism, but also developed a chauvinistic corollary. From the early post-revolutionary days, the international proletariat was urged to defend the interests of the Russian Republic—the *otechestvo*, fatherland, of the workers of the world. The appeal to both Russians and non-Russians was the same—and it was ostensibly based not on Russian national interest, but on the proletarian interests of all the world's workers. The Soviet state was equally the state of all workers, defending their interests and representing their hopes. But increasingly, under Stalin, such internationalism came to be a means of obtaining international support for the defense of Russian soil. (During the

[24] An oft-reported, but probably apocryphal story. As Louis Fischer put it (*The Life of Lenin* [New York: Harper & Row, 1964], p. 159), Lenin "doubted the viability of the Soviet regime" unless Europe sprang to revolutionary action. He and his cohorts "scanned the western horizon for red flames."

[25] The word "Soviet," so closely bound up with Russian communism, has little to do with Marx's Marxism. The soviets (Russian for "councils") were working-class and soldiers' organizations fashioned in the Revolution of 1905. Lenin disliked them, fearing that he could not control them and wanting to avoid groups that he could not control. However, in 1917 he decided they were a vehicle that could aid in the seizure of power and he, therefore, adopted them as his own. Subsequently the term, regarded as a popular one, was widely used. The unity it supposedly represented was institutionalized in the soviets, which are, in theory, the chief legislative arm of the current governmental system in Russia.

late 1920's and early 1930's, such a development was already discernible, but it was clouded by the ideological overlay.) With the coming to power of Hitler, however, the symbols of Russian patriotism, kept under wraps since 1917, were uncovered. Russia was officially called *rodina,* the motherland, as it had been in tsarist times; tsarist heroes, previously anathema to the Bolsheviks—men such as General Suvorov and Admiral Ushakov, as well as Peter the Great and even Ivan "The Terrible"—were now "rehabilitated." The purpose was to unify the Russian people in defense of their ancestral homeland, to use national rather than international symbols because the former elicited a more powerful response. Eventually even the *International,* the hoary hymn of the international movement, was replaced by a *national* anthem. In more recent years, the Soviet system has continued to manipulate both internationalism and nationalism for its own interests. It has never abandoned the pose of internationalism, but superimposed upon it—actually a much more significant factor—has been Russian nationalism: more specifically, Great Russian nationalism.

Russia, in terms of nationality, is not a homogeneous entity. Though figures vary, there are at least 150 different nationalities in the U.S.S.R. Of these the Great Russians, Ukrainians, and White Russians make up approximately eighty percent of the population. But there are also Lithuanians, Latvians, Estonians, Armenians, Georgians, Kalmyks, Tatars, Turkomens, and so forth. Most of these peoples have long traditions of independence and some have been part of Russia for only a century or less.

Marx regarded national differences as outmoded and destined to disappear. Lenin publicly displayed a similar attitude, but by the second decade of the twentieth century he realized that considerable support for the revolution could come from national groups such as Poles, Latvians, Georgians, and Jews, who had opposed the nationally repressive policies of the Tsar and who, to greater or lesser degrees, desired independence. To gain support in nationalist circles, Lenin—using Stalin, a Georgian, as frontman—began to advocate national self-determination for the minority nationalities. This seemed to mean that, after the revolution, a minority nationality could decide to remain a part of the greater entity or choose independence. In practice, after 1917, Lenin used every device at his command, including military coercion and terror, to keep the minorities within the Soviet state. Thus, from the beginning, the Soviet nationalism policy largely has been a snare and a delusion.

In point of fact, Soviet nationality policy has often been even more repressive than that of the tsars. Though elaborate attempts have been made to indicate that there is wide national autonomy, at least cultural autonomy, in the U.S.S.R., the suppression of all significant autonomous elements has been determined and persistent. Each sizable national group in the Soviet Union, except the Jews, has its own supposedly autonomous republic, region or area, depending upon its size; but all are controlled from Moscow or by Moscow's agents. The minority group in its own "autonomous" locality must learn Russian as well as its own language, but a Great Russian living there need learn only Russian. In culture, the guideline is national in form, socialist in content, which means that, in a play, the characters may be dressed in native costume of long past days of independence, but the values expressed must be those of the regime. The Russians are always friends, the rich are always bad, and the poor are always good; a political moral must always be taught.

Using more powerful devices than the tsars ever had, the Communist party of the Soviet Union has attempted to impose a uniform culture, often imposing dominant Great Russian values on all the people of the Soviet Union. The radio, press, and television repeat endlessly and with little variation the party line. On the job, at play, in the streets, the average Soviet citizen is endlessly confronted with the same message. No tsarist indoctrination ever approached such universality. But despite such full-scale efforts, the old values have not been eradicated. The nationalistic impulse still thrives. Ukrainians dislike Tadzhikis; Tadzhikis dislike Kazakhis; they all dislike Great Russians; and so on. Yet the formal party emphasis on equality of races and the opportunity given adaptable minority members to rise in the system (as well as a variety of technological and historical factors) have drawn the peoples of the country closer together. It is likely, though scarcely verifiable since the Soviets do not permit such research, that the average member of a minority group increasingly feels himself a part of his country. Marxism in Russia, then, has had an impact upon the building of a sense of nationhood,[26] but, again, this was not the intent of Karl Marx.

The Russian revolution, in its essence, was Lenin's revolution. While the collapse of tsarism was only minimally his doing, he marshaled the forces to take advantage of the chaos following the Tsar's overthrow. He devised

[26] At this point it seems appropriate to note that particularly in underdeveloped nations, Marxism and nation building have often been closely linked. As new nations come into existence they seek to avoid ties with their old colonial masters. They cannot exist without outside assistance and the communist world is often their most available alternative. As new nations, they seek power as quickly as possible and the Soviet Union says it has the key for accomplishing this goal. Moreover, in the struggle for independence, the Communist claim of being anticolonial and anti-imperialist (though the Soviet Union resolutely held on to the old tsarist colonies in Central Asia) has attracted many independence-minded colonials to their creed. But the primary attraction is usually not that of building communism but of achieving nationalist ends, the opposite of Marx's goals.

the organization, planned the strategy, provided the determination which brought the Bolsheviks to power in 1917. But neither his organization of the Bolshevik faction, nor its strategy, nor his personal determination had anything to do with Marx. Thus, as in other ways to be presently indicated, while Lenin termed the 1917 revolution a Marxist revolution, this was a gross distortion of the facts. The Russian revolution had almost nothing to do with Marx—and, indeed, were it not that Lenin designated himself as a Marxist and became Marx's apologist, explaining away Marx's prophetic failures and unceasingly affirming the correctness of Marx's analysis—Marx might well be a little better known than such other social philosophers of the nineteenth century as Saint-Simon and Bakunin.

The Stalinist Reality

Having declared the 1917 revolution to be a Marxist revolution, it now became necessary for believers to prove Marx's other prophecies were being borne out as well. Marx prophesied, for instance, that the revolution would occur in a heavily developed country beset by insuperable problems of overproduction. But Russia had neither warehouses bursting with goods nor the capacity to produce all-but-unlimited supplies. On the contrary, it was largely the shortage of goods and food that brought Russia to revolution. This lack could be compensated for temporarily by the division of the landed estates and by the ransacking of the manor houses of the wealthy. But such confiscations could not be repeated, though the Bolsheviks would attempt it; [27] nor was it the foundation upon which to build communism, as Lenin well knew.[28]

Since Russia was not a developed country, it was necessary to convert her into one. This was not only because industrialization represented the Marxist path to the future but because of Russia's unique and isolated position. If Russia, for the time being, was to be the only Marxist country, then it must show the rest of the world the advantage of its way. It must move forward so that others might rapidly follow in the direction of modernization and industrialization. Moreover, if Russia was the only Marxist country, there was the continuing danger posed by capitalist encirclement. The capitalist powers might at any time decide to crush the new Soviet state. She must, therefore, be in a position to fend off such attacks. This, too, required industrialization.

Marx, however, had said nothing about the necessity to industrialize

---

[27] As in the periodic resumption of "class warfare" in the countryside.
[28] *What the "Friends of the People" Are and How They Fight Against the Social Democrats.*

after the revolution; thus Russia's industrialization required innovation. Indeed, perhaps the salient feature of Russian communism as it is presently understood in much of the contemporary world, is its modernizing techniques and processes.

By the time of Lenin's death in 1924, or shortly thereafter, the extent to which the Russian experience had departed from the Marxist model was unmistakably clear to perceptive observers. The revolution had broken out and been confined to a relatively backward country in which the proletariat was a distinct minority—and even that minority was far from being solidified in support of the revolutionary party. When Lenin returned from Switzerland in April, 1917, on a sealed train provided by the Germans, there were fewer than 25,000 members of his party. By November, the ranks had increased only to a quarter million, less than one-quarter of one percent of the total population of Russia. Though there was widespread argumentative give-and-take in the party at that time, the will of the party was centered in Lenin. It was *his* revolution, and he almost always had the last word. In the Civil War of 1918–21, Lenin—ensconced in Moscow while other leaders were out in the field—became increasingly accustomed to making unilateral decisions.[29] It became the characteristic manner of decision-making in the Soviet system.

Thus, there was only one political party and only one leader in that party. How this occurred, other than as suggested above, is a study in political dynamics too involved to be related here.[30] But it did occur. The party controlled the country. And one man, Lenin, controlled the party. Again, this is scarcely what Marx had foreseen and certainly not what he wanted. Though Marx had written of the dictatorship of the proletariat, he had meant rule by the many over the few, not vice versa—and that only for a short duration. Of course, the Russian Communist party of Bolsheviks declared itself to be the representative of the many; but in effect, it represented only itself and its interest in maintaining and augmenting the power it had seized. The picture that developed was not of a party of the people, but of a party substituting its conception of the people's interests (as well as its own interests) for the perceptions of the people; then of the leaders of the party putting their perceptions (and interests) first; and, finally, of one man superimposing his own views (and interests) above all the rest.

That the breach between ruler and ruled in Russia did exist and was

[29] Leonard Schapiro, *Communist Party of the Soviet Union* (New York: Random House, 1960), p. 239.

[30] Isaac Deutscher, *The Prophet Unarmed* (New York: Oxford University Press, 1954); Adam Ulam, *The Bolsheviks* (New York: Macmillan, 1965); Leonard Schapiro, *The Origin of the Communist Autocracy* (Cambridge: Harvard University Press, 1955).

serious was indicated by the Kronstadt uprising of March, 1921, in which 14,000 of the formerly staunchest supporters of the Leninist regime now fought it to the death. These soldiers and sailors of peasant background were not opposed to communism, but only to those who were ruling Russia in its name, exhibiting less concern for the Marxist promise of workers' power than for their own power. Even before Kronstadt, Lenin had concluded that steps must be taken to conciliate the population. Exhausted by seven years of war, revolutions, and then Civil War, the Russian people desperately desired an end to violence and a return to normalcy. The economy was devastated; food shortages had led to an evacuation of the larger cities. Lenin therefore decided to move backwards. Small businesses seized in the flush of communist victory should be returned to their owners. Peasants, whose crops had been forcibly expropriated by Red Guard detachments from the cities, were promised no further levies and were urged to produce large crops and "enrich themselves."

The retreat embodied in this New Economic Policy (NEP), Lenin argued at the tenth party congress in 1921, was absolutely necessary in order to stabilize his regime. The encouragement of the petty bourgeoisie and the peasants, however, was to be only temporary. (A prime example of "Two steps forward, one step back" strategy. One must retreat in order to advance again.) He planned, as soon as it was feasible, to get on with the business of modernization, which required more, not less, control. But within a little over a year he had a stroke. Twenty months later he was dead.

Lenin's NEP was successful in large measure in righting the Russian economy. By 1926, in most areas, Russian production had been restored to 1913 levels, the year before war came to Russia. But, as the studies of leading Russian economists indicated at the time,[31] Russia, in both relative and absolute terms was falling further and further behind the West. One figure, used by a chief opponent to Stalin in 1925, indicated that Russian per capita productivity had dropped since the beginning of World War I from one-eighth to one-tenth of that in the United States.[32] For a regime dedicated to proving that its system was the most advanced in the world while faced with the constant threat of outside intervention by that same West which was so decisively outproducing it, this was a devastating fact.

Given the fact that Russia had to industrialize if it was to compete with and outdistance the West, the question became how to acquire the capital

---

[31] The best known was E. Preobrazhensky, who had Trotsky's ear.

[32] Isaac Deutscher, *The Prophet Unarmed* (London: Oxford University Press, 1959), p. 209.

necessary to underwrite the required growth. The suggestion of literally selling off the crown jewels, and other objets d'art and artifacts of now-defunct regal and aristocratic splendor, was dismissed because it could not provide the large sums demanded (though it was utilized for special objectives). Invite foreign capitalists to invest? Russia might again be subject to capitalist exploitation (if indeed capitalists would be willing to invest in a country which had only recently confiscated all foreign-owned installations).

Should the peasants be assured greater profits, leading to greater production, which could become a source of capital formation? There was strong support for such a solution, even at the loftiest levels of Soviet power. But opponents pointed out that to get the peasant to produce and market more, it was necessary to offer him something on which he could spend his rubles: namely, consumer goods. To provide consumer goods, it was necessary to develop consumer industries; and what Russia required was not consumer industries but capital industries. Russia needed the opening of coal mines and ore mines, the building of steel mills and railroads, if she were to compete in the twentieth century and defend herself. Only later could the luxury of consumer goods expansion be offered.

Soviet specialists have long argued whether the Russian leaders of the late 1920's, given the requirement of industrializing Russia as rapidly as possible, had any viable alternative to the method which they finally adopted for the accumulation of capital, the forced collectivization of agriculture. This was an attempt to obtain maximum production from the peasantry without providing any tangible return to them, in order to accelerate the development of heavy industry. Some Western scholars argue that Russia in 1926 was well on the way to significant industrial growth—and that the chaos occasioned by forced collectivization and subsequent steps interrupted that development.[33] Such is a minority opinion, however. Given the backward state of Russian industry, given the attitudes of the Russian peasantry, given Russia's isolated position in the world, given the prejudices of Marxist ideology and the will to power evidenced by Russia's Bolshevik leadership, the path chosen by those leaders may have been the most satisfactory alternative open to them, even taking into consideration the bloodletting that followed the decision to collectivize.

Underlying the collectivization-industrialization process adopted by Russian communism (generally regarded as one of the hallmarks of contemporary communism) was a lack of humaneness not present in Marx. Marx's work was directed at freeing the masses and ameliorating their suffering.

---

[33] An excellent discussion of the problem is to be found in Theodore Von Laue, *Why Lenin? Why Stalin?* (Philadelphia: J. B. Lippincott, 1964).

While he acknowledged that the condition of the masses would worsen before it improved, he intended to end their suffering as quickly as possible. Certainly Marx nowhere contemplates a system of strict controls instituted by a small minority over the masses, even in the name of the revolution. Yet that is what occurred in Russia.

Lenin, on the other hand, manifested a certain disdain for the masses. He did not trust them to bring about the revolution. He claims that all is done for the masses; but it appears that in reality the seizure and maintaining of power—if not Lenin's primary initial purpose—soon assumes that dimension. It is power, and not the cause of the masses, that preoccupies him and his successor. And to achieve power in 1927–28 demanded collectivization and industrialization almost regardless of human costs.

The theoretical underpinning of collectivization-industrialization held that capitalism had accumulated its capital over centuries ("primitive capital accumulation"); but if underdeveloped Russia were to overtake and surpass the capitalist West, it had to aggregate capital much more rapidly. This was to be accomplished partly by conducting agriculture as efficiently as possible, thus justifying collectivization. Presumably, large-scale agriculture was more efficient than the tilling of small private plots because the former makes possible the most effective use of agricultural machinery, thus supposedly guaranteeing larger crop returns. Collectivization also simplified the job of supervision and minimized the obstructionist tendencies of the peasantry.

Once the farms were collectivized, the peasant's job was to work as hard and produce as much as possible. Most of his produce would go to the state which, in turn, would pay him as little as possible. From the net gain to the state, industrialization would be financed.

The net effect of such a party attitude towards agriculture has been to make the farm the dead end of Soviet life. Young people possessed of ability or initiative usually hasten to leave the countryside as quickly as they can. Indeed, the natural course of events in industrializing countries is for large numbers of people to be attracted into the cities. In the U.S.S.R., the process has been accelerated by the neglect of the farm. Fifty years after the revolution, many farms with hundreds of thousands of residents remain almost as they were in 1917—without electricity, with the most primitive communications system, with little medical aid.

From time to time after the death of Stalin the party seemed to recognize that greater agricultural production demanded greater attention to the capital needs of the farm and the psychology of the farmer. But to produce more inorganic fertilizers, to increase payments to the peasant, to provide him with more consumer goods, required that the party withdraw funds from other projects and areas that had stronger priorities. And so the party has hauled and filled on this issue, caught between what it apparently must do to solve the agricultural dilemma and what it wants to do. Whether even huge investments would solve the perennial Soviet agricultural problem is by no means certain. No amount of investment is likely to change the climate of Russia, and most of Russia lies north of Minneapolis. Nor is additional investment likely to improve the quality of life in the collective sufficiently to keep most talented young farmers at home. But on the basis of what has transpired in the latter 1960's, agriculture does appear likely to receive more sympathetic attention designed to improve farmer morale.

Not only agricultural workers were expected to work as hard and receive as little as possible; [34] industrial workers were to be treated likewise. Once industrialization was under way, the potential for gain from the exploitation of labor expanded. All capital obtained was to be plowed back into the further expansion of industry, which in turn led to still greater expansion. As practiced in the Russian workers' state, the exploitation of labor smacked of the worst practices of the developmental stage of capitalism in the West.

In the Soviet scheme, planning is central. Contrary to the prototype of capitalism, in which each entrepreneur decides what to produce and where capital should be invested, the basic tenets of Marxism-Leninism call for rigid planning of the economy. In Russia, this meant using accrued capital almost entirely for heavy industry. The production of one steel plant was used to build another steel plant or coal-mining machinery or locomotives or armaments, but rarely to produce new textile equipment or cars or housing. The latter received higher priority only when *absolutely* necessary, as determined by the Kremlin, which frequently overrode the more "rational" judgments of the planners for its own purposes.

Problems of the System—and Solutions

Despite the disruption of the Stalin purges in the late 1930's and the severe losses suffered in World War II, Russia became the second largest producing nation in the world. In some industries, such as coal and steel, she even began to outproduce the United States.

Such successes have—even beyond the Eastern European countries upon which Russia forcibly imposed her model—recommended the Soviet system for industrial development to other countries and leaders. In an age when

[34] "As little as possible" meant enough to keep the worker alive and reasonably healthy rather than a life of reasonable comfort. The chief incentives used were inexpensive appeals to ego-hunger: names in newspapers, medals, and so forth. Even so, the industrial worker received far more of these proportionately than did the peasant, because it was the former's contribution that most concerned the regime.

industrialization and power were viewed as synonymous, those who pursued power recognized that rapid industrialization was indispensable. To more than a few the Russian model has seemed to fit their circumstances. And though the heavy cost in human terms of the Russian way has generally been understood, many men have come to view it as *the* way to build up their countries. Beginning in the late 1950's, however, the Chinese argued that *their* way, an adaptation of the Russian method, was a better model for most underdeveloped countries because the latter, like China, were starting at a far more primitive level than 1917 Russia and because the Chinese had more recently traversed the path of early development. But whether it was the Russian model or its Chinese variant that was considered, the argument for forced industrial development was an appealing one to nations struggling to industrialize and win a place in the sun.

Despite the apparent success of the Russian model, though, the Russians themselves have had to veer away from it. At best, it has proved a successful model only for the establishment and *early* development of industry. Even then it has involved a loss of freedom which many societies might not be willing to accept.

Indeed, the question of individual freedom is one of the most difficult which communist regimes have had to contend with. Marx saw the revolution as liberating mankind. Laws that previously had served the bourgeoisie and constrained the proletariat were to serve the opposite purpose before they disappeared. Regardless of his predilection for personal power, Lenin also wrote of the withering away of restraint before the revolution. But the first months of the revolution convinced him that the masses were not yet ready for the responsibility which self-restraint imposed. Control of industry by the workers, he wrote in 1918, is a false and dangerous fiction.[35] Control by the party is required. Opposed by the Whites, by national groups, by opposition parties, by uncooperative peasants and disgruntled workers, Lenin quickly turned to force for suppressing the opposition. When the collectivization-industrialization cycle began, the coercive apparatus which Stalin needed was already in existence—to be aimed not at the bourgeoisie, but at the peasantry. Increasingly, too, it was aimed at the erstwhile proletariat, in whose name the revolution had been carried out.

Particularly in those regions of Russia where the traditions of small independent farms were strong, the opposition to collectivization was intense. If the authorities wanted him to surrender his land and live on a cooperative, the peasant thought the government should supply him with the necessary seed grain, cattle, horses, sheep, and barnyard fowl to make the collective a success. Certainly he had no intention of *giving* his possessions to

[35] *Immediate Tasks of the Soviet Government.*

the collective. He would rather destroy them. And this the peasantry in many parts of Russia proceeded to do. Between 1929 and 1933, the number of cattle was reduced from 68 to 38 million; the number of sheep and goats was reduced from 147 to 50 million; and the number of horses was reduced from 34 to 16 million.[36]

Stalin reacted by sending in political and military detachments to bring the peasantry to heel: farms were burned, tens of thousands of peasants were executed or shipped to slave-labor camps. There is a strong continuing suspicion in some quarters that Stalin refused to relieve the lower Volga famine of 1931–33, which took upwards of a million lives, in order to discipline the recalcitrant peasants of the area.[37]

But even these victims of collectivization were relatively few compared to the millions terrorized in the later 1930's. While Stalin had been responsible, as Lenin before him, for the death of opposition forces, both had attempted to stay clear of internecine warfare within the party. There was a continuing concern lest the revolution begin devouring its own children. But it gradually became clear to Stalin that if he was to insure the support of his policies against the opposition that recurrently appeared within the party, he must terrorize the party even as he had terrorized the peasantry.[38]

The number of people arrested in the Great Purge and in the continuing purge which lasted until Stalin's death may never be known.[39] It has been estimated that as many as one out of every ten Russians was arrested for political crimes at one time or another. In the Great Purge, which lasted from 1936–38, the wave of arrests gained a momentum of its own. The dread knock on the door in the middle of the night became as common in Russia in the 1930's as in Germany. Millions were involved. Scarcely a family was spared. Most of those taken into custody were innocent as was admitted by Khrushchev in 1956.[40] Russia was swept up in a frenzy of accusation reminiscent of the Salem Witch trials almost three centuries before. But now millions, not just a few score of people, were involved.

While many thousands of former high-ranking officials of the Soviet sys-

[36] J. Stalin, *Problems of Leninism* (New York: International Publishers, 1934).

[37] Boris Souvarine, *Stalin* (New York: Alliance, 1939), p. 552.

[38] See "A Comparison of Politburo Actors in the First and Fifth Decades of Soviet Power," Dan N. Jacobs, in *Fifty Years of the Soviet Union*, ed. K. London (Baltimore: John Hopkins University Press, 1968), pp. 45–75.

[39] A wide variety of literature on the purges has appeared. The Robert C. Tucker–Stephen F. Cohen edition of *The Great Purge Trial* (New York: Grosset & Dunlap, 1965), a stenographic account, is recommended. N. Leites and E. Bernaut, *Ritual of Liquidation* (Glencoe, Ill.: Free Press, 1954), is valuable for its psychological insights, as is Arthur Koestler's novel *Darkness at Noon* (New York: Macmillan, 1941).

[40] N. S. Khrushchev, "Secret Speech" in *The New Communist Manifesto*, ed. Dan N. Jacobs, 2nd rev. ed. (New York: Harper and Row, 1965), pp. 132–139.

tem were executed, most of those arrested were sent to camps in remote areas. Since a regime bent on increasing its industrial might could not permit such a large percentage of its male population to be removed from the labor force, the camps were put to work on production projects. The White Sea ship canal, for example, was the product of such slave labor. Slave laborers were put to work felling trees, mining gold, digging coal and diamonds—doing any of the onerous jobs required in the desert or frozen wastelands to which they were sent.

The slave-labor camps became part of the regular production apparatus of the Soviet Union. Each camp commander had quotas to fulfill. As elsewhere in Soviet society, living conditions were as meager as possible while labor demands were maximized. Under these conditions, many became ill or died. The prisoners who could still work, however, were driven yet harder, thus increasing the sick list. Since quotas had to be met, this could only be done by bringing in more prisoners.[41]

Even with large numbers of Russians behind barbed wire fences, it has often been observed that those outside had scarcely more freedom.[42] Changing of jobs was forbidden; tardiness at work was sometimes punishable by death, as was absenteeism. The secret police or their agents were everywhere. An atmosphere of suspicion and terror prevailed. In some circles it had been anticipated that the heroic behavior of the Russian people during World War II would lead to more considerate treatment from the party. But Stalin was motivated by power, domestic and international, not by considerations of humanity. Life in Russia after World War II became still more grey, still more grim, still more foreboding.

How was it possible to correlate the realities of life under communism with the Marxist promise? Marx had promised the withering away of the

---

[41] While there was no dearth of information in the West in the mid-1930's on the widespread existence of Soviet slave-labor camps, not until the Cold War were the charges taken seriously. The existence of these camps is attested to by more than a hundred published English-language autobiographies of former inmates. In a sense, the Soviet Union itself capped the story when it permitted the publication of A. Solzhenitsyn's autobiographical novel *One Day in the Life of Ivan Denisovich* (New York: Frederick A. Praeger, 1963), which dealt with the struggles for survival in the Siberian camps. Khrushchev himself intervened to have this volume published in the U.S.S.R. It was the only Solzhenitsyn novel published in Russia as late as 1969, though several of his works had been printed abroad and received high critical acclaim. Solzhenitsyn, who had faced death in World War II, in the slave-labor camps and from cancer, refused to conform to the demands of the system, though subjected to heavy pressures. His international reputation made it difficult to imprison him, especially after he was awarded the Nobel prize in 1970.

[42] Indeed, inside the Soviet Union, it was widely believed that there was more freedom inside the camps, since those already arrested could no longer fear arrest. See A. Solzhenitsyn's *The First Circle* (New York: Harper, 1968).

state, and of coercion; Lenin had emphasized his faith in the same vision. Yet three decades and more after 1917, the state had become more powerful than ever and coercion, stronger and more pervasive. In practice it was possible simply to overlook what Marx had said, but it was not possible for the Soviet leaders to be completely disdainful of the theory which legitimized their power. Without Marx they were mere power-seekers, not agents of the historical process. Therefore, the current condition of the Soviet Union had to be fitted into the Marxist scheme.

In part, this was done by denying, hiding, or disguising the coercion that existed. In part, it was done by asserting again and again, that the U.S.S.R. was the freest nation in the world. In Orwellian terms,[43] slavery was freedom.

For example, the so-called Stalin Constitution of 1936, still in effect in Russia more than a decade after the downgrading of its originator, was represented as being the "freest" in the history of the world. Its authors [44] culled the constitutions of capitalist and previous societies and included in Chapter X, under "Fundamental Rights and Responsibilities of the Soviet Citizen," a wide and imposing selection of the rights guaranteed by Western constitutions, adding a few extra rights, such as the right to employment. In the Soviet Constitution freedom of speech, press, assembly, and of street demonstrations are guaranteed. But these freedoms were not realistic in 1936, or in any subsequent year. The guarantee, however, served at least two functions: it helped the image of the Soviet Union abroad, particularly in those circles that wanted to believe that the U.S.S.R. had the freest system extant; and it stood as a promise to the Soviet people—millions of them evidently regarded it as such—that, though these freedoms did not now exist, they would be brought to fruition in the communist future. In short, the Constitution was, at least with respect to Chapter X, a promissory, not a descriptive, document.

Chapter X of the Stalin Constitution also guaranteed the "freedom of religious worship." This was, in practice, systematically violated: the regime pursued a consistently antireligious policy. Yet it was obliged to retreat somewhat from its once-intransigent position, a position originating with Karl Marx and ideologically supported by his successors.

Marx was convinced that religion was one of the impediments to the revolution, for it allegedly taught that man should be content with his lot,

[43] George Orwell was a noted essayist and novelist of the 1950's. Particularly in *Animal Farm* (New York: Harcourt, Brace, 1949), he popularized the notion of communist "double-think," which equates war with peace, slavery with freedom, etc.
[44] Many of the framers of the 1936 Constitution were removed from power by Stalin and lived under suspicion. They were permitted to contribute their idealism to the system in this document, after which they fell victim to the purges.

whatever the poverty and suffering involved, since his reward would come in the next world. Such attitudes, held Marx, could only lead to a spirit of resignation and passivity, thus bolstering the ruling classes. In effect, then, religion and its leaders bulwarked the state; religion itself, in Marx's words, was the "opiate of the masses."

From its establishment, in fact, the Soviet system opposed religion, partly because of Marx's stand and partly because bolshevism opposed any institution it did not control. The regime closed churches and monasteries, outlawed religious instruction of the young, and conducted determined antireligious propaganda. It claimed, even in the general press, that religion and drunkenness share the same roots, that religion perverts children and so forth.[45] But in spite of the decades-long efforts, the party now confesses that religious beliefs persist even within the party, as well as among the workers and peasants. It urges, from time to time, the need for continuing efforts to extirpate these beliefs.[46]

But the Soviet regime is reasonably realistic. While its hostility to religion remains, it does not pursue its goal in unmeasured fashion, lest it antagonize large numbers of the Soviet citizenry over what it regards as a secondary issue. Therefore, while it still threatens with words, and sometimes, with deeds, it permits churches, particularly those of the Orthodox faith, to operate. Indeed, since the mid-1930's, it has provided financial assistance for the traditional Russian Orthodox Church, as previous governments had done for over three hundred years. If it must tolerate any religion, the party prefers the Orthodox Church because it has long been subjected to secular authority, has few traditions of independence, and is a *Russian* church. On the other hand, Roman Catholics, Jews, Mohammedans, Baptists, Jehovah's Witnesses, and other groups are opposed because they have histories of independence and/or foreign contacts.

For a Russian who openly acknowledges his Catholic, Jewish, Baptist, Islamic, etc., affiliation, there is always the possibility of persecution. Certainly, the future is unpromising for him. Even if he or she could gain admission to a university, which is improbable, a good job upon graduation would be unlikely. For the professing Orthodox, too, there is little chance of rising to high station in Soviet life. But despite the official antireligious posture of the system, even party officials and their children often wish to have their marriages performed not in the state-supported Marriage Palaces, but in churches amidst the awe-inspiring trappings of the old Russian religion. In recent years, prosperous and prominent Soviet families have organized unobtrusive auto safaris to towns far from Moscow, Leningrad,

[45] *Izvestia*, December 19, 1965.
[46] *Pravda*, January 12, 1967.

or Kiev, where they can celebrate their marriages and baptisms in the traditional Russian manner within the onion-skinned domes.

The Withering Away of the State

Marx anticipated that the state would "wither away" shortly after the revolution. But the state apparatus and the bureaucracy, instead of withering away, were progressively strengthened. How could this be explained? The Stalinist response was persuasive, because initially it contained a strong element of truth. The strengthening of the state was necessary, said Stalin, because of "capitalist encirclement." "Constant vigilance" was required to fend off the predatory capitalist enemies. Moreover, the greater the disintegration of capitalism, the greater the danger; for like the wounded tiger, the nearer the capitalist beast moves towards extinction, the more dangerous he becomes,[47] the more willing to make one last desperate leap to dispatch the foe. Thus, the weaker capitalism is, the greater the necessity to strengthen the apparatus of the socialist fatherland against it. But when the capitalist beast has been exterminated, the state *will* wither away.

Whether pre- or post-revolutionary, the emphasis in Marxism-Leninism, and now in Stalinism was upon the future. Prior to the revolution the proletariat had to undergo great suffering before the liberating balm of revolution could be applied. After the revolution it became necessary for the proletariat to suffer for the benefit of future generations. To make the sacrifices which collectivization-industrialization and Stalin's drive for absolute security necessitated, Stalin emphasized the internal and external threats to his regime and to the Russian fatherland. He also provided numerous, mostly noneconomic, rewards and promised a glorious future. But from time to time he felt obliged to demonstrate that some of those promises were indeed being realized, that the goal of communism was being reached. Thus in 1936, Stalin announced that socialism had been achieved and the building of communism was now under way. For the average Russian, life was not significantly better after 1936 than before. For most, the greatest suffering lay ahead. But the objective situation required evidence of progress, and so it was produced in word, if not in fact.

A quarter of a century later, Khrushchev, Stalin's successor, also feeling constrained to indicate progress towards the goal of communism, announced that a new stage in the development of communism had been attained: that

---

[47] The wounded-tiger hypothesis is best described by Nathan Leites in his *A Study of Bolshevism* (Glencoe, Ill.: Free Press, 1953), and its shorter version *The Operational Code of the Politburo* (New York: McGraw-Hill, 1951).

of the "state of all the people." [48] This was allegedly the first stage of the state after the end of the dictatorship of the proletariat, and on the way towards communism and the withering away of the state. Of course, the mere assertion that a new stage on the way to communism had been entered did not of itself bring communism any closer—at least not communism according to Marx.

Khrushchev's Party Program [49] of 1961 generally defined what the "entrance" into communism would be like. He announced that it would operate in two stages, one to be completed by 1970 and the second a decade later. It was to be characterized by ample living space, increased social security benefits, free streetcar, bus, and train rides, and so forth.

According to Khrushchev's description of the entrance into communism, Russia would still fall short of that stage of overproduction which Marx expected. There was, for example, no discussion of open warehouses with ample stores for all. Instead Khrushchev's description bore a striking resemblance to the contemporary state of the capitalist West where workers were concerned. Still, for the workers of Russia, weary of decades of deprivation and eager to enjoy life in their own generation, it may have sounded encouraging. In any event, however, Khrushchev's successors abandoned his timetable and buried his doctrine of the "state of all the people" and its concomitant concept of the entrance into communism.

In describing the entrance into communism in strictly materialistic terms and in setting the time of its arrival, Khrushchev was coming to grips again with a problem that had plagued the Soviet state from its very beginning, had become acute in the late 1920's, then was "solved" by Stalin until it cropped up again in the late 1940's—namely, the need to engage the energies of the Russian masses. Stalin had settled for the acquiescence and compliance of the Soviet citizenry. But by about 1948, it was becoming apparent that such attitudes were no longer sufficient for the continued development of the new Russian industrial giant.

[48] "New Party Program" in *The New Communist Manifesto*, ed. Dan N. Jacobs, 2nd rev. ed. (New York: Harper & Row, 1965). Khrushchev himself was probably never clear as to what was meant by the "state of all the people," except that it indicated a milestone in communist progress. Khrushchev also indicated that while he still believed that the state would wither away at some indefinite future time, the organizational and directing presence of the party would be required indefinitely. Engaged in struggles to establish his authority at home as Stalin's successor and abroad against the Chinese, Khrushchev was convinced at the time, evidently, that it was time to say something "ideological." Marx established the precedent that a great communist leader must be ideologically creative. Actually, from Lenin on, each successive Russian party chief has been less ideologically talented, but nevertheless each has tried to indicate the authenticity of his credentials. The problem has been particularly acute for the more recent contemporaries of Mao Tse-tung, since he does have credentials as an ideologist.

[49] *Ibid.*

Changing Models

Post-World War II Russian society, as has been noted, was dominated by fear and foreboding. Those who peopled it were the "survivors." They had survived collectivization-industrialization; they had survived the Great Purge and its successors; they had survived World War II. They were exhausted—but prepared to do what must be done to continue to survive. But if Soviet development was to make further progress, a different kind of response was required from the Soviet citizenry. There was need for active support, involvement, and identification—at all levels.

In the late 1940's and early 1950's, important branches of Soviet science were hamstrung, in large part by the arbitrary positions established by Stalin. In genetics, in physics, in linguistics, Stalin had approved certain theories and eliminated others (and their advocates), often elevating the adherents of doctrines that were scientifically invalid but politically attractive to commanding positions. By budgetary means and intervention in personnel recruitment, among other methods, Stalin also determined which sciences were to be favored and which neglected. If a discipline was judged to be nonessential, funds would be withheld for its pursuit.

Economists whose studies did not satisfy Stalin's prejudices were demoted, imprisoned, and even shot. Generally, the statistics on Soviet economic development were completely undependable. The primary purpose behind the then-prevalent doctoring of statistics was to deceive the capitalist world, but at times those involved in the day-to-day conduct of Soviet industry were also misled.

There were problems in planning, as well. When the level of industrial development was low, it had been relatively simple to set up priorities and determine what would be produced and in what quantities. But as productive capacity grew, as the number of items produced multiplied, and as technology became increasingly complex, the allocation of resources became bewilderingly complex—particularly when every aspect had to be planned minutely. Complicating all of the planning was the ever-present possibility that political considerations would upset technologically dictated adjustments.

Necessary as change had become, Stalin remained wedded to his own model. Though preparations for change were constantly considered, few real changes could be made (except in token form) until Stalin's death in 1953.

The Soviet Union was—and is—the most political of states. The chief values of its leadership have steadfastly been political. Every group, person, or institution in it has been under the control of the party—whether a philatelic society, Boy Scout troop, or parent-teacher association. All groups were to be originated by the party and controlled by it for party purposes. Otherwise, they were a potential source of opposition to the state. Despite Soviet assertions to the contrary, it is the political component, not the economic one, that has been the prime concern of the Leninist structure come to life. And it was for *political* reasons that changes—economic and others—were first introduced in the post-Stalinist period.

With Stalin dead, his possible successors clearly feared public reaction to the change in regimes. The heirs apparent had been closely associated with Stalin for years, many for decades. They were aware of the intensity of feeling against Stalin that had developed out of collectivization. They knew of the warmth with which the German invaders had been met in some parts of Russia in the 1940's. Moreover, traditionally in Russia, change in regimes produced a "time of troubles" when the frustrations of the masses were unleashed. Such a development was feared in 1953.

An additional complicating factor was the leadership's mixed feeling towards Stalin. The members of the party hierarchy had long lived under the shadow of Stalin and the constant threat of elimination by him. As Khrushchev stated in the "Secret Speech" in 1956,[50] when one was summoned to Stalin's office, he never knew if he would emerge a free man. For a quarter century, the cult of Stalin's personality had been energetically and systematically developed by the party's leadership; and they fell victim, in a sense, to their own creation. Though they feared, they also stood in awe.

The remaining Soviet leadership, then, was unsure of itself. Could it do the job? Would the populace rebel? Since it needed popular support, it offered concessions, partly in the form of more consumer goods. But as party leaders were angling for popular support of the regime, the struggle to inherit Stalin's mantle also depended partly on public support. For a leader to succeed Stalin, a following was required; concessions might also be useful in creating that following.

Initially Khrushchev, for political and ideological reasons, opposed such concessions; they were identified with his principal opponent—Malenkov. Accordingly, Khrushchev sought support from the old Stalinists who still controlled the party and who opposed changing economic priorities. For these men, development of heavy industry still came first, and Khrushchev temporarily espoused their position. But having dispatched Malenkov, Khrushchev himself began to advocate economic and other concessions to enhance his own position. In the process of advocating this policy, Khrushchev apparently became convinced that it was necessary, not only for his own power aspirations, but for the advancement of the Soviet system.

[50] N. S. Khrushchev, "Secret Speech" in *The New Communist Manifesto*, ed. Dan N. Jacobs, 2nd rev. ed. (New York: Harper & Row, 1965), p. 163.

The Soviet people had to make greater efforts if the system was to move ahead. Cajolery, threats, and violence would no longer suffice. The stick was producing diminishing returns; the carrot now must be used—the carrot of more and better food, clothing, housing, and transportation.

Implementing of this policy required altering some basic Stalinist dogmas: that the masses must be worked as hard as possible for as little as possible; that consumer industry must be subordinated to capital industry; that the center must maintain absolute control of all areas. Those who opposed the new formula argued that changes in the system were not needed; that the existing system had produced victories in the past and would produce them again. Moreover, it was feared, one concession would call for another and yet another. Once the dam had broken nothing could hold the flood of change back. In the resulting chaos the party would be undermined, its leadership threatened and the "progress" of the past fifty years destroyed.[51]

The advocates of change steadfastly argued that they were not altering priorities: capital industry would still come first.[52] But despite the denials, it was clear that catering to consumer demand would impinge upon the investment available for capital development. Increased attention to housing, automobiles, clothing, and furniture was bound to be at the expense, at least temporarily, of steel foundries and hydroelectric dams, as well as new weaponry.

But perhaps even more fundamental than the concern over the economic implications of catering to consumer demand was that involved in the fear of "freedom" which changed economic concepts seemed to require.

In the Stalinist model, all was centrally controlled to satisfy the political objectives of the regime. But as industry grew increasingly complex, the men at the top became less capable of perceiving what was indeed in the interests of production. More decision-making needed to be delegated to those at a lower level, who were more familiar with the problems of the particular industry. But this meant decentralization of authority and more freedom for local officials, a prospect that awakened the most primitive fears of the top leadership. Continued centralization threatened the continued growth of Soviet industry; decentralization was an implicit threat to the authority of those in power.

[51] The economic, as well as some political, aspects of the debate over change are presented in P. Hardt, D. M. Gallik and V. G. Treml, "Institution Stagnation and Changing Economic Strategy in the Soviet Union," in U.S. Congress, Joint Economic Committee, *New Directions in the Soviet Economy,* 89th Congress, 2nd session (Washington: Government Printing Office, 1966), pp. 19–62.

[52] As, indeed, it has. Only by 1968 had the annual increase in consumer goods expressed in percentage outdistanced that in capital goods—and it was emphasized that this was only a temporary situation. In absolute terms, capital industry output still came first.

The Life of the Mind

The regime solved its dilemma by compromise. It moved toward decentralization, but not enough to secure the results it sought. And it stood ready to reassert the complete control of the center whenever political considerations required this.

Similar dilemmas have existed for the top leadership in other areas. Even Stalin had recognized that Soviet science could not operate in a vacuum, if only because it was so far behind the West. He did allow Soviet scientists to have access to Western scientific journals, but contact with Western scientists or with more general Western literature was not permitted. So long as the level of scientific development in the U.S.S.R. was relatively low, Soviet science might operate tolerably well under such circumstances. But as scientific capabilities more closely approached those of the West, the need for the cross-fertilization of ideas became pronounced. Moreover, Soviet scientists, proud of their accomplishments, wanted to become part of the world scientific community. Authority felt compelled to relent; a few Soviet scientists were permitted to travel abroad to attend professional meetings. Once outside Russia, they became more fully aware of the burdens under which Soviet sciences and all Soviet society operated. The scientists began to demand the same rights as their non-Soviet counterparts enjoyed, and the same access to information, scientific and otherwise, that their colleagues enjoyed elsewhere. And because the Soviet leaders needed total commitment from and the best opportunities for its scientists, it acceded to such demands—albeit reluctantly, slowly, and in piecemeal fashion.

As unwillingly as Soviet power reduced its control in industry and science, it yielded still less in spheres where the need was less compelling in the view of the Soviet leadership. Particularly was this true of literary freedom. Absolute subservience of the media was a fundamental characteristic of the Stalinist approach. All publication was under state control, except for the very few handwritten or handprinted illegal, underground publications that have appeared from time to time in very small quantities. All newspapers—such as *Pravda* and *Izvestia,* all journals—such as *Kommunist* and *Agitator,* all books were to present the party line.

Literary work during the Stalin period was supposed to exemplify "socialist realism," which portrays life not as it is, but as it ought to be and will be when communism has been achieved. Under socialist realism, a boy is attracted to a girl, not because she is lovely to look upon or because she is nice, but because she can dig sugar beets faster than anyone else on the collective. A girl is attracted to a boy not because he is handsome or *sympatico* or is likely to be a good provider, but because he is the best machine tractor operator in the district. And when they are together they talk not about personal matters—marriage, finding an apartment, raising a family—but about increasing their contributions to the plan and the party.

In socialist realism there are no greys; all is black or white. The heroes are always heroic; and the villains are always villainous. Virtue always wins and evil is always dispatched. The underlying assumption of socialist realism is that everyone and everything must contribute to the development of the system. Every piece of literature should be an object lesson in correct deportment, an image for Soviet man to emulate. To play on the theme of private values—or on the frustration of good, or the triumph of evil, or the prevalence of the irrational—works contrary to that which the system seeks to foster in future generations. The "new Soviet man"—about whom the ideologists never tired of writing—must be exposed only to positive influences as his models.

From the beginning of the Soviet state, some writers found it impossible to conform to this code. Many of the best emigrated. Even so, Soviet literary life was vigorous and creative in the 1920's. But the advent of socialist realism in the 1930's brought a crackdown on those who would not conform. The quality of Soviet writing deteriorated abruptly. Those writers who could and would turn out the types of plays, novels, and poetry that were demanded were mostly hacks; therefore, little significant literature emerged from the literary mills of the Stalin period. Some writers of talent tried to adjust, usually unsuccessfully. Others, such as Boris Pasternak, turned to translating in order to support themselves while they wrote seriously only for their "desk drawer"—material to be seen only by themselves and a few intimates. Still other men of talent found themselves inmates in Stalin's prisons.

Russian writers, in common with the rest of the country, emerged only slowly from the constricting fear that had spread over Russia in Stalin's later years. In 1955, one of the older writers, Ilya Ehrenburg, who had been among Stalin's most abject apologists, gave title to the change that was beginning when he wrote a novel called *The Thaw*. Increasingly, as the 1950's moved into the 1960's, increasing numbers of Russian writers struggled to break away from socialist realism. They sought to describe the world, not as the party saw it, but as they themselves saw it, occasionally even emphasizing private values.

Consistent with Russian tradition, the struggle for self-expression was led by the poets. Men like Yevtushenko and Voznesensky pointed in verse to the inadequacies and injustices of their country, and, while not directly accusing the regime—indeed, emphasizing their loyalty to it—the implication was clear. Hundreds of young people gathered to hear the poets read their lines in Mayakosky Square. Thousands attended their readings in halls and stadia in Moscow and Leningrad and elsewhere. However, Yevtushenko, Voznesensky,[53] and other like-minded writers sometimes suffered for their outspokenness. They have on occasion been forbidden to travel abroad, were sometimes exiled to Siberia, placed in insane asylums, or their works were not published for a period of time. But many who were driven out of Moscow eventually returned—and some, at least, had their works published.

The Dilemmas of Power

Under Stalin, if a poet had dared to write that he liked New York (as did Voznesensky) [54] or doubted the direction in which the regime was moving and, especially, if anyone dared publish his work abroad, the matter would have been simply and expeditiously handled: either slave-labor camp or execution. But after Stalin, the widespread use of such extremes was abjured. True, socialism didn't require poets as it required scientists. It could ruthlessly suppress them—and the only loss would be to the morale of the society. But if the effort necessary to make the U.S.S.R. the leading society was to be supported by the Russian people, morale factors were significant. Furthermore, it would be impossible to grant sufficient freedom for the flowering of science while ruthlessly restricting the freedom of nonscientists.

One specific Soviet example indicates the difficulty of depriving one group of freedom while granting it to another. In painting, as in writing, the guidelines in Russia have been dictated by socialist realism. This has meant that all painting has been representational and objective—with the emphasis upon strong, athletic, confident men and women, and heathy, happy children. Nonobjective painting has been strictly outlawed, being

[53] Writers like Yevtushenko and Voznesensky have been published in the Russian press because they emphasize their loyalty to the revolution and the regime and Russia, because not all of their works are controversial, because they have found friendly editors willing to take a chance, because they have achieved reputations, etc. Other writers, however, have concluded that their works would never be published in the Soviet Union. They have smuggled their works abroad to be published in France, Italy, Britain, or America. When apprehended, such men have usually been sentenced to long terms at hard labor.

[54] A. Voznesensky, "The Triangular Pear," in *Antiworlds,* ed. Patricia Blake and Max Haywood (New York: Anchor Books, 1967).

described as the "effluvia" of a decadent society.[55] Then, in late 1965, in Moscow, a group of artists opened an exhibit of very mildly nonobjective art,[56] which was immediately closed by the police. A few days later the exhibit reopened in the halls of the Academy of Physical Sciences, under the sponsorship of Peter Kapitsa, a distinguished Soviet physicist. Of course, party authorities had the power to close the exhibit at the Academy, too. But at what cost? The scientific community would have been aroused and the regime's posture of liberality would have been shattered. The exhibit was allowed to remain open—and was witnessed by thousands of spectators.

The Kapitsa incident indicates another facet of the problem of authority in the U.S.S.R.: the party seeks to maintain its former authority but without so much reliance on force; without the constant threat of execution or jail, some Russians will not be intimidated by the party; but if force is unduly used to secure compliance, the possibility of optimally engaging the energies of society is negated.

Impaled on the horns of this dilemma, the regime vacillated. Although Khrushchev was widely regarded as a boor, at best, and a bloody dictator at worst—in retrospect it can be seen that the realities and prospects of freedom improved under him (though certainly not linearly). Under his successors, however, the situation was reversed. At first, Brezhnev and Kosygin, uncertain of their positions and more opposed to Khrushchev personally than to the general drift of his policies, moved very cautiously and often imperceptibly. But in early 1968, the party hierarchy became badly frightened by developments in Czechoslovakia. The rapid deterioration of the Czech party position in the face of demands for reform convinced a controlling share of the top party leadership that freedom could bring the same result in the Soviet Union, as well.

Determined to prevent this, Brezhnev made it clear in March and April, 1968,[57] that there was to be no downgrading the role of the party, either now or in the future. All authority came from the party, he said, and all decisions were its prerogative to make.

Events during the spring and early summer of 1968 tended to confirm the shift to a conservative direction. And the invasion of Czechoslovakia by Soviet, Hungarian, East German, and Polish troops in August indicated how greatly the Soviet leadership feared the effect that domestic developments within Czechoslovakia would have on internal Russian poli-

---

[55] Khrushchev once castigated a nonobjective picture as having been daubed by the "tail of a donkey." *Encounter*, Vol. XX, no. 4 (April, 1963), p. 28.

[56] *New York Times*, June 4, 1966.

[57] See the March 30, 1968, speech to the Moscow City Committee of the CPSU.

tics. During the last few years of the 1960's, also, the internal security forces in the Soviet Union were considerably strengthened and labor camps, which had been deactivated to a great degree in the 1950's, were reopened. Literary rebels were treated with less leniency. The party affirmed its Marxist-Leninist orthodoxy. And, as if to remove any lingering doubts as to the party's intent, Stalin's image as a positive figure—particularly as a leader during World War II—was revived.

Yet, in spite of the unmistakable attempts of the regime to return to at least quasi-Stalinism, it would be a mistake to assume that it wished to fully restore the atmosphere of the Stalin period. The contemporary leaders were no Stalins; they lacked his authority and his controls. Nor were the Soviet people the same as they had been two decades earlier. They were less easily controlled. The deadening impact of the Stalin era had been lifted to a large degree and few under thirty had experienced its brutality. Thus while the stick was applied more in this regime than under Khrushchev, the carrot would play a larger role than it had under Stalin.

There can be no doubt that there were strong forces in the Soviet Union in the later 1960's which wished to redirect the party's course far more sharply towards the past. The party had the power to so move, but only at the heavy price of economic stagnation and increased public apathy, if not hostility. The price was too high.

The Role of the Party

The party thus found itself in a position where its role, given its various goals, no longer could be as absolute as in the past. Soviet society was comprised of a variety of groups—scientists, intelligentsia, consumers, industrial management, military, peasants, youth—all of whom exerted pressure. They were not organized as pressure groups in the Western sense. But the regime was aware that it could flout the interests of such groups only at considerable peril. Increasingly, its role became not so much to arbitrarily order as to integrate and moderate demands. The party did not cherish this role, and often resisted it; but there seemed no long-run alternative, unless the system was bent on its own destruction.

In taking on the role of mediator among various interest groups, the party, in a sense, was behaving increasingly like the modern democratic model. That is not to say that it was going to become democratic. The Soviet Union remained a one-party state with only spurious elections. But the Soviet system had changed; a new model was being developed. Its precise shape was uncertain, but it would differ greatly from its Stalinist predecessor.

What also seemed certain, short of an improbable revolution, was that the change would be justified in Marxist-Leninist terms. Ideology, as previously noted, is the basis of party legitimization. Every action must be supported by and supportive of Marxism-Leninism.[58] Thus any direction in which the system moves will necessarily receive theoretical sanctification—though generally after the fact. Marx did not interfere with what Lenin felt he had to do; nor Lenin with what Stalin felt he had to do; nor Stalin with Khrushchev; nor Khrushchev with his successors. Each leader or leadership-group did what it thought necessary—and then constructed an ideological rationale.

Party theoreticians have at times been hard put to cope with the changes that political necessity seemed to dictate. For example, prior to August, 1939, and the Russo-German pact, Naziism was daily lambasted in the Soviet press as the worst enemy of communism and mankind. Novels portrayed the fascists as swine and the motion picture industry produced films preparing the Russian people for war against Hitler. But suddenly Russia and Germany were reconciled, a reconciliation Stalin hoped would protect Russia while the Western European powers destroyed one another. Antifascist editorials were muted; the novels were withdrawn from circulation; the films were not exhibited. Two years later, when Hitler invaded, the process was reversed and the pre-1939 articles, books, and films emerged once again.

While the theoreticians with their card files of Marxist-Leninist quotations appropriate for every occasion ultimately have proved equal to the task of justifying the various tergiversations of the party line, the followers of that line have not always been able to make the leap—the suspension—of judgment required. For many reasons, Russian communism in the 1920's and 1930's was able to gather an international coterie of supporters, people willing to defend its every move, determined to disbelieve the accusations of its critics, refusing to acknowledge that the practices of Russian bolshevism were in glaring contrast to the utopian dreams of Marx's communism. Even so, millions of such adherents were *not* able to rationalize the pact with Hitler or the later attack upon Hungary. Particularly were they disenchanted by Khrushchev's "Secret Speech" at the party congress in February, 1956, in which the image of the divine Stalin was defaced and shattered beyond repair.

If almost everything that the party had drummed into the people about

---

[58] Lenin wrote so voluminously and was such a freewheeling pragmatist, that substantiating statements can be found in his writings for almost any course of action. Marxist-Leninist action, however, must never be taken because it is expedient. That would be "opportunism," one of the worst crimes in the communist lexicon.

Stalin for decades was a lie—that instead of being all-seeing, all-kind, all-brave, he had been a cowardly, shortsighted, paranoic murderer—then why believe what the party said today, or tomorrow? The blinders which most people had placed upon their own consciousness for purposes of self-protection were now removed. Stalin was revealed for what he was—and the Soviet system, to a lesser degree—for what it was. No matter how hard the apologists might try, the one could not be disengaged from the other, for Stalin had made the system what it was.

In the international communist movement, the disclosures about Stalin stunned loyal party members. Tens of thousands of the disillusioned broke with the party. Inside Russia, efforts were made to keep Khrushchev's revelations secret, lest admission of Stalin's crimes demoralize the people and weaken the regime. Slowly the news leaked out, however. The net effect of the revelations everywhere was to reduce the authority of the Kremlin and place its leaders and the system under suspicion.

Youth and Changing Values

Marxist-Leninist theory is one of the mainstays of the Soviet educational curriculum. Soviet education, like every other aspect of life, is under the total domination of the party. Education is, obviously, of great importance to the system because it shapes the minds of the citizenry and prepares workers to fill necessary jobs. The latter task has narrowly focused the educational system on slotfilling. Since one hundred thousand petroleum engineers are required some years hence, the required number of people must enroll in petroleum engineering this year. And since only one hundred historians and anthropologists will be needed, there will only be one hundred openings in the universities for people interested in these disciplines. And so forth. If students want to specialize in French literature and the party wants physicists instead, students must adjust to the system. In the post-Stalinist years, as the rigidity of the system was reduced, there were more opportunities for those interested in the humanities and social sciences. But the overwhelming emphasis upon education to serve industry persisted. Indeed, the prospect of opportunity and economic rewards, rather than official orders, attracted young people to the desired fields.

But whether one is to be a chemist, a mathematician, a sociologist, a worker on the assembly line or a peasant in the field, one must receive ideological grounding in Marxism-Leninism. It is taught at every level from grade school through the university and there is a Higher Party School where one becomes a specialist in it. Every Soviet student is expected to be thoroughly familiar with it. In the past, knowledge of it had been one of the prerequisites to success and there was an obligation to be familiar with current interpretations. The diminution in the authority of Stalin and his successors diminished the authority of the doctrine, however. Much of university-bound youth has become bored with ideology. Classes on Marxism-Leninism, at the most prestigious institutions, are usually regarded as to be avoided whenever possible.[59]

Among that group of Soviet youth from whom tomorrow's leaders were most likely to come there was increasingly a sense of unrest about their government and its ideology. There was the feeling that what Marx had to say a century ago had little pertinence for contemporary life. The Marxist "classics" were felt to be obsolete, with no message for today's world of automation and journeys to the moon.

It was a fact that the dominant trends in Soviet life increasingly differed from those which the earlier Soviet system had stressed. The ideological thrust had sought to subordinate the individual for the sake of the masses. Preoccupation with one's own affairs was attacked as the malaise of the decadent bourgeoisie, of life under capitalism. The primacy of public values was strengthened by the lack of attainable private values and there were few places where one might find privacy; four or more people living in a single room was the norm. Life was lived publicly, and always under the supervision, real or anticipated, of the secret police. There were few private goods to be had, and even when they were available, one was apprehensive lest accumulation of them bring suspicion upon self and family.

But with a declining use of coercion and a greater availability of consumer goods, the private interests of the Soviet public, intentionally or otherwise, were increasingly being served. Apartments for single families were becoming available. The street no longer had to serve as the living room of the Soviet citizen, who now increasingly had his own private living room in his own apartment. There was the possibility of saving for a *dacha* (country house), an automobile, new furniture, a television set, a refrigerator, and a vacation abroad. The individual turned his attention toward his own interests and private goals—and away from those of society as a whole. The Soviet people became, as the Chinese communists charged, "bourgeois," [60] dominated by values of personal acquisition and personal success.

As already suggested, the regime encouraged such values, because hopefully they would elicit greater effort from the populace. To get a new auto, a new television set, a new refrigerator, one would work with the energy needed to serve the purposes of the regime. The acquisition of goods in-

[59] William Taubman, "Dialectics Is a Drag," *Saturday Review,* February 17, 1968.
[60] June 14, 1963, letter of the Central Committee, Communist Party of China to the Central Committee, Communist Party of the Soviet Union. Point 24 in particular.

creased the stake of their owners in the existing system. Moreover, they would be so involved in acquiring property that they would overlook some of the shortcomings of the system. But while the regime succeeded to a degree in obtaining the cooperation and support of the masses by encouraging private tastes, it also undermined the applicability and meaningfulness of the equality-centered, world-revolution-oriented Marxist hypothesis. The Marxist ideal of a classless society has not been practiced in Russia since 1918, and has been practiced even less in the Khrushchev and post-Khrushchev years. While the average male worker in the Soviet Union had a net income of $106.16 per month in mid-1966 [61] (as compared to $453.41 in the U.S.), the income of a scientist, for example, was five or more times as great. On the farm, the agricultural specialist or technician has always received several times more per time unit of labor than his less skilled co-worker. While it may be somewhat easier to move from class to class in Soviet than in American society, classes do exist—and class lines are becoming more rigid as those at the top seek to maintain a similar position for their own offspring. Khrushchev, among others, noted this tendency, and even attempted to reverse it—without notable success apparently because the Russians at or near the top were more interested in their own private worlds than in being equal. The spread of communism would be nice, but to the average Russian this priority was far below that of acquiring a new motorcar.

The low level of interest in Marxist theory has been further accentuated by the poor calibre of its teachers. By and large, those with high teaching aptitudes have specialized in the more traditional academic subjects. Instruction in Marxism-Leninism thus has been left to ambitious but often incompetent persons who have seen this path as their best road to success.[62] If they did a workmanlike job here, were punctual, and had a good attendance record, more remunerative and prestigious party jobs might be forthcoming.

The foregoing does not mean that the Soviet student doesn't know his Marx and Lenin. He has memorized what was needed to pass examinations because this was necessary to advance to the next educational level, and a failing grade would arouse party suspicions jeopardizing his future. But he would have preferred to study something more relevant to contemporary life, something less boring.

[61] Radio Liberty dispatch, November 2, 1967.
[62] B. Mochalov, "Party Work in Institutions of Higher Education," *Kommunist*, No. 10 (July, 1966); *Current Digest of the Soviet Press*, XVIII, No. 36 (September 28, 1966), 3–6.

Decision Making

But if Russian Marxist ideology has a low profile for communist youth and if the leaders of communist states have essentially been pragmatists, is ideology of no consequence? The answer is one of degree. Ideology is of some consequence, but only in certain limited areas.

Soviet leadership cannot abandon ideology. Marxism-Leninism confers legitimacy upon both system and authority. Moreover, the contemporary leaders have come of age believing in Marxism-Leninism; their path to power has been in its name. Older men are not likely to cast aside their ideological cargo in their later years. Therefore, their acts must be verbally squared with Marxist theories. But it is the "acting" that comes first and the "squaring" that comes after.

While it is likely that the power elite can understand, in the abstract, how and why they and their predecessors have had to interpret Marxism, it is unlikely that they conceptualize the violence they have done to Marx's theory. These are practical men engaged in the day-to-day business of running an increasingly complex state. They are self-appointed inheritors of Lenin's power. It would be psychologically painful, if possible, for them to concede weaknesses in the foundations of their power or confess to significant departures from its propositions. They might agree that they have had to make adjustments, but these are matters of interpretation necessitated by specific circumstances. They have never departed from Marxism-Leninism. Their goals remain unchanged. They are convinced they are good Marxist-Leninists. They hold on to many of the shibboleths of the past. Yet, in practice, Russia since 1917 has given abundant examples of pet party beliefs being surrendered on the altar of necessity.

For Soviet leadership, ideology does not, in most respects, seriously cramp decision making. Ideology does, however, contribute to the Russian value system and the Russian view of the world. For example, there apparently is not much sympathy in the Soviet Union for private ownership of factories or of railroads or the telephone or telegraph system.[63] The Marxist bias against private ownership of the means of production is widely shared in the U.S.S.R., though it should be pointed out that the concept of private property was never a very deep-seated one in Russian society[64] and that

[63] Alex Inkeles and Raymond Bauer, *The Soviet Citizen* (Cambridge: Howard, 1959), pp. 242–246. As more recent economic concessions have contributed to the accumulation of private property, the regime has solved the ideological dilemma by designating privately-owned autos, country homes, etc., as "personal" property and, therefore, presumably, acceptable.

[64] John Maynard, *Russian in Flux* (New York: Macmillan, 1948), pp. 26–28.

many factories as well as the means of communication were state-owned even before November, 1917. On the other hand, in agriculture, it would appear that one of the best chances for increasing output would be to increase the private sector. But establishment commitment to collectivization remains so great as to make the possibilities for adopting that solution very remote.

There is also in the Soviet Union the general conviction that communism *is* the "wave" of the future.[65] Capitalism is doomed; it is decadent; it will collapse. "We will bury you." [66] Communism will triumph.

But even here one finds that circumstances have forced alterations in the doctrine. For capitalism has proved stronger than Marx or Lenin had anticipated. Moreover, its advanced technology has developed the nuclear bomb and the capacity to deliver it. "Their" possession of the bomb makes it dangerous to provoke the capitalists since nuclear war could destroy communism as well as capitalism. Therefore, said Khrushchev—and his revisionism in this issue has not been renounced by his successors—the two systems must "coexist" [67] for the time being. Communism, however, will still ultimately conquer by the superiority of its example.[68] By making communist society exemplary, other peoples will seek to emulate it. Struggle must still be emphasized, but it is the struggle to achieve, and not the struggle to destroy capitalism; the struggle for, not the struggle against.

If at almost every turn, practice has altered not only basic Marxist ideology, but even the adaptations that followed as well, what is left, ideologically speaking? There are a series of values and expectations, based more or less on Marx; and there is a system for speedy industrial development that has nothing to do with Marx—that is now increasingly recognized even by communists as being outdated for Russia, but which still may have meaning for less highly developed countries. Other than this, there is little except self-interest, party interest, national interest—and it is on the basis of these that life is lived and decisions are made in the Soviet Union. Some observers, particularly Soviet ones, object to assertions of the downgrading

65 N. S. Khrushchev, *New York Times,* September 20, 1959, Sect. IV, p. 1.

66 *Ibid.* In so stating, Khrushchev clearly meant that communism would win out over capitalism in a generalized, historical sense, not that the Soviet Union would bomb the United States out of existence. He was enunciating his Marxist-Leninist certainty. But a great many people put a more literal and violent interpretation on his statement.

67 Lenin also spoke of "peaceful coexistence," but such coexistence was a temporary expedient employed by a communist power for reasons of tactics. It was not to become a way of life, as Khrushchev and more recent Soviet practice have indicated.

68 N. S. Khrushchev, September 30, 1959, at a banquet in his honor in Peking. He repeated this statement on many different occasions.

of Marxism-Leninism in Russia.[69] Some Western scholars believe its demise to be even more certain than herein indicated. But the trend does seem clear, all assertions from Soviet sources to the contrary.

The Future of Marxism-Leninism

If ideology plays the role indicated in the Soviet Union, a still less determining role in Eastern Europe, and has been altered almost beyond recognition in the People's Republic of China, does this mean that the ideology of Karl Marx is dead, or at the most, moribund? The answer would seem to be in the negative.

In Western Europe, in particular, the established communist parties have come to recognize that, if their parties have a political future, it is to be found in adjusting to local situations and not in pursuit of Leninism or Stalinism. The Western European parties over the years have suffered greatly from the abject homage they have paid to Soviet authority. They now recognize that they cannot come to power, or even continue the present level of political prosperity which the Italian and French parties enjoy, without putting the needs of their own countries ahead of those of the Soviet party and state. As their attentions have turned inward and they have begun to operate not as revolutionary parties but within the democratic context, they have begun to return to some of the values which Marx held paramount and to operate in a context in which his ideas and ideals have relevance. Marx thought that his revolution would occur only after an industrial system had been developed that was so productive that the needs of all the people could be provided by it—a stage that only now is beginning to be realized in a few Western countries. While it is difficult to divorce Marxism from Lenin and Stalin, to the extent that this can be done, "pure" Marxism becomes a much more viable alternative for discussion. There is a running argument, of course, as to whether the totalitarianism that justifies itself as Marxist is indeed implicit in Marxism. It certainly is not explicit. Marx himself would never have conceded it.

Perhaps most important for the survival of Marxism is the message of hope and the rallying point which it provides for the powerless of the world —at least in those lands where a regime calling itself Marxist has not yet been installed. Marx in his ideology defines what is wrong with the world; he tells why man is suffering, how he has been defrauded. He explains what can be done to alleviate the misery of the human condition and flatly as-

[69] Some Western scholars would agree with the emphasis on "pragmatism" here, but they would place additional emphasis on Marxism-Leninism's role in establishing the basic attitudes within which pragmatism operates.

serts that his felicitous solution is sure to come. His is a doctrine that promises the total destruction of all that is mean, selfish, and petty and its replacement by justice, freedom, and harmony. Marx offers every man's dream to those accepting his hypotheses, and he guarantees its fulfillment. He does this at great length for those who require an intellectually sophisticated foundation: he does it with passion and a literary flair for those more susceptible to emotional appeal. In a world in which the majority of mankind lives in misery and in which those desiring power and denied it yearn for an ideological support for their frustrations and ambitions, the made-to-order arguments and promises of Marxism will probably continue to find receptive ears, perhaps even more receptive than in the immediate past, whatever disfigurements Marxism has suffered in practice. For it can always be argued that the error was not in Marx but in his disciples [70]—and that we, the new disciples, will be forever true to his vision.

Soviet communism is only one manifestation of the practical and ideological fruits of Marxism. Before exploring the impact of Marxism on power in other countries, however, it may be well to examine the philosophy and practice of "guerrilla communism." The latter has proved successful in a number of countries and its appearance is one of the more fascinating aspects of modern ideology.

Bibliography

Armstrong, John A. *Ukrainian Nationalism.* 2nd ed. New York: Columbia University Press, 1963.
Bialer, Seweryn, ed. *Stalin and His Generals.* New York: Pegasus, 1969.
Billington, James H. *The Icon and the Axe.* New York: Alfred A. Knopf, 1966.
Brzezinski, Zbigniew, and Samuel P. Huntington. *Political Power: USA–USSR.* New York: Viking, 1964.
Campbell, Robert W. *Soviet Economic Power.* 2nd ed. Boston: Houghton Mifflin, 1966.
Deutscher, Isaac. *Trotsky.* 3 vols. New York: Oxford University Press, 1954, 1959, 1963.
Fainsod, Merle. *How the Soviets Are Ruled.* Rev. ed. Cambridge: Harvard University Press, 1963.
Feifer, George. *Justice in Moscow.* New York: Simon & Schuster, 1964.
Hayward, Max, ed. *On Trial: The Soviet State versus "Abram Tertz" and "Nikolai Arzhak."* New York: Harper & Row, 1966.
Hazard, John N. *The Soviet System of Government.* 4th rev. ed. Chicago: University of Chicago Press, 1968.

[70] Tito, for example, held that there was nothing wrong with Marx, but only in the actions of those who attempted to apply his ideas, especially after Lenin's death. On the "New Left," too, there are those who make similar assertions about Marx.

Jacobs, Dan N. *The New Communisms.* New York: Harper & Row, 1969.

Johnson, Priscilla, and Leopold Labedz, eds. *Khrushchev and the Arts—The Politics of Soviet Culture, 1962–1964.* Cambridge, Mass.: The MIT Press, 1965.

Leites, Nathan. *A Study of Bolshevism.* Glencoe, Ill.: Free Press, 1953.

Lowenthal, Richard. *World Communism: The Disintegration of a Secular Faith.* New York: Oxford University Press, 1964.

Meyer, Alfred G. *The Soviet Political System.* New York: Random House, 1965.

Mihajlov, Mihajlo. *Moscow Summer.* New York: Farrar, Strauss & Giroux, 1965.

Morton, Henry W. and Peter H. Juviler, eds. *Soviet Policy Making.* New York: Frederick A. Praeger, 1966.

Parry, Albert. *The New Class Divided: Science and Technology versus Communism.* New York: Macmillan, 1966.

Schapiro, Leonard B. *The Communist Party of the Soviet Union.* New York: Random House, 1960.

Skilling, H. Gordon. *The Governments of Communist East Europe.* New York: Thomas Y. Crowell, 1966.

Solzhenitsyn, Alexandr I. *The First Circle.* New York: Harper & Row, 1968.

Tucker, Robert. *The Soviet Political Mind.* New York: Frederick A. Praeger, 1963.

Ulam, Adam B. *The New Face of Soviet Totalitarianism.* Cambridge: Harvard University Press, 1963.

Chapter 5

Guerrilla Communism: China, North Vietnam, Cuba

The term "guerrilla communism" is intended to suggest the union of communist ideology and guerrilla warfare.[1] It is a commonplace of the twentieth century that the communists have preempted guerrilla warfare as the chief method of revolutionary struggle.

Although guerrilla warfare is accorded a lengthy history in the annals of military affairs, both the name and the methods were formalized only in the Spanish resistance to the Napoleonic invasion of 1808–14. A derivative of *guerra* (the Spanish word for war), the term "guerrilla" means, in literal translation, "little war." Such a war was waged in the Spanish countryside by partisan fighters who continued to harass the French army after the regular Spanish troops had been defeated.

Guerrilla (or "irregular," "unconventional," "insurgency," "partisan") warfare has since become a central concern of military theorists of every persuasion. Writing in the 1820's, for example, Karl von Clausewitz devoted a portion of his classic work *On War* to the analysis of this type of military operation.[2] Primary responsibility for developing the theory and practice of guerrilla warfare, however, must be assigned to communist thinkers. As early as 1849 Karl Marx exhibited an acute understanding of the nature and potentialities of irregular warfare. He wrote: "A nation fighting for its liberty, ought not to adhere rigidly to the accepted rules of

---

[1] To my knowledge "guerrilla communism" is used for the first time in Lucian Pye, *Guerrilla Communism in Malaya* (Princeton: Princeton University Press, 1956).

[2] Chap. 26: "Arming the Nation."

warfare. Mass uprisings, revolutionary methods, guerrilla bands everywhere —such are the only means by which a small nation can hope to maintain itself against an adversary superior in numbers and equipment. By their use a weaker force can overcome its stronger and better organized opponent." [3]

Lenin also drew a sharp distinction between regular and irregular warfare, repeatedly stressing the importance of the latter. Revolutionary struggle, he wrote in 1906, must pay particular attention to guerrilla warfare:

Military tactics are determined by the level of military technique. . . . Military technique today is not what it was in the middle of the nineteenth century. It would be folly for crowds to contend against artillery and defend barricades with revolvers. . . . These [new] tactics are the tactics of guerrilla warfare. The organization required for such tactics is that of mobile and exceedingly small units, units of ten, three, or even two persons. [4]

In a classic passage written in 1920, Lenin forecast the spirit and rationale of the military doctrine to be adopted by communist leaders everywhere:

To tie one's hand beforehand, openly to tell the enemy, who is at present better armed than we are, whether and when we shall fight him, is stupidity and not revolutionariness. To accept battle at a time when it is obviously advantageous to the enemy and not to us is a crime; and those political leaders of the revolutionary class who are unable "to track, to maneuver, to compromise," in order to avoid an obviously disadvantageous battle, are good for nothing. [5]

As it evolved in the twentieth century, guerrilla communism has come to assume several interrelated characteristics. First, it has been associated almost exclusively with the underdeveloped or semideveloped countries of the world; in that sense, it represents an application of Marxist-Leninist ideology to "developing" and "colonial" countries. Second, guerrilla communism has a rural, rather than an urban, orientation; it looks to the countryside, not the cities. Third, it necessarily relies upon the rural peasantry, not an urban proletariat. Fourth, it rests upon a protracted military conflict undergoing distinct stages of development.

The foremost theoretician-practitioner of guerrilla communism is undoubtedly Mao Tse-tung. He formulates an explicit and self-conscious

---

[3] Quoted in C. Aubrey Dixon and Otto Heilbrunn, *Communist Guerrilla Warfare* (New York: Frederick A. Praeger, 1954), p. 19, n. 1.

[4] "The Lessons of the Moscow Uprising" (September, 1906), *Selected Works* (New York: International Publishers, 1943), III, p. 351. See also Lenin's "Partisan Warfare," translated in *Orbis*, II (Summer, 1958), 194–208.

[5] " 'Left-Wing' Communism: An Infantile Disorder" (May, 1920), *Selected Works*, X, 118–19.

statement of the ideology and practice of guerrilla communism, and he proclaims it as a model for all developing countries. Accordingly, this chapter begins by delineating in some detail the evolution of guerrilla communism in China and its chief components as identified by Mao Tse-tung. It then proceeds to an analysis of guerrilla communism in two other revolutionary situations: the Vietminh revolution, which, with some exceptions, closely followed the Chinese model; and the Cuban revolution, which seriously challenged it. The overall objective of the chapter is to describe, compare, and contrast the conditions under which guerrilla communism took roots in the three countries; the ideology that sustained it; and the strategy and tactics that were essential to its success.

China

Chinese communism consists, primarily, of Mao Tse-tung's attempt to apply to the "colonial, semicolonial, and semifeudal" [6] country of China a theory of revolution originally designed for advanced industrial societies. This attempt is consistent with the communist assertion, first enunciated by Lenin, that Marxism must be integrated with the specific conditions of the country in which it is to be employed: communism, Lenin repeatedly asserted, "is not a lifeless dogma but a guide to action." Accepting this proposition, Mao insists that Marxism-Leninism must be fused with specific historical conditions and given a "definite national form" before it can be put into practice. He wrote as early as 1938:

Being Marxists, Communists are internationalists, but we can put Marxism into practice only when it is integrated with the specific characteristics of our country and acquires a definite national form. The great strength of Marxism-Leninism lies precisely in its integration with the concrete revolutionary practice of all countries. For the Chinese Communist Party, it is a matter of learning to apply the theory of Marxism-Leninism to the specific circumstances of China. For the Chinese Communists . . . any talk about Marxism in isolation from China's characteristics is merely Marxism in the abstract, Marxism in a vacuum. Hence to apply Marxism concretely to China so that its every manifestation has an undubitably Chinese character . . . becomes a problem which it is urgent for the whole Party to understand and solve.[7]

[6] A "colony," according to Mao, is controlled by a single imperialist power, whereas a "semicolony" is under the simultaneous influence of several imperialist countries. A "semifeudal" country is one in which elements of capitalism exist side by side with elements of feudalism.
[7] "The Role of the Chinese Communist Party in the National War" (October, 1938), *Selected Works*, 4 vols. (Peking: Foreign Languages Press, 1961–65), II, 209. Hereafter this work will be cited by volume number only.

Mao's integration of Marxism with the historical circumstances of China is the subject of this section.

Conditions in China

Communism began seriously to attract the Chinese intellectuals after the Russian revolution of 1917. The dynamics of the communist movement, however, may be traced to the middle of the nineteenth century— to the Opium War of 1839–42, and the ensuing embarrassment and humiliation of the Chinese people. Thwarted in attempts to sell opium freely in China and to use it as a medium of exchange for Chinese goods (silk and tea, for example), the British began smuggling the drug into Chinese ports. Chinese efforts to halt this traffic were consistently defeated by Britain's superior naval power. The Anglo-Chinese Treaty of Nanking (1842) ceded Hong Kong to Great Britain and opened Chinese ports to foreign trade. Thus began a century of exploitation under a system of "unequal treaties" that divided China into foreign concessions outside of Chinese jurisdiction and immune to Chinese law. A most important consequence—one which played a key role in the emergence of Chinese nationalism—was the destruction of the ancient concept of the Middle Kingdom: China as the mighty center of the world.

The Western penetration of China and the introduction of foreign capital and products led to increasing foreign exploitation, economic maldistribution, and social unrest. Defeat at the hands of Japan in the war of 1894–95 (over the control of Korea and Taiwan) further humiliated the Chinese people and demonstrated the ineptness of the Manchu regime. The failure of the Manchu rulers to throw out the foreign "barbarians" ignited the antiforeign Boxer Rebellion of 1900, in which hundreds of civilians and missionaries were killed. It took foreign troops—American, British, French, German, and Russian—to end the Rebellion. The conviction grew that only massive reform could return to China its strength, integrity, and self-respect.

The key figure in the nationalist movement was Sun Yat-sen, who brought to the revolutionary process the ideological, political, and organizational leadership it had lacked. Educated in Hong Kong and Hawaii, converted to Christianity at the age of eighteen, and impatient with Chinese traditions, Sun sought to create a new China representing a fusion of oriental and Western values—a China free of foreign rule, politically strong, and economically prosperous. His objectives were spelled out in the Three People's Principles of "nationalism," "democracy," and "people's welfare." "Nationalism" meant political independence and national unity, to be attained by elimination of imperialism and warlordism. "Democracy" called for a responsible, popular, republican government in China. "People's welfare" involved redistribution of the feudal land, nationalization of the basic industries, and creation of a modern and efficient economy. These objectives were to be accomplished in three successive stages: military unification, political tutelage, and constitutional democracy.

The accidental explosion of a bomb on October 10, 1911, ignited a popular uprising in Hankow that spread rapidly across many provinces and eventually marked the overthrow of the Manchu regime. Sun Yat-sen, who at the time happened to be on a fund-raising mission in the United States, returned to China and was inaugurated provisional president of the Republic on January 1, 1912.

Throughout his life, Sun persisted in efforts to unify China, create a viable national government, and establish an effective National People's Party (the Kuomintang or KMT). In this he asked for support from the West. Having been turned down, he called upon the Soviet Union. Adolf Joffe, a leading Soviet diplomat, was sent to China in 1922; he was followed a year later by Mikhail Borodin, a leading revolutionary. The latter proved exceedingly helpful in establishing the Whampoa Military Academy, organizing political agitation and propaganda, and reorganizing the KMT along communist lines (which organization, by the way, is still retained on the island of Taiwan).

Sun's death in 1925 precipitated a conflict within the KMT over the line of succession, from which Chiang Kai-shek (then commander of Whampoa Academy as well as Sun's son-in-law) emerged victorious. This event marked a triumph for the right, conservative wing of the KMT over its left, liberal wing, which Sun had represented.

Evolution of Communist Strategy

In the first two decades of the twentieth century, the student, intellectual, and leftist elements in China, imbued with the spirit of anti-imperialism, became the leaders of a full-scale nationalist movement. They espoused a series of social, political, and economic reforms under the slogan "Science and Democracy," reflecting the influence of the West. Chinese nationalism reached a peak of intensity in 1915 as a reaction against the Twenty-One Demands presented by Japan, which included the assumption of German concessions in Shantung and the monopoly of certain industries in the Yangtze valley. The decision of the Versailles peacemakers to transfer to Japan the former German rights in Shantung (as a means of inducing the former to participate in the Paris Peace Conference) triggered the May Fourth Movement of 1919, generally regarded as a turning point in Chinese history. The movement began in Peking and spread rapidly to other parts of the country. Defying the authorities, Peking and Shanghai students marched into the streets and called for a general strike that lasted about a month in the latter city. Some joined nationalist groups; others became members of such leftist organizations as the Young Socialists and the Federation of Labor Unions. As a whole, the May Fourth Movement represented a revolt against defeat and humiliation, a protest against economic hardships and exploitation, and a reaction against the privileged position of foreign merchants and investors.

The Russian communists and the Communist International (Comintern) watched developments in China with great interest. In 1920 the second Comintern congress formally adopted Lenin's long-standing thesis expounding a two-stage theory of revolution in backward countries, according to which a "bourgeois-democratic" revolution would be followed by a "proletarian-socialist" revolution. Since the communists were relatively weak, Lenin argued, they could not single-handedly bring about a revolution. As an initial step, it would be necessary to form alliances with all other classes and groups (especially the bourgeoisie and the peasantry) in a national and patriotic struggle against imperialist and feudal oppression.[8] Having attained sufficient strength, the proletariat would then move the revolution to the next stage and establish its own dictatorship. The Comintern dispatched an agent—Gregory Voitinsky—to China to organize the Communist party.

The formal beginning of the communist movement in China may be dated with the founding of the Chinese Communist Party (CCP) in 1921. By this time communism had become a familiar ideology to many Chinese intellectuals and a number of communist study groups had been founded in the major cities. On July 1, 1921, about a dozen representatives from the various communist groups met in a girls' school in the French section of Shanghai to give the party its formal organization and adopt its first constitution. Ch'en Tu-hsiu, a respected intellectual, was elected general secretary. Mao Tse-tung, then a relative unknown, represented his home province of Hunan, where he had been active in patriotic and leftist move-

---

[8] One of the major differences between a communist revolution in an advanced as opposed to a backward country lies in the classes on which the revolutionaries must necessarily rely. In advanced industrial countries there are presumably two main classes, the proletariat and the bourgeoisie. In colonial, semicolonial, and semifeudal countries, by contrast, capitalist classes coexist with precapitalist classes: there is a vast peasantry, a strong landlord class, a small bourgeoisie, and a comparatively insignificant proletariat. Each of these classes is further segmentized. The bourgeoisie, for example, is divided into the big bourgeoisie, the middle (or national) bourgeoisie, and the petit bourgeoisie. Being exceedingly small, the proletariat cannot engineer a revolution on its own strength alone; it must rely on all other classes and groups that may, for whatever reason, support its cause.

ments since 1917. He had lived in Peking in 1918–19 and had held a minor post in the Peking University library, where he had met various leftist intellectuals, and where he had read widely in Western literature, Marxist as well as non-Marxist.

Under Comintern direction, the CCP commended Sun Yat-sen's stand against imperialism and feudalism, and actively sought an alliance with the nationalists. The communists made clear, however, that any cooperation was a matter of expediency and would not be permitted to cloud the communist objective of eventual seizure of power. At the same time, there developed within the CCP the first in a series of internal struggles. One segment of the party, which reportedly included Mao, criticized Ch'en Tu-hsiu and his associates for the "right" deviation of failing to stress sufficiently the leadership role of the Communist party in any united front arrangement. Mao's group then attacked a third faction led by Chang Kuo-t'ao for committing the "left" deviationist error of stressing the purity of the communist movement and opposing alliance with other parties and groups.

Sun Yat-sen welcomed cooperation with the communists in the hope of destroying the warlords and attaining national unity. Thus when the KMT (Kuomintang) held its first national congress in Canton in January, 1924, CCP members were admitted to membership as individuals, while the CCP continued its own independent life as well.

The first CCP–KMT alliance proved catastrophic for the communists. Having succeeded Sun Yat-sen, Chiang Kai-shek decided to terminate relations with the communists. In March, 1926, while reiterating his faith in the united front principle, Chiang conducted a purge against the communist leaders in the Kuomintang. The CCP became apprehensive, but the Comintern (now under Stalin) insisted on the continuation of the united front with the nationalists. This insistence, far from being geared to Chinese realities, was the consequence of a major struggle between Stalin and Trotsky over the question of leadership after Lenin's death in 1924. Distrustful of the bourgeoisie in general, Trotsky opposed CCP alliance with KMT. Although by late 1927 Stalin had consolidated his position within the Soviet party, any alteration of his views would have constituted an implicit endorsement of the Trotsky argument. Later, he quietly accepted some of Trotsky's beliefs.

In April, 1927, Chiang Kai-shek staged a massive night coup in Shanghai, killing thousands of communists, virtually eliminating all labor leaders, and nearly finishing off the labor movement in that city. Thus ended the CCP–KMT alliance and the first united front. The incident was a blow to Stalin's position on the Chinese revolution. It also destroyed much of the proletarian base of the Chinese Community Party.

Although this period was disastrous for the CCP, the communists learned some important lessons from it. They discovered the need for military strength and for mass support, the latter to be gained through alliance with all segments of the population except the big bourgeoisie. They insisted on the necessity of CCP leadership of the united front. They began to grasp the advantages of basing party strength in rural areas during the early stages of a communist revolution—an unorthodox idea by any communist standard and a departure from Moscow teachings.

As early as 1926 Mao Tse-tung had turned his attention to the problem of revolution in the Chinese countryside. His *Report on an Investigation of the Peasant Movement in Hunan* (March, 1927) examined and glorified the role of the peasantry in the communist revolution. Mao saw the peasant movement as a "mighty storm" that would sweep all forces of oppression before it. The importance of the rural areas and the key role of the peasantry became the basis of Mao Tse-tung's revolutionary strategy. Since the proletariat was an insignificant minority in China, the "communist" revolution had to be based on some other class.

In September, 1927, Mao organized a peasant uprising to coincide with the autumn harvest in Hunan. Having failed, he led a contingent of armed peasants into the rugged Chiang-kang mountains on the border of Hunan and Kiangsi. There he created a revolutionary base, set up a worker-peasant government, and launched a program of land redistribution. For the next four years, in relative isolation from government troops, Mao and his associates concentrated on building a Red Army and expanding the rural base areas ("soviets" or, later, "liberated areas").

During the same period Mao devoted a great deal of attention to the development of a host of revolutionary techniques. He stressed the ineptness of the "White" (KMT) regime and forecast an eventual communist victory. Special emphasis was placed on armed struggle, peasant guerrilla warfare, and the capturing of the cities from the countryside. Mao insisted, however, that armed struggle was not the only function of the Red Army—that economic, political, propaganda, and organizational tasks were equally important.

The White regime, Mao quickly found, far from being a cohesive political force, was divided by constant strife. When the ruling classes are in conflict with one another, he argued, the Red regime can pursue a "comparatively venturesome" policy; when there is relative stability in the ruling regime, the revolutionaries must adopt a tactic of "gradual advance" and concentrate on consolidating the base areas. Realizing the relative weakness of the communists, Mao called for patience, devotion, and hard work. Given the leadership of the Communist party, he insisted, all difficulties would be overcome.

In 1927 Chiang Kai-shek established the nationalist government in Nanking. The Nanking government (1927–37) was anything but permissive or democratic, with Chiang's policies, though declared to be based on Sun Yat-sen's ideas, never actually proceeding beyond the stage of "political tutelage"—that is, party dictatorship. The KMT exercised complete control over governmental and administrative agencies. Aided by German military advisers, one of Chiang's main ambitions was to build a powerful army under his personal control. Party, government, and army became indistinguishable; Chiang simultaneously headed all three. By the early 1930's the Nanking government was rapidly losing public support.

In December, 1930, Chiang began a series of five campaigns to wipe out the communists and destroy their strongholds. Employing overwhelming military power and a German-devised policy of multiple blockades, he was able to overpower the communist forces in the last of these campaigns. In 1934, the Red Army faced the alternative of either being completely destroyed or breaking through Chiang's lines and establishing a base elsewhere. Thus began, on October 15, 1934, the famous Long March from southeast China (Kiangsi) to northwest China (Shensi), covering some 6,000 miles of deserts, mountains, and rivers. Committing military blunders and following a predictable course, the Red Army suffered heavy casualties. The severity of the situation compelled a meeting of the Politburo of the CCP Central Committee at Tsunyi (Kweichou Province) in January, 1935. At that meeting Mao Tse-tung succeeded in consolidating his forces, crushing the opposition, and emerging as undisputed leader of the communists—a position he was to hold for about three decades. Meanwhile, in 1936, the CCP established its new headquarters in Yenan, Shensi province.

When the Japanese launched an invasion of northeast China in September, 1931, the communists immediately stressed national unity and resistance to the foreign aggressor as matters taking precedence over all other tasks. As early as 1933, the CCP offered a new alliance with the KMT on the condition that the latter would end its attack on the Red Army, but the KMT refused. Chiang's initial decision was not to concentrate on resisting the Japanese invaders until he had first suppressed and defeated the communists—a decision that was resented by some of his close associates. He changed his position and consented to a new united front only after he had been kidnapped and detained by one of his own (apparently procommunist) officers, Chang Hsueh-liang, in December, 1936. Under the terms of the new alliance, Chiang agreed to relax his military blockade of the communists, in return for which the CCP agreed to abandon its policy of insurrection, place the Red Army (now reorganized into the Eighth Route

Army and the New Fourth Army) under KMT command, and relax its policy of land redistribution in the countryside. Not even the combined CCP–KMT strength was sufficient to withstand the Japanese armies, however. Gradually, the communists withdrew to their stronghold and settled down for a long drawn-out conflict with Japan.

The Japanese armies quickly overran northern China and captured the capital city of Nanking in December, 1937. By 1939 the Japanese forces controlled most of the major cities. The increasing corruption within the KMT and the worsening of domestic economic difficulties (particularly inflation) marked a rapid deterioration in Chiang's position, while the CCP gained in power and prestige. By 1940–41, Chiang became so fearful of the growing strength of the communists and their ability to attract public support that he reinstituted the policy of military blockade. In January, 1941, KMT troops launched a fierce assault against the New Fourth Army and thus began a semiconcealed intermittent civil war—a war within a war.

In northern and central China, the communists were exceedingly effective in exploiting the weaknesses of the KMT. The CCP attracted widespread public support by projecting itself as the leader of a great patriotic struggle against Japan and picturing the KMT as traitor of the people's cause. It embarked on a large-scale policy of land reform in the "liberated areas." It dramatized and propagandized the autocratic and dictatorial rule of the KMT. And it capitalized on the enormous prestige of Sun Yat-sen by formally adopting the Three People's Principles as its "minimum program."

When the Japanese surrendered in August, 1945, the CCP was fully prepared to turn the anti-Japanese war into a "people's war" against the KMT. Before unleashing a full-scale civil war, Mao proposed a coalition government with the KMT in which the communists would have an effective voice. For six weeks (August 28–October 11, 1945), Mao Tse-tung met with Chiang Kai-shek at Chungking (southwest China) to negotiate the details of the coalition government and nationalization of all armed forces. But no concrete agreement was reached, partly because Chiang's real intentions appear to have been to dissolve and absorb the CCP troops. For his part, Mao insisted on maintaining sufficient communist military and political strength eventually to overthrow the Chiang regime.

In the civil war that ensued, KMT troops rapidly recaptured cities in south China; but the situation was different in the north, where the Red Army had long maintained powerful bases. The balance of forces between the communists and the nationalists, although several times in favor of the latter in 1945, quickly began to change and reached a rough parity by mid-1948. From late 1947 on, Chiang's troops suffered consistent defeats at the hands of the Red Army, now called the People's Liberation Army (PLA). By 1949, the communists had completed the conquest of Manchuria and had occupied Canton, Hankow, Nanking, Peking, Shanghai, and most other major cities. The nationalists, rapidly changing capitals, finally found themselves on Taiwan. Mao Tse-tung proclaimed the People's Republic of China on October 1, 1949.

The most significant reasons for the success of the communists included: (1) the ineptness of the Chiang regime and the unpopularity of KMT dictatorship; (2) the progressive worsening of domestic conditions and the consequent alienation of large segments of the population; (3) the Japanese invasion, which helped weaken the nationalists and render the Chiang government unable to control northern China, where the CCP became entrenched; and (4) the revolutionary strategy of Mao Tse-tung and the CCP promises to return to the Chinese people their national pride and integrity.

The Doctrine Formalized

The most important features of Chinese communism ("Mao Tse-tung's thought") are to be found in the following areas: the theory of imperialism, the concept of united front, and the nature and function of military activity. Also notable is the attempt to project on the global level the entire revolutionary strategy of Mao Tse-tung.

THE THEORY OF IMPERIALISM. Mao's conception of imperialism is an extension of the Leninist theory—applying that theory to revolutionary circumstances in a colonial, semicolonial, and semifeudal country.[9] Throughout his analysis, Lenin's attention was directed to the capitalist countries and to the development of capitalism into its international monopoly stage, imperialism. Accepting Lenin's propositions, Mao proceeds to analyze the implications of the Leninist theory, not from the point of view of capitalism-imperialism, but from the standpoint of the backward countries, particularly China. Applying the "law" of uneven political and economic development to a colonial and semicolonial country—a "law" devised by Marx and Lenin to describe the global development of capitalism—Mao arrived at the conclusion that since China is unevenly developed, and since the power of the enemy is concentrated in the urban, industrialized centers, the revolutionaries would have to retreat to the countryside, rely on the local population for all their needs, consolidate and strengthen their position, surround the cities, gradually undermine the position of the

---

[9] See n. 6 above.

enemy, and finally strangle him. The Chinese countryside, Mao insisted, provides "the indispensable, vital positions of the Chinese revolution"— the reason being that "revolutionary villages can encircle the cities, but revolutionary cities cannot detach themselves from the villages. . . ." [10]

Only after the revolutionary regime has gathered sufficient strength can a shift to the urban centers be made. In China, this shift corresponded to the virtual seizure of political power throughout the country. Thus on February 8, 1949, Mao Tse-tung announced that "From now on, the formula followed in the past twenty years, 'first the rural areas, then the cities' will be reversed and changed to the formula 'first the cities, then the rural areas.' " [11]

THE UNITED FRONT. The united front is a policy of class alliance that seeks to bring together and unify all potential social forces in the struggle against a common enemy. This, according to Mao Tse-tung, is a special feature of revolutionary movements in colonial and semicolonial countries. (In advanced capitalist countries, a complete polarization of all social forces had presumably taken place, whereas in backward countries, some precapitalist classes continue to exist.[12]) In colonial and semicolonial countries the victory of the revolutionary movement is predicated upon the firm alliance of all social classes and groups that may for one reason or another coöperate with the Communist party. The problem of identifying the revolutionary social forces in the various stages of revolution, mobilizing them, uniting with them, and employing their combined strength is the problem of united front policy.

There is no doubt that Mao Tse-tung's conception of united front owes a profound debt to Lenin and Stalin. On some points, however, his thoughts go beyond the Soviet propositions. This is particularly the case with his treatment of the role and function of the peasantry, and his analysis of the national bourgeoisie.

Lenin and Stalin did emphasize the role of the peasantry and did conceive of the revolutionary groups as basically made up of workers and peasants. However, Leninist-Stalinist theory exhibited certain reservations regarding the potentialities of the peasantry, whereas Mao's faith in the peasants as a revolutionary force is virtually unqualified. Lenin and Stalin viewed the peasantry as incorrigible seekers of private property—and therefore ultimately untrustworthy. By contrast, Mao actually used the

---

[10] "Appendix: Resolution on Certain Questions in the History of our Party" (drafted by Mao and adopted by the CCP Central Committee on April 20, 1945), III, 198.

[11] "Turn the Army into a Working Force" (February, 1949), IV, 337.

[12] See n. 8 above.

time-honored term "vanguard" to refer, not to the proletariat, but to the poor peasants.[13]

Although the position of the national bourgeoisie was progressively undermined in China, the formal aspects of the alliance continued to persist until the mid-1960's. The extension of this policy was determined by the concrete utility of the national bourgeoisie to the regime. Although this class was viewed as feeble and vacillating, its existence was justified in terms of its contribution to the economic development of the country and its virtual monopoly of modern managerial and technological knowledge. Accordingly, the Chinese communists sought to "educate" and "remold" this class to accept socialism peacefully and to participate actively in the building of socialism in China. This was nothing short of an attempt to eliminate capitalism by peaceful means, a proposition without precedent in the history of communist thought.

THE ROLE OF THE MILITARY. The decisive role of the military as a dynamic force of revolutionary development was clearly spelled out by Lenin and Stalin. Lenin's fascination with the military model was at least as great as Mao's. Such basic notions as the general importance of the military in revolutionary activity and the essentially political nature of armed struggle were explicitly set forth by Lenin. Mao's contribution here lies in developing the conception of a protracted "people's war" and the strategy of peasant guerrilla warfare.

"Political power," Mao writes after Lenin, "grows out of the barrel of a gun." But he adds immediately: "Our principle is that the Party commands the gun, and the gun must never be allowed to command the Party." [14] He insists, in other words, on the unity of the military and the political, and the subordination of the former to the latter. Military activity is not a substitute for, and does not preempt, other forms of activity. All forms of activity, furthermore, must be judged by political criteria; and military operations must have concrete political ends.

A principal objective of the military's political work is "unity between the army and the people." This task derives from the premise that the military struggle is not an isolated struggle, that without mass mobilization armed activity cannot succeed. "The richest source of power to wage war," Mao declares, "lies in the masses of the people." [15] Mao's untiring emphasis on maintaining the closest possible ties with the masses cul-

[13] "Report on an Investigation of the Peasant Movement in Hunan" (March, 1927), I, 32.
[14] "Problems of War and Strategy" (November, 1938), II, 224.
[15] "On Protracted War" (May, 1938), II, 186.

minated in the formation of the "Eight Points for Attention," first stated in 1928 and reissued with minor changes in 1947. The eight points read:

(1) Speak politely.
(2) Pay fairly for what you buy.
(3) Return everything you borrow.
(4) Pay for anything you damage.
(5) Don't hit or swear at people.
(6) Don't damage crops.
(7) Don't take liberties with women.
(8) Don't ill-treat captives.[16]

The army, in short, must be transformed into a "people's army" and the war into a "people's war." The army must help the people in their work, and protect their economic and political interests. Mao repeatedly points out that although militarily strong, the basic political weakness of the Kuomintang and the Japanese armies lay in their isolation from the masses.

The operational principles of Mao Tse-tung's military thinking were developed over a long period of time, reflecting the gradual maturing of the Red Army. The undeviating line in all military operations was summed up in three propositions: "we should resolutely fight a decisive engagement in every campaign or battle in which we are sure of victory; we should avoid a decisive engagement in every campaign or battle in which we are not sure of victory; and we should resolutely avoid a strategically decisive engagement on which the fate of the whole nation is staked." [17]

The overwhelming power of the enemy and the uneven development of the country dictated the conclusion that the revolutionary struggle would have to be protracted in nature. A protracted war undergoes (from the standpoint of the revolutionaries) three stages of development: strategic defensive, strategic stalemate, and strategic counteroffensive. Being weak, Mao argued, the revolutionaries were bound to lose ground in the initial phase of the conflict. In the meantime, it was necessary to develop a war of maneuver over a vast territory, to harass the enemy and undermine his effectiveness and morale. This required mass political mobilization, a united front of "the whole people," and the development of peasant guerrilla warfare on a national scale. Having attained sufficient strength through these means, the revolutionaries would then launch a counteroffensive to destroy the enemy. Given the necessary time, Mao insisted, a transforma-

[16] "On the Reissue of the Three Main Rules of Discipline and the Eight Points for Attentions—Instruction of the General Headquarters of the Chinese People's Liberation Army" (October, 1947), IV, 155.
[17] "On Protracted War," op. cit., p. 180.

tion in the balance of forces between the revolutionaries and their enemy was bound to take place.

The most important form of armed struggle in a colonial and semi-colonial country is guerrilla warfare. A main requirement of protracted war is to develop popular, mass guerrilla warfare to consolidate one's own position and undermine the effectiveness of the enemy. The operational principles of guerrilla warfare have been summarized by Mao Tse-tung on a number of occasions. The most important set of tenets takes the shape of a well-known formula: "The enemy advances, we retreat; the enemy camps, we harass; the enemy tires, we attack; the enemy retreats, we pursue." [18]

Guerrilla warfare is the weapon of the militarily weak; it is fought vis-à-vis a superior enemy. The major task in such warfare is the preservation of one's effective strength, not the holding of the cities. Mao argues that since guerrilla warfare requires space for maneuvering, it would not be feasible in a small country such as Belgium. Geographic limitations, however, may be overcome by a variety of conditions, among them, inept domestic government or foreign support of the guerrillas.

The principal use of guerrilla warfare is not in destroying the enemy but in harassing him, confusing him, disrupting his lines of communication, forcing him to disperse his strength, and most importantly perhaps, undermining his morale. Destruction of the enemy takes place through conventional warfare. Guerrilla warfare, in other words, is not a substitute for regular warfare.

THE GLOBAL DIMENSION. The Chinese revolution, Mao Tse-tung has said, is an integral aspect of an epoch of world upheaval that began with the Russian October Revolution of 1917. The October Revolution, he argues, changed the course of world history and introduced an era destined to culminate in the victory of the proletarian revolution at the global level. The Chinese revolution, furthermore, extended and deepened the influence of the Russian revolution. The significance of the Chinese revolution, according to Mao, lies not only in carrying forward the tradition of the October Revolution but also in its special attraction for, and applicability to, other colonial and semicolonial countries. The Chinese revolution, in other words, is held up as a model for backward countries.

In recent years, the Chinese communists have sought to project on the global level the entire revolutionary strategy of Mao Tse-tung. The most authoritative attempt was undertaken by the Chinese defense minister, Lin Piao (now Mao's heir apparent), in September, 1965. In a document of major importance, Marshal Lin insisted that "Mao Tse-tung's theory of the establishment of rural revolutionary base areas and the encirclement

[18] "A Single Spark Can Start a Prairie Fire" (January, 1930), I, 124.

of the cities from the countryside is one of outstanding and universal practical importance for the present revolutionary struggles of all the oppressed nations and peoples." He added:

Taking the entire globe, if North America and Western Europe can be called "the cities of the world," then Asia, Africa and Latin America constitute "the rural areas of the world." . . . In a sense, the contemporary world revolution also presents a picture of the encirclement of cities by the rural areas. In the final analysis, the whole cause of world revolution hinges on the revolutionary struggles of the Asian, African and Latin American peoples who make up the overwhelming majority of the world's population. The socialist countries should regard it as their internationalist duty to support the people's revolutionary struggles in Asia, Africa and Latin America.[19]

Such is the Chinese desire to universalize the revolutionary strategy of Mao Tse-tung. What worked in the domestic arena, it is contended, can be extended and operationalized at the international level. This view leaves aside the elementary problem of China's inability to control the foreign policies of other countries or to dictate a common posture to be adopted vis-à-vis the "imperialist powers."

North Vietnam

Conditions in Vietnam

The Vietminh revolution of 1946–54 was an intense nationalistic response to the long French domination of Indochina. Vietnam was a unified and centralized nation by 1802. With the coming of the French colonial wars in 1858–83, however, Vietnam lost its name, unity, and independence. For approximately eighty years it was known as Tonkin (the North), Annam (the Center), and Cochinchina (the South). Throughout this period, an incipient nationalism gathered momentum, which finally burst forth in the World War II period. During the Vietminh assertion of control the alternatives of the Vietnamese people were relatively clear: to follow nationalist albeit communist leaders, or to remain under French colonial control.

A vast array of conditions—economic, psychological, social, political—coalesced to set the stage for the revolution. The major economic difficulties revolved around the French tax and land policies. Taxation was based more on French fiscal needs than on the native population's capacity to contribute. The French had a monopoly on alcohol, salt, opium, and tobacco; the taxes on these products provided a significant portion of the colony's revenues. The French settlers paid almost no taxes.

[19] Lin Piao, "Long Live the Victory of People's War!" *Peking Review,* VIII, No. 36 (September 3, 1965), 24.

The French land policies were also poorly conceived. The output re-quired of the peasants drove them into debt or into renting land they had previously owned. The rent and the interest on loans were so high that thousands of debt-ridden peasants were forced off their land.

As the condition of the peasantry progressively worsened, the resultant gap between expectation and achievement created serious psychological frustration throughout the countryside. Conditions were no better in the urban centers, where the educated native elite was confronted with a per-sistent discrepancy between political aspiration and political achievement. John T. McAlister has argued persuasively that a denial of political power to the intelligentsia—and the resultant discrepancy between socioeconomic status and political influence—was a most important source of discontent leading to revolution.[20] Indeed, much of the impetus for the Vietminh revolution came from the relatively small segment of the Vietnamese popu-lation which had experienced some social mobility and economic achieve-ment through colonial institutions, but no commensurate political power.

Revolutions occur, in part, when large segments of an oppressed popula-tion anticipate relief through open defiance of the existing regime and an appeal to an alternative one. Such a realization probably did not become widespread in Vietnam until the Japanese occupation of World War II. The comparative ease with which the Japanese subjugated the French ex-ploded the myth of French military invincibility. During this period various nationalist groups merged into the League for the Independence of Viet-nam, founded by Ho Chi Minh (see below, p. 160). Thus emerged the possibility of a viable indigenous alternative to French colonialism.

French colonialism was phenomenally inefficient and unresponsive in Vietnam. The oft-promised tax and land reforms never materialized. In some seventy years of colonial rule the French constructed dozens of pris-ons but only one university. Only a fraction of the Vietnamese children got even an elementary education. Early attempts to create a University of Hanoi and a native high school system met with strong opposition from the French settlers, chiefly on the grounds that education meant one coolie less and one rebel more. Such measures as were taken—e.g., sending bright Vietnamese students to France—were too little and too late. The victory of Japan over Russia taught the Vietnamese that Western knowledge was a most important weapon for defeating the Western powers. As a result, many natives left for Japan; underground study groups and newspapers began to appear; traveling lecturers began to stress the importance of an

[20] John T. McAlister, Jr., *Viet Nam: The Origins of Revolution* (New York: Al-fred A. Knopf, 1969), esp. pp. 325 ff.

educated native elite—all spurred by the realization that education had been denied as a means of suppression.

Some of the reasons for French callousness and unresponsiveness included the repressive aims of French colonialism, the profit motive of the French settlers, the fear of an educated indigenous elite, and the enforced repression of native Vietnamese political influence.

When Ho Chi Minh proclaimed Vietnamese independence on September 2, 1945, and Bao Dai (the puppet emperor installed by the departing Japanese) abdicated in Ho's favor, support for the Vietminh regime became synonymous with the defense of the country's newfound freedom. There was no viable noncommunist alternative and a return to colonial subjugation was unthinkable. The move toward independence was a crystallization of developments that had taken shape for decades.

Ideology

The most important component of the Vietminh ideology was nationalism. The leadership was communist and Marxist, to be sure, but their motivation as well as that of the masses was first and foremost a desire for national autonomy and the elimination of French colonialism. The ideology was tied to a militant psychology and to communist guerrilla warfare. Communist propaganda untiringly condemned the French imperialists and their desire to keep all peoples of Indochina in slavery, stressed the brotherhood of all peoples and their common cause against colonialism, projected the communists as ceaseless fighters for national independence and people's welfare, and emphasized the army's love for the people and the people's love for the army.

The most critical role throughout the Vietminh revolution was played by Ho Chi Minh. (Vo Nguyen Giap's military contributions are also crucial and will be considered in a later section.) Ho's political career began about World War I. He was a member of the congress that founded the French Socialist Party in 1920; later he traveled to Moscow as a party delegate and remained there to study communism. In 1925 he went to China, ostensibly to work at the Soviet Consulate in Canton but in reality to operate as a Comintern agent. In 1930 he founded the Indochinese Communist Party. From this small party Ho forged an organization that eventually controlled North Vietnam, influenced the Laotian and Cambodian communists, and drove the French out of Indochina. Throughout, he remained in complete control of the Vietminh revolution.

By the mid-1930's the communist ideology was widespread, albeit thinly, throughout Indochina. Attempts were made to infiltrate local governments and to form secret underground organizations where recruitment, training, and propaganda proceeded ceaselessly. At first the inspiration for the communist movement in Vietnam came from Russia. However, since the Soviet emphasis on a proletariat was inappropriate in Vietnam, the communist orientation was altered in favor of the Chinese model.

With the outlawing of communism in Vietnam at the outbreak of World War II, many Vietnamese communists fled to China. In May, 1941, Ho Chi Minh held a conference in Kwangsi province attended by former members of the Indochinese Communist Party as well as by left-wing and nationalist organizations. The conference resulted in the formation of the League for the Independence of Vietnam (the *Viet Nam Doc Lap Dong Minh Hoi*), thereafter commonly known as the Vietminh. Although from the start the Vietminh was led and dominated by the communists, its declared objective was the freedom of Vietnam. Communist ideology was played down because the leaders were in Nationalist China and because they hoped for Chinese as well as American aid. Ho Chi Minh and his fellow communists privately resolved, however, that the Vietminh would follow a communist doctrine.[21] The core of this doctrine was to wage a protracted war based on guerrilla warfare.

On August 7, 1945, a day after the bombing of Hiroshima, Ho Chi Minh announced the formation of the Viet Nam People's Liberation Committee as his provisional government. Giap's guerrillas, now some 5,000 strong, on that day assumed the title of the Viet Nam Liberation Army. Ho and Giap had patterned their forces on the Chinese experience, as described in Mao Tse-tung's writings on guerrilla warfare; this experience emphasized the need for internal political cohesion and solidarity, mobilizing and organizing the masses, and establishing and equipping secure base areas. Mao's Eight Points for Attention (see p. 155 above) became a guideline in all military activity.

With the abrupt surrender of the Japanese, the Vietminh infiltrated quickly into Haiphong, Hanoi, and many other areas in the north in order to claim the powers of government. The Vietminh apparatus worked exceedingly well, and by the end of August, 1945, Ho Chi Minh was in control of all Tonkin and northern Annam except for Hanoi and Haiphong. Ho's victories brought forth a ground swell of nationalist feeling. On September 2, 1945, having just dissolved the old provisional Liberation Committee, he proclaimed the existence of an independent Democratic Republic of Vietnam, and severed all ties with France. The French, however, reestablished control, banned the communist party, and forced Ho to continue the struggle for national independence.

21 See, for example, Edgar O'Ballance, *The Indo-China War, 1945–1954: A Study in Guerrilla Warfare* (London: Faber and Faber, 1964), pp. 38–39.

Strategy and Tactics

The chief objectives of the Vietminh organization were to facilitate political control and to develop an effective military system. Political organization, as we have seen, played a key role in propaganda and mobilization, even though from 1945 to 1951 the party was outlawed and the communists had to operate in a clandestine fashion. In 1951, Ho Chi Minh announced the formation of the *Lao Dong* (Workers Party), which was the first overt appearance of the communist party since its "dissolution" six years earlier.

The military was from the start subject to political control and centralized authority. The political officers were the most influential element in the military structure, having veto power over decisions made by their military counterparts.

Gradually, as the revolution progressed and they became less necessary politically, noncommunists were eased out of the political-military structure. By the end of the 1940's, the Vietminh tightly controlled the political-military apparatus and actively pursued communist objectives consistent with nationalist goals.

The Vietminh military operations were masterminded by General Giap, and their effectiveness rested on several interrelated factors.[22] One set of factors related to Vietminh tactical principles. The first of these was speed of movement. Forces would concentrate rapidly, take position and strike quickly and decisively, and disappear almost instantaneously. Marching at night, the Vietminh would develop a position without alerting the enemy. The attack would take place early in the morning. The assault and the retreat would be executed with maximum speed. The Vietminh were seldom caught without a plan of retreat.

Another principle was that of surprise. A favorite device was to leak inaccurate information to the enemy in order to mislead him into an ambush; to this end, fake documents were planted on double agents, for example. Another means of confusing the enemy was to attach to regional units the numerical designation of regular troops.

A further principle was undermining enemy morale. Communist agents would infiltrate French camps to encourage treason and to spread propaganda. Threats of violence and terror were made against pro-French elements and on occasion bribes were offered for cooperation.

Finally, the Vietminh would attack only if the manpower ratio was in

[22] I rely on George K. Tanham, *Communist Revolutionary Warfare: From the Vietminh to the Viet Cong,* rev. ed. (New York: Frederick A. Praeger, 1967), pp. 73–97.

their favor, or if, through surprise or ruse, they had gained a decisive advantage over the enemy. This involved an intelligence system of an efficiency which the alien French could not command.

The Vietminh intelligence system was quite elaborate. The *Quan Bao* (Military Intelligence) was composed of party members especially chosen for their physical, mental, and moral qualifications and given special training. On occasion these agents used comparatively modern methods (e.g., radio intercept) to obtain information; more characteristically, however, they relied on direct interrogation of both the local civilians and enemy personnel—a task at which they excelled. For example, they would interview prisoners of war several times for long periods and at hours when the prisoners' resistance was lowest. Sometimes they would display sarcasm toward the prisoners, hoping to generate anger and impatience, in the course of which the prisoners would reveal more than they intended. Agents were sometimes slipped into prisoners' cells to pose as other prisoners.

The detailed planning of the Vietminh can be seen in their offensive and defensive tactics. All military operations were based on Mao Tse-tung's formula: "The enemy advances, we retreat; the enemy camps, we harass; the enemy tires, we attack; the enemy retreats, we pursue" (see p. 156 above). Several considerations were important for an offensive: the right choice of time, a careful plan, adequate preparations, and high combat spirit. Guerrillas would watch a garrison over a period of time in order to discover when it was most susceptible to attack. Observers took note of when the guards were changed, which guards were lax in their duties, and when key officers would be absent. The communist intelligence also noted the weakest points of defense, installations to be neutralized, and the best routes of retreat. In preparing for the battle the Vietminh would sometimes rehearse the attack, using specially constructed mockups of the garrisons. The troops were indoctrinated on the importance of their objectives and whipped into high combat spirit.

The Vietminh usually attacked at night because the French were considered inferior night fighters and because their air and artillery support was less effective at that time. Usually the main effort was concentrated on a very narrow front while other smaller groups created diversions. Four groups were frequently used in an offensive. The first manned the heavy weapons and tried to neutralize key enemy positions such as the radio, the command post, the heavy guns. The second group consisted of assault engineers or dynamiters who ran forward or infiltrated the enemy lines and exploded dynamite at critical points. The third group moved forward on a narrow front generally in three waves in an attempt to overwhelm the post. The fourth was a reserve unit that supported the main assault group and picked off the enemy as he counterattacked.

Ambushes were laid for enemy relief forces. As a relief column approached, it met a Vietminh force blocking the road. As the column halted it was met with fire not only from this group but also from two others located on either side of the road and one to the rear of the column.

The typical defense operation was based on Mao's principle of retreat and of luring the enemy into an isolated and hostile environment. Some of the best defense tactics were illustrated in the villages. Individual shelters and hiding places, usually underground and connected by tunnels, were constructed so that a defender could fire from one place, disappear into the ground, and then fire again from another. To add to French confusion each village had a different defense pattern.

The battle of Dien Bien Phu was a most atypical operation in the Vietminh revolution—totally at variance with the strategy of protracted warfare. It was a classic nineteenth-century battle involving a surrounded defense position which sustained constant attacks from artillery and land forces. The French decided to defend Dien Bien Phu because—having two airstrips and serving as intersection of three roads—it could be used to block Vietminh movements in and out of Laos. Moreover, the French believed that General Giap could not divert the number of men necessary to take the fortress and that any positional warfare would hurt the Vietminh more than the French.

From January to May, 1954, the Vietminh pounded the French positions while digging a huge trench around Dien Bien Phu. The French morale remained high, though they were jolted by the intensity and accuracy of Vietminh firepower. Psychological pressures mounted as Giap began to close in simply by digging from the encircling trench toward the French. The final series of assaults began on May 1. Gradually, French positions began to collapse and French outposts were overrun by Vietminh forces. On May 7, the Vietminh broke through the heart of the defenses and the struggle ended that evening.

The battle of Dien Bien Phu was fought consistent with Giap's conviction that a decisive battle may shorten a protracted war.[23] Having been wary of protracted sieges since a series of defeats at the hands of the French in 1951, Giap gradually concluded that a successful general offensive involving positional warfare would make easier the taking of Hanoi and would deal a blow—politically, psychologically, and militarily—suf-

[23] Cf. Chalmers Johnson, "The Third Generation of Guerrilla Warfare," *Asian Survey*, VIII (June, 1968), 435–37.

ficiently crippling to be felt in Paris and thus shorten the duration of the war. This is the chief modification introduced by the Vietminh in the Chinese model of guerrilla communism.

The Geneva negotiations began shortly after the fall of Dien Bien Phu. Giap and his troops had given the Vietminh negotiators a much stronger political and psychological posture vis-à-vis the French.

Cuba

Conditions in Cuba

By the mid-1950's—a few years after the 1952 coup d'état that established the dictatorship of Fulgencio Batista—Cuba was ripe for revolution. Economically, Cuba was a semideveloped or partly developed country occupying an intermediate position between the advanced countries of Western Europe and North America on the one hand and the developing areas of Asia and Africa on the other. The Cuban economy was highly unstable, however, and several economic tensions created strain on the socioeconomic system. One of the main tensions was between the city and the countryside. The countryside lagged seriously behind the cities in housing, education, employment; agrarian reform had no place in Batista's program. The rural population had so little to lose under the Batista regime that once it began to weaken, they hastily abandoned it.

A serious gap between the organized workers and the rootless unemployed accentuated the unstable character of the Cuban economy. The organized worker was able to neutralize to some extent the adversity that accompanied the unstable economy, but the rootless unemployed was completely helpless. The chronic unemployment rate was about nine percent, and the status of a substantial segment of the agricultural work force was dependent upon prices, supply, and demand abroad.

Another tension involved the aspirations of the newer middle class for change and the resignation of the older middle class to the status quo. While the older middle class was not content with the Cuban society of the 1940's and 1950's, it was hesitant openly to espouse or participate in revolution. By contrast, a rising generation of educated Cubans were determined to build a new Cuba and reform its socioeconomic system. It was necessary for the younger generation to convince the older middle class to embrace revolution.

The most serious precipitators of revolution in Cuba, however, were political not economic. The political history of twentieth-century Cuba is the history of dictatorship, corruption, incompetence, and—not surprisingly—little social and economic reform. The Batista administration was no exception. Batista, who first came to power in 1934, remained the leading political figure until 1959, although he relinquished the presidency in 1944 only to regain it in a coup in 1952. Indeed, the most instrumental figure in bringing about a revolution in Cuba was Batista, not Fidel Castro. The persistent tyranny and gross inefficiency of the Batista regime provided the catalyst that made it possible for a charismatic leader to bring together the various disaffected groups in Cuban society. The Cubans turned against Batista for various reasons: because he became overly corrupt, because of his dictatorial policies, out of hopes for a revitalized Cuba. The Batista rule, in short, gave the disaffected groups a symbol on which to focus their frustrations and hopes.

Another condition of political revolution in Cuba was the reaction against foreign domination and control. The United States was deeply involved—economically, politically, and militarily—in Cuban affairs. American investors had enormous holdings in Cuba's national wealth and dominated the Cuban economy. By the late 1950's, however, a trend toward greater Cuban economic autonomy appeared to be emerging. The U.S. control of the sugar industry, for example, had declined from about seventy percent in 1928 to about thirty-seven percent in 1958.[24] The United States continued to retain firm political control, however.

What particularly annoyed the Cuban intellectuals and revolutionaries of the 1950's was the United States' policy—under the Mutual Security program and Mutual Assistance pact—of training the Cuban army and providing extensive military assistance (planes, tanks, ships, missiles, etc.) to the Batista regime—all for the purpose of "hemispheric defense." The revolutionaries protested that U.S. arms were being used to suppress popular sentiment against Batista. Some believed that a secret agreement had been reached between Havana and Washington, according to which Batista was to create the facade of constitutional government in return for accelerated U.S. military support, together with a U.S. pledge to take action against Cuban revolutionary sympathizers soliciting funds and purchasing arms in the United States.

In many ways the actions of the U.S. government at this time helped create or kindle Cuban nationalism and make "Yankee imperialism" a vital force in the closing stages of the Cuban revolution. The exact nature and extent of Cuban nationalism's role in the early stages of the revolution is not altogether clear, however. Some scholars maintain that, although the United States was the natural scapegoat for Cuban troubles, the relative

[24] Theodore Draper, *Castroism: Theory and Practice* (New York: Frederick A. Praeger, 1965), p. 109.

well-being of Cuban society militated against the development of mass anti-American sentiment as a basis for revolutionary activity. Because the Cuban people in general understood the primary goal of the revolution as the ouster of Batista rather than the eradication of American control, nationalism played only a small role in the *beginning* of the revolution. Many of the men who participated in Castro's revolution, however, were weaned on the belief that American imperialism was the major cause of Cuba's shortcomings. They equated socioeconomic reform with national economic independence, to be attained by eliminating foreign influence and remolding the existing system.

Ideology

The ideology of the Cuban revolution is closely identified with Fidel Castro. Born in 1926, Castro showed little interest in politics until 1945, when he entered the University of Havana Law School. There he was exposed to a new generation of Cubans who rebelled against "Cuban decadence" and sought a revitalization of national spirit and public life.

In 1947 Castro joined an expeditionary force of about a thousand men about to sail for the Dominican Republic to overthrow the dictator Trujillo. The invasion was intercepted by frigates of the Cuban navy on orders from the Cuban President, Ramon Grau San Martin, and Castro just managed to escape by swimming ashore. (The tactic of invasion from another land was to be employed later unsuccessfully by a force led by Castro from Mexico against the Batista government in December, 1956.)

In 1952, shortly after his graduation with a law degree, Castro was campaigning for a congressional seat in the upcoming June elections when Batista's coup destroyed his plans for political office. Castro presented a petition to the Supreme Court demanding that the Batista government be declared unconstitutional and illegal, but to no avail.

Castro's special talent lay in his ability to guide a revolution rather than to articulate a well-defined revolutionary ideology. This is consistent with his own perception of himself as a man of action and not an intellectual. Castro's pragmatism permitted him the luxury of molding and remolding his programs to fit changing conditions in Cuba. The relative detachment from a definitive ideology allowed for great latitude to maneuver and to adapt.

The amorphous character of Cuban revolutionary thought makes it difficult to identify *an* ideology of revolution. No single well-defined ideological premise dominated the revolutionary movement. There were various ideologies within the overarching ideology of nationalism, itself largely latent or submerged in the initial phases of the revolution. Theodore Draper believes, for example, that Castroism "has been made up of elements from different traditions and movements; it has mainly contributed means and sought elsewhere for ends." He concludes: "Historically, then, Castroism is a leader in search of a movement, a movement in search of power, and power in search of an ideology. From its origins to today, it has had the same leader, and the same 'road to power,' but it has changed its ideology." [25] Specifically, Castro was a democrat and a nationalist before turning to socialism and Marxism-Leninism.

Throughout the 1950's, Castro consistently attacked the Batista regime and called for a democratic Cuba. He sought constitutional government, land reform, a wider distribution of the national wealth, and an end to corruption and ineptitude. His public appeal for democracy, freedom, and social justice generated popular support throughout Cuba.

Throughout this period the underlying dynamic of Castroism was a latent or submerged nationalism. However, just as Castro could not have come down from the Sierra Maestra in 1959 proclaiming himself a Marxist-Leninist, he could not, in the early stages of the revolution, have expounded nationalism as effectively as he did after attaining power. Although a majority of the Cuban people wanted Batista overthrown, they did not necessarily see Batista as an American puppet. While Castro and his colleagues may have seen the end of U.S. domination as the panacea to Cuba's problems, they apparently realized that the majority of the Cuban people did not share this view. In a word, nationalism played a dual role in the Cuban revolution: it was the rallying cry of the revolutionaries, but for the Cuban people as a whole, it played a latent, submerged role—a role, however, that became manifest as the revolution progressed.

Castro rarely alluded to or manifested familiarity with the works of Marx, Lenin, Mao, and others. As Regis Debray has argued, it was probably advantageous to the Cuban revolution that Castro did not become imprisoned by these works.[26] Castro needed ideological flexibility more than commitment to any formal ideology.

By mid-1960 a definite change was taking place in the ideological posture of the Cuban revolution. At a youth congress in Havana in August 1960, Ernesto Guevara, then Minister of Industries, stated: "What is our ideology? If I were asked whether our revolution is Communist, I would define it as Marxist. Our revolution has discovered by its methods the paths that Marx pointed out." [27]

[25] *Ibid.*, pp. 50, 48–49.
[26] *Revolution in the Revolution? Armed Struggle and Political Struggle in Latin America* (New York: Grove Press, 1967), pp. 98 ff.
[27] Quoted in Theodore Draper, *Castro's Revolution: Myths and Realities* (New York: Frederick A. Praeger, 1962), p. 3.

At about the same time Castro seems to have concluded that the goals of his revolution would not be attained unless the Cuban economy was socialized. Thus in October, 1960, the Castro regime nationalized most Cuban, American, and Cuban-American enterprises. In a matter of days, virtually the entire Cuban bourgeoisie was eliminated. Castro stated: "We ourselves don't know quite what to call what we are building, and we don't care. It is, of course, socialism of a sort." [28]

On December 2, 1961, Castro delivered his famous "I am a Marxist-Leninist" address. The official adoption of Marxism-Leninism was consistent with Castro's programs of extensive land reform, radical redistribution of wealth, eradication of illiteracy and disease, and the socialization of the economy. He legitimized Marxism-Leninism in terms of the evolving needs of the Cuban society, not in terms of an abstract commitment to that ideology.

Castro, then, used certain ideologies (democracy and nationalism) to capture popular support and attain political power, and certain other ideologies (socialism and Marxism-Leninism) to retain and solidify his political control. Instead of adhering to any definite ideological posture, which would have restricted his freedom of movement and may even have conflicted with the unique characteristics of Cuban society, Castro subscribed to an amorphous ideological baggage.

Strategy and Tactics

The Cuban revolution may be said to have been formally launched with Castro's attack on the Moncada army post on July 26, 1953, seventeen months after Batista's seizure of power. Though unsuccessful, this event popularized Castro's movement, enabled him to emerge for the first time as an independent political figure with a personal following, and gave the "26th of July Movement" its name.

Sentenced to a fifteen-year prison term for anti-Batista activities, Castro was released in May, 1955, under a general amnesty. He soon departed for Mexico, where he trained an expeditionary force for a future invasion of Cuba. From Mexico he planned, in collaboration with local rebels, a November 30th, 1956, uprising in Oriente province to coincide with a planned invasion of Cuba. But the invasion was delayed, and Castro and his men did not land until December 2, 1956. By that time, Batista's army was fully alerted and the invasion forces were immediately crushed. Castro and eleven of his men managed to escape into the Sierra Maestra.

On March 12, 1958, Castro addressed the Cuban people over the rebel radio, declaring "total war" against Batista and calling for a general strike

[28] *Ibid.*, p. 10.

on April 9. The strike failed because, among other things, the trade unions, who were prospering under Batista, refused to participate. The abortive strike prompted Batista to initiate massive counterterror against the revolutionaries, killing many innocent Cubans and eroding middle-class and other support for the ruling regime.

The failure of the general strike propelled Castro toward guerrilla warfare. While some writers, especially Che Guevara, have made guerrilla warfare into the key revolutionary activity in all Latin America, Castro accepted it only after other tactics had failed—and this near the end of the struggle. Only after failing in two conventional-type attacks and the general strike did Castro "adopt" guerrilla warfare as his primary tactic.

Batista's response to guerrilla warfare was a more intensive program of counterterror. The army and secret police struck back indiscriminately and senselessly. The orgy of murders, tortures, and brutalities made life intolerable for the Cuban people. The working class, the middle class, and the intellectuals turned anti-Batista. Even the Batista army became demoralized and lost its combat effectiveness. By mid-1959 the revulsion against the Batista regime was virtually total.

Fidel Castro, Che Guevara, and Regis Debray have all attempted to theorize about the Cuban revolution and to extend their generalization to Latin America as a whole. Theodore Draper has usefully summarized Castro's basic insights in the following terms:

1. "The masses make history," but they must be "launched into the battle" by "revolutionary leaders and organizations."

2. The Cuban masses had been launched into the struggle by "four, five, six, or seven" guerrillas.

3. The "objective conditions" for such a struggle exist in "the immense majority of Latin American countries" and only the "subjective conditions"—that is, the "four, five, six, or seven" willing to launch the armed struggle—are lacking.

4. "Peaceful transition" may be "possible," but there is not a single case of it on record, and in any event, armed struggle must take place in most Latin American countries.[29]

In this way Castro stakes out—as had Mao Tse-tung before him—a claim both to the uniqueness of the Cuban revolution and its applicability to other Latin American societies where similar conditions exist.

Che Guevara derives three fundamental lessons from the Cuban revolution, applicable to all Latin America:

1. Popular forces can win a war against the army.

2. It is not necessary to wait until all conditions for making revolution exist; the insurrection can create them.

[29] Draper, *Castroism* (above, n. 24), pp. 40–41.

3. In the underdeveloped America the countryside is the basic area for armed fighting.[30]

The second point departs sharply from Mao's conception of protracted warfare, especially the stage of strategic defensive. According to Guevara, the "necessary minimum" for revolutionary activity is that the "people must see clearly the futility of maintaining the fight for social goals within the framework of civil debate." [31]

Perhaps the most far-reaching contribution to Cuban (and Latin American) revolutionary theory has been made by Regis Debray, a French philosophy student and an admirer of the Cuban experience. Debray's book *Revolution in the Revolution?* is purportedly based directly upon the Cuban experience and has been formally sanctioned by Fidel Castro himself.

According to Debray, the Cuban experience demonstrates that revolution in Latin America cannot follow the pattern established by either the Bolshevik or the Chinese revolutions. The Cuban revolution is a "revolution in the revolution," different from all revolutions before it. Debray lists four "imported political concepts" that, if employed, would lead to failure in Latin America. These are armed self-defense, armed propaganda, a fixed guerrilla base, and the control of the party over the military.

Armed self-defense fails because militarily this strategy is not mobile, does not take the initiative, and is not consciously intent on the conquest of political power as a primary objective. This strategy gives the government forces the initiative and enhances their ability to cut off supplies to the defense areas, bomb these areas, and isolate them. In short, this strategy denies the guerrillas their proper role as an active revolutionary force.

Armed propaganda fails as a strategy because the rural population of Latin America, though extensive, is sparse and lives in remote areas. While this method can be used in the revolutionary program, it must follow, not precede, military action. The best propaganda technique, according to Debray, is military activity, which serves to destroy the supposed invincibility of the government troops and establishes the military objectives of the guerrillas.

There can be no fixed guerrilla bases in Latin America because of the absence of suitable territory in most countries, the low density of rural population, the absence of common borders with friendly countries, the numerical superiority of government forces and their command of airborne troops and efficient communication systems. The guerrilla force must be extremely mobile; and it should establish bases, as in Cuba, only

[30] *Guerrilla Warfare* (New York: Vintage Books, 1961), p. 1.
[31] *Ibid.,* p. 2.

after many months of fighting, when the security of the base can be guaranteed.

The relationship between the party and the guerrillas, finally, is the most significant and novel concept in the Cuban revolution. Not until the Cuban experience did anyone question the supremacy of the party in all matters of revolution. Since then Castro and other Latin American revolutionaries have embraced the belief that the Marxist-Leninist party need not necessarily serve as the political vanguard. As Debray states, "There is no exclusive ownership of the revolution." [32]

Although theoretical and historical orthodoxy has asserted the supremacy of the party over the army, Debray believes, "historical circumstances have not permitted Latin American Communist Parties, for the most part, to take root or develop in the same way." [33] Just as Mao and Giap modified Lenin's theories to fit the conditions of China and Vietnam, it is Debray's contention that Castro had to modify the theories of Mao and Giap to fit Cuba. The Cuban example is a direct reversal of Mao Tse-tung's dictum that under all conditions "the Party commands the gun, and the gun must never be allowed to command the party" (see p. 154 above). Successful revolutionary activity in Latin America requires the opposite practice: the political apparatus must be controlled by the military. While the success of the revolution lies in the realization that guerrilla warfare is essentially political, the party and the guerrilla must become one and the same, with the guerrilla in command.

Successful execution of revolutionary policies demands a unified command with responsibility to maximize the effective use of scarce resources. The guerrilla cannot tolerate a duality of functions and powers, but must become the political as well as military vanguard of the people. In Latin America today, as shown by the Cuban revolution, it is necessary for the party and the military to become unified in the guerrilla movement: *"The guerrilla is the party in embryo."* [34] This union of Marxist theory and new revolutionary practice is the novelty of the Cuban revolution, says Debray. The armed destruction of the enemy—the public demonstration of his fallibility—is the most effective propaganda for the local population. Consequently, in Latin America today, the chief concern must be the development of guerrilla forces and not the strengthening of political parties.

In Cuba, Debray points out, military and political leadership are combined in the person of Fidel Castro. He quotes Castro: "Who will make the revolution in Latin America? The people, the revolutionaries, with or

[32] *Revolution in the Revolution?* (above, n. 26), p. 125.
[33] *Ibid.*, p. 101.
[34] *Ibid.*, p. 106. Italics in original.

without a party." [35] Castro's thesis, Debray believes, is not that there can
be a revolution without a vanguard, but that the vanguard need not necessarily be the Marxist-Leninist party. "In Cuba it was not the party that was
the directive nucleus of the popular army, as it had been in Vietnam according to Giap; the Rebel Army was the leading nucleus of the party, the
nucleus that created it." This, Debray concludes, is Cuba's "decisive contribution to international revolutionary experience and to Marxism-Leninism." [36]

The deviations in orthodoxy can be explained and justified, according
to Debray, by the unique conditions of Latin America. Each particular
revolution must be coordinated by the contingencies forced upon it by the
environment. Flexibility of response rather than rigidity of doctrine must
prevail. The Cuban example, and not the Russian or the Chinese, is the
appropriate one for Latin America. While there cannot be another Cuban
revolution, its lessons are of the most immediate relevance for Latin American countries.

Conclusion

The Russian Revolution established communism in Europe, the Chinese
Revolution in Asia, and the Cuban Revolution in Latin America. Guerrilla
communism as a revolutionary doctrine was first formulated during the
Chinese revolution, modified in the Vietminh experience, and challenged
in Cuba. The conditions of revolution were similar in all three countries
except that economic factors played a less prominent role in Cuba than
in China and Vietnam. The ideology of revolution was nationalist and
communist in all three instances except that the Cuban revolutionary ideology was much more amorphous than the others. All three ideologies left
room for maneuver and compromise. In all three revolutions communism
was sometimes soft-pedaled in order to maximize popular support and
avoid alienating hostile forces domestically and internationally. Each revolution gave birth to a political hero (Mao, Ho, and Castro) and a corresponding military hero (Chu Teh, Giap, and Guevara, respectively).

Mao Tse-tung's statement of guerrilla communism revolves around the
key concepts of imperialism, united front, and protracted military struggle.
Since the country is unevenly developed and since the combined power of
imperialism and the domestic reactionary classes is concentrated in the
urban centers, he concludes, the revolutionaries must retreat to the countryside, establish inaccessible bases in the most rugged areas, gradually consolidate and strengthen their position, surround the cities, and gradually

[35] *Ibid.*, p. 98.
[36] *Ibid.*, p. 106.

choke the enemy to death. The core of this strategy is a protracted military conflict based on peasant guerrilla warfare, mobilization and organization of the local population, the fanning of their patriotism and nationalism, and complete reliance on them for food, supplies, and manpower. Mao proclaims this strategy as a model universally applicable to all colonial countries.

The Vietminh revolution and the Vietminh leaders closely followed the Chinese pattern, though reliance on nationalism and anti-imperialism was probably more systematic and self-conscious in Vietnam than in China. The chief strategic departure from the Chinese model, crystallized in the battle of Dien Bien Phu, stemmed from Giap's conviction that a decisive battle at the right time and place would generate sufficient political, psychological, and military impact to demoralize the enemy and shorten the duration of the revolution.

The Cuban revolution and the Cuban leaders posed a sharp challenge to the Chinese prototype of guerrilla communism. Castro, Guevara, and Debray all believe that revolution in Latin America cannot follow the pattern established by either the Bolshevik or the Chinese revolutions. Just as Mao and Giap revised Lenin's theories to fit conditions in China and Vietnam, the Cuban leaders changed the theories of Mao and Giap to fit conditions in Cuba. Specifically, they reversed the relationship between the military and the political, and stressed the primacy of the military in guiding and directing revolution.

The Chinese and Vietminh revolutions were based almost exclusively upon the peasantry, whereas in Cuba peasants played an insignificant role. The Cuban revolutionary struggle was led by a relatively small group of armed men who captured the sympathy and support of the urban middle class. Without the desertion of the middle class, the Batista regime would probably have survived. And yet, having come to power and having declared himself a Marxist-Leninist, Castro had no alternative but to downgrade the role and status of the middle class.

The Chinese reaction to the Cuban challenge to Mao's revolutionary prototype was quite predictable. An unsigned article in the official weekly *Peking Review* approvingly discussed a statement by the Communist party of France denouncing the "fallacies of Regis Debray." The Chinese portrayed Debray's book as "a big counter-revolutionary mystification and . . . in essence an attack on Marxism-Leninism, Mao Tse-tung's thought." They dismissed Debray's "purely military viewpoint" and his "preposterous" attack upon the "correct theories of Chairman Mao Tse-tung's." [37]

[37] See "Marxism-Leninism, Mao Tse-tung's Thought, Is Universal Truth," *Peking Review*, XI, No. 30 (July 26, 1968), pp. 11–12.

Che Guevara's failure in Bolivia does, however, indicate possible weaknesses in the Cuban revolutionary strategy as conceptualized by Castro, Debray, and Guevara. It demonstrates that—however dedicated to proclaimed values of freedom and humanity—a small guerrilla force, in an unfamiliar and hostile environment, isolated from a distrustful local population whose language the guerrillas did not speak, and relentlessly pursued by a vastly superior government force trained by a modern military equipped with an array of counterguerrilla techniques—such a force is doomed to defeat. But all this is beyond the immediate focus of the present chapter.

Bibliography

China

Brandt, Conrad, Benjamin Schwartz, and John K. Fairbank. *A Documentary History of Chinese Communism*. Cambridge: Harvard University Press, 1952.

Ch'en, Jerome, *Mao and the Chinese Revolution*. New York: Oxford University Press, 1964.

Cohen, Arthur A. *The Communism of Mao Tse-tung*. Chicago: University of Chicago Press, 1964.

Johnson, Chalmers A. *Peasant Nationalism and Communist Power: The Emergence of Revolutionary China, 1937–45*. Stanford: Stanford University Press, 1962.

Mao Tse-tung. *Selected Works of Mao Tse-tung*. 4 vols. Peking: Foreign Languages Press, 1961–65.

Rejai, Mostafa, ed. *Mao Tse-tung on Revolution and War*. New York: Doubleday, 1969.

Scharm, Stuart, ed. *The Political Thought of Mao Tse-tung*. New York: Frederick A. Praeger, 1963.

Schurmann, Franz, and Orville Schell. *The China Reader*. 3 vols. New York: Random House, 1967.

Schwartz, Benjamin I. *Chinese Communism and the Rise of Mao*. Cambridge: Harvard University Press, 1952.

Snow, Edgar. *Red Star Over China*. New York: Grove Press, 1961.

North Vietnam

Buttinger, Joseph. *Vietnam: A Political History*. New York: Frederick A. Praeger, 1968.

Fall, Bernard, ed. *Ho Chi Minh on Revolution*. New York: Frederick A. Praeger, 1967.

Fall, Bernard. *Street Without Joy: Insurgency in Indochina, 1946–1963*. Harrisburg, Pa.: Stackpole, 1964.

Fall, Bernard. *The Two Vietnams: A Political and Military Analysis.* New York: Frederick A. Praeger, 1967.

Fall, Bernard. *The Vietminh Regime.* New York: The Institute of Pacific Relations, 1956.

Giap, Vo Nguyen. *People's War, People's Army.* New York: Bantam Books, 1968.

Hoang Van Chi. *From Colonialism to Communism: A Case History of North Vietnam.* New York: Frederick A. Praeger, 1964.

Honey, J. P. *Communism in North Vietnam.* Cambridge: The M.I.T. Press, 1963.

McAlister, John T., Jr. *Viet Nam: The Origins of Revolution.* New York: Alfred A. Knopf, 1969.

O'Ballance, Edgar. *The Indo-China War, 1945–1954.* London: Faber and Faber, 1964.

Tanham, George K. *Communist Revolutionary Warfare: From the Vietminh to the Viet Cong.* New York: Frederick A. Praeger, 1968.

Cuba

Debray, Regis. *Revolution in the Revolution?* New York: Grove Press, 1967.

Draper, Theodore. *Castroism: Theory and Practice.* New York: Frederick A. Praeger, 1965.

Draper, Theodore. *Castro's Revolution: Myths and Realities.* New York: Frederick A. Praeger, 1962.

Guevara, Ernesto. *Guerrilla Warfare.* New York: Vintage Books, 1961.

Guevara, Ernesto. *Reminiscences of the Cuban Revolutionary War.* New York: Grove Press, 1968.

Huberman, Leo, and Paul M. Sweezy. *Cuba: Anatomy of a Revolution.* New York: Monthly Review Press, 1961.

Matthews, Herbert L. *Castro: A Political Biography.* London: Allen Lane, 1969.

Mills, C. Wright. *Listen Yankee: Revolution in Cuba.* New York: Ballantine Books, 1960.

Plank, John, ed. *Cuba and the United States.* Washington: The Brookings Institution, 1967.

Smith, Robert. *The United States and Cuba: Business and Diplomacy, 1917–1960.* New York: Bookman Associates, 1960.

Suarez, Andres. *Cuba: Castroism and Communism, 1951–1966.* Cambridge: The M.I.T. Press, 1967.

Taber, Robert. *M-26: Biography of a Revolution.* New York: Lyle Stuart, 1961.

Chapter 6

Democracy:
A Faith in the Common Man

Democracy: Sacred and Profaned

Democracy—the word, the values, the institutions and practices—has won widespread acceptance only in this century, despite an etymology traced back to the ancient Greeks. And even though the twentieth century has been labeled the age of faith in the common man,[1] it has not been kind to that belief. Instead, democracy often has been subjected to ridicule of its tenets, attacks upon its institutions, condemnation of its consequences, prostitution of its name, obfuscation of its meaning, doubts about its contemporary revelance, and loss of faith in its possibility. Much of the international conflict of our times has been between democracy and its antitheses.

A powerful and emotion-laden word-symbol, "democracy" is both profaned and held sacred. It has been profaned by modern elitists and totalitarians alike, attacking its values as false and its institutions as unworkable. They have condemned the democratic principles of political equality and popular political participation as leading to "mediocracy," and scorned democracy's predominant concern with individual freedom as "atomistic" and "anarchic." In opposition, they have offered a statist system in which all-encompassing powers are concentrated in a small, self-selected, and self-perpetuating elite. The German Nazis and Italian fas-

[1] Carl J. Friedrich, *The New Belief in the Common Man* (Boston: Little, Brown, 1942).

cists, for example, railed against "individualistic" and "vulgar" democracy for bringing their countries to ruin after World War I, and attacked the alleged impotencies of the Western democracies. The communists, on the other hand, have condemned "bourgeois democracy" as a sham political structure engineered by the capitalists to facilitate their continued exploitation of the workers; they assail the Western imperialist powers for exploiting their economic, if not political, empires.

Indeed, twentieth-century man has experienced profound misgivings about the contemporary viability of democracy. Doubts and denials as to its workability are voiced ironically in relation to both the developed and developing nations. Regarding the developed nation, it is said that the complexities and requirements of an advanced society (urbanized, industrialized, technologized, bureaucratized) render democracy impossible of execution and undesirable in its effects. What is needed is expertise not Jacksonian equalitarianism, technical skills not common sense, central planning not Jeffersonian localism, big administrative organization not town meetings, computerized decisions not popular referenda.

Less developed nations are characterized as not having the minimum political, economic, and social conditions prerequisite to democracy. They lack national unity, consensus on national values and goals, adequate communications and literacy to make political discussion possible and political choice meaningful, traditions of political self-restraint to permit stable and peaceful political competition and transitions of political power, and enough economic well-being to soften conflict and build a stabilizing middle class. Moreover, the argument continues, a strong, centralized, and authoritarian government is needed to establish these essential preconditions to democracy.

Thus while much of the twentieth century has been marked by a contagious belief in the common man's capacity to achieve a just society and humane progress through democratic politics, it also is marred by disillusionment with that belief. We experience what the political scientist Neal Riemer aptly calls an "unhappy democratic consciousness."

If we perceive rightly the terrors of the twentieth century, it is hard to believe in rationality, intelligence, and good will, in the responsible use of freedom, in the Brotherhood of Man—let alone the Fatherhood of God. If we perceive these terrors rightly, we see man fleeing from freedom to totalitarian dictatorship; we see irrational hate, lust, greed, and pride leading to aggression at home and abroad under communism, fascism, apartheidism, nativism, imperialism; we see good will mocked, intelligence deprecated, and justice scorned.[2]

[2] Neal Riemer, *The Revival of Democratic Theory* (New York: Appleton-Century-Crofts, 1962), p. 36.

The twentieth century also has brought confusion to the meaning of "democracy" (for although democracy, like virtue, is often deprecated, few dare reject its label). To be sure, the John Birch Society and its radical right allies proclaim that democracy "has never worked satisfactorily as a form of government," and are spurred hot-haste to alert Americans to the subtle communist conspiracy "to convince the American people that we are supposed to be a democracy." [3] But today few people do not profess to be democrats; few countries disclaim the title "democracy"; and few regimes do not assert that popular support and rule in the interests of the people are the bases of their legitimacy. Thus, the Nazis in Germany recited the ills of democracy but sought plebiscitary democracy by demonstrations of mass acclaim, and "elections" as evidence of virtually unanimous consent to Hitler's regime. Mussolini contemptuously dismissed democratic values and institutions but declared that "if democracy means not to relegate the people to the periphery of the State, then Fascism could be defined as an 'organized, centralized, authoritarian democracy.' " [4] While the communists employ "bourgeois" or "formal democracy" as an epithet, they christen their totalitarian single-party states as "socialist" or "people's democracies." Mao Tse-tung assaults Western democracy but declares that the first stage of the communist revolution in China is "no longer democracy in a general sense, but democracy of the Chinese type, a new and special type—New Democracy." "The state system—joint dictatorship of all revolutionary classes. The political structure—democratic centralism. This is New Democratic government; this is a republic of New Democracy. . . ." [5]

Among the newly independent and developing nations similar ingenuity has been used to keep the name "democracy" while prefacing it with qualifying adjectives to explain compromising political arrangements. Sukarno, when President of Indonesia, condemned Western "free fight" democracy "where half plus one is always right" and called upon his people "to change it into Indonesian democracy, guided democracy, or democracy with leadership." [6] Former President Ayub Khan of Pakistan, having decided that democratic institutions of national scope were beyond the capacities of his people, established a scheme of basic democracies [7]

[3] Cited in Gene Grove, *Inside the John Birch Society* (Greenwich, Conn.: Fawcett Publications, 1961), pp. 98, 100.

[4] Cited in Dell G. Hitchner and William H. Harbold, *Modern Government: A Survey of Political Science* (New York: Dodd, Mead, 1962), p. 98.

[5] Cited in Paul E. Sigmund, Jr., *The Ideologies of the Developing Nations* (New York: Frederick A. Praeger, 1963), pp. 44, 50—from *On New Democracy* (Peking: Foreign Languages Press, 1960).

[6] Cited in Sigmund, *ibid.*, p. 62—from a lecture given to students of Hasanuddin University on October 31, 1958.

[7] See in Sigmund, *ibid.*, pp. 107–120.

at the level of the local community. Egypt's Nasser spoke of "old, fake democracy," banned all political parties, and transformed his party into a National Union: "a national and patriotic organization" to unify Egypt for the success of its political and social revolutions. This he called "party-less democracy"—"a new experiment which will guard us at the same time against the faults of the single party and against the inconveniences of a system of several parties—an experiment which answers the need for an organism with which all the children of the nation will be associated." [8] In Africa, Sekou Toure of Guinea has defined "dictatorship" as "the concentration of powers exercised by a man or group of men over the whole," and "democracy" as "the exercise of national sovereignty by the people." [9] Coupling the words, he calls his regime "democratic dictatorship." And, as a final example, Cuba's Castro describes his political order as "true democracy"—"the leadership of the state through a party." [10]

Since lip service to the honorific character and emotional symbolism of democracy promotes greater popular support for rulers and more willing participation in the achievement of national goals, nondemocratic rulers find it hard to forego the name and at least the stage props of democracy: if not the solemn and solitary act of casting ballots and the dreary task of counting them, then at least the pageantry of mass meetings with the psychedelia of banners flying, the blare of bands playing, the fever of frenzied oratory, and the crowds chanting their version of "unanimous consent."

Thus, while democracy has been profaned it has remained symbolically sacred, and, as a consequence, has become confused. Our task will be to achieve some clarity as to the meaning, framework of ideas, and interface between the ideal and reality of democracy.

The Foundations of Democracy

Democracy is a political system in which "the people" (citizenry) voluntarily consent to and are major participants in their governance. In elementary analysis, political systems may be classified in terms of the locus and scope of political power. In a democratic system, the citizenry hold the controlling shares of political power; and public authority is limited, recognizing a relatively broad area of private freedom. Democracy, in

[8] Cited in Sigmund, *ibid.*, p. 129—from a speech delivered at the opening of the High Dam project on November 26, 1959.

[9] Cited in Sigmund, *ibid.*, pp. 162 and 163—from *La Lutte du Parti Democratique de Guinee pour l'Emancipation Africaine* (Conakry: Imprimerie Nationale, 1959).

[10] Cited by Tad Szulc, "This is Castro—Three Years After," *The New York Times Magazine*, December 31, 1968, p. 26—from a speech of December 2, 1961.

this sense, is a system of self-determination: in the private sphere significant areas of life are left to individual freedom of choice; in the public sphere the citizens, directly or indirectly, determine the offices and policies of government. This admittedly general definition of "democracy" leads to the questions: (1) what are the normative and empirical assumptions on which democracy is founded? and (2) what are the prescriptive principles that translate democracy into a working political order?

The Basic Normative and Empirical Assumptions of Democracy

At the very foundation of democracy is the primary value of individualism. The values and procedures of democracy begin and end with the individual, and the basic unit of a democratic society is the individual human being defined as a *person* with a separate identity and worth. The individualism of democracy contrasts sharply with the corporatism of other political systems, which fixes men in the mass—their identities and worths deriving from their membership in a larger social whole.

Based upon this initial value, democrats assert and accept the value of each individual's self-fulfillment as the ultimate purpose to be served by the state. As stated by Sir Ernest Barker, "The development of the capacities of personality, in its members, is the ultimate purpose served by the state and the final political value." [11] Therefore, the democratic society is organized to exclude barriers to individual self-development.

Democracy is, in fact, built upon a structure of postulates about the nature of man. Historically, democrats have generally believed that men are by nature rational, moral, free, endowed with rights, and equal. The last of these postulates—that men are equal—should be elaborated upon. Democrats do not posit an actual equality of human beings in their physical, intellectual, and emotional endowments. Rather, they assume that each man is the equal of every other man in possessing moral and rational faculties, freedom and rights, power and capacity to share in his governance, and the claim to an opportunity for self-realization. Furthermore, they assume that despite wide variations in the human condition all men possess·potentialities that merit equal respect, and that each man should have an equal opportunity to achieve his potential. Democracy thus is not based on individualism alone but also on *individuality*—on recognition of and respect for the uniqueness of each man. Indeed, the equality of democracy is an equality of differences not of sameness.

Men achieve their individualism, self-realization, freedom and equality, of course, in society with its ordered relationships and political institu-

[11] *Principles of Social and Political Theory* (Oxford: Oxford University Press, 1951), p. 136.

tions. Therefore, it is necessary to face the issue of the relationship between freedom and authority, equality and rulership, and to ask what political system, what structure of political ideas and institutions, best serves these values and best conforms to the nature and potential of man. The advocates of democracy believe and insist that their preferred system best accords with man's minimal needs and maximum capacities.

The Fundamental Principles of Democracy

The principles outlined below flesh out the meaning of democracy. The structure includes the basic ideas which comprise traditional democratic ideology—the ideas of democratic thinkers responsible for the first or classical formulations of democracy. The structure undergirds an *ideal* political order, in which the people hold ultimately decisive political power and enjoy a relatively broad area of private freedom.

POPULAR SOVEREIGNTY. The first principle of democracy is that of popular sovereignty: the idea that ultimate political power—political power in its original form—resides in each man and in all men. As stated by John Locke in his *Second Treatise of Civil Government,* "To understand political power aright, and derive it from its original, we must consider what estate all men are naturally in, and that is, a state of perfect freedom to order their actions, and dispose of their possessions and persons as they think fit, within the bounds of the law of Nature, without asking leave or depending upon the will of any other man."

Thus, it is assumed that man is not born subject to a superior human authority but rather is born with the power and capacity to regulate his adult life and behavior. This principle was traditionally expressed through a scheme of a universal and transcendent (superior) natural law. Space limitations preclude examination of the debate over natural law. Suffice it to say that popular sovereignty has been seen as a necessary and logical starting point for democracy. If man is to be free and politically self-governing, and if he is to be so as a matter of right and not at the sufferance of another, then power must be his in the first place—by the very nature of his existence. This has been a fundamental article of democratic faith.

HUMAN FREEDOM IN SOCIETY. Democrats insist that each individual should have the liberty and opportunity to formulate and pursue his own legitimate purposes. As Locke put it, man's right to "his life, liberty, and estate" is his "property." Freedom demands the absence of unreasonable external restraints and the presence of meaningful opportunity. In a democratic society, the individual is to have the largest possible measure of liberty and opportunity to speak, to act, to decide. Moreover, a causal relationship is postulated between freedom and social progress. The freedom of its citizens permits a society to be more inventive, productive, moral, and interesting than one in which conscience, speech, and action are ordered by some higher authority. On the other hand, freedom is based on the limitations as well as the capacities of men. It recognizes that all men are fallible, and that, therefore, no state of knowledge can be regarded as unqualifiedly true, no set of conditions can be regarded as inevitable and permanent, and no person or group of persons can be regarded as having a monopoly on truth, wisdom, or the ability to rule. As the ethics and method of science are instruments of self-correction and progress in knowledge, so the ethics and method of freedom are instruments of self-correction and progress in a democratic society.

Democrats, of course, recognize that liberty in society cannot be absolute, and that no man can be wholly free. Absolute liberty becomes anarchy since each person is the final arbiter of his own rights; it is also the effective rule of the strong over the weak. The exercise of freedom must be compatible with the equal rights of others, including the right to a reasonable amount of security. However, democratic restraints are minimal, and the law which limits liberty is equitably and self-imposed. In setting the boundaries on liberty, John Stuart Mill wrote in *On Liberty:* ". . . the sole end for which mankind are warranted, individually or collectively, in interfering with the liberty of action of any of their number, is self-protection. That the only purpose for which power can be rightfully exercised over any member of a civilized community, against his will, is to prevent harm to others."

Finally, the principle of freedom must apply directly to the politics of a democratic society. Freedom of thought, expression, and action must be guaranteed in political affairs. Men must have free access to political information; be free to hold and express political ideas; support, criticize, and oppose political figures and programs; associate for political purposes; seek political influence and public office; and cast free ballots in honest elections.

HUMAN EQUALITY IN SOCIETY. Democrats hold that each person must be guaranteed equal rights in society. They advocate social and economic equality—equal rights and opportunities to pursue social status and material well-being, and political equality—equal rights and opportunities to share in their governance. The latter is most commonly expressed in terms of universal and equal suffrage, and equality before the law. The decisions of democratic politics shall be made among persons with equal formal weights in determining the ultimate results, and the protections and benefits of government and the law shall be equally available to all persons. Although admitting that men are not identical—and that they differ considerably in their individual values, talents, interest, needs, and pleasures—democrats nonetheless assert that men are part of a common humanity, and that sharing of membership in the human race is more significant than specific differences among men.

This is not, as Plato bemoaned in *The Republic,* "dispensing a kind of equality to equals and unequals alike," but reflects a belief that neither birth nor wealth nor color nor religion nor violence shall erect artificial and arbitrary barriers to the inherent equality of men. If inequalities of condition are to emerge in society, they are to reflect achievement, not ascription or force. These inequalities of condition, however, must not themselves become barriers to the equal rights and opportunities of men.

CONSENT AND CONTRACT: THE BASE OF RULE. Central to the structure of democracy is the principle that men are born free and not subject to the rule of others, and that therefore the only legitimate basis for rule over men is their consent to be ruled. In order to make the principle of consent operational in an ultimate sense, classical democratic philosophers, particularly John Locke (in *The Second Treatise of Civil Government*) and Jean Jacques Rousseau (in *The Social Contract*), developed the idea of social contract. Men, they asserted, had (at least in an analytic sense) a prepolitical state of being—a "state of nature"—in which they were free, equal, and possessed of rights. They governed their own conduct, through reason comprehended "the laws of nature" by which they ordered their lives, and thus lived in reasonable harmony with each other. However, there were inconveniences and inadequacies in this prepolitical state, since each man was the interpreter and enforcer of his own rights, and since some men violated the rights of others. This "want of a common judge," as Locke put it, led men by mutual agreement to a social contract to join together into a civil society. Men, therefore, create and empower the state to better protect and more securely enjoy their freedoms, rights, and equality through the enactment and enforcement of civil laws.

The ideas of consent and contract, and of an existence for men and their freedom prior to and independent of the state, are logical components of classical democratic ideology. If ultimate political power resides in all men, only their consent can confer legitimate power upon the state. Men involuntarily subject to the rule of others are neither sovereign nor free nor equal. Rights granted by other men, rather than inhering in all men, are insecure. Government without consent is an affront to human worth and dignity. Finally, the principle of consent and contract involves not only mutual agreement to the original act of creating the political order, but also continuing consent to its existence and performance, and to its policies and officers. It is the prescription, as stated by Colonel Rainboro, leader of the rebellious soldiers of Cromwell's army, ". . . that every man that is to live under a government ought first by his own consent to put himself under that government." [12]

THE STATE AS TRUSTEE OF DELEGATED POWERS. The principle that the state is trustee of the people with powers delegated to it by the people derives from the consent basis of the state. Owing its existence to its citizens, and having no authority or purposes except those assigned to it by the citizens, the state continues at their pleasure. Thus the state and its government are (1) instruments created by men for their own purposes; (2) trustees of delegated powers and functions; (3) limited to these powers and functions. As stated by Robert M. MacIver, "Under the democratic system government becomes the agent and the people the principal who holds it to account. The community establishes its formal superiority over the state." [13]

CITIZEN PARTICIPATION AND CONSENT IN GOVERNANCE. Democracy requires that the citizenry be guaranteed opportunities to participate, and exercise final authority, in political decisions relating to public leadership and policy. Men are not subject to law and authority unless they have consented to their establishment. Democrats therefore conclude, as did Lincoln, that the principle that men "have the right of regulating their own affairs, is morally right and politically wise." [14] Democrats, furthermore, lodge their faith not just in the inherent moral and rational potentialities of men but also in education to develop those potentialities and communications to create an informed citizenry. Jefferson, for example, prescribed free schools and a free press to maintain the health of a free society.

AN ENVIRONMENT OF DIVERSITY AND CONFLICT. Democracy assumes diversity and conflict in society. The uniqueness of men, their cherished individualism and freedom, create a multiplicity and clash of ideas and interests, as people seek to translate their ends into public policy and their ambitions into dominance in government. A free, open, pluralistic society encourages political conflict, and raises the question: How shall the political process resolve conflicts in a manner consonant with the basic norms of democracy?

DEMOCRACY AS A WAY OF GOVERNING: THE PRIMACY OF PROCEDURES. Democracy involves a way of governing—a way of resolving the conflicts in society and making decisions about public policy and officials. Decisions relating to society's desired ends and the means to attain them are arrived

[12] A. S. P. Woodhouse, ed., *Puritanism and Liberty,* 2nd ed. (Chicago: University of Chicago Press, 1951), II, 301.

[13] *The Web of Government* (New York: Macmillan, 1947), p. 197.

[14] "Speech at Bloomington, Illinois," September 26, 1854, as reported in *The Peoria Weekly Republican,* October 6, 1854.

at by processes in which the citizens have the controlling influence. The democratic process, in its barest rudiments, is guided by certain basic procedural norms.

Fair Hearing and Deliberation before Decision. Democracy requires that the diverse and conflicting claims to political truth and advantage be accorded fair hearing, and that full and open public deliberation be insured, before decision. It is a system of nondogmatic politics, managing substantive issues with an empirical and pragmatic approach. Since there are many and opposing ends and interests among men, and since all men have equal rights to self-realization, none can legitimately lay exclusive claim to virtue, truth, or the benefits of society. No political philosophy or program answers all the questions and problems of political life. Each person, whatever his status, has something to contribute and a stake in political decision. In the ideal democracy, as suggested by A. D. Lindsay, "everyone should have somehow made his contribution to that decision." [15] Democracy views conflicts in politics as disagreements of interests and preferences, and consequently, views political "truths" and decisions as tentative, subject to reconsideration and change. In democracy, resolution of political issues comes not via the designs of one or a few men but through gathering all of the facts, encouraging the widest expression of views and alternatives, and requiring consent through the mobilization of majority support.

Moderation and Accommodation before Decision. Democracy requires of its citizens moderation and restraint in their politics. It calls for individualism tempered with a willingness to listen to the other fellow's side of the issue and with some concern for the public interest. The democrat's recognition of the fallibility of men and their equal right to pursue their separate paths demands not rigidity but flexibility of mind. Deliberation and persuasion, while they are a prelude to the counting of noses, imply not intractability but a way to arrive at some common grounds of agreement. The norm of moderation, and the art of compromise, are essentials of democracy. However, since unanimity is rare, an appropriate decision-making process must be established.

Decision by Election. Democracy is a process by which ultimate decisions resolving political conflicts are made by elections. The culminating drama of democratic politics is the counting of equally-weighted ballots. Thus, in a democracy, political decisions are legitimate because they are based on consent—a consent preceded by free and open discussion and confirmed by election. But what shall be the character of these decisions, and what weight shall carry the day?

[15] *The Essentials of Democracy,* 2nd ed. (London: Oxford University Press, 1935), p. 35.

Open and Tentative Decisions. No man or elite is infallible, and neither is the electorate participating in a particular election. The continuing character of democracy is retained because its decisions are temporary, subject to review and revision. Democracy affords each generation its right and opportunity to determine anew its goals and the means to fulfill them. Citizens in a democracy are not bound in a suicide pact with their predecessors. The dynamic of democracy is to be found in its openness to change, to new ideas and new practices.

Decision by Majority Support, Limited by Minority Rights. The principle of majority rule and minority rights prescribes that when a public decision is being made, and opinions are divided, the alternative preferred by the larger number of participants in that decision shall prevail—except that the minority's rights shall be protected. In prevailing, the alternative supported by the majority is for that time conclusive and binding on the entire community. As Locke said, "And thus every man, by consenting with others to make one body politic under one government, puts himself under an obligation to every one of that society to submit to the determination of the majority, and to be concluded by it; . . . . For where the majority cannot conclude the rest, there they cannot act as one body, and consequently will be immediately dissolved again."

Majority rule is a technique for implementing popular sovereignty and political equality. If political power in its ultimate form resides equally in each person, the alternative decision preferred by the larger number must be selected and enforced. Majority rule, therefore, is an arithmetic necessity and means simply that fifty-one shall take precedence over forty-nine. In resolving political conflict unanimity is unlikely, an equal division of votes is indecisive, less than a majority prevailing gives some people greater weight (more than equality) in the decision, and a requirement of an extraordinary majority in the decision (a more complicated issue) gives a few people the veto over the larger number.

There are limits to what the majority can do. It cannot oppress the minority: expropriate their property, diminish their citizenship, infringe their rights, or deny them the freedom to oppose and seek to become the majority. Jefferson stressed this in his inaugural address of 1801: ". . . though the will of the majority is in all cases to prevail, that will, to be rightful, must be reasonable; that the minority possess their equal rights, which equal laws must protect and to violate which would be oppression." [16] However, the rights of the minority are to be secure, to be

[16] Adrienne Koch and William Peden, *The Life and Selected Writings of Thomas Jefferson* (New York: Random House, 1944), p. 371.

heard, and to seek to prevail; not to rule, or to forcibly resist so long as its rights are protected. Just as the majority has the obligation to respect the rights of the minority, so the minority has the obligation to respect the majority's right to rule. In sum, democracy is in peril either if the majority is tyrannical or if it cannot function.

Majority rule is a continuing and not a sometime norm of democracy. Just as no man or given electorate is infallible, so neither is any given majority. The prerogative of the majority is to govern temporarily. Majority rule permits the larger part of the people to exercise its will at a given time, but the right remains to undo what is done. The minority retains the right to oppose and seek to become the majority, and the majority (and minority) cannot alter, dispense with, or destroy the norms and procedures by which majorities are freely, periodically, and openly arrived at. If it does so, its claim to legitimacy ceases to be valid within the framework of democracy. As Lincoln said in his first inaugural address, "A majority held in restraint by constitutional checks and limitations, and always changing easily with deliberate changes of popular opinions and sentiments, is the only true sovereign of a free people." [17]

THE BASES AND LIMITS OF POLITICAL LEGITIMACY AND OBLIGATION. Conformity to "higher law" and governance by consent are the classical criteria of democracy for determining political legitimacy and the obligations of citizens to loyalty and obedience. As suggested previously, classical democratic thinkers posit a higher law—an eternal, universal, and superior law of nature—which invests men with freedom, equality, and rights, and which they comprehend through "right reason." This higher law is binding on men, their governments, and public officers. The terms of the social contract, and the ordering and conduct of the state and its government, must conform to it. If this higher law is violated, the transgressing political system, regime, or official ceases to be legitimate. Violative acts reflect "raw power," and individuals are not bound to obey them. Indeed, in a conflict between the commands of this higher law and those of the laws of men, the individual may be morally obligated to disobey or resist civil law.

Moreover, the social contract, in turn, serves as a superior law for the political order. The constitution establishes the purposes, organization, and parameters of power, and guarantees the rights of the people; regimes and public officials must obey its prescriptions and prohibitions. The people, as the principals to the contract, agree to submit to authority—provided

[17] Carl Sandburg, *Abraham Lincoln: The War Years* (New York: Harcourt, Brace, 1939), I, 132.

that government as their agent abides by this "supreme law of the land," fulfills its purposes, conforms to its procedures of consent, and confines itself to the powers delegated.

Thus, democracy includes the self-preservative of a hierarchy of law which men must obey in public authority as well as private life. Violations of these superior laws and the trusteeship of government are civil and political "wrongs"; and procedures are provided to prevent, protest, and redress such violations. If the procedures of redress or consent are absent, foreclosed, or made shams, then the claim to legitimacy and obligation to obey terminate. Individuals in that society may engage in civil disobedience or resistance, or revolution, to establish or reestablish a democratic order. They may assert and exercise "the Right of the People to alter or abolish it, and to institute new Government, . . ." on democratic foundations.

THE DEMOCRATIC FAITH IN MEN AND PROGRESS. The democrat's faith in men and their ability to achieve progress must be restated here because it is the *omega* as well as the *alpha* of democratic ideology. Democrats believe that men can live in freedom and peace; regulate their own lives and engage in voluntary cooperation; share in their governance, discuss temperately, and choose wisely; and enjoy equality and improve the human condition. Contemporary democrats may not share the supreme confidence of their eighteenth-century predecessors in "the omnipotence of human reason," but they reject Plato's portrayal of self-ruling masses as "peasants at a festival." The democratic faithful are unable in logic and unwilling in commitment to abandon their belief in the essential capacity of men to govern themselves intelligently.

The Classic Period: Direct Democracy through Popular Government

Up to the twentieth century the history of democracy primarily concerns the development of the ideas and institutions of direct democracy relative to popular rule; it is in the twentieth century that we get revision in the direction of popular control. Direct democracy—also called "classical" or "pure democracy," in its undiluted form—involves the full exercise of popular sovereignty, the citizenry directly exercising the powers of the state and conducting its affairs. In the New England town meeting, for example, the citizens periodically gather in assembly to decide policy and enact laws, levy taxes, authorize expenditures, select public officials and hold them accountable. The brief narrative of the development of classical democracy which follows focuses on selected main-threads of a long, and for many centuries, not very successful history.[18]

Athenian Democracy

The word *democracy* was coined by the Greek historian Herodotus in the fifth century, B.C., to signify "popular rule" (*demo* meaning "the people," and *kratein* meaning "to rule"). In the democracy of the ancient Greek *polis* or city-state, as exemplified by Athens, the citizens (1) were equal in their political rights and before the law; (2) discussed and debated public issues in the Assembly, and by majority vote directly decided some issues, exercised ultimate control over others, and elected public officers accountable to them; (3) enjoyed political and civil freedom, including the right to criticize and oppose; (4) were protected against tyranny by respect for the law and by recognized legal restraints on government.

The citizens of Athens had "kingly dignity": all were equal in their right to share in public deliberation in the Assembly, in the weight of their votes, and in their eligibility for public office. To insure that circumstances as well as law did not exclude citizens of modest means from office or participation, most offices were salaried and compensation was provided for attendance in the Assembly in later years. To afford all citizens an equal chance to hold office, many positions, like magistrate and Council member, were filled by lot from panels of elected candidates; terms of office were short; and individuals could only hold an office once.

The major institution of citizen participation in Athenian democracy was the General Assembly, in which all citizens were members. It regularly met ten times each year to make policy and choose officers. The Assembly's process was deliberative, and its method of decision was by election, in which each citizen had an equal vote and the majority prevailed. A Council of Five Hundred, responsible to the Assembly and including fifty representatives from each of the ten Athenian tribes, proposed policy to the Assembly, supervised the execution of Assembly decrees, and performed other executive functions. In addition, there were courts or juries, composed of hundreds of citizens chosen by lot from elected panels, which heard and decided disputes under the law.

Athenians enjoyed freedom of political expression. Certainly the harsh criticisms of Athenian democracy by Plato and Aristotle indicate that this freedom was substantial. Plato in *The Republic* complained that there was too much individual freedom: ". . . the city is full of liberty and free

---

[18] A more detailed summary of the "Evolution of Democratic Ideas in the West," from which much of the material in this section is drawn, may be found in M. Rejai, *Democracy: The Contemporary Theories* (New York: Atherton, 1967), pp. 1–20.

speech and everyone in it is allowed to do what he likes . . . each man in it could plan his own life as he pleases." The Athenians sought to protect themselves against oppressive rule by valuing respect for the law, providing procedures for fair trial, and recognizing and enforcing limits to the authority of the *polis* and public officers. The need for security against tyranny was stressed by Plato in *The Laws;* for his part, Aristotle in *The Politics* developed the idea of constitutionalism—government checked by established and enforced restraints.

This happy picture of democracy in ancient Athens in the fifth and fourth centuries, B.C., must realistically be tempered with several qualifications. First, the Greek concept of citizenship was narrow, and limited that status to a minority of Athenians by excluding women, children, resident aliens, and slaves. Citizenship, moreover, was a matter of birth, and was rarely acquired. Even within the citizenry there was a fairly rigid social stratification, each class having its own tasks within its own sphere. Second, the city-state was viewed as an organic entity, superior to the individual and other institutions. The *polis* was the state, the nation, the society—all in one—and there were no independent centers of power. Athenian citizenship did not involve the freedom *from* community derived from the subsequent Hebrew-Christian tradition. Rather, it meant freedom *in* community: civic loyalty, the duty of active participation in public affairs, and service and devotion to the *polis*. Indeed, Aristotle described a citizen as one who participates, for any period of time, in public office. Third, democracy in Athens did not always live up to its ideal. The reality of the principle of the active, equal, and free involvement of all citizens was that only a minority of this minority were ever in attendance at any one time in the Assembly, that political leadership was largely provided by the aristocracy, and that there were periods of political repression. Fourth, many Greek thinkers were not favorably disposed towards democracy. Plato, Aristotle, Thucydides, to name a few, were highly critical of it. While Pericles lauded the "happy versatility" of his fellow Athenians, Plato saw the ordinary citizen as incompetent to rule himself, unable to see beyond his personal and immediate interests, and susceptible in mass meetings (as in the Assembly) to the appeals of demagogues. While Pericles revered Athens as a democracy "because the government is in the hands of the many, not the few," Plato saw democracy as unable to produce continuity of policy and lacking a focus of political responsibility. Fifth, Athenian democracy was practiced in a small city-state, and this peculiar form of democracy cannot be transferred to a large, populous modern industrial state, or to one searching for modernity.

Nevertheless, the ancient Greeks contributed mightily to laying the foundations of democracy. They believed that their fellow citizens were capable of self-rule and civic responsibility. They valued political freedom by encouraging not only participation but critical participation in public life. They valued education as indispensable in transforming latent human potential into manifest effective citizenship. The Greek Sophists argued that the political arrangements and laws of men originate in agreement among individuals, and that they are binding only on those who consent to such agreement. And, finally, the ancient Greeks believed that democracy was the political order best suited to produce political stability—through its protections against injustice and abuse of authority, its opportunities for political persuasion and accommodation, and its claim to obedience by consent. Athenian democracy, in sum, included: ". . . the direct control or making of the political decisions by the assembled citizens; the political equality of all citizens; the liberties, including the freedom to oppose; and the taking of decisions by a majority vote." [19]

Further Early Development of Democracy

The Romans, faced with the task of unifying and governing a far-flung empire, contributed to democracy the more formal and legalistic elements of constitutionalism and the supremacy of the law. To Cicero, the best known of the Roman lawyers, the universe and human society are governed by an eternal and superior natural law. Men comprehend this natural law through reason, regulate their lives according to it, and are endowed by it with certain "natural rights." While Cicero viewed human society as a natural institution, he held the state to be a product of consent. Political authority thereby derives from the citizenry who possess rights prior to it and who must have equal rights before its law. The actions of government are authoritative and binding only to the extent that they conform to the higher laws of nature and the foundation of consent.

From early Judaism and Christianity democracy derived the beliefs in the brotherhood of all men as children of God, the moral and spiritual equality of all men before God which cannot be overridden by any earthly differences or human power, the instrumental function of the state to maintain peace and order so that men might pursue higher spiritual ends, and the conditional quality of political legitimacy and obligation.

The feudalism of the Middle Ages can hardly be classified as democratic; but it nevertheless was based on informal and formal contracts governing the relationships between king and lord, and lord and vassal. These contracts established mutual and binding obligations; those aggrieved by al-

[19] Henry B. Mayo, *An Introduction to Democratic Theory* (New York: Oxford University Press, 1960), p. 41.

leged breaches of such obligations, be they king or lord or vassal, had recourse to "trial by peers" in court. These feudal courts were forerunners
of trial by jury and other elements of due process of law, and of king's
councils and parliamentary legislative bodies.

It was in the Middle Ages—and especially through the handiwork of
St. Thomas Aquinas—that natural law was converted into the divine reason
of God, which was binding on both the subjects and holders of political
authority. Therefore, neither the authority of rulers nor the obligation of
subjects was absolute. As John of Salisbury said, tyrannicide, the rightful
slaying of a ruler, was justified if the ruler violated the superior laws of
God or exceeded his earthly authority.

The period of the Renaissance and Reformation—which came with the
growth of towns and commerce, the emergence of a middle class of merchants and bankers, the ascendancy of the secular order over the temporal,
and the demise of feudalism and the rise of the nation-state—also added
to the foundations of democracy, despite the predominantly nondemocratic
character of the prevailing political orders. To such writers as Bodin, Gro-
tius, Machiavelli, and Hobbes, the state was independent of temporal control but was itself sovereign and absolute. But even during these periods,
expression was given to the consent-and-contract origins of political authority, and to the need for the representation of various classes or groups in the
institutions of public policy-making. The Renaissance was an age of individualism, in which freedom, self-development, and self-realization were
glorified. Characteristic of the age were a reaction to absolutism and dog-
matism, the emergence of the scientific spirit and freedom of inquiry—especially in the intellectual and artistic fields—and optimism about the
future of man. Such ideas of course are of great importance in the history
of democracy. Important too are the Reformation ideas of the primacy of
personal conscience and the possibility of a direct relationship between man
and God. The Protestant challenge to absolute temporal authority and demand for religious liberty are, in fact, milestones in the history of democracy, as is the development in some Protestant churches of congregational
principles of organization.

The Democratic Revolution of the Seventeenth and Eighteenth Centuries

The more immediate origins of democracy are to be found in the democratic revolutions of the seventeenth and eighteenth centuries—especially in
England, the United States, and France. During this time the claims and
practices of state sovereignty, absolute monarchy, and aristocracy of birth
met at last with crescendos of opposition and ultimate overthrow. The
ideological instrument of rebellion was the framework of ideas of the social

contract as expressed by Locke in *The Second Treatise of Civil Government,* Rousseau in *The Social Contract,* and such supporters of the American grievances and revolution against British rule as Alexander Hamilton, John Adams, Samuel Adams, Thomas Paine, and Thomas Jefferson. Space precludes even cursory descriptions of the individual contributions of the consent-and-contract writers of this period. However, each in his own way expressed the structure of democratic ideas discussed in the previous section (pp. 180–188).

Perhaps the most dramatic and concise statement of the democratic ideology of consent-and-contract is that of Jefferson in the American *Declaration of Independence.* Rephrased in the French *Declaration of the Rights of Man and Citizen,* employed as justification for the democratic revolutions in Europe in the 1830's and 1848, an important base for *The Universal Declaration of Human Rights* of the United Nations, and eulogized by leaders of anticolonial revolutions, it is worth rereading for its importance, as well as its economy and eloquence of expression:

We hold these truths to be self-evident, that all men are created equal, that they are endowed by their Creator with certain unalienable Rights, that among these are Life, Liberty and the pursuit of Happiness. That to secure these rights, Governments are instituted among Men, deriving their just powers from the consent of the governed. That whenever any Form of Government becomes destructive of these ends, it is the Right of the People to alter or to abolish it, and to institute new Government, laying its foundations on such principles and organizing its powers in such form, as to them shall seem most likely to effect their Safety and Happiness.

Here is stated a revolutionary new basis of political legitimacy and obligation to the state—the consent and agreement of free and equal men.

The Nineteenth-Century Establishment of Democracy

In the nineteenth century, the ideas of democracy were systematically elaborated, and its institutions refined and more broadly established. In England the franchise was expanded, and parliamentary institutions and powers and the competitive political party system were broadened and more firmly implanted. Philosophers like John Stuart Mill added to the ideological arsenal of democracy. In *On Liberty* Mill urged the intrinsic worth of each human personality, and the absolute rights of freedom of conscience and expression. To Mill the elements of democracy—universal suffrage, popular participation in governance, elections—were made meaningful only by the guarantee and exercise of personal liberty. He saw social progress as the product of the free development of free men.

In the United States in the nineteenth century, the institutions and guarantees of democracy were established in the federal Constitution and in those of the several states; in the broadening of suffrage; in the organization of political parties and their processes for selecting candidates and formulating programs; and in enlarging the participation, direct and indirect, of the people in their governance. Jefferson elaborated further on the Lockean scheme, giving specificity in ideas and action to the general principles of government by consent. He believed a universal and moral law of nature imparted to men freedom, inviolable rights, and the capacity for self-rule. Sovereignty, according to Jefferson, rests in the people who create and thereby fix the powers and purposes of their governments. The proper function of government is to preserve the freedom and liberties and secure the happiness of its citizens, and it properly becomes the object of criticism and the subject of opposition and rebellion if it exceeds or reneges upon its trust. Perhaps Jefferson's most distinctive contribution was his seemingly unbounded and optimistic faith in the ability of the American people, if educated and informed, to govern themselves. Similarly, Lincoln, in addressing himself to the "moral, social and political evil" of slavery, spoke of the "sacred right of self-government" and the moral and political wisdom of men "regulating their own affairs." [20]

Twentieth-Century Revisionism and Popular-Rule Democracy

This democracy, as Lincoln put it, is one of "government of the people, by the people, for the people." It is *of* the people in its being derived from their consent in its creation, *by* the people in its functioning by their participation, *for* the people in its purpose of serving their will and fulfillment. The key to the popular-rule model of democracy, however, is its emphasis on government *by* the people. Citizenship in it is intensely personal and demanding. It assumes that citizens will be highly motivated politically and will participate fully and continuously in public life; that citizens will have access to adequate political information and will use it for enlightened political decision-making; that citizens will be able to communicate their political views to others; that citizens will have access to the centers of decision-making; and that, given an environment of freedom, citizens are capable of generating and choosing among alternatives, perceiving which are in their interests, and harmonizing their interests with the public welfare. Popular-rule democracy, then, demands the direct, constant, and enlightened participation of citizens in their governance.

The argument has been raised that this picture of classical democracy, especially in its expectations of citizen involvement, is distorted because in

[20] "Speech at Bloomington, Illinois," *op. cit.* (above, n. 14).

fact it does not require that the citizens themselves directly govern. Rather, it requires that they decide which policies and programs they prefer and choose governors to carry out their will. Thus, the principle of representation must be added to the framework of democratic ideas and institutions. There is, of course, a historical basis for this addition. The democratic revolutions in England, the United States, and France sought to overturn absolute rule based on divine grace and birth, and establish government by consent through freely elected representative legislatures. Moreover, the idea of representation was an important component of the philosophies of such advocates of democracy as Locke, Rousseau, and Jefferson.

Representation reduces the role of the citizen and creates a structure in which the major offices of government are elected by, accountable to, and removable by the citizenry, now an electorate. The holders of these offices are representatives of the electorate, chosen to reflect and carry out the expressed will and policy preferences of their constituents. They are freely chosen and removable by the electorate by majority vote in periodic and frequent elections, and their actions are determined by majority decisions.

While representation served to make democracy operational as a political system, the conception of representation expressed in classical democracy did not satisfy the critics. It unburdened the ordinary citizen of the chores of direct participation in decision-making assemblies, but still left him with a heavy political load to bear. Joseph A. Schumpeter, for example, described the classical democracy of the eighteenth century as "that institutional arrangement for arriving at political decisions which realizes the common good by making the people itself decide issues through the election of individuals who are to assemble in order to carry out its will." He saw "our chief problems about the classical theory centered in the proposition that 'the people' hold a definite and rational opinion about every individual question and that they give effect to this opinion—in a democracy—by choosing 'representatives' who will see to it that that opinion is carried out. Thus the selection of the representatives is made secondary to the primary purpose of the democratic arrangement which is to vest the power of deciding issues in the electorate." [21]

Moreover, it is necessary to examine the institutional arrangements which this conception of democracy has produced. In the United States in the nineteenth century, the advocates of popular rule assumed that the skills of governing are common to all men. This brought Jacksonian rotation-in-office; the multiplication of elected offices; short terms of office and ineligibility for reelection; initiative and referendum for constitutional amend-

[21] *Capitalism, Socialism and Democracy,* 3rd ed. (New York: Harper & Row, 1950), p. 269.

ments, policy enactments, tax levies, and bond issues; recall of public officials; and popular control of political party choices of candidates, programs,
and officers through delegate conventions and primary elections.

This assumption concerning the universal possession of governing skills
has been a favorite whipping boy of the enemies of democracy, who attack
it as being disastrously blind to the needs of modern times and society;
erroneously based on the unproven, if not disproven, competence of "the
people" to govern themselves; and inevitably leading to lack of national
purpose or accomplishment, and to anarchy or mob rule. More importantly,
however, some of those committed to democracy have been highly critical
of the popular-rule model. First, they reject overoptimistic expectations
concerning the capacities of all people to govern themselves—to be informed, interested, active, and creative in politics. This is bluntly put by
E. E. Schattchneider: "The beginnings of wisdom in democratic theory is to
distinguish between the things the people can do and the things the people
cannot do. The worst possible disservice that can be done to the democratic
cause is to attribute to the people a mystical, magical omnipotence which
takes no cognizance of what very large numbers of people cannot do by the
sheer weight of numbers. At this point the common definition of democracy
has invited us to make fools of ourselves." [22] Democratic critics of popular
rule have particularly stressed that by unrealistically attributing political
initiative to the citizenry, classical democrats failed to recognize the vital
need for and realities of leadership in society, and failed to cope with the
real problem of insuring that such leadership is produced and maintained
within the framework of democratic principles.

Democratic critics of direct democracy have restated the old argument
that such a political order is impossible in societies of large size and population, which require more elaborate organization of their political processes.
Classical democracy focuses almost exclusively on the individual as the
predominant unit of politics, and cannot cope in modern and highly differentiated society with the presence and power of politically active interest
groups and classes. Perhaps direct democracy is adequate for a small society
with minor conflicts, and simple policy problems. But it is inadequate for a
large, complex modern industrial society with diverse groups and classes,
with basic conflicts of goals and interests, and with complex policy issues
that require high levels of expertise for their resolution. In short, politics
cannot be left as an avocation for all citizens; it must, in reality, become a
vocation for at least some of them.

Within this framework of criticism, the question is: How can a special

[22] *The Semisovereign People: A Realist's View of Democracy in America* (New
York: Holt, Rinehart & Winston, 1960), p. 139.

group of people—politicians—assume the major burden of governing and the foundations of democracy be retained? Schumpeter, having noted that in classical democracy the selecting of representatives is secondary to the electorate's action on political issues, suggests: "Suppose we reverse the roles of these two elements and make the deciding of issues secondary to the election of the men who are to do the deciding. To put it differently, we now take the view that the role of the people is to produce a government. . . . And we define: the democratic arrangement is that institutional arrangement for arriving at political decisions in which individuals acquire the power to decide by means of a competitive struggle for the people's votes." [23]

The classical model in which each citizen had the opportunity to freely participate with equal power in the decisions of government, and in which self-government and an emergent common will would promote the good of the individual and the community, proved to be an utopian democratic ideology separated by a wide gap from democratic reality. In the United States, as Lindsay pointed out, new conditions led to "the transformation of democracy into something very different from anything Jefferson and Lincoln ever dreamed of." [24]

Before dealing with this "very different" democracy, perhaps a brief word is in order in defense of classical democracy. Its advocates are often treated harshly. Schattschneider, for example, delivers this unkind cut: "The classical definition of democracy as government by the people is predemocratic in its origins, based on notions about democracy developed by philosophers who never had an opportunity to see an operating democratic system." [25] This is true, but the context and circumstances of the origins of democratic ideas must also be considered. The framers of classical democracy were struggling to overturn the existing orders of feudalism, aristocracy, and absolute rule. They sought the most powerful ideological weapons, denied the moral rectitude and empirical validity of the prevailing ideology, and countered with its opposite. They opposed individualism to the rigid class structures and corporatism; they opposed universal rationality to the claims of divine ordination and assertions of mass incompetence; they opposed equality to societal orders of superiority and inferiority by birth; they opposed self-rule to absolute subjection. To shatter the order of their reality they espoused ideas that not only contradicted it but also contradicted part of the common realities of life in any societal order. In so doing, they join an illustrious fraternity of revolutionary thinkers.

[23] Schumpeter, *op. cit.* (above, n. 21), p. 269.
[24] Lindsay, *op. cit.* (above, n. 15), p. 9.
[25] Schattschneider, *op. cit.* (above, n. 22), p. 130.

The cause for concern, therefore, is not with direct democracy through popular rule as originally espoused, but with its contemporary advocacy and applicability. Prophets long dead ought not be saddled with responsibility for what those who claim to be their disciples say and do.

Modern Democracy: Representative Government through Popular Control

If direct democracy through popular rule is inadequate and inappropriate today as a form of government, is there a democratic order that can govern a modern society and govern it well? Is it possible to build and operate a political system that is based on popular consent and faithful to the fundamental principles of democracy, which still provides the leadership, skills, and organization needed to govern a modern society?

The proponents of representative democracy through popular control of government agree with Schumpeter that the role of the people in selecting representatives must be made primary to their deciding issues if democracy is to be workable. "The problem," as Schattschneider states it, "is not how 180 million Aristotles can run a democracy, but how we can organize a political community of 180 million ordinary people so that it remains sensitive to their needs. This is a problem of *leadership, organization, alternatives and systems of responsibility and confidence.*[26]

Democratic Leadership and Representation

In the management of public affairs, as in other areas of human activity, some people are more skillful than others; and everyone benefits if the more skillful conduct the public business. Moreover, majorities and minorities are not spontaneously generated in society. Political leaders and activists, a relatively small segment of the body politic, play a crucial role in the mobilization and functioning of majorities and minorities. Similarly, policy and program alternatives do not spontaneously rise out of some emergent collective common will. It is this same relatively small corps of political leaders and activists that raise political issues and suggest answers, inform and arouse public opinion, lead the debate, and organize supporters.

Not all patterns of leadership, of course, are compatible with democratic values. Democracy requires that the system of leadership recruitment be open, that the right and opportunity to seek the leader role not be arbitrarily denied to any individual or category of persons. Democracy describes a leader as someone who has formally won popular support, be it of a majority or a minority. The procedures of democracy are organized to pre-

[26] Schattschneider, *op. cit.* (above, n. 22), p. 138.

serve this relationship of support between leader and followers. The non-democratic leader need not formally demonstrate popular support, since his incumbency may reflect his power to heap vengeance on his foes, or his status as a demigod.

The ingredient of active leadership alters the concept of democratic representation from a passive representation of agency to an active one in which representatives and candidates shape as well as follow public opinion. This, it is argued, does not eliminate an effective and decisive role for the citizenry. To the contrary, it better utilizes their personal and political resources, and enhances their role in the political system by making it more manageable. The power of the people is not increased by giving them more things to decide but by giving them the ultimately important things to decide.

Democracy through Popular Control of Government

Democracy prescribes that government be (1) responsive to the people —ready, able, and willing to listen to and meet their needs and reasonable demands; and (2) responsible to the people—formally accountable to their authoritative judgments of its performance. In turn, responsive and responsible government does not necessarily require that the people must rule, but that they exercise a relatively high degree of control over their governors. The role of the people, as seen by John Dewey, is that of "selecting officials and regulating their conduct as officials." [27] Often quoted to express this view of democracy is Robert M. MacIver's statement that the people control in a democracy by "determining who shall govern and, broadly, to what ends." The basic norm of modern democracy, as he sees it, is that the people, "by a system of elections, shall determine the choice of government and the general direction of governmental policy. This is the democratic liberty to make and unmake government." [28] Among the earlier proponents of democracy there were those who recognized the importance of popular control in the institutionalization of democracy. Jefferson, for example, suggested that the judgment as to whether governments are more or less democratic be made on the criteria of whether "they have more or less of the element of popular election and control in their composition. . . ." [29]

Democracy: The Choosing and Changing of Governments

If the governed need not and cannot make policy directly, how shall they keep their governors responsive and responsible to them? They can choose and change their governments—intervene periodically and frequently to

[27] *The Public and Its Problems* (New York: Holt, 1927), p. 15.

[28] MacIver, *op. cit.* (above, n. 13), pp. 198, 201.

[29] Cited from a letter "To John Taylor," May 28, 1816, in Rejai, *op. cit.* (above, n. 18), pp. 66–67.

decide which set of leaders, offering which qualities of leadership and general policy program, shall govern.

The power of the people to choose and change government means, in a practical sense, the power to remove a government from office and replace it. E. F. M. Durbin observed from British history

that the essential thing to attain and preserve is the power of the people to *dismiss* a government from office. This negative power is in reality an important positive power, because ordinary men and women are moved more deeply by the disapproval of measures they dislike in practice, than by their less definite conception of what they desire in the future. Political change in democracies is more frequently induced by a slow accumulation of resentment against an existing government or institution, than by the growth of a positive idea of new social forms. Experience is more real than imagination, to unimaginative people.[30]

The major offices of government—those central and determining in the making of public policy—must be subject to periodic and frequent elections. The length and terms of tenure must be sufficient, on the one hand, to permit the holders to perform their offices; but not so long, on the other hand, as to permit tenure to become entrenchment in office. The goal of maintaining the manageability of the tasks of the electorate means that reasonable limits must be placed on the number of elected offices and the frequency of elections. However, important nonelective offices must fit within the structure of responsiveness and responsibility by being made subordinate and accountable to those popularly elected.

Democratic Popular Control through Political Competition

Democratic popular control of government comes through the people having the opportunity to choose among real political alternatives competing for popular support. It is, in other words, from meaningful differences in qualities of leadership and policy programs offered by political groups and candidates that the electorate derives the power to choose and give consent. Schattschneider defines democracy as *"a competitive political system in which competing leaders and organizations define the alternatives of public policy in such a way that the public can participate in the decision-making process."* He warns that *"the people are powerless if the political enterprise is not competitive.* It is the competition of political organizations that provides the people with the opportunity to make a choice. Without this opportunity sovereignty amounts to nothing." [31]

[30] *The Politics of Democratic Socialism* (London: Routledge and Kegan Paul, 1940), p. 237.
[31] Schattschneider, *op. cit.* (above, n. 22), pp. 141, 140. Italic his.

The character of the popular-control model is summarized by Seymour M. Lipset: "Democracy in a complex society may be defined as a political system which supplies regular constitutional opportunities for changing governing officials, and a social mechanism which permits the largest possible part of the population to influence major decisions by choosing among contenders for political office." Among the conditions which give effect to democracy he includes: "one set of political leaders in office," and "one or more sets of recognized leaders attempting to gain office." [32]

Vital to democracy, therefore, is the presence of an organized, viable, respected, and secure opposition. Lipset cautions that "if conditions for perpetuating an effective opposition do not exist, the authority of the officials in power will steadily increase, and popular influence will be at a minimum.[33] A viable opposition is dependent upon political freedom—especially minority rights, political equality, open and peaceful competition for public support and office in an environment of political pluralism, and the right of minorities not only to compete electorally but also to be represented and heard in government in some reasonable relationship to their popular support.

Political freedom to discuss, and debate and differ over, the crucial issues central to the politics of the time must function in the center and at the periphery of politics. This freedom must include, as Supreme Court Justice William O. Douglas said, "the right to differ as to the things that touch the heart of existing order." [34] Further, it must include freedom to hold, express, and seek support for views not only in the traditional center of the political spectrum but also at its radical fringes. Freedom for political unorthodoxy, as the Supreme Court has said of American democracy, is a "fixed star on our constitutional constellation." [35]

Democratic Popular Control through Popular Consultation

Modern democracy depends not only on popular control through frequent and periodic competitive elections, but also on a continuing relationship of interdependence between the people and their leaders through popular consultation. It requires government which is continuously responsive— "subservient and sensitive to the whole complex common life of society." [36]

[32] *Political Man* (Garden City, N.Y.: Doubleday, 1960), p. 45. Similarly, Anthony Downs describes functioning democracy as having one party or coalition of parties in office, one or more parties out of office, and periodic elections by means of which power is transferred. See *An Economic Theory of Democracy* (New York: Harper, 1957), pp. 22–24.

[33] Lipset, *ibid.*, p. 46.

[34] *Beilan v. Board of Education*, 356 U.S. 399 (1958).

[35] *West Virginia Board of Education v. Barnette*, 319 U.S. 624 (1943).

[36] Lindsay, *op. cit.* (above, n. 15), p. 283.

Alternatives to leadership and policy develop, and governmental decisions are made, in a setting in which public opinion is sounded out as well as led —on a continuing day-to-day and year-to-year basis. Consequently, democracy requires not only freedom of political communication but also well-developed networks of communication media and two-way communication linkages between the governed and their governors.

Perhaps the difficulty of precisely describing this element of modern democracy can be partly overcome by noting that every society develops some means of self-observation to regulate and record its operation.[37] The data of such observation—depending on the character of the political system—are the bases of its political decisions, the legitimacy of its acts, and the writing of its history. Thus what a society seeks to learn about itself and avoids learning are intimately tied to what that society is and is not, what it wants to be and doesn't want to be, how it functions and doesn't want to function. The social statistics of monarchies and aristocracies of birth therefore are genealogies. Modern totalitarian states collect dossiers on their peoples and create security networks to control them. The vital data of a democracy are its election returns and its public opinion surveys and polls. In the United States, for example, considerable money and energy are spent on attitude and opinion research and on political polling. Why do we bear the expense and permit this prying into our minds and preferences? We tolerate the costs and questioning because we consider this information important in maintaining the responsiveness of American democracy. Social science inquiry in the United States is empirical, quantitative, and policy-oriented because these provide the kind of data a democratic society wants to know about itself. In short, social scientists and pollsters count noses because in a democracy, in the final analysis, the counting of noses is decisive.

When Is a Political Order Democratic?

It is beyond the scope of this introduction to democracy to deal with specific democratic institutions and procedures—with the substantial variety of constitutional frameworks, governmental institutions (legislatures, executives, bureaucracies, judiciaries), political party systems, election processes, interest group networks, and organs of political communication and opinion which implement democratic principles and which are found in particular nations. While the framework of democratic values and norms has been outlined herein, information about particular political institutions and systems must be obtained elsewhere.

[37] See Daniel Lerner, "Social Science: Whence and Whither?" *The Human Meaning of the Social Sciences,* ed. Daniel Lerner (New York: Meridian, 1960), pp. 13–39.

It is possible and useful, however, to discuss briefly criteria which have been proposed as minimal and optimal to determine the presence and extent of democracy—whether a particular political order *is* democratic, and *how* democratic it is in comparison to others or to an ideal standard.[38]

Perhaps the simplest approach to use is the principle of exclusion—that is, to state criteria which determine the political orders that are *not* democratic. The Italian political scientist Giovanni Sartori attempts this technique of negative attribution: "The difference between democracy and its opposite lies in the fact that in a democracy power is scattered, limited, controlled, and exercised in rotation; whereas in an autocracy power is concentrated, uncontrolled, indefinite, and unlimited. What democracy *is not* is, in one word, autocracy." [39] While Sartori's scheme may permit crude dichotomous classification into democracies and autocracies, it does not provide even rudimentary bases of measurement by which political orders could be evaluated along a continuum from the most autocratic to most democratic. Moreover, the organization and exercise of power in the real world is too complicated for the empirical application of Sartori's simple standards in specific situations.

The characteristics of the popular-control model of democracy of Lipset previously discussed have been operationalized by the sociologist Phillips Cutright to measure degree and stability of democracy—the extent to which countries institute and maintain competitive party systems and open elections. Cutright developed a scoring system "rewarding" with points nations which have established and retained explicitly democratic institutions, and "penalizing" with no points those which do not have democratic forms, or those which "backslide." His scoring system might be of interest.

1. Legislative Branch of Government

Two points for each year in which a parliament existed in which the lower or the only chamber contained representatives of two or more political parties and the minority party or parties had at least 30 percent of all seats. One point for each year in which a parliament existed whose members were the representatives of one or more political parties, but where the "30 percent rule" was violated. No points for each year no parliament existed or for years when either of the above types of parliaments was abolished or discarded by executive power. Parliaments whose members are not members of political parties are given a zero. Parliaments that are not self-governing bodies (e.g., the mock parliaments of colonial governments) are given a zero.

[38] An excellent collection of articles dealing with this issue is provided by Charles F. Cnudde and Deane E. Neubauer, eds., *Empirical Democratic Theory* (Chicago: Markham, 1969).

[39] *Democratic Theory* (New York: Frederick A. Praeger, 1965), pp. 151–152.

2. Executive Branch of Government

One point for each year the nation was ruled by a chief executive who was in office by virtue of direct vote in an open election where he faced competition or was selected by a political party in a multi-party system, as defined by the conditions necessary to get 2 points on the legislative branch indicator above. If the parliament ceased being a multi-party parliament because of executive action, the chief executive stopped getting points. One half point each year the chief executive was not selected by virtue of his hereditary status but was selected by criteria other than those necessary to attain one point as given above. Colonial governments receive one half point per year. No points if the nation was governed by an hereditary ruler.[40]

Points are also assigned to political systems on the basis of one set of officials in office, one or more sets of political leaders out of office, and reliance on political parties and free elections as the legitimate political institutions for society—thereby permitting the development of a continuum for comparative purposes.

In another empirical study, the political scientist Deane E. Neubauer shifts attention from criteria designed basically to distinguish democratic from nondemocratic governments, to those that permit more refined comparisons among democratic governments. He states,

The most characteristic feature of democratic regimes is the election of key governmental personnel. . . . The form of election alone, however, does not guarantee their democratic substance. Democratic elections are those in which opposition groups are given some opportunity to contest office with ruling groups. Two key indicators of a country's tolerance of electoral opposition groups are the existence of actual electoral competition and the existence of multiple sources of public information.[41]

Based upon these assertions, Neubauer constructed an index composed of four indicators which measure the relative amounts of electoral equality and competition present in a given political system: (1) percent of the adult population eligible to vote; (2) equality of representation; (3) information equality—degree of pluralistic ownership of the press; and (4) electoral competition by political parties. The formulas for calculating these measures are complex and cannot be restated herein, but the resulting rank ordering and competitive scores of the countries studied by Neubauer can be noted.

[40] "National Political Development: Measurement and Analysis," *American Sociological Review*, XXVIII (April, 1963), 256.

[41] "Some Conditions of Democracy," *American Political Science Review*, LXI (December, 1967), 1005.

ORDERING OF SAMPLE COUNTRIES ON INDEX
OF DEMOCRATIC PERFORMANCE [42]

1. Great Britain	236.3
2. France	231.4
3. Finland	229.4
4. Sweden	225.8
5. Netherlands	220.9
6. Belgium	214.9
7. Japan	212.7
8. Luxembourg	210.1
9. Norway	209.7
10. New Zealand	209.4
11. Denmark	205.7
12. Israel	203.2
13. West Germany	199.4
14. Italy	198.6
15. Canada	196.8
16. United States	190.9
17. Venezuela	188.3
18. Austria	186.9
19. Chile	184.6
20. Ireland	181.4
21. India	172.7
22. Switzerland	169.3
23. Mexico	121.9

Finally, the political scientist Anthony Downs offers this enumeration of the characteristics which in practice distinguish democratic government from other forms. A government may be classified as democratic, under this formulation, if it exists in a society in which the following conditions prevail:

1. A single party (or coalition of parties) is chosen by popular election to run the governing apparatus.
2. Such elections are held within periodic intervals, the duration of which cannot be altered by the party in power acting alone.
3. All adults who are permanent residents of the society, are sane, and abide by the laws of the land are eligible to vote in each such election.
4. Each voter may cast one and only one vote in each election.
5. Any party (or coalition) receiving the support of a majority of those voting is entitled to take over the powers of government until the next election.
6. The losing parties in an election never try by force or any illegal means to prevent the winning party (or parties) from taking office.

[42] Neubauer, *ibid.*, p. 1007. For a critique of Neubauer's study by Phillips Cutright and Neubauer's reply, see *American Political Science Review*, LXII (June, 1968), 578–581.

7. The party in power never attempts to restrict the political activities of any citizens or other parties as long as they make no attempt to overthrow the government by force.
8. There are two or more parties competing for control of the governing apparatus in every election.[43]

Each of these "tests of democracy" offers standards by which particular political systems may be evaluated in terms of their conformity to democratic prescriptions of governance by popular consent and control. A political order, then, can be said to be democratic if in reality the people are linked to their government so that they can and do set and attain their goals through political institutions. The extent and quality of democracy depends upon the extent and quality of the linkages of consent and control connecting the people to their government.

The Preconditions and Prospects of Democracy

The Preconditions of Democracy

During recent years, with the rise of totalitarian regimes, the dismantling of colonial empires and the accompanying search of newly independent states for national development and viable political forms, and the disappointingly frequent failure of democracy to take root in these and other nations, there has been considerable interest and empirical inquiry as to whether there are prerequisites to democracy—preconditions essential to its emergence and survival. Why some political systems are democratic and others nondemocratic is not a new question in the history of democratic thought. However, empirical investigation into the environmental conditions, if any, upon which the institutionalization and maintenance of democracy might be dependent is of more recent vintage. It is important to note that if only specialized societal environments can produce and sustain democracy, then the potential for the spread of democracy is limited.[44]

PHYSICAL SCALE AND DEMOCRACY. It was long believed that democracy was associated with small geographic size and small population. Jefferson's belief is well known—that democracy flourishes best when hardy and independent yeoman live in "ward republics" sufficiently small so that each

[43] Downs, *op. cit.* (above, n. 32), pp. 23–24. He notes for item 3 that in some democracies women and permanent resident aliens or both are not allowed to vote. Robert A. Dahl also offers a set of definitional characteristics of "polyarchy" (democracy) in *A Preface to Democratic Theory* (Chicago: University of Chicago Press, 1956), p. 84.

[44] Much of the material on the preconditions of democracy is drawn from Rejai, *op. cit.* (above, n. 18), Part Two; and Cnudde and Neubauer, *op. cit.* (above, n. 38), Part Three.

citizen can participate in community affairs. Similarly, De Tocqueville praised small-scale democracy for permitting the people to directly govern themselves. In the United States the myth of "grassroots democracy" has a traditional and powerful attraction, one contemporary writer stating that "democracy is more likely to survive, other things being equal, in small states." [45]

Other things, of course, are rarely equal, and, given the growth of democracy in the United States as the nation occupied a continent, other factors seem more basic as preconditions for that growth than physical scale. Roscoe C. Martin, based upon study of the adherence to democratic principles of local government in the United States, denies that "Lilliputian government is more democratic *per se* than big governments." He concludes that

smallness in size and multiplicity in number of rural governments provide neither the guarantee of the existence nor a standard for measuring the effectiveness of local democracy. There are other and more meaningful criteria, among them the nature of popular participation, the representativeness of policy-making bodies, and the kind and efficacy of the control exercised over administrative bodies. The relationship between the degree of democracy and the complexity of local governmental machinery is much more likely to be inverse than direct.[46]

RELIGION AND DEMOCRACY. Democracy frequently is associated with the Judeo-Christian heritage—or sometimes more particularly with Christianity, Protestantism, or Catholicism.[47] It is argued that these religious faiths have provided the Western democracies with an essential base of beliefs: in the dignity and equality of the individual, compassion and justice, love of fellowman, human freedom, respect for authority. Others deny that religious faith or a particular religious belief are preconditions of democracy. Currin V. Shields, for example, states, "Democracy is a purely secular creed, devoid of religious implications. Democratic beliefs about the prin-

[45] Ernest S. Griffith, "Cultural Prerequisites to a Successfully Functioning Democracy: A Symposium," *American Political Science Review*, L (March, 1956), 102. Also see Robert A. Dahl, "The City in the Future of Democracy," *American Political Science Review*, LXI (December, 1967), 953–970.

[46] *Grass Roots* (University, Alabama: University of Alabama Press, 1957), pp. 56, 58.

[47] See Griffith, *op. cit.* (above, n. 45); Jacques Maritain, *Christianity and Democracy* (New York: Charles Scribner's Sons, 1945); Reinhold Niebuhr, *The Children of Light and the Children of Darkness* (New York: Charles Scribner's Sons, 1945); and *Christian Realism and Political Problems* (New York: Charles Scribner's Sons, 1953); R. H. Tawney, *Religion and the Rise of Capitalism* (New York: New American Library, 1947); Max Weber, *The Protestant Ethic and the Spirit of Capitalism*, trans. Talcott Parsons with a foreword by R. H. Tawney (New York: Charles Scribner's Sons, 1958); and J. H. Hallowell, *The Moral Foundation of Democracy* (Chicago: University of Chicago Press, 1954).

ciples of political conduct are derived, not from the dogmas of religion, but from the practices of politics." [48]

SOCIOECONOMIC CONDITIONS AND DEMOCRACY. Attention in recent years has focused on the socioeconomic environment of democracy, and the question: Are there social and economic factors which correlate, positively and negatively, with democratic values and institutions? Lipset provided the first significant empirical examination of the hypothesis that democratic political development is related to the presence of relatively high levels of economic development. Using the indices indicated as measures of economic development, he found, "In each case, the average wealth, degree of industrialization and urbanization, and level of education are much higher for the more democratic countries. . . ." [49] Democracy, he concluded, "is related to the state of economic development. . . . The more well-to-do a nation, the greater the chances it will sustain democracy." Only in a relatively prosperous society with a reasonably fair distribution of wealth does the mass of the people have the freedom from raw want, the self-confidence, self-restraint, and time and inclination to participate in democratic politics. "A society divided between a large impoverished mass and a small favored elite results either in oligarchy . . . or tyranny. . . ." Wealth, urbanization, and industrialization, on the other hand, serve to develop "a growing middle class. A large middle class tempers conflict by rewarding moderate and democratic politics and penalizing extremist groups."

In a prosperous urban and industrial society, Lipset continues, a large part of the people are brought into contact with diverse groups and ideas, provided greater economic security, and become beneficiaries of more widespread education. The result is a multiplicity of organizations independent of government control (private associations, interest groups, business associations and unions, political parties, etc.). "Such organizations serve a number of functions: they inhibit the state or any single source of private power from dominating all political resources; they are a source of new opinions; they can be the means of communicating ideas, particularly opposition ideas, to a large section of the citizenry; they train men in political skills and so help to increase the level of interest and participation in politics." In this setting, according to Lipset, the "lower strata" are able "to

[48] *Democracy and Catholicism in America* (New York: Macmillan, 1958), p. 272. Also see John Pamenatz, "Cultural Prerequisites to a Successfully Functioning Democracy: A Symposium," *op. cit.* (above, n. 45).

[49] Lipset, *op. cit.* (above, n. 32), p. 50. Also see Robert A. Dahl and Charles E. Lindblom, *Politics, Economics, and Welfare* (New York: Harper & Row, 1953); Daniel Lerner, *The Passing of Traditional Society* (New York: Free Press, 1958); and Edward A. Shils, *Political Development in the New States* (The Hague: Mouton, 1962).

develop longer time perspectives and more complex and gradualistic views of politics. A belief in secular reformist gradualism can be the ideology of only a relatively well-to-do lower class."

Lipset found his most significant relationship to exist between democracy and level of education. "The higher one's education, the more likely one is to believe in democratic values and support democratic practices." He notes that education "presumably broadens man's outlook, enables him to understand the need for norms of tolerance, restrains him from adhering to extremist doctrines, and increases his capacity to make rational electoral choices." Lipset concludes, "If we cannot say that a 'high' level of education is a *sufficient* condition for democracy, available evidence suggests that it comes close to being a *necessary* one." [50]

It seems quite clear that a relationship exists between a country's level of social and economic development and its likelihood of being democratic. Indeed, the very low probability of a very poor country's being democratic, given the preponderance of poor countries in the world and the limited prospects for their improvement, must discourage those hoping for the spread of democracy. It should not be assumed, however, that increments of social and economic development are continuously correlated with increments of democratic political development. A recent study indicates that while an overall relationship exists between socioeconomic development and democracy, a "threshold" phenomenon also seems to exist; once this threshold level of socioeconomic development has been reached, other factors are more important in determining democratic development and performance.[51] Therefore, while a relatively high level of socioeconomic development is perhaps a necessary condition for democracy, it is not a sufficient one.

CONSENSUS, PERSONALITY, AND DEMOCRACY. Consensus, or agreement on fundamental values and the "rules of the game," frequently is assumed to be a necessary condition for the functioning and stability of democracy—especially in placing certain restraints on political competition and keeping it within peaceful and tolerable limits.[52] Carl J. Friedrich, on the other hand,

[50] Lipset, *ibid.*, pp. 48, 50, 66, 67, 61, 56. Verification of this general relationship between economic and democratic development is offered by Cutright, *op. cit.* (above, n. 40); and Donald J. McCrone and Charles F. Cnudde, "Towards a Communications Theory of Democratic Political Development: A Causal Model," *American Political Science Review*, LXI (March, 1967), 72–79.

[51] Deane E. Neubauer, *op. cit.* (above, n. 41). Also Phillips Cutright's critique and Neubauer's rejoinder in *American Political Science Review*, LXII (June, 1968), 578–581.

[52] See J. Roland Pennock, *Liberal Democracy: Its Merits and Prospects* (New York: Rinehart, 1950); and David B. Truman, *The Governmental Process* (New York: Alfred A. Knopf, 1951).

argues that consensus is unnecessary if not undesirable in a democracy because it may stifle diversity and dissent. Moreover, he states that such a prerequisite might foreclose the possibility of democracy "because it cannot be assumed that there will be any agreement upon what is fundamental." [53]

Empirical studies conducted by political scientists James W. Prothro and Charles M. Grigg indicate that while a modest area of agreement may exist among American voters on the fundamentals of democracy when these are stated as abstract principles (e.g., voter affirmations of belief in the principle of freedom of speech), there is no agreement on the application of these principles as specific precepts and practices (e.g., negative replies by the same people to such questions as whether communists should be permitted to speak). They conclude that the voters "were closer to complete discord than to complete consensus. . . ." [54] However, they observed, as did Lipset, that education is the most important variable for determining consistency or inconsistency between agreement with abstract democratic principles and their specific applications. In another important study, Herbert McClosky found consensus on democratic values and norms lacking among the American general public, but present to a degree among political leaders and activists.[55]

Does a lack of consensus on the fundamentals of democracy pose serious difficulty for its practice and continued existence? Prothro and Grigg, observing that democracy functions in the United States despite this lack of agreement, suggest that other significant factors must be operative to sustain the democratic political system. They cite the comparative price tags of expressed belief versus action. It is far less costly for the individual to express an antidemocratic belief than it is to engage in explicitly antidemocratic behavior. Therefore, apathy—failure to act on belief—may well perform an important function in democratic politics by keeping undemocratic behavior out of the political arena.

Similarly, McClosky argues that dissensus among voters should not cause excessive alarm because

those who are most confused about democratic ideas are also likely to be politically apathetic and without significant political influence. . . . In the United States, at least, their disagreements are *passive* rather than *active*, more the result of political ignorance and indifference than of intellectual conviction or conscious identification with an "alien" political tendency. Most seem not even to be aware of their deviations from the established values. This suggests

[53] Friedrich, *op. cit.* (above, n. 1), p. 173.
[54] "Fundamental Principles of Democracy: Bases of Agreement and Disagreement," *Journal of Politics,* XXII (May, 1960), 291.
[55] "Consensus and Ideology in American Politics," *American Political Science Review,* LVIII (June, 1964), 361–382.

that there may, after all, be some utility in achieving agreements on large abstract political sentiments, for it may satisfy men that they share common values when in fact they do not.

McClosky notes that it is the smaller political strata "rather than the public who serve as the major repositories of the public conscience and as the carriers of the Creed. Responsibility for keeping the system going, hence, falls most heavily upon them." Those who choose to participate most in politics are those most committed to democratic norms; when the ordinarily unconcerned and inactive citizenry is politically aroused it is from political elites that they largely take their cues as to acceptable and effective political activity. McClosky, however, doubts whether consensus is necessary even among leaders and activists in a democracy. "The opinion has long prevailed that consensus is needed to achieve stability, but the converse may be the more correct formulation, i.e., that so long as conditions remain stable, consensus is not required; it becomes essential only when social conditions are disorganized. Consensus may strengthen democratic vitality, but its absence in an otherwise stable society need not be fatal or even particularly damaging." [56]

In a related but separate vein, a complex of personality factors have been stipulated as necessary for a viable democracy.[57] Democratic man, it is argued, must be (relatively, of course) secure and free from anxiety, adaptive to change and new experiences, receptive to divergent points of view and tolerant of opposition, flexible of mind, cooperative in interpersonal relations, respectful but not worshipful of authority, confident in his potentialities and in those of others. In contrast to the "openness" of the democratic personality, the authoritarian personality is portrayed as insecure, rigid, intolerant, distrustful, conforming, and hostile.[58]

[56] McClosky, ibid., pp. 376, 374, 377. Also see Robert A. Dahl, Who Governs? (New Haven: Yale University Press, 1961), pp. 311–325.

[57] See Gabriel A. Almond and Sidney Verba, The Civic Culture (Princeton, New Jersey: Princeton University Press, 1963); Zevedei Barbu, Democracy and Dictatorship: Their Psychology and Patterns of Life (New York: Grove, 1956); Alex Inkeles, "National Character and Modern Political Systems," in Francis L. K. Hsu, ed., Psychological Anthropology: Approaches to Culture and Personality (Homewood, Illinois: Dorsey, 1961); Harold D. Lasswell, "The Democratic Character," in The Political Writings of Harold D. Lasswell (New York: Free Press, 1951); Daniel Lerner, op. cit. (above n. 49); and Karl Mannheim, Freedom, Power, and Democratic Planning (New York: Oxford University Press, 1950).

[58] See T. W. Adorno, Else Frenkel-Brunswik, Daniel J. Levinson, and R. Nevitt Sanford, The Authoritarian Personality (New York: Harper, 1950); Barbu, op. cit. (above, n. 57); Morris Janowitz and Dwaine Marvick, "Authoritarianism and Political Behavior," Public Opinion Quarterly, XVII (Summer, 1953), 185–201; Milton Rokeach, The Open and Closed Mind (New York: Basic Books, 1960); and Don Stewart and Thomas Hoult, "A Social-Psychological Theory of the Authoritarian Personality," American Journal of Sociology, LXV (November, 1959), 274–279.

The Prospects of Democracy

Do contemporary conditions and trends permit the survival and spread of democracy? Do democratic values reflect the aspirations and meet the needs of late-twentieth century man? In the few pages remaining, these complex and controversial issues can be dealt with only by raising some representative questions and factors.

Today, as yesterday, democracy is a minority political system. Only in about two dozen of the more than twelve dozen independent nations of the world have the people—over the past two decades—regularly enjoyed the right to participate in free elections. Moreover, little real interest or hope exists for the emergence of democracy in nations with established nondemocratic political orders. The focus of attention and hope—and disillusionment—has centered, rather, on developing nations. "Development" or "modernization," as the terms are used by scholars and practitioners, includes (1) economic growth—agricultural modernization, industrial development; (2) social transformation—social differentiation, urbanization, national integration; and (3) political change—increased political participation by more of the citizenry.[59] However, the expansion of participation in governance—including free and open elections with competitive political parties—seems to have consistently the lowest priority, with the justification offered that nation-building and economic development require elite control and centralized authority unencumbered by the bickerings, inconveniences, delays, and wastes of democratic processes. Moreover, the gap between rich and poor nations seems to widen rather than narrow, offering little hope that the socioeconomic conditions favorable to democratic development will soon be present in the third world. Finally, even if this situation were to improve substantially, the question of the transition from authoritarian to democratic rule remains unanswered. It is unlikely that those elites in power will—at the "right moment"—volunteer to broadly share power and subject themselves to formal accountability. The transition, if it occurs, will be difficult and often violent, involving more revolution than transition. In sum, there will be continued and perhaps expanded use of the rituals rather than the realities of democracy, but there is little basis for optimism that the registry of democracies will include many new enrollees.

The conditions, trends, and issues of modern life also raise challenges

[59] See Gabriel A. Almond and G. Bingham Powell, Jr., *Comparative Politics: A Developmental Approach* (Boston: Little, Brown, 1966); A. F. K. Organski, *The Stages of Political Development* (New York: Alfred A. Knopf, 1965); Lucien W. Pye, *Aspects of Political Development* (Boston: Little, Brown, 1966); and Fred W. Riggs, "The Theory of Political Development," in *Contemporary Political Analysis,* ed. James C. Charlesworth (New York: Free Press, 1967), 317–349.

for the democratic prospect in the United States and other advanced democratic societies. First, the physical and structural scale of contemporary society—not only in population and geographic size, but also in large-scale organization and bureaucracy—makes democratic participation, consent, and
control difficult. Can a nation continental in size with a present (and rapidly
increasing) population of over two hundred million enjoy democracy, even
if the role of the citizenry is limited largely to the election of governors?
Given the growth in size and authority of governmental bureaucracy, are
the governors indeed elected? Are these key bureaucratic policy-makers in
fact subject to effective popular control, or are they substantially independent of the electorate and elected officials?

Second, is democratic pluralism working its "magic" of "countervailing power" [60] to insure and promote justice in society? Are the various interests and strata in society able to make themselves "heard and felt" in
politics, or are some groups far more capable of attaining their goals
through public policy at the expense of others? [61] Are there people in society
who are invisible and outside the equation of power, and what realistic
means do they have of making themselves "heard and felt"—the politics of
representation or the politics of protest? [62]

Third, the accelerated pace of scientific and technological advance has
posed problems for democracy. Have the resulting increases in the complexity and urgency of public policy issues, and the need for expertise in
governmental policy-making, diminished the reality of democracy? Can a
society be dependent upon, and benefit from, the special knowledge and
skills of its scientists and professionals, and at the same time keep them
sensitive to the values and needs of the citizenry? Indeed, given the growing
technical content of public policy, it is not out of order to ask whether
elected officials themselves can exercise effective legislative and executive
control over governmental policy and expert advisers and administrators.
Senator J. William Fulbright argues:

[60] See John K. Galbraith, *American Capitalism: The Concept of Countervailing
Power* (Boston: Houghton Mifflin, 1956); Theodore J. Lowi, *The End of Liberalism*
(New York: W. W. Norton, 1969); Grant McConnell, *Private Power and American
Democracy* (New York: Alfred A. Knopf, 1966); and William E. Connolly, ed.,
The Bias of Pluralism (New York: Atherton, 1969).

[61] See G. William Domhoff, *Who Rules America?* (Englewood Cliffs, N.J.:
Prentice-Hall, 1967); C. Wright Mills, *The Power Elite* (New York: Oxford University Press, 1956); and, for a critique of the "power elite" concept, Nelson W.
Polsby, *Community Power and Political Theory* (New Haven: Yale University Press,
1963).

[62] See Michael Lipsky, "Protest as a Political Resource," *American Political Science Review*, LXII (December, 1968), 1144–1158; and Jerome Skolnick, *The Politics
of Protest: Violent Aspects of Protest and Confrontation—A Staff Report to the
National Commission on the Causes and Prevention of Violence* (Washington: Government Printing Office, 1969).

The case for government by elites is irrefutable insofar as it rests on the need for expert and specialized knowledge. The average citizen is no more qualified for the detailed administration of government than the average politician is qualified to practice medicine or to split the atom. But in the choice of basic goals, the fundamental moral judgments that shape the life of a society, the judgment of trained elites is no more valid than the judgment of an educated people. The knowledge of the navigator is essential to the conduct of a voyage, but his special skills have no relevance to the choice of whether to take the voyage and where we wish to go.[63]

Do the gravity as well as the complexity of the issues of contemporary democratic politics—thermonuclear war and domestic violence, a trillion dollar economy and poverty, crowded megalopoli and environmental pollution—call into serious question the capacity of the citizenry to cope with them, even if just by listening to the debate and "choosing up sides"? And what of the consequences for democracy of recent advances in the science and technology of mass persuasion communications? Has expertise in the engineering of consent and its application in the mass media, especially television, rendered democracy more vulnerable to the dangers of demagoguery, or to "Gaullist"-type regimes in which a strong chief executive deals directly with the citizenry, and the legislature and political parties suffer in their representational and other roles? Has that same expertise and application increased the importance of "big money" in politics, and created newly (and disturbingly) important power groups in society—the public relations experts, and the mediamen?[64]

Fourth, does democracy require no more than intermittent popular selection of rulers under a highly imperfect system of representation in which too many people go unnoticed, unheard, unrepresented? Those who see themselves as outside of the Establishment—the young, the black, the Mexican-Americans, the poor—deny that it does. Their concern with problems of societal scale, dependence on technocrats, and the limits of effective popular control has led to a resurgence of enthusiasm for participatory democracy, for "all power to the people." They insist that greater scope be given to the

[63] *The Elite and the Electorate: Is Government by the People Possible?* (Santa Barbara, Calif.: The Center for the Study of Democratic Institutions, 1963), pp. 4–5.

[64] See *Financing Presidential Campaigns: Report of the President's Commission on Campaign Costs*, Alexander Heard, Chairman (Washington: Government Printing Office, 1962); *Voters' Time: Report of the Twentieth Century Fund Commission on Campaign Costs in the Electronic Era*, Newton N. Minow, Chairman (New York, 1969); Stanley Kelley, Jr., *Professional Public Relations and Political Power* (Baltimore: Johns Hopkins University Press, 1963); Robert MacNeil, *The People Machine: The Influence of Television on American Politics* (New York: Harper & Row, 1968); and Gene Wyckoff, *The Image Candidates* (New York: Macmillan, 1968).

individual to participate directly in the making of those decisions that affect him.[65] This should not be confused with the arrangements in ancient Greece under which all citizens came together to discuss and decide. In participatory democracy, in fact, only those directly affected by particular policy decisions are to participate—as in community action programs, community control of schools and urban redevelopment, welfare rights organization, and in the demands of black and student power. Just how popular consent through participation is to be institutionalized remains unclear, as is the question of defining who is affected. In modern society, with its complex networks of interdependencies, it is difficult to decipher the impacts and ramifications of policy. Decisions affecting one group or locale also affect others; because of limited resources, a decision to allocate benefits to one group affects the shares of others. Moreover, data comparing participation in local and national politics do not support the hope that people will participate more thoroughly and effectively at these more proximate levels of politics. In the United States in recent years the effort to encourage direct election by the poor of their representatives on municipal poverty boards brought only a 3–4 percent participation.

Fifth, have the pressures, uncertainties, and alienation of modern life too greatly impaired democratic civility? Have the animosity and rigidity they have produced ("nonnegotiable demands" seems a common bargaining posture today) become inimical to the continued functioning of democracy? Democracy combines respect for tradition and openness to change. Consequently, its normal expression is one of gradual and piecemeal reform within the framework of traditional values and forms. Many on the contemporary radical left and radical right find this way of proceeding inadequate and undesirable—either too little too late or too much too soon. Can democracy survive the attacks of those who call for one or the other of the two faces of political violence—revolution or repression?

Finally, do the self-doubts of modern man cloud the democratic prospect? Democracy is founded on faith in the common man, and it faces its gravest peril when men lose faith in themselves and their capacities to share meaningfully in a governance directed toward individual fulfillment and human progress. Thus, democracy today faces severe trials and an uncertain future. It has faced and met similar challenges before—global war, civil strife, economic collapse. As in the past, the future of the democratic experiment rests in the imaginations and commitments of men devoted to making democracy work.

[65] See Henry S. Kariel, *The Promise of Politics* (Englewood Cliffs, N.J.: Prentice-Hall, 1967); and the discussion of the New Left in Chap. 9.

Bibliography

Bachrach, Peter. *The Theory of Democratic Elitism*. Boston: Little, Brown, 1967.

Barker, Sir Ernest. *Reflections on Government*. New York: Oxford University Press, 1942.

Becker, Carl L. *Modern Democracy*. New Haven, Conn.: Yale University Press, 1941.

Berelson, Bernard. "Democratic Theory and Public Opinion." *Public Opinion Quarterly*, XVI (Fall, 1952), 313–330.

Braybrooke, David. *Three Tests for Democracy*. New York: Random House, 1968.

Brzezinski, Zbigniew, and Samuel P. Huntington. *Political Power: USA/USSR*. New York: Viking, 1965.

Cassinelli, C. W. *The Politics of Freedom: An Analysis of the Modern Democratic State*. Seattle: University of Washington Press, 1961.

Chambers, William N., and Robert H. Salisbury, eds. *Democracy in Mid-Twentieth Century*. St. Louis, Mo.: Washington University Press, 1960.

Cnudde, Charles F., and Deane E. Neubauer, eds. *Empirical Democratic Theory*. Chicago: Markham, 1969.

Commager, Henry S. *Majority Rule and Minority Rights*. New York: Oxford University Press, 1943.

Dahl, Robert A. "Further Reflections on the Elitist Theory of Democracy." *American Political Science Review*, LX (June, 1966), 296–305.

———. *A Preface to Democratic Theory*. Chicago: University of Chicago Press, 1956.

———. *Who Governs?* New Haven, Conn.: Yale University Press, 1961.

Davis, Lane. "The Cost of Realism: Contemporary Restatements of Democracy." *Western Political Quarterly*, XVII (March, 1964), 37–46.

Downs, Anthony. *An Economic Theory of Democracy*. New York: Harper, 1957.

Durbin, E. F. M. *The Politics of Democratic Socialism*. London: Routledge and Kegan Paul, 1940.

Ehrmann, Henry W., ed. *Democracy in a Changing Society*. New York: Frederick A. Praeger, 1964.

Frankel, Charles. *The Democratic Prospect*. New York: Harper & Row, 1964.

Friedrich, Carl J. *The New Belief in the Common Man*. Boston: Little, Brown, 1942.

Givertz, H. K. *Democracy and Elitism*. New York: Charles Scribner's Sons, 1967.

Hattersley, A. M. *A Short History of Democracy*. Cambridge: Cambridge University Press, 1950.

Kariel, Henry S., ed. *Frontiers of Democratic Theory*. New York: Random House, 1970.

Key, V. O., Jr. *Public Opinion and American Democracy*. New York: Alfred A. Knopf, 1961.

Lakoff, Sanford A. *Equality in Political Philosophy*. Cambridge, Mass.: Harvard University Press, 1964.

Lindsay, A. D. *The Essentials of Democracy*. 4th ed. London: Oxford University Press, 1935.

———. *The Modern Democratic State*. New York: Oxford University Press, 1943.

Lippincott, Benjamin E. *Democracy's Dilemma*. New York: Ronald, 1965.

Lipset, Seymour M. *The First New Nation*. New York: Basic Books, 1963.

———. *Political Man*. Garden City, N.Y.: Doubleday, 1960

Lipson, Leslie. *The Democratic Civilization*. New York: Oxford University Press, 1964.

MacIver, Robert M. *The Web of Government*. New York: Macmillan, 1947.

Mayo, Henry B. *An Introduction to Democratic Theory*. New York: Oxford University Press, 1960.

Meiklejohn, Alexander. *Political Freedom*. New York: Harper & Row, 1960.

Mill, John Stuart. *Utilitarianism, Liberty, and Representative Government*, intro. by A. D. Lindsay. New York: E. P. Dutton, 1951.

Mills, C. Wright. *The Power Elite*. New York: Oxford University Press, 1956.

Moore, Barrington, Jr. *Social Origins of Dictatorship and Democracy*. Boston: Beacon Press, 1966.

Padover, Paul K. *The Meaning of Democracy: An Appraisal of the American Experience*. New York: Frederick A. Praeger, 1963.

Pennock, J. Roland. *Liberal Democracy: Its Merits and Prospects*. New York: Rinehart, 1950.

Rejai, M. *Democracy: The Contemporary Theories*. New York: Atherton, 1967.

Riemer, Neal. *The Revival of Democratic Theory*. New York: Appleton-Century-Crofts, 1962.

Sartori, Giovanni. *Democratic Theory*. New York: Frederick A. Praeger, 1965.

Schattschneider, E. E. *The Semisovereign People: A Realist's View of Democracy in America*. New York: Holt, Rinehart & Winston, 1960.

Schumpeter, Joseph A. *Capitalism, Socialism and Democracy*. New York: Harper & Row, 1950.

Simon, Yves R. *Philosophy of Democratic Government*. Chicago: University of Chicago Press, 1951.

Smith, T. V., and Edward C. Lindeman. *The Democratic Way of Life*. New York: New American Library, 1951.

Spiro, Herbert J. *Responsibility in Government: Theory and Practice*. New York: Van Nostrand Reinhold, 1969.

Thorson, Thomas L. *The Logic of Democracy*. New York: Holt, Rinehart & Winston, 1962.

Tingsten, Herbert. *The Problem of Democracy*. Totowa, N.J.: Bedminster Press, 1965.

Walker, Jack L. "A Critique of the Elitist Theory of Democracy," *American Political Science Review*, LX (June, 1966), 285–295.

Wheeler, Harvey. *Democracy in a Revolutionary Era*. Santa Barbara, California: Center for the Study of Democratic Institutions, 1970.

Chapter 7

Democratic Capitalism

The breakup of feudalism and the emergence of an urbanized, industrialized, mobile society set the stage for the growth of a democratic ideology. But differing interpretations of the compatibilities of various economic systems with the democratic idea—and with general notions of justice—have led to subideologies of major importance. Two of these, democratic capitalism and democratic socialism, will be analyzed in this and the succeeding chapter.

The politico-economic ideas we associate with capitalism did not precede and therefore mold the main outlines of Western industrial societies; rather, they largely developed as an explanation for, and a defense of, an industrial system produced by economic imperatives of a nonideological character. That is, the prospects of economic gain, under changing conditions, caused men to evolve certain economic practices and institutions for realizing those gains. Once the machinery had been created, men sought to legitimize and bulwark their creation with an adequate and comforting philosophy.

Although largely *post hoc,* this philosophy has not been without impact on history. As it evolved, became refined, was disseminated, and became a widely accepted body of thought, it helped shape men's perspectives and provided them with premises and value judgments which vitally affected their attitudes toward their economic system and its relationship to government. The loyalties it engendered significantly influenced the social and political climate within which the system functioned.

Although "capitalism" basically refers to an economic rather than a political system, the term has become enmeshed with a series of political ideas which supplement and reinforce the system. The blending of these interrelated political and economic ideas can be referred to as a "subideology." This subideology of capitalism has sometimes evoked as much passion, produced as much dogma, and had as much integrating influence on individuals' social outlook as the larger ideology to which it related.

There are almost as many definitions of "capitalism" as writers on the subject. The prudent author may well content himself with Webster's *Third New International Dictionary* attempt: ". . . an economic system characterized by private or corporation ownership of capital goods, by investments that are determined by private decision rather than by state control and by prices, production and the distribution of goods that are determined mainly in a free market."

The reader will observe that the lexicographers quite properly inserted "mainly" in the last phrase. They might well have added several other "mainlys," since practically all systems usually classified as "capitalist" have some public ownership, and some investment made by public rather than private decisions. One of the most difficult (indeed, impossible) semantic tasks is that of determining just when a "capitalist" system becomes a "socialist" system. How much public ownership, investment, and control are compatible with a capitalist system? About twenty percent of Britain's economy is said to fall under public ownership. Is Britain a capitalist country? No authoritative dividing line has been established to distinguish between a capitalist and a socialist country. This being the case, the term "capitalist" shall hereafter be applied where a heavy preponderance of economic activity takes place under private ownership and control—the reader (hopefully) bearing in mind the necessary arbitrariness of the term.

The Economic Creed

The central features of the capitalist system in its classical form are the dominance of private property; the dynamics of the profit motive; the existence of a free market; the presence of competition. In order for these elements to work properly, entrepreneurs must be free to innovate, workers free to seek a higher wage, and investors free to seek their highest rewards.

The capitalist model assumes that private ownership and control of property will maximize men's interest in its care and productive potentialities. The model also assumes that the profit motive provides the most potent incentive to economic activity, efficiency, and progress. By harnessing this motive, the system works most closely in harmony with the nature of man, as an economic animal.

The market system is at once the stimulator, regulator, coordinator, and harmonizer of men's economic activities—a system which works with consummate and almost mysterious cunning (Adam Smith referred to an "invisible hand") to promote the best economic interests of all. Prompted and disciplined by the laws of supply and demand, men perpetually readjust their economic efforts in order to make that contribution which provides maximum personal rewards and simultaneously meets the needs of others.

The system has thus been seen to be a thing of rare beauty. Adam Smith celebrated its marvels in his famous *The Wealth of Nations,* a volume which not only made the classic explanation of the system, but set the tone and direction of economic thought for well over a century. As Smith saw it, the market system contained a self-generating and self-correcting mechanism as faithfully attuned to natural laws as was the motion of the planets traversing their celestial rounds. So well did it function that the proper role of government was to keep hands off ("laissez-faire"), lest it upset the delicate balances which assured the harmony of the whole.

In the words of economist John Kenneth Galbraith, "There is something admirably libertarian and democratic about this process. It is not hard to understand why, among the devout, the market, no less than Christianity and Zen Buddhism, evokes such formidable spiritual feeling." [1]

(Laissez-faire, it should be noted, never really existed in practice, although government intrusions into the economy were at a minimum in the last half of the nineteenth century in Great Britain and the United States. Tariffs and federal aid to the railroads were glaring exceptions in the United States.)

The Political Creed

Capitalism, as previously noted, is an economic, not a political system. But with the development of capitalism, a supporting body of political ideas arose. Among the political concepts which accompanied the growth of capitalism were the following:

First, there was a presumption that private property should be unregulated, since it is the means by which the individual advances the economic well-being of both himself and his society. Abuses will temporarily crop up in the capitalist system, but since the market has its own subtle ways to chasten the erring, government should hold its well-meaning impulses in check. Nature is infinitely more wise, left to herself, than men's presumptuous efforts to correct her seeming defects. Following this concept, then, government's role shriveled to the traditional dimensions of maintaining law and order, upholding the sanctity of contract (of particular importance

---

[1] "The New Industrial State," *Atlantic Monthly,* CCXIX (April, 1967), 55.

to capitalism), providing protection from external threats, regulating currency, and raising taxes.[2]

The market has its own implacable coercions, but these would apply impersonally and impartially. They would produce less socially dangerous resentments than the compulsions and restraints of a noncapitalist state. Men can usually accept with better grace the hardships, failures, and inequalities imposed by the laws of nature than misfortunes more readily attributable to public officials.

Second, decentralization of economic power was considered to be the best defense against its abuse. Under capitalism, no individual can exploit the consumer or his employees for long. The latter can turn elsewhere if unfair prices or wages exist. And since government does not control the means of production, it cannot so readily force men to submit to injustice by resort to economic pressure. When no person or institution possesses much economic power, the possibilities of either public or private oppression are greatly diminished.

Third, inequality of wealth was regarded as a normal and desirable state of affairs. It is the aspiration for and realization of inequality which enables the system to function and gives it vitality. Wealth naturally gravitates to those who serve society's needs best and poverty becomes the just fate of those who contribute little. Rewards are thus apportioned in accordance with a kind of "natural" system of justice. Government interference with the judgments of the market, therefore, can only disrupt a system whose apparent harshness ("survival of the fittest") conceals a hidden beneficence. Justice, yes, but not rigidly so. In the words of one writer, "The capitalist belief in abundance allows the rewards to be generous and not exact. There is an element in it that appeals to the gambler as well and looks amiably upon the success of the man who, by the luck of timing or his shrewd judgment of the market, 'strikes it rich' . . ."[3]

Finally, the market system was believed to be the most democratic way to organize an economic order. No elite can prescribe economic priorities to fit its notion of justice or social need; rather, each individual casts his vote for production priorities whenever he makes a purchase. Since both efficiency and maximum profits are promoted by mass production and mass

[2] Adam Smith conceded that government had "the duty of erecting and maintaining certain public works and certain public institutions which it can never be for the interest of any individual, or small number of individuals, to erect and maintain, because the profit could never repay the expense to any individuals or small number of individuals, though it may frequently do much more than repay it to a great society." *Wealth of Nations*, Book IX, Chap. IX.

[3] Nathaniel Stone Preston, *Politics, Economics and Power* (New York: Macmillan, 1967), p. 46.

distribution, the system inherently seeks a constantly widening market rather than being content to minister to a privileged minority. Thus capitalist dynamics naturally served one democratic premise—that the economic gains of society should largely be mass gains.

Not all of these concepts appeared when the characteristic features of the modern capitalist economy were first emerging. But the generalizations set forth were widely accepted by educated men in the nineteenth century, were assiduously taught in the schools, and were propounded in the press. Many of them are still stoutly defended today.

The Development of Capitalism

A species of commercial capitalism existed in Phoenicia, Greece, Carthage, and Rome. Industrial capitalism, however, did not make an appearance in those cultures. As for the Middle Ages, the philosophy of the medieval church was inhospitable to capitalism: it condemned usury, deplored deviations from a "just price," and disparaged the dignity of the commercial professions. Moreover, the feudal system—with its innumerable tolls and fees, its system of serfdom, its restrictions of the guilds, and the general rigidities of its social and economic system—stood as a barrier to the development of capitalist enterprise.

A capitalist economic system, however, was spurred by the discovery of vast quantities of gold and silver in the New World, a discovery which inflated prices sharply without simultaneously producing an increase in workmen's wages.[4] The "profit inflation" which followed provided capital with which to fuel an industrial revolution once conditions were ripe. These conditions included the "inventing of inventions"—perhaps the most momentous intellectual breakthrough in the history of mankind. Its revolutionary implications—for a species accustomed to doing things in time-hallowed ways and hostile to the very idea of change—cannot be exaggerated. (Contrary to earlier assumptions that capital accumulation would be capitalism's principal means of advancing economic welfare, more progress now comes from invention and innovation than from additional capital assets.)

The development of the nation-state—with the power and will to destroy the feudal heritage by eliminating trade barriers, establishing a uniform currency, maintaining domestic order, promoting education for the commercial classes, and providing improved communication and transportation facilities—also played a central part in shaping an environment conducive to the genesis of a new economic system.

Meanwhile, the medieval church's condescending attitude toward trade

---

[4] *Encyclopaedia Britannica*, IV, 840.

and commerce was being effectively challenged by a Calvinist ideology which glorified the qualities demanded by capitalism. Calvin extolled hard work, sobriety, thrift, and efficiency. Successful enterprise suggested that God's favor rested upon you, an indication—though not a proof—that you were among those predestined to eternal salvation. But prosperity should not be manifested by ostentatious consumption: profits should not be spent on carnal satisfactions, but reinvested in the enterprise. Wealth should be used to produce more wealth. (Previously, a great deal of capital had been poured into costly but economically unproductive cathedrals and used for other ecclesiastical purposes.) As a consequence, several centuries of capital accumulation began to reap economic dividends in the eighteenth century.

The development of modern capitalism is usually associated with the Industrial Revolution—and the Industrial Revolution with the emergence of the large-scale factory. Factory manufacturing on a substantial scale first took place in England in about the mid-eighteenth century; a century later it was the "key economic institution of England, the economic institution which shaped its politics, its social problems, the character of daily life— just as decisively as the manor or guild had done a few centuries earlier." [5]

The factory was destined to raise living standards to undreamed of levels, but its initial impact was not altogether salutary. Although the abuses and evils associated with early capitalism created an image of that system now largely dispelled in the West, it is an image still fresh and vivid in the minds of many non-Westerners, to whom capitalism remains a dirty word. Late eighteenth and early nineteenth-century industrial England gave rise to a rash of literature deploring the social effects of the factory system. Factories were often noisy, dirty, smelly, dimly lit. Machinery was unguarded and crippling accidents were common; so were occupational diseases, especially lung ailments. Women worked from dawn to dark in factories and mines, taking only a few days off to deliver their children. Children worked similar hours, escalating to as many as sixteen hours per day during rush seasons. Some began their labors at ages four to five (especially pauper children). Often children slept in shifts, using beds still warm from the previous shift. If injuries disabled (child or adult), the worker was discharged without compensation. Wages for children were pitifully low, and were little better for adults.

The factory worker and his family went home at night to slum conditions of an appalling nature. Overcrowding was severe; houses were badly ventilated, poorly lit, and poorly constructed; garbage and sewage were often

[5] Robert Heilbroner, *The Making of Economic Society* (Englewood Cliffs, N.J.: Prentice-Hall, 1965), p. 82.

dumped in the streets for lack of an alternative. The stench was often almost unbearable. Weekend drunkenness was the workman's principal recreation; prostitution was common (in some slums, one house in ten were said to be brothels); vice and crime flourished.

Although the picture was an ugly one, it would be wrong to conclude that the worker's lot had uniformly deteriorated. In some instances standards of living had fallen, but in others, workers' lives had improved.[6] Urban slums were sometimes superior to the wretched rural slums the worker left behind. Clothing, diets, and hospital facilities were sometimes better than rural people had known before. Some owners were more humane than others. In general, standards of living rose steadily in the nineteenth century.

Could anything be done about the abuses of the factory system? No, according to economists Thomas Malthus and David Ricardo, following the general lead of Adam Smith. Improve the condition of the working man, warned Malthus, and you will stimulate fecundity, leading to population increases inevitably outstripping food increases. The upshot: famine must do its necessary work to reestablish a balance between food resources and population—unless war or pestilence steps in first.

Ricardo agreed, arguing that above-subsistence wages would prompt larger families, an overabundance of labor, and wage declines to subsistence levels or less. The "Iron Law of Wages"—Ricardo's theory as developed by his successors—inevitably doomed the worker to a marginal existence, except as brief periods of greater affluence were followed by the imperative correctives of sufficient suffering to restore the birth rate to a subsistence equilibrium.

Various writers, such as Herbert Spencer and William Graham Summer, later adapted Charles Darwin's evolutionary theories to demonstrate that the poor, being manifestly less fit than others, should be left to their hapless fate while the process of "survival of the fittest" continued its ageless work of improving the hardihood, adaptability, and capacity of the species. Social Darwinism was a grim theory, but one to which many industrialists could readily adjust. Maximum profits in accordance with the laws of nature and nature's god? A comforting view indeed!

The pessimists, however, were not to prevail. Whatever the economists might say, many Britons refused to accept their conclusions. In England, Charles Dickens' powerful pen aroused sympathy for the poor; John Ruskin, Thomas Carlyle, and Matthew Arnold railed against industrialism and the lot of the worker. Royal Commissions investigated the workmen's plight, issuing reports that stung the conscience of Parliament (and pleased

    [6] *Ibid.,* pp. 85–6. Also see John Chamberlain. *The Roots of Capitalism* (Princeton, N.J.: D. Van Nostrand, 1959), pp. 98–101.

the aristocracy and landed gentry, annoyed as they were with the parvenus of the industrial class). Well before Karl Marx and Friedrich Engels attacked capitalism, a reform movement—emerging side by side with the capitalist system—had begun its long and fitful process of correcting the excesses and abuses of capitalism. In 1802, legislation forbade the employment of children for over twelve hours a day, followed in 1819 by legislation tightening enforcement. The Factory Acts of 1833 provided further restrictions on child labor; subsequent legislation protected women, insured the right of workers to form labor unions, and called for government inspection of factories.

In Germany, Bismarck, alarmed by the growth of socialist sentiment, proceeded to shore up the state against this "threat" by granting the worker a system of workmen's compensation, health insurance, and old age insurance (1883–89). Once this was done, the Iron Chancellor declared, "the Socialists will sing their siren song in vain and the workingmen will cease to throng to their banner." Early in the nineteenth century Britain followed suit with sickness and accident insurance, unemployment compensation, a minimum wage law, and a system of public employment bureaus. Thus, Adam Smith's model of the shrunken government gave way before governments' estimates of the pragmatic necessities of their time.

Meanwhile capitalism was demonstrating its tremendous capacity as a matrix of economic progress. Britain and the United States, the major strongholds of relatively unfettered capitalism, had become the richest and most powerful nations in the world. Other Western European powers, although hampered by a slow start, were also making great strides.

Trusts and Antitrust

By the latter part of the nineteenth century, it was clear that the capitalist system was not evolving in accordance with the master plan perceived by the natural law philosopher–economists. In the United States, competition in many industries had generated a degree of economic insecurity which capitalists found intolerable. Cutthroat competition and price wars threatened not only the profit levels but the very existence of many heavily capitalized enterprises. To "rationalize" a chaotic situation, "trusts" were formed, by which stockholders in competitive firms turned over their stock to managers of a trust, receiving in return trust certificates entitling them to a share of the profits but no economic control over the firms coming under the trust's canopy. Trusts came to dominate many fields in the latter nineteenth century—sugar, cement, oil, steel, whisky, tobacco, meat packing, electrical goods, and others.

Although Big Business did not achieve dimensions in Western Europe comparable to those in the United States—partly because of smaller national markets—concentration of industry went steadily forward there, also. Instead of "trusts," however, European businesses formed cartels. These usually involved formal agreements between companies in a given industry dividing markets and fixing prices at levels providing both security and comfortable profits for all. The result was to considerably reduce both the insecurities and the invigorating character of competition.

In 1890 Congress passed the Sherman Antitrust Act, outlawing "every contract, combination in the form of trust or otherwise, or conspiracy in restraint of trade . . ." and making it a crime to "monopolize, or attempt to monopolize or combine or conspire with any other person or persons to monopolize. . . ."

For years the act was unenforced. Presidents Theodore Roosevelt and William Howard Taft, however, won some notable victories over giant corporations which had used their economic power too harshly. The Supreme Court did considerable zigging and zagging in its interpretation of the act —and of its successor, the Clayton Act of 1916. In general, the Court concerned itself with the abuse of power rather than with sheer bigness itself. Size alone was no offense, said the Court, if this was won by legitimate methods and power was used in proper ways.

During the 1920's and most of the 1930's the Sherman Act again fell into eclipse, only to take on renewed importance under trust buster Thurman Arnold in 1938 and under his successors in the Truman and Eisenhower Administrations.

Antitrust was not the only area in which business was obliged to accept a measure of public discipline after 1885. Sensitized and aroused by crusading muckrakers, who exposed abuses perpetrated by various business buccaneers, Congress responded by: (1) outlawing specific abuses in the railroad industry, and establishing the Interstate Commerce Commission to keep a watchful eye on it; (2) passing a pure food and drug act; (3) approving controls over the stockyards and meat packing industry; and (4) requiring railroads to accept responsibility for workmen's compensation.

Although these measures were often bitterly opposed by industry, a combination of public indignation and interest group pressures overrode their objections.

The Depression: A Time of Testing

There has never been a period in American history when the capitalist system was in serious danger of being supplanted, although the system itself was continuously being modified. Despite the various "panics" in the nineteenth century, confidence in the system was largely unshaken. At least until the 1930's, Marxism had made no appreciable impact upon either the intelligentsia or the working class; democratic socialism, anarchism, and syndicalism had won only small bands of supporters. Most of the muckrakers had no intention of weakening the system. They were not philosophic or activist revolutionaries, but pragmatists intent upon correcting specific abuses. Most Americans simply took capitalism for granted, assuming its general beneficence and superiority over any other system.

Faith in the system was not shattered by the Great Depression, but it was considerably shaken. The stock market crash, the collapse of thousands of banks, a radical upsurge in the number of business bankruptcies and farm foreclosures, the violence of the farm "Holiday" movement, thirteen million unemployed, breadlines—all of these, combined with the lengthening of the depression, raised serious doubts about the economic system. Was Marx—just maybe—correct in his prediction that capitalism, because it was internally rotten and shot full of contradictions and illusions, was doomed to increasingly severe crises and eventually to collapse? Although the bulk of the American people thought the economy would soon return to normal, a significant minority of intellectuals began to question the fundamental validity of the system. Many of these were not Marxists, but Marxism had been afforded its first real opportunity to make converts in America. Democratic socialism, led by the redoubtable Norman Thomas, was also pressing its case.

The Roosevelt New Deal brought about only a partial recovery (almost nine million remained unemployed in 1940), but it did help restore popular faith that the economy would right itself. The wide variety of measures enacted during the New Deal to directly or indirectly reduce individual economic insecurity and promote a more responsible exercise of private economic power, were ultimately destined to strengthen the capitalist system by abating grievances which, cumulatively, could weaken attachment to any system. In summary, the New Deal, followed by the extension of the welfare state under subsequent administrations, doubtless bolstered popular support for the capitalist system even as it altered the free market in a host of ways.

Despite the impressive array of public services and economic protections provided by the New Deal, the future of capitalism in 1945 seemed far from assured. Europe during the 1930's had experienced a depression as devastating as the United States had and the loyalty of Europeans to the capitalist system—never as great as in the United States—had been seriously undermined. Labor and socialist parties became major contenders for power throughout most of Western Europe. Nationalization of major industries was central to their goals, along with a degree of central economic planning usually regarded as incompatible with capitalism. The growth of fascism in Italy and Spain, and of Naziism in Germany, showed that capitalism could be retained, nominally, but made so subservient to state goals that it lost many of its most distinctive qualities. Finally, the growth of communism in East Europe and of major communist parties in Western Europe presented the greatest threat of all—since communism was based on the total repudiation of the capitalist structure and the capitalist spirit.

The major danger to capitalism in both the United States and Western Europe lay in the possible inability of the system to maintain full employment and an acceptable rate of economic growth. Only the war had ended the depression in the Western Hemisphere; could a peaceful postwar world avoid another economic disaster? The issue was of critical importance, because even in capitalism's strongest domain, the United States, it was doubtful that the system could survive a repetition of the Great Depression. In Europe there was not much doubt at all—the system couldn't.

Postwar Europe did avoid another economic collapse, but socialist governments and policies forged ahead nonetheless. The partial nationalization of industry went forward on many fronts; centralized planning of investment and the establishment of national economic goals to guide private economic decisions also became common.

In the United States the much-feared postwar depression also failed to materialize. A heavy backlog of public and private needs accumulated from depression and war years combined with a massive accumulation of wartime savings to keep economic activity high. When the economy showed signs of weakness, the Korean War provided a fresh spending stimulus which recharged the economic batteries. But could the capitalist system maintain full employment and a high rate of economic growth in the absence of war?

The question was resolved in the 1950's and 1960's through application of the economic theories of John Maynard Keynes. Writing to George Bernard Shaw in 1935, Keynes predicted that the book he was then writing would revolutionize economics.[7] It was an audacious prophecy, but it proved to be an understatement. More than revolutionizing economics, *The General Theory of Employment, Interest and Money* (1936) dealt a lethal blow to the hopes of doctrinaire socialism in the West.

Keynes challenged the notion that the capitalist system had self-correcting tendencies insuring that purchasing power would normally be adequate

[7] Robert Heilbroner, *The Worldly Philosophers* (New York: Simon & Schuster, 1953), pp. 258–59.

to stimulate full employment; he denied that the disaster of the 1930's was a temporary aberration which could hardly happen again. He insisted that the economy could stabilize at a level well below full production, largely because people sometimes hoard their savings instead of investing them. Although his theories are very complex, his fundamental recommendation was that government, whenever private demand was insufficient to fully utilize men and machines, should compensate for this deficiency by either reducing taxes and running a deficit, or increasing spending to incur a deficit. Once aggregate demand, drawing on both public and private spending, reached an adequate plane, the economy would return to full production.

The belief that government, like family households, should always balance its budget, was so powerfully entrenched that policies based on Keynes's views encountered stubborn resistance from the public in general and from conservative political forces in particular. Long after most economists had adopted Keynes's theories, Congress and President Eisenhower were either unconvinced or unwilling to risk public displeasure by consciously using a public deficit to stimulate the economy. Most of Western Europe, however, acted upon Keynesian principles throughout the 1950's and achieved not only continuous full employment, but a rate of economic growth well above that prevailing in the United States. (West Germany, a holdout against Keynesian economics, deliberately resorted to deficit financing in 1967 when a recession threatened.) Although America ran a persistent series of deficits during the postwar period, these were accidental rather than purposive and were commonly deplored.

In 1963, President Kennedy finally asked for a major tax cut to stimulate our lagging economy. Congress balked, but after Kennedy's assassination, granted Lyndon Johnson an $11 billion tax cut designed to pull the economy out of stagnation, prevent the recessions which had dogged postwar America (1948–49, 1953–54, 1957–58, and 1960–61) and reduce the rising levels of unemployment. The resulting burst of prosperity, unmatched in all American history, sufficiently vindicated the American Keynesians to virtually insure that their policies would be followed in the future.[8] Even Richard Nixon was prepared to adopt Keynesian policies if the 1970 recession failed to yield to more orthodox prescriptions.

The gratifying postwar economic performance of Western Europe in the 1950's largely put an end to agitation for the public ownership of industry. Nationalization for nationalization's sake might appeal to old-guard socialists, but to the younger generation and to less committed socialists, public ownership came to seem irrelevant.

[8] Interestingly, American businessmen long rejected Keynesian economics, even though their self-interest should have dictated an enthusiastic reception.

Currently Western Europe is concerned with another problem. Heavy American investment in European industry, combined with a phenomenal American growth rate in the 1960's which pushed the U.S. gross national product close to the trillion dollar mark, has aroused deep apprehension on the Continent. Fearful that U.S. industry is pulling decisively ahead in developing the technologies of the future (especially in computers, electronic processing equipment, and aerospace), J. J. Servan-Schreiber warns that Western Europe must close the widening gap or be consigned to a dwindling economic and political role.[9] He sees the necessity of educating a much larger percentage of European youth (only one fourth as many go on to higher education as in America), training far more scientists and engineers, emphasizing training in managerial skills, doubling investment in research and development, and devising supranational political institutions which enable the fullest exploitation of technological possibilities.[10] Thus Europe, much as it resents American economic superiority and disdains American culture, may find itself compelled to follow "capitalist" America's lead or be hopelessly outclassed in the economic race. Few Europeans suggest that either old-fashioned or newfangled socialism can enable West Europe to compete with America.

But even if Western Europe chooses to follow in America's footsteps, the growing concern with controlling industrial pollution, plus the need to curb persistent inflation, may drive Western governments ever more deeply into economic intervention. The blend of private enterprise and governmental direction will apparently lean ever more heavily toward the latter as this century progresses.

Capitalism: Myth and Reality

Earlier, we described the classical model of capitalism, setting forth the major principles and premises which constitute the capitalism subideology. It will be instructive to compare the current characteristics of the American economy with the theoretical construct of the eighteenth and nineteenth centuries.

Although there are some eleven to twelve million business enterprises in the United States (including three million farms), the rise of the corporation has obscured the individual entrepreneur so prominent in early capitalist theory. Corporations currently do about seventy-five percent of all the

---

[9] *The American Challenge* (New York: Atheneum, 1968).

[10] See also Walter Goldstein, "Europe Faces the Technology Gap," *Yale Review*, LIX (Winter, 1970), 161–178.

business in America, earn over half of the national income, and—in the stock socialist phrase—control "the commanding heights of the economy."

An important point of difference between the corporation and the entrepreneur is that corporations operate under the principle of limited liability. Whereas an individual businessman who goes bankrupt may face the loss of all his private property to satisfy his creditors, the corporation stockholder is liable only to the extent of its assets. Because less individual risk is involved, corporations are able to take more collective risks.

Yet, while able to take more risks, the modern corporation also differs from the traditional risk-taking entrepreneur in that it makes every effort to minimize risks. It does this by "vertical integration"—by gaining sufficient control of raw materials and sales outlets to insure greater security for its total operation; by relying ever more heavily on internal financing rather than going into the stock market for expansion capital; by insuring adequate demand both through massive advertising campaigns; and by supporting governmental programs for stabilizing the economy as a whole. Rather than entrust its fate to a free market which mercilessly penalizes mistakes in judgment and inefficiency of operation, the modern corporation does everything in its power to cushion itself against the shocks and perils of a free market.

While the classical model of capitalism assumed a direct correspondence between individual financial ownership of an enterprise and the control of that enterprise, the modern corporation has separated ownership from control. The large corporation is run not by its thousands (or millions) of stockholders, but by professional managers who exercise full control over its operations. So long as they make a profit, and the stockholders get reasonable dividends, their control is virtually absolute. Yet the management may not have the same hierarchy of goals as the stockholders. John Kenneth Galbraith believes that corporation managers ". . . now exercise largely autonomous power, and not surprisingly, they exercise it in *their* own self-interest. And this interest differs from that of the owners . . . security of return is more important than the level of total earnings. . . . And growth is more important to managers and technicians than maximum earnings." [11]

The management may seek stability of earnings to insure that the stock-

[11] "Market Planning and the Role of Government," *Atlantic Monthly*, CCXIX (May, 1967), 79. Gregory Grossman agrees that some firms are content with a "satisfactory" rate of profit, or with maintaining a "traditional" share of the market. —*Economic Systems* (Englewood Cliffs, N.J.: Prentice-Hall, 1967), p. 47. However, see the discussion between Robert M. Solow and Galbraith in *The Public Interest*, No. 9 (Fall, 1967), 100–119. Also see a subsequent discussion between Robin Marris and Solow in *The Public Interest*, No. 11 (Spring, 1968), 37–52.

holders will leave them alone. And, consistent with the traditional American belief that "bigger is better," the managers seem to find maximum ego satisfaction in a year-end financial statement reflecting impressive company growth. The lure of maximum company profit, therefore, does not always direct priorities in the classic sense. However, Galbraith overlooks the important influence which security analysts and institutional investors of mutual funds, pension funds, and investment trusts have upon management autonomy. He also draws a sharper distinction between a growth goal and a long-run profit goal than many economists will accept.

In contrast to the older image of the individual entrepreneur shrewdly calculating his gains and losses from this decision compared to that, and personally making the final judgment with an eye on profits, the modern private corporation absorbs the individual into a vast apparatus in which his contribution is only indirectly related to his cash returns. If he works in the research and development division of the firm, he may be the most innovative and creative person in the plant, but the nexus between his efforts and his monetary rewards is tenuous. He does not directly and immediately benefit from increased company profits. The impersonality, the extreme specialization of labor, the diffusion of decision-making, the magnitude of the operation—all tend to mute the individual profit motive and transmute it into something not too different from the incentive within the big public corporation, wherein good work may also lead to a promotion or salary increase or various psychic satisfactions.

Many of the modern private corporations are massive—bigger than the early capitalist theoreticians ever imagined. General Motors has capital assets of $13 billion and earns over $2 billion a year in net profits. American Telephone and Telegraph has the world's largest capital assets—over $37 billion. The five hundred biggest industrial concerns control two-thirds of all the manufacturing assets in the nation; the top fifty control one-third; and the top five, one-eighth.[12] Nor is this phenomenon confined to the United States. Concentration of manufacturing industries is even farther advanced in Japan and Canada. In West European countries also, a small number of firms frequently dominate the production of major industries.

Economic Giantism

The role of massive corporations in the American economy deserves special attention. Why have they become so large? Is bigness a virtue? How has

[12] Most writers believe economic concentration has increased little if any over the past fifty years. See G. Warren Nutter, *International Encyclopedia of Social Sciences,* VII (1968), 221.

it affected competition? How much political power does big business have?

In a relatively free economy there is a natural tendency for the more efficient competitors to grow at the expense of the less efficient. That is, competition tends to destroy competition, and the victors gain strength from the wreckage of their unsuccessful rivals.

Bigness also enjoys certain inherent advantages insofar as potential efficiency is concerned. The large corporation can buy more cheaply, because it buys in large quantities. It can afford to advertise more extensively, spend more on research, organize a better nationwide sales organization, recruit promising talent in a more systematic nationwide manner, probe foreign markets more successfully. It can engage in mass production, with the economies and efficiencies associated therewith. It can integrate control over raw materials, the manufacturing process, and the sales process without yielding potential profits to other firms which might otherwise participate in the total operation. It can diversify operations sufficiently to compensate for losses in one field with profits in another. Sometimes this is done by "conglomerate" mergers of essentially unrelated economic enterprises. It has greater stability and can thus offer potential employees attractive security and fringe benefits. Its very prestige as a big, nationally known outfit has recruiting power. In these and other ways, the development of bigness is natural to a society with a vast domestic market, free from cramping tariffs and tolls.

Other factors have played a part in developing our huge corporations. During wartime, government contracts tend to flow first and fastest to them, since they are geared up to the mass production scale which modern warfare demands. This tends to make the big bigger. The patent laws also work to the benefit of the "bigs," since they can spend heavily to develop patents which confer a competitive advantage or buy up patents for the same purpose.[13] About twenty-five percent of modern corporation growth comes from mergers, in which one firm buys another—because the joint operations will contribute to greater efficiency, eliminate competition, or satisfy the itch for growth. (Since 1950, mergers which "substantially" reduce competition have not been permitted.)

That a close correlation exists between increasing size and increasing efficiency is demonstrable only up to a point. Many economists believe that a medium-sized firm is as efficient or more efficient than a giant corporation. In the *International Encyclopedia of Social Sciences,* Joe S. Bain contends

---

[13] See Walter Adams and Horace M. Gray, *Monopoly in America* (New York: Macmillan, 1955), for a general exposition of the theory that government policy has contributed greatly to economic concentration in America.

that "Economies of the multiplant firm appear to have been greatly over-rated by various observers making casual judgments." [14]

Very few corporations enjoy a monopolistic position in the strictest sense of the word. But oligopolies—where a handful of firms dominate an industry—have become a common feature in the economy. With oligopoly has come a serious threat to one of the basic elements of the competitive system —price competition. Instead of competing by price, oligopolies often develop a system of "price leadership," whereby one firm establishes a price level providing comfortable profit probabilities, and the others "follow the leader." The price is often set with a particular profit "target" in mind. [15] No formal agreements are made between the firms—there is just a tacit understanding that since price cutting will only redound to the disadvantage of all, why not be sensible and behave like gentlemen? Price leadership is the American counterpart to the European cartel, and it has led some critics to deplore the decline of competition in the United States.

It is not at all clear, however, that competition has actually declined. Competition can be and often is as fierce among three or four competitors as among fifty, as is demonstrated in the auto industry—or by Hertz and Avis Rent-A-Car! Big firms are likely to pour more money into research, yielding improvements or new products attractive to the consumer.

Price competition is not the only significant form of competition. Competition based on differences in quality can be of equal importance, as well as offers of superior servicing or the supply of custom-made goods to meet industrial specifications. Moreover, competition can be effectively furnished by substitute products or services. For example, Drive-It-Yourself competes with taxis, Haul-It-Yourself with trucks, Do-It-Yourself kits with painters and carpenters, motels with hotels, house trailers with houses and apartments, television with movies, planes with buses and railroads, natural gas and oil with coal, paper and tin containers with glass, synthetic fibres with cotton and wool, frozen with canned goods, plastics with metals, soccer with baseball, Hondas with Mustangs, savings and loan associations with banks.

Better transportation enables (nonghetto) consumers to shop around for better buys, thus sharpening competition; chain stores and supermarkets compete with small grocers and drugstores; discount houses and mail order houses compete with department stores; as tariffs fall, foreign competition

---

[14] IV (1968), 494. Efficiency, Bain says, normally "requires firms with outputs no larger than one plant of minimum optimal scale." On the other hand, he does not associate major diseconomies with giantism, either. (From 10–30% of American manufacturing output is said to be produced by firms too small for maximum efficiency.)

[15] For a particularly conspicuous example, see Herman Roseman, "The Price of Peace," *Reporter*, XXII (February, 1960), 13–15.

increases. In a myriad ways, it is alleged, competition is intensifying rather than declining in the United States.[16]

In any case, there is often a temptation to exaggerate the shrinkage of competition and the free market. John M. Blair, chief economist for the Senate Subcommittee on Antitrust and Monopoly for over ten years, observes that in addition to services, the professions, handicrafts, and some retail trades, ". . . the free market functions tolerably well in such additional fields as construction, most foods, most textiles, apparel, lumber, furniture, printing, some paper products, stone and clay products, nonferrous metals (except aluminum), fabricated metals, most machinery, many electronic products and some chemicals. The area of the economy in which competition is very much alive is certainly as large as the area in which it is quiescent." [17]

Relatively easy entry into an industrial field was one of the presuppositions of the early writers on capitalism; today the capital investment required to compete with many oligopolies is so immense that new competition is effectively foreclosed—except as the giants branch out into new fields. The capacity of the big corporations to spend huge sums on advertising contributes heavily to this, since struggling new firms can rarely afford the money required to compete with the saturation advertising of the giants.

Rugged Individualism?

In the classical model, wages as well as prices were set in a free market. Today wages are not usually determined by businessmen negotiating with individual workers. Instead, giant labor unions bargain with businessmen, establishing wage levels which govern the entire corporation or even an entire industry. The unions also exercise a voice in the making of many economic decisions—a voice designed to promote employee security and well-being rather than maximum company profits. An undetermined percentage of executives, moreover, are willing to sacrifice some potential profits because the ethos of our time calls upon them to exercise "social responsibility" rather than calculate every decision exclusively by profit criteria.

Advertising, now a $17 billion business in the United States, serves an-

[16] A concise and persuasive statement of this position was made in economist Sumner Slichter's "The Growth of Competition," *Atlantic Monthly*, CXCII (November, 1953), 66–70. Joe S. Bain speaks for many economists when arguing that there has been no substantial decline in competitiveness over the last thirty or forty years—*Industrial Organization* (New York: John Wiley, 1959), Chap. 6.

[17] "Galbraith's Two Hats," *Progressive*, XXXI (August, 1967), 36.

other function unrelated to classical capitalism. Acting in response to instructions from businessmen, advertisers create a market for certain products rather than merely responding to existing demand. Planning for a period of many years, corporations invest millions in a new product or a variation of an old product. They cannot afford, considering their investment, to place their trust in spontaneous customer acceptance of the product. By employing all the beguilements of modern advertising, the consumer is teased, tantalized, wheedled, and coaxed into purchasing the product. Major advertising campaigns are not always successful; nor can advertisers long sell a clearly inferior product. To a considerable degree, however, an affluent society can be persuaded to buy a skillfully advertised product which might be largely ignored in the absence of advertising. Thus the consumer's reign over the marketplace becomes something less than sovereign.

Other factors should be noted. The modern businessman cannot afford to rely upon the accident of purchasing power balancing the supply of goods and services offered by a full employment economy. Under Say's law (that the production of goods and services generates the purchasing power needed to consume them), no problem could exist—at least not for long. But when the depression shattered this "law" once and for all, stopgap measures were used to deal with the crisis. Immediately after World War II, Congress passed the Full Employment Act of 1946, which affirmed the government's responsibility to insure adequate employment opportunities. The insecurities of the market system, once believed to have a salutary effect on the economy by purging its inefficient firms, prodding the survivors into still better performance, and stimulating the uneasy worker to greater efforts, have not been eliminated by governmental programs; but they have been substantially reduced. The individual firm can still go broke, but widespread bankruptcy occasioned by a slump in consumer demand is most unlikely to recur in the foreseeable future.

The image of ruggedly independent entrepreneurs rising or falling strictly on the basis of market demand for their products is also modified by the presence of numerous government subsidies to firms which would fail without them. The shipping industry and the airlines receive subsidies enabling them to stay in business. The construction industry enjoys government mortgage guarantees which have contributed greatly to its level of operations and profits. Innumerable newspapers and magazines are able to operate because the United States Treasury subsidizes the delivery of their product through postal rates lower than the cost of carrying such mail. Tariffs (a form of producer subsidy) enable some industries to survive international competition. Government stockpiling of certain metals and materials is used not merely to promote the national security but also to bolster sagging prices which threaten profits. Farmers receive irrigation water at far below cost. In scores of ways, governments prop up various businesses rather than permit the rigor of the free market to take its toll.[18] (Most American industries, it should be added, are not subsidized.)

Even in agriculture, often thought of as the fortress of rugged individualism, the free market has taken its lumps. A substantial portion of agricultural prices are still set in the free market, but government acreage controls, price supports, and emergency purchase operations have placed floors under many farm commodities corresponding to wage floors established by collective bargaining and minimum wages. Much of the fabulous progress made by American agriculture this century has come about not from private enterprise but from government research and experiment stations.

Eli Ginzberg has estimated that roughly forty percent of the jobs in the American economy derive from the "not for profit sector." [19] This includes not only all the millions of workers who are employed by federal, state, and local government; but also employees of unions, trade associations, professional societies, co-ops, most colleges, hospitals, foundations, libraries, research organizations, Blue Cross, Blue Shield, etc., and that important segment of the private economy which produces sophisticated weaponry, outer space equipment and other goods purchased only by governments. (Obviously space and defense goods are produced for profit, but most of them are purchased by government through negotiation, often based on a cost plus arrangement.) With federal, state, and local budgets running to nearly $300 billion, the operations of the free market have been distorted and its orbit has shrunk sharply.

The most conspicuous form of socialism (public ownership of industry— TVA and other public dams; the Government Printing Office; the Atomic Energy Commission; municipal water, power, and transportation systems) remains a minor part of our total economy system. Governments generally have resorted to public ownership only if a service was traditionally governmental or inherently monopolistic, or had proven unprofitable for private enterprise, yet was essential to the public welfare.

In summary, the classical model of a free market and a freely competitive system dominantly characterized by small enterprise, highly individualized initiative, and a hands-off government, has been radically altered by economic and political developments of the past century.

[18] For a full description of government subsidies, see *Subsidy and Subsidy-Effect Programs of the U.S. Government,* Joint Economic Committee, 89th Congress, 1st Session (Washington: Government Printing Office, 1965).
[19] *The Pluralistic Economy* (New York: McGraw-Hill, 1965), p. 209.

Economic Power and Political Power

No study of modern capitalism can afford to ignore the interrelationships between business power and political power. One of the principal charges leveled against capitalism by its Marxian and some of its non-Marxian critics is that economic power is inevitably converted into political power. The capitalists, despite their cleverness in concealing their string-pulling operations, are said to call the major political shots in America by their control of the mass media, of powerful interest groups, and of key legislators. As long ago as January 8, 1890, the editor of the *Atlanta Constitution* declared "Politicians may talk, but businessmen will act, control and dominate the destinies of this common-sense country." Much more recently, C. Wright Mills paid tribute to the extraordinary political power of the corporate rich in *The Power Elite*.[20]

The following generalizations, while sometimes lacking empirical proof, would probably be supported by most professional students of interest groups in the United States.

In many small-to-middle-sized communities, large corporations which supply much of the employment for those communities are likely to have impressive political influence whenever they choose to exert it—particularly if the issue is of direct concern to them. This influence may be used with discretion or it may be used in a heavy-handed manner to keep unions at bay, win or maintain special tax or other privileges, dictate local candidates for public office, and generally control local policies of economic importance.

On the state level, business organizations are among the most potent interest groups. As an extreme example, Harry M. Caudill has written that ". . . the state and local governments [of Appalachia] are little more than fronts for the absentee corporations which control the economic destinies of the region. The wealth—and it is almost immeasurable—is in 'foreign' ownership as surely as are most of the riches of Central America." [21] The lack of public concern with state legislation, the high percentage of businessmen serving as state legislators, the weakness of labor lobbies in the states, the competition between states to attract industry by giving business a favored position—all help explain the undoubted importance of business power on the state level.

[20] *The Power Elite* (New York: Oxford University Press, 1956), Chaps. 7, 10, 12. Mills's thesis is challenged by Robert Dahl, "A Critique of the Ruling Elite Model," *American Political Science Review*, LII (June, 1958), 463–469; and by Daniel Bell in *The End of Ideology,* rev. ed. (New York: Free Press, 1962), pp. 47–74.
[21] "Misdeal in Appalachia," *Atlantic Monthly*, CCXV (June, 1965), 44.

Nationally, the most prominent groups representing American business are the National Association of Manufacturers and the United States Chamber of Commerce. These organizations are professionally staffed, well financed, and politically active. No responsible student, however, believes they dominate the Congress. The NAM (representing large business) is not even regarded as one of the more powerful interest groups, largely because it has won the dubious reputation of having opposed almost all "progressive" measures during the twentieth century. The Chamber (representing smaller business) exercises somewhat greater, but by no means awesome power.[22]

Business organizations representing specific industries are regarded as much more potent than the NAM and the Chamber. Yet industries often have conflicting interests which cancel out their lobbying efforts, as when the railroad and trucking industry interests collide, or the coal industry interests conflict with the natural gas interests, or firms with export interests oppose firms having import interests.

On the federal level, Andrew Shonfield notes that ". . . to an outside observer it seems . . . that private enterprise has had some striking successes in actually capturing a number of enclaves inside the structure of the Federal Government. And even where its marauding parties have not been able to establish full rights of conquest, they do seem in several instances to have taken up permanent residence inside and to be living on terms of equality with those officially in charge." [23]

In many cases, of course, the political power of business is counterbalanced by the political weight exercised by labor unions. In other instances (e.g., the defense industries, coal, and shipping), unions have established incestuous relations with management which largely destroy the "counterbalancing" effect unions are supposed to exercise.

Grossman contends that "Perhaps the most significant feature of postwar capitalism has been the politico-economic equilibrium among, and mutual acceptance of, business (especially big business), government and organized labor in the advanced countries." [24] However, the political self-interest of the chief executive and of members of Congress, it might be noted, obliges corporations to pursue broader goals than the expansion of business profits.

Few bills imposing important restrictions on American business have

[22] Small business in recent decades has often proved to be more conservative than big business. See Arnold M. Rose, *The Power Structure* (New York: Oxford University Press, 1967), p. 115; and Robert Heilbroner, *The Limits of American Capitalism* (New York: Harper & Row, 1966), p. 41.

[23] *Modern Capitalism* (New York: Oxford University Press, 1965), p. 334.

[24] *Economic Systems, op. cit.* (above, n. 11), p. 29.

passed Congress during this century. Yet when abuses have become sufficiently flagrant, or the public was sufficiently aroused, business has not been able to block reforms. The muckrakers *did* succeed in obtaining remedial legislation; and the Roosevelt administration *was* able to regulate the stock market, the sale of securities, holding companies, wages and hours, and to obtain major organizing and bargaining rights for labor unions. Business was unable to prevent the passage of many other welfare state measures to which it was opposed, both during the Roosevelt administration and during the first eighteen months of the Lyndon Johnson administration. Business, furthermore, has been obliged by public pressure to spend far more money on pollution control than it would like. Auto safety measures, following growing public unrest over 55,000 fatalities a year, have been forced upon the auto industry. So have exhaust emission controls. Fair employment laws were enacted during the civil rights revolution of the 1960's, despite business distaste for such legislation.

Still the picture is very mixed. For example, the major drug companies have successfully fought off modest controls over abuses spotlighted by Congressional investigations; and the tobacco companies were long able to blunt the drive for effective control over their advertising practices.[25] The major oil companies have been able to maintain controls over oil production and transportation, along with oil depletion allowances of scandalous nature, which vastly enhance their profits and cost the consumer billions of dollars annually.[26]

Although the American tax structure bristles with inequities which benefit the affluent (primarily among the ranks of business), such as the excessive oil depletion allowance, tax-free state and local government bonds, capital gains windfalls, and various "tax havens" for the sharp operator, the beneficiaries (often big campaign contributors) have been extraordinarily effective in strangling or blunting proposed reforms.[27] Probably in no other area are American business and its allies in so complete command of a significant public policy as in the tax structure. On the other hand, business chafes under a forty-eight percent federal corporation tax, which it is quite incapable of reducing, except as part of a general tax reduction program. In brief, business wins many legislative battles and loses many others.

25 For an excellent analysis of the cigarette strategy, see Elizabeth Brenner Drew, "Quiet Victory of the Cigarette Lobby," *Atlantic Monthly*, CCXVI (September, 1965), 76–80.

26 Ronnie Dugger, "Oil and Politics," *Atlantic Monthly*, CCXXIV (September, 1969), 66–88.

27 See Philip M. Stern, *The Great Treasury Raid* (New York: Random House, 1964).

While the urban press is usually run by wealthy businessmen, and usually supports business interests, the most influential newspapers are not narrowly dominated by a business viewpoint. The most influential columnists and writers for the prominent national magazines are not partial to business interests. It has long been commonplace to concede that the press, though largely Republican, does not have a great impact upon national elections. No pattern can be found between press support and national election returns.[28] While the major publishing houses are themselves big business, their leadership seldom agrees with the NAM. In any case, they are delighted to publish the works of any writer who will lambaste American business or any segment thereof—if the book will sell! Moreover, attacks generally sell while defenses do not.

On the antitrust front, business pressures have enjoyed mixed results. As already indicated, friendly administrations have often ignored the law or softpedaled its enforcement. Yet there have been other periods when enforcement has been severe enough to bring cries of anguish and complaints of persecution from business. Thurman Arnold, Wendell Berge, Judge Samuel Barnes, and Robert Bicks were trustbusters from 1938 to 1960 whom no knowledgeable person would accuse of being subservient to big business. When Mr. Bicks prosecuted executives of twenty-seven electrical companies for collusive violations of the Sherman Act, leading to convictions and jail sentences for a number of them, this was a chastening (and highly un-Marxian) experience for American business.[29] Business has also resented the Celler Act of 1950 forbidding mergers which have a substantially adverse effect on competition in any line of business in any region of the country. Yet it recognizes the futility of seeking to repeal the law.

While the major outlines of business expansion have not been altered very much by the Sherman Act, there is no real doubt that antitrust has made businessmen more prudent about their competitive practices and less inclined to consummate mergers which might enhance their profits, but would also bring antitrust officials to their doorstep.

On several notable occasions, Presidents Kennedy and Johnson were able to force business to reverse price decisions which threatened inflationary

---

[28] Frank L. Mott, "Newspapers in Presidential Campaigns," *Public Opinion Quarterly*, VIII (1944), 358.

[29] A good, brief analysis of antitrust enforcement in America can be found in Richard Hofstadter, "Antitrust in America," *Commentary*, XXXVIII (August, 1964), 47–53. Hofstadter concludes that antitrust has "ceased to be an ideology and has become a technique . . . it has gained in effectiveness at the very moment it has lost public interest."

consequences. Yet in general, business has been able to control its price structure in accordance with its own profit estimates, without yielding very much ground to Presidential pressures.

The independent regulatory commissions, established to insure that American business in general, and certain industries in particular, operate within the "public interest," have had an uninspiring record. Potential appointees are carefully screened by the industrial interests involved and those believed "hostile" to the industry are unlikely to be appointed, or if appointed, to be confirmed. Many appointees, acquiring expertise during extended commission tours, also acquire a sympathetic view of the industry's "problems" in the conscious or unconscious hope of obtaining lucrative positions with the industry when their terms expire. It is common to speak of the commissions as "mothering" the industries under their jurisdiction rather than vigorously regulating them. Yet gross abuses are probably limited somewhat by the presence of these commissions.

Does American business have a considerable control over American foreign policy? It depends on how one defines "considerable." The decades of "Yankee imperialism" in Latin America are too well known to need recapitulation; the American dollar was consistently supported by the American flag. Currently it is impossible to state, with adequate evidence, how much influence business exerts in this area. American oil interests abroad, since oil is critical to national defense and future industrial needs, undoubtedly attract formidable American political power in their support. But with countries everywhere demanding the right to control all foreign enterprise within their boundaries, neither American businessmen nor the State Department is able to overcome that sovereign claim.[30]

Heilbroner asserts that ". . . the politics of nationalism has asserted its pre-eminence over the politics of imperialism, with the salutary consequence of a diminution in the role of business as the active initiator of foreign economic policy."[31]

American trading interests, contrary to a widely held misconception, are often of a liberalizing nature, since American businessmen are more interested in making a profit via international trade than in adhering to strict ideological lines. Thus many businessmen may favor trading with communist countries, while national business spokesmen make emotional speeches about the apocalyptic character of the communist menace.

[30] Edwin S. Dale, "The U.S. Economic Giant Keeps Growing," *New York Times Magazine,* March 19, 1967, p. 136. Dale's penetrating review generally minimizes the influence of American economic power in world politics.
[31] *The Limits of American Capitalism, op. cit.* (above, n. 23), p. 107.

No responsible historian would contend that American military involvement in World War II, Korea, Lebanon, Cuba, the Dominican Republic, or Vietnam was primarily dictated by American business interests. Business often had a stake, but its voice was not decisive; political rather than economic considerations were dominant in each instance.

Probably business' biggest political asset lies in the extent to which the average American shares the businessman's values and attitudes. Americans are convinced that the private enterprise system has brought them unparalleled prosperity; believe the profit system "works"; regard wide income differentials to be normal and proper; want business to be as "free" as possible; and are wary of Big Government, bureaucracy, centralized political power, and high taxes. These attitudes powerfully undergird business interests; they severely limit the scope of potential legislation affecting business. They make economic planning, European style, politically impossible in the United States.

Still, as Adolf Berle notes, the big corporations function within a framework of public consensus which, although rarely articulated, operates as a continuing restraint upon business power.[32] An excellent example is found in the case of Ralph Nader. Stung by Nader's documented charges that the auto industry was unconscionably resistant to elementary safety construction needs, General Motors put private detectives on his trail in an effort to discover something about his private life which could be used to discredit his damaging charges. But when false accusations were made about Mr. Nader, and the nature of General Motors' project came to light, the result was revealing. For all that its huge economic wealth, power, and prestige were pitted against one lone young man, General Motors was obliged to beat a precipitous retreat in the face of a chorus of public denunciation of its tactics. The president of General Motors publicly apologized for his company's action. The upshot was the strengthening of the movement for an effective auto safety law which cost the reluctant industry many millions of dollars (promptly passed on to the consumer, however). Similarly, the cigarette industry was eventually forced to yield to public criticism of radio and TV advertising. The pollution-control movement also demonstrates that business is no match for an aroused public.

A reasonably accurate summary of the political power of American business is not easy to make. Heilbroner notes that ". . . what is noticeable among the majority of big businessmen in America is a striking absence of real political commitment."[33] He finds business political power declining

[32] *Power Without Property* (New York: Harcourt, Brace, 1959), pp. 90–91.
[33] *The Limits of American Capitalism, op. cit.* (above, n. 23), p. 39.

but believes that "of all interest groups in the nation, no other is so potent as business." [34] While conceding that business has considerable political clout, Arnold Rose concludes that "power is so complicated in the United States that the top businessmen scarcely understand it, let alone control it." [35]

Perhaps one might safely say that American political attitudes are favorable to capitalistic ends, that business can well defend its legitimate interests and, in the absence of public concern, some less-than-legitimate interests. But when the American people are persuaded that serious abuses exist or that welfare legislation is needed, business opposition does not prevail. No interest group—whether business, labor, agriculture, or the military—is bigger than Washington when Washington responds to an aroused public.

That the capitalist system is well adapted to the rapid development of a country's resources—at least under some conditions—is not challenged. The wealth and economic dynamism of countries like the United States, Canada, West Germany, Switzerland, and Japan are not without major significance. Each of these countries relies heavily on private enterprise and a relatively free market to produce its goods and services.

Japan provides an impressive example of the kind of economic progress which can be made when a basically private enterprise system is combined with indirect but influential governmental support and direction of the economy. From 1955–64, Japan's rate of economic growth was without parallel in the history of any nation. It achieved annual growth rates of up to 11 percent and has sustained a high rate of economic expansion throughout the entire post World War II period. Although Japan also had annual rates of growth averaging 3.3 percent from 1879–1913 and 4.4 percent from 1913–38, it has far outdistanced this record since 1945. What accounts for this truly remarkable feat? [36]

In addition to the intangible characteristics of the national character, a number of factors seem to be involved. The Japanese give education the highest social priority, achieving a literacy rate of 98 percent and sending roughly twice as high a percentage of its youth into higher education as does Western Europe. Unlike many developing nations, the Japanese were not obsessed with industrial development at the expense of agriculture but devoted substantial research and financial resources to the agricultural sector. As a result, Japanese farms are among the most productive in the world.

Japanese savings rates are the highest of any nation. The Japanese

[34] *Ibid.,* p. 49.
[35] Rose, *op. cit.* (above, n. 23), p. 490.
[36] Much of the following four paragraphs draw heavily from Benjamin Higgins, *Economic Development,* rev. ed. (New York: W. W. Norton, 1968), pp. 644–649, 698–700.

regularly pour a tremendous amount of money into investment, the ratio of gross investment to gross national product reaching as high as 38 percent. (It is often estimated that less developed nations need to invest 12–13 percent of their output into capital goods and equipment if they are to achieve a so-called takeoff stage.) In addition, the Japanese are celebrated for their capacity to absorb and effectively utilize the technical advances of other nations. Although the Japanese wage rate is not as low as is commonly believed—if generous fringe benefits are calculated—those rates still have given the Japanese an advantage in exploiting the brisk post World War II world market. Success in controlling the birth rate (largely through very high abortion rates) has helped maintain a labor force proportion of the population which is conducive to maximum economic progress. And the forced demilitarization of Japan following Hiroshima released billions of yen for nonmilitary purposes.

What part did government play in all this? General Douglas MacArthur had supervised the dissolution of many major industrial combines, leading to a more competitive structure of business enterprise. Statistical projections of anticipated output, wages, prices, and investment by the Japanese government have helped industry plan more effectively. Particular attention is given to predicting which industries are likely to be most profitable and which least profitable a decade hence. Japanese businessmen take these prophecies seriously and act accordingly.

As with most of the socialist governments of Western Europe, the government has established no coercive national economic plan; but governmental guidance of economic development through consultations, recommendations, tax policies, and other fiscal inducements has helped to bring about a pattern of economic activity highly advantageous to rapid growth. Through its control of the Bank of Japan, the government has had a considerable impact upon industrial loans, using its influence to encourage high-priority industries. Mergers which would help firms become more competitive in the world market have been encouraged by generous lending policies. The Japanese civil service is believed to be one of the world's most efficient, and its cooperation with and encouragement to preferred industries have played an important part in shaping Japanese economic decisions. Finally, Japanese workers, who devote their lives to serving a single firm (which in turn assures their economic security) do not fear technological unemployment nor resist automation.

Overall, the dynamism of a relatively free economy, accompanied by the quiet but effective guidance of a statistically well informed and economically literate government, largely accounts for the prodigious economic achievements of postwar Japan. The government was able to succeed in part, however, because it has postponed any serious effort to solve many of its pressing domestic problems. For example, two-thirds of the inhabitants of Tokyo lack sewer services and Tokyo's air pollution is only exceeded by that of some other Japanese cities.

The next most notable record of economic growth in the postwar world was provided by West Germany. While its performance was not quite as spectacular as that of Japan, its nonetheless remarkable progress has furnished a great deal of cheer for those who claim that "enlightened capitalism" is far from obsolete in the modern world.

Hitler's Germany had eschewed public ownership, but had placed the economy under a web of restrictions and controls largely designed to insure the sustenance of Hitler's war machine. After the war, and especially when Ludwig Erhard became Minister of Economics, the German recovery program stressed the role of relatively free private enterprise in rebuilding the nation and raising German living standards.

German recovery was the product of various elements. The German has long been regarded as perhaps the hardest working person in all Europe; his diligence, vigor, and quality of workmanship have been the envy of other nations. Like Japan, Germany's exclusion from the arms race turned out to be an enormous asset, since its resources could be devoted fully to consumer goods industries, the infrastructure needed to support them, and to necessary social services. American economic aid in the amount of $5 billion also gave considerable stimulus to the German economy. The Germans diverted up to 25 percent of their gross national product into investment, a sum well above that of almost every country except Japan. This was made possible, in part, by a very high level of taxes, reaching approximately 33 percent of GNP. Much of this was invested in education, transportation, and communications—which of course was highly beneficial to the economy. With the bomb-devastated nation in need of almost total rebuilding, the demand for goods and services was almost unlimited for many years.

With so much of German industry rebuilt from scratch, the Germans were able to construct the most modern manufacturing plants and to install the most modern equipment, which in turn helped make German industry extraordinarily efficient.

Under Erhard's urging, Germany also passed an antitrust act in 1957. Germany once had been among the most cartel-ridden countries in Europe; about 2,000 cartels were present in 1925. Many of these were broken up during the allied occupation, but attempts to reestablish cartels continued. The German antitrust law was not severely restrictive, permitting so-called crisis cartels and certain forms of retail price fixing. Nor did it prevent the growth of giant industry; by 1960 the 100 largest firms produced 40 percent of German industrial output. Still, it had symbolic importance; although its future impact, as demonstrated by American experience, depends on the vigor of its enforcement.

In his highly regarded work, *Modern Capitalism,*[37] Andrew Shonfield says that Erhard talked a stronger free enterprise line than he practiced. He was not an overall planner but a "jogger and nudger." [38] For example, Erhard (and other German officials) offered liberal tax concessions to builders and low interest loans to home buyers, which enabled West Germany, between 1949–55, to build a new dwelling for every five Germans! Agriculture, as with virtually all European countries, was bulwarked by a variety of price supports and subsidies. Shonfield notes that ". . . the German Government set up a series of targets for economic recovery—basic industries, exports, housing—and concentrated the resources of the nation on them, one after another. Public saving, combined with the great ploughback of profits by firms fed on tax concessions, provided the finance for these extensive investments . . . direct subsidies, cheap loans and special tax allowances" were employed on behalf of "a variety of favoured economic activities." [39] Among the latter were steel, coal, iron, electricity, and certain enterprises importantly engaged in export operations.

Currently, the German Ministry of Economics, ". . . aided by a Washington-style council of economic advisors . . . prepares an annual projection of the coming year's increases in output, productivity, wages and prices." [40] This council provides orientation data enabling German industry to chart its future more profitably, a practice closely paralleling that of other European countries.

Capitalism has not been wholly responsible for United States prosperity; our abundant resources (and their ruthless exploitation), our large domestic market, immigration policies conducive to rapid economic growth, federal subsidies to railroads, the absence of foreign invasions and of a cramping feudal legacy have played a part. So did the use of slave labor, low paid nonslave labor, the coincidence that America was shaping the major outlines of its economic system when the Industrial Revolution was at high tide—and so have innumerable laws assisting and chastening American business. Nonetheless, only the hopelessly biased would dispute that capitalism can sometimes generate a phenomenal amount of economic horsepower. Even Karl Marx's *Communist Manifesto* conceded that "[The capitalist class] during its rule of scarce one hundred years, has created more

[37] *Modern Capitalism* (New York: Oxford University Press, 1965).
[38] *Ibid.,* pp. 292–23.
[39] *Ibid.,* pp. 283–84.
[40] Philip Siekman, "Germany Catches Its Second Wind," *Fortune,* LXXIX (April, 1969), 89–91.

massive and more colossal productive forces than have all preceding generations together."

How has America's wealth been divided, under our capitalist system?
The *Statistical Abstract of the United States* furnishes the following information: [41]

Income Level (1969)	Percent of Families
Under $3,000	12.5%
$3,000–4,999	12.8
$5,000–6,999	16.1
$7,000–9,999	24.3
$10,000–14,999	22.4
$15,000 and over	12.0

Whether this is or is not a healthy distribution is a matter of opinion.
Currently, however, the nation is making a modest effort to reduce the ranks
of the twenty-five million persons who fall below the poverty line. And national income seems to be as widely distributed in the United States as in
any country in the world.[42] Moreover, inequality of income has declined
over the past forty years.[43]

The Ideology, the System and the Future

At the outset, this chapter dwelt upon the capitalist subideology which
developed in the days of Adam Smith—and upon the way it broadened in
subsequent decades. Into what form has that subideology developed?

Many businessmen and millions of Americans doubtless subscribe to
most of the tenets of the capitalist faith delineated at the outset of this chapter. This is still the old-time religion, so far as they are concerned. While
they might make modifications here and there (such as dropping the "natural
law" element), the early capitalist doctrines still constitute the essential
truths and guidelines of their belief. They may vaguely realize that the ideology does not faithfully correspond to the realities; they may even approve
of many of the developments which have distorted the capitalist system to its
present hybridized character. But they retain an emotional commitment to
capitalist fundamentalism.

[41] *Statistical Abstract of the United States* (1969), Table 473, p. 322.
[42] Herman P. Miller, *Rich Man, Poor Man* (New York: Thomas Y. Crowell,
1964), pp. 11–13.
[43] Calvin Hoover, *International Encyclopedia of Social Sciences* (1968), II, 301.
And even though America is regarded as a capitalist nation, the percentage of national income accruing to employees is almost as high as that of any country in the
world. Preston, *op. cit.* (above, n. 3), p. 78.

More thoughtful and knowledgeable students of the American system would hold that "capitalism" is quite an inadequate descriptive term for an economic system which intermingles public and private enterprise, involves a substantial measure of government regulation, has evolved the welfare state, guarantees relatively full employment, and subsidizes numerous private enterprises. And yet many well-informed Americans who understand what has happened to the American and European economies retain a profound commitment to a system which *primarily* is based on private property and private enterprise, permits entrepreneurs to produce what they please in a *primarily* free market, with the government's control *primarily* of an indirect nature. They still feel these conditions maximize individual economic freedom, provide a valuable barrier against unnecessary bureaucracy and unnecessary governmental restraint, decentralize economic power in the most workable fashion, grant the consumer the widest variety of choices and the highest overall standard of living. They believe it enhances individual initiative and creativity and enables the economic system to adjust to the changing requirements of a dynamic age in the most flexible fashion. They believe the current economic mix to be highly compatible with a democratic political system.

Does capitalism respond unduly to the cash demands of the marketplace rather than to needs of a more fundamental nature than those represented by middle and upper income spending patterns? The present system leaves it to government, through its budgets, to insure the provision of those items which have the highest social priority but which are not adequately supplied by the free market (education, highways, conservation, minimum living standards for the poor, housing, pollution control, urban renewal, medical care, etc.), permitting the marketplace to respond freely to the private dollars which remain. This is believed to guarantee the best balancing of our public needs and our private desires. If the general public is unwilling to support nondefense public spending on a scale required by a rationally defensible conception of the public interest, then the public is to blame rather than the economic system. Many members of the New Left have failed to grasp this point, preferring to indict "the system" rather than the average American.

At this stage of American history (and perhaps European, too) the major political arguments revolve about the establishment of social priorities, and the amounts to be allocated in their support. There is little debate, however (except among New Left adherents), over the desirability of permitting private enterprise to preside over the production of most goods and services in a market which if considerably less free than in the classical sense, is still quite free when contrasted with totalitarian economies.

The most serious criticism of today's modified capitalist system tends to stem from moral rather than economic considerations. Critics ask hard questions about the effects of capitalism upon the ethos of a people. Does it focus men's interests abnormally upon the spirit of competitive advantage, acquisitiveness, and materialism at the expense of concern for community well-being and social justice? Does the pervasive character of the profit system unduly encourage the envisioning of the good life in terms of ever-increasing consumption? Does even the artist tend to be corrupted by the thought—"But will it sell?" [44] Does the ubiquity of advertising and the commercial spirit subtly coerce men's interests and loyalties into patterns which militate against the highest potentialities of the mind and spirit? In brief, perhaps the most telling criticisms of capitalism are not those identified with Marx, but those which challenge the imponderable effects of a highly competitive system upon the psyche and the perspectives of a people. Or does capitalism simply bring out into the open pressures, conflicts, stresses, and ego drives which will have other but equally destructive manifestations in another system? Some thoughtful people believe the latter is a realistic interpretation of the nature of man.

What is the future of capitalism? Nothing is more hazardous than economic and political prophecy. For the present, of course, many of the underdeveloped countries perceive only the evils of capitalism. Tending to associate it with Western imperialism, with exploitation, with great inequalities of wealth and status, and with the abuses of nineteenth-century capitalism, they prefer something (often vague) called "socialism." To them socialism implies economic democracy, cooperation, the sharing of wealth, equality, and the concentration of society's resources upon economic enterprises which have the greatest importance to rapid development. Thus capitalism might appear to have a bleak future in much of the world.

This pessimism may prove excessive, however. Milton Friedman argues that the developing countries which have made the most impressive progress in recent years are those which rely most heavily on the market system. He contends that Malaya, Singapore, Thailand, Formosa, Hong Kong, and Japan are prospering under primarily free markets, while India, Cambodia, Indonesia, and Communist China are lagging behind because of overreliance on central planning.[45] Also, Charles Lindblom has noted that while many leaders of the developing nations are "prisoners of early Marxian doctrine on planning or prisoners of English socialism of the style and date

[44] Marya Mannes, "The Exercise of Conscience," *Vital Speeches,* May 1, 1961, pp. 441–443.

[45] Milton Friedman, "Myths That Keep People Hungry," *Harper's,* CCXXXIV (April, 1967), 16–24.

of Harold Laski," attitudes may change. He makes a persuasive case that since both Western and communist countries are "rediscovering" the values of the market, this rediscovery "is certain to impress them [leaders of developing nations]." And since the developing countries lack the administrative skills and organization for "executing any kind of plan," since the market provides the best "method of extricating a traditional peasantry from older institutions and habits of life that retard development," since they lack the living standards which make possible forced savings—communist style—and since certain kinds of central planning are compatible with the market mechanism, he is optimistic about the market's future in those countries. Lindblom concludes that "the market mechanism is now everywhere becoming recognized as a fundamental method of economic organization which no nation can ignore and which every nation can well afford to examine freshly." [46]

Inasmuch as many developing nations' economies will remain mainly agricultural for years to come and collectivized agriculture has proved to be the weakest link in the communist economy, privately owned and operated agriculture may remain predominant in the East as well as the West. A respected economist has further observed that the advantages of private enterprise over public enterprise in small-scale business are now "quite evident to anyone without ideological blinkers." [47] Since some communist states tacitly recognize this fact, private enterprise may well have a considerable future in the service trades and light industry of the developing countries.

Undoubtedly a great deal of experimentation will accompany the long succession of revolutionary upheavals which lie ahead in many developing nations, upheavals which are inevitable because popular impatience—faced with the agonizingly slow progress which impends—will lend itself to frustrations and social discontents having explosive consequences. The likelihood seems great that popular dissatisfactions with economic development will lead to a proliferation of communist regimes. But whether these regimes will practice totalitarian economics, or settle for something called "communism" which actually bears little resemblance to the form of government found in Stalinist Russia or Maoist China, remains to be seen.

Western-style capitalism seems more secure than it has been for a long while (partly because it no longer operates along the lines of classical capitalism). Yet even at its hour of apparent vindication, forces exist which may not displace capitalism, but render the profit sector progressively less sig-

[46] Charles Lindblom, "The Rediscovery of the Market," *The Public Interest,* IV (Summer, 1966), 89–101.
[47] Grossman, *op. cit.* (above, n. 11), p. 112.

nificant. The enormous potentialities of modern technology make it probable that, in a couple of generations, a relatively small percentage of people will be able to produce the goods and services which businessmen now supply. Instead of forty percent of our productive activities falling within the nonprofit area, a steadily larger percentage of human labor will be diverted there. The more this area expands, the less crucial becomes the function and status of the capitalist elements of the economy. Instead, the role of the artist, the writer, the designer, the entertainer, the city planner, the scientist, the educator, will be held in ever higher esteem. Men will increasingly value work, not for the income it yields, but for the creative satisfactions it brings.[48]

Robert Heilbroner sees science as the vehicle by which our economy and our aspirations will be transformed. For science not only will enable a small percentage of the population to supply our economic needs, it also captures the imagination and loyalties of the young and talented. In Heilbroner's words,

. . . science and its technical application *is* the burning idea of the twentieth century, comparable in its impact on men's minds to the flush of the democratic enthusiasm of the late 18th century or to the political commitment won by communism in the early twentieth. The altruism of science, its "purity," the awesome vistas it opens, and the venerable path it has followed, have won from all groups, and especially from the young, exactly that passionate interest and conviction that is so egregiously lacking to capitalism as a way of life.[49]

Today's college generation, however, is beginning to ask searching and skeptical questions about science and scientism which suggest that science may command less loyalty than Heilbroner believes. The growing humanistic doubts about the preeminence of science and technology as guides and goals for the human spirit suggest no resurgence of capitalism. Rather, they imply a further diminution of its priorities and philosophy.

Heilbroner further notes that

The world of science, as it is applied by society, is committed to the idea of man as a being who shapes his collective destiny; the world of capitalism to an idea of man as one who permits his common social destination to take care of itself. . . . Before the activist philosophy of science as a social instrument, this inherent social passivity of capitalism becomes archaic and eventually intolerable. The "self-regulating" economy that is its highest social achievement stands

---

[48] John K. Galbraith, *The Affluent Society* (Boston: Houghton Mifflin, 1963), Chap. XXIV; David Bazelon, "The New Class," *Commentary*, XLII (August, 1966), 48–53.

[49] *The Limits of American Capitalism, op. cit.* (above, n. 23), p. 128.

condemned by its absence of a directing intelligence, and each small step taken to correct its deficiencies only advertises the inhibition placed on the potential exercise of purposeful thought and action by its remaining barriers of ideology and privilege. In the end capitalism is weighed in the scale of science and found wanting, not alone as a system but as a philosophy.[50]

Mr. Heilbroner's judgment may or may not be correct. But judging by observable present and highly probable future trends, the long-run prospects are that capitalism will not be overthrown by any revolutionary movement (violent or nonviolent), but that it will simply shrink to a position of minor social importance in advanced industrial nations. The likely new order would appear to be a pragmatic compromise between democratic capitalism and democratic socialism, with the aesthetic and ethical components of the latter taking on increasing importance. As economic necessity becomes less demanding and the uses of leisure more central, society will seek to accommodate man's love for beauty, for creative opportunity, and for justice by a socio-economic system better adapted to those ends.

Bibliography

Berle, A. A. *The 20th Century Capitalist Revolution*. New York: Harcourt, Brace, 1954.

Chamberlain, John. *The Roots of Capitalism*. Princeton, N.J.: D. Van Nostrand, 1959.

Friedman, Milton. *Capitalism and Freedom*. Chicago: University of Chicago Press, 1963.

Galbraith, John K. *American Capitalism*. Boston: Houghton Mifflin, 1961.

Galbraith, John K. *The New Industrial State*. Boston: Houghton Mifflin, 1967.

Ginzberg, Eli, *et al. The Pluralistic Economy*. New York: McGraw-Hill, 1965.

Hansen, Alvin H. *The Postwar American Economy*. New York: W. W. Norton, 1964.

Heilbroner, Robert L. *The Limits of American Capitalism*. New York: Harper & Row, 1966.

Heilbroner, Robert L. *The Making of Economic Society*. Englewood Cliffs, N.J.: Prentice-Hall, 1965.

Kolko, Gabriel. *Wealth and Power in America*. New York: Frederick A. Praeger, 1962.

Lilienthal, David. *Big Business: A New Era*. New York: Harcourt, Brace, 1954.

Myrdal, Gunnar. *Beyond the Welfare State*. New Haven: Yale University Press, 1960.

Preston, N. S. *Politics, Economics and Power*. New York: Macmillan, 1967.

[50] *Ibid.*, pp. 132–133. Also see Michael Harrington, *The Accidental Century* (New York: Macmillan, 1965).

Rose, Arnold. *The Power Structure*. New York: Oxford University Press, 1967.
Salvadori, Massimo. *The Economics of Freedom: American Capitalism Today*. Garden City, N.Y.: Doubleday, 1959.
Shonfield, Andrew. *Modern Capitalism: The Changing Balance of Public and Private Power*. New York: Oxford University Press, 1965.
Wallich, Henry C. *The Cost of Freedom: A New Look at Capitalism*. New York: Harper & Brothers, 1960.
Wright, David McCord. *Capitalism*. Chicago: Henry Regnery, 1962.

Chapter 8

Democratic Socialism

Webster's *Third New International Dictionary* defines socialism as "any of various economic and political theories advocating collective or governmental ownership and administration of the means of production and distribution of goods." Socialist historian Carl Landauer prefers a quite different definition: "Socialism is a system of communal (or social) ownership, established for the purpose of making (or keeping) the distribution of income, wealth, opportunity and economic power as nearly equal as possible." [1]

As with capitalism, the number of definitions of "socialism" is legion; one of the problems in defining the term derives from the fact that socialism has reflected so many different visions and assumed so many different forms. For example, we have had Utopian socialism, Marxian socialism, Christian socialism, revisionist socialism, Fabian socialism, guild socialism, and syndicalism as well as various hybrids and subspecies of these. This chapter will concern itself with democratic socialism, the most successful non-Marxian form of socialism.

While "socialism," generically, refers to an economic concept, "democratic socialism" refers to an ideology resting on both economic and political assumptions. The meaning of *democratic* socialism has varied from decade to decade, from nation to nation, and from interpreter to interpreter. Nevertheless, certain persistent elements have characterized the term throughout most of its history.

In exploring the ideological anatomy of democratic socialism, it may be useful to list certain of its characteristics—comparing and contrasting them

[1] *European Socialism: A History of Ideas and Movements* (Berkeley and Los Angeles: University of California Press, 1959), I, 5.

with communism in the Soviet Union where such comparison is relevant. (During much of the nineteenth century, the terms "socialism" and "communism" were often used interchangeably.)

(1) Democratic socialism is unequivocally devoted to the democratic political system. It fully supports the individual rights of free speech, free press, free assembly, free elections, religious freedom, cultural freedom, and due process of law. It rejects, both in theory and practice, the legitimacy of a violent assumption of power by a minority. It is, in brief, a full-bodied democratic faith, as the term "democratic" is understood in the West.

(2) In contrast to communism, democratic socialism does not envisage the state as a transitionally necessary evil, but as the indispensable instrument through which the people can achieve and maintain socialist objectives. It has no illusions that the elimination of private property would exorcise the root sources of human evil and render organized coercion unnecessary.

(3) Democratic socialism has not (in recent decades, at least) called for the total nationalization of economic life.

(4) The concept of class struggle, while not absent from democratic socialist theory, does not bulk as large as in communist theory. Where present, it is usually transmuted into less harsh and intractable forms than strict Marxist theories require.

(5) Democratic socialists are not wedded to any theory of economic determinism. Unlike communism's "scientific socialism," evolving from historic necessity and the inexorable laws of social development, democratic socialism proceeds from the will and efforts of men.

(6) Democratic socialism has no Holy Prophet or Holy Scriptures to provide it with infallible interpretations of history and guides to action. It has no Marx or Lenin or Mao Tse-tung as an object of reverence, who can be used to promote unity, kindle zeal, and condemn heresy.

This means that democratic socialism, as an ideology, is more low-keyed, more adaptable, less doctrinaire than orthodox Marxian socialism. Judge Learned Hand once declared, "The spirit of liberty is that spirit which is not too sure it is right"; democratic socialism is compatible with that spirit.

On the other hand, democratic socialism does share some theoretical conceptions commonly associated with communism. It has favored public ownership of major national industries. It has a long history of distaste for the profit system and for the competitive spirit which underlies capitalism. It sees a necessity to reeducate men so that they habitually give higher priority to considerations of public need and lower priority to purely private advantage. It is committed to extensive national planning, believing that the market system misallocates resources to the production of frivolous or secondary goods and services at the expense of more pressing needs such as housing, education, conservation, urban redevelopment, etc. It believes depressions are avoidable only if the state gives broad direction to the economic order. It favors a distribution of wealth which permits only modest income differentials between the more prosperous and less prosperous. (The U.S.S.R. does not follow this principle in practice.) It believes in a comprehensive "welfare state." It wants to eradicate special privileges and create more equal opportunities for all. Its sympathies rest with the working class. On the Continent (although not in Great Britain and the United States), it has had a distinctly anticlerical flavor.

But while they have some common precursors and some common beliefs, communists and democratic socialists have for the most part been arch-enemies. After the Bolshevik revolution, each regarded the other as the major threat to its own future; and each has directed its most vituperative attacks at the other. The communists saw democratic socialism as a heretical, diversionary movement, faithless to Marx, which would only delay the processes of history; the democratic socialists saw communism as a ruthless, dogma-shackled movement threatening democratic values, which were equally as valid as socialist economic goals.

The Early Ancestry of Socialism

The growth of the democratic idea in the nineteenth century led some observers to conclude that political democracy was incomplete without economic democracy. Political democracy, it was alleged, was subverted by the political power of the economic masters. Thus, the former might present an attractive facade, but the economic realities—which were largely the realities of existence—remained grim and disillusioning. Only socialism, through its focus on the economic rights and material well-being of all the people, could fulfill the deeper implications of democracy.

Just as the idea of equality has been a taproot of democracy, its interpretation also became the taproot of socialist thought. The conviction that all men are essentially equal led to the view that society should seek not only equal political rights and equal human dignity, but also a system which distributed material goods in some rough harmony with this premise.

While the French Revolution contained profoundly democratic political concepts, its theoretical foundations were profoundly individualist in economic terms. It assumed an economic system based on private property—a system receptive to "laissez-faire" because property owners would profit from this philosophy. But when the Industrial Revolution bore the fruits of the factory system, with its abuses and inhumanities, the institution of private property came in for reassessment. While some critics with a radical democratic outlook sought to ameliorate the evil of laissez-faire, others began to see private property itself as the fundamental cause of injustice and suffering. The division between those who would reform the existing system and those who would destroy its keystone—the institution of private ownership of productive property—marked the beginnings of socialist thought in Europe. The latter group of critics, it should be noted, were not only impressed with the ineradicable evils of private property but with the visions of abundance made possible by the Industrial Revolution. For the first time, the elimination of mass poverty came to seem feasible.

In summary, the democratic idea, the Industrial Revolution, and man's endless quest for greater justice combined to produce the movement called "socialism."

Identifying all the individuals and groups which played leading roles in the historic evolution of socialism is beyond the scope of this chapter. Among them, a few of the more significant will be touched upon, however.

Plato regarded the common ownership of property as the ideal arrangement for producing human virtue and social harmony, but conceded that this might be impracticable. In *The Republic* he proposed that the governing and warrior classes should forego the ownership of private property altogether, while in *The Laws* he called for the division of land into equal allotments, with a citizen's purely personal property limited to an amount the value of which was not more than four times the worth of his allotment of land. Plato regarded economic inequality as the principal source of civic discord, and wanted to restrict this inequality to a comparatively harmless level.

Among the first socialist groups, the early Christians once "held all things in common," seeking to give practical application to the principles which they associated with Jesus. The experiment was short-lived, but the idea persisted throughout the Middle Ages that communal ownership of property was the most ideal arrangement; private property was an unfortunate institution brought about by the fall of man.

The first political movement reflecting this conception occurred in the mid-seventeenth century. Gerard Winstanley, speaking for an English group called the Diggers, argued that nature itself prescribes common ownership of property, since such ownership constitutes the natural state of man.[2] He contended that the possession of private property leads to most of the greed, violence, corruption, and exploitation which plague mankind.

[2] The Diggers were not uncompromising socialists; they only sought to cultivate the common (unenclosed) land on a communal basis.

And he believed true freedom was impossible unless men had equal access to the bounties of nature. In his model society, all the fruits of the land would be held in common, to be drawn upon by each as need indicated. At about the same time, also in England, a representative of the Levellers was giving expression to a political idea which the socialists were later to appropriate in the economic realm: "Really I think that the poorest he that is in England hath a life to live as the greatest he. . . ." John Lilburne, a Leveller spokesman, wanted to do away with political privilege in England—to win universal manhood suffrage and full equality before the law.

A still more central source for socialism was to be found in France. Daniel Bell has written, "If the heart of socialism is to be found in the idea of community . . . the seeds of modern socialism are to be found in Rousseau." [3] The latter's egalitarianism as well as his emphasis on the primacy of the community were spiritually consistent with socialist sentiments. Perhaps more important was his devastating attack upon the notion that the ownership of private property, because it is a "natural right," is superior to the claims of society. Rousseau asserted that all men's "rights" come *from* society, rather than antedating society. Natural man could not even conceive of a "right"; only as a member of society could he learn a language, become civilized, and acquire a conception of his rights. Since rights proceed from society, society can determine the metes and bounds of those rights. "The right which each individual has to his own estate," as Rousseau put it, "is always subordinate to the right which the community has over all." [4] Rousseau's thoughtful analysis thus provided the key for the legitimization of public ownership, although he seemed to favor a system assuring all Frenchmen a fair share of productive property rather than the collectivization of such property.

During the French Revolution François Babeuf, perhaps the first full-fledged activist socialist, sought the elimination of private property and the establishment of equal living standards. Like many another socialist, he believed this would rid society of "crime . . . greed, jealousy, insatiability, pride . . . in short, of all vices." But Babeuf's "Conspiracy of Equals" in 1796 had no mass base and ended at the guillotine. [5]

[3] *International Encyclopedia of the Social Sciences* (New York: Macmillan, 1968), XIV, 507.
[4] See Rousseau's *Discourse on Inequality* for the full elaboration of this view.
[5] For a good brief account of Babeuf's role in the French Revolution, see Edmund Wilson, *To the Finland Station* (Garden City, N.Y.: Doubleday, 1940), Part II, Chap. I. Babeuf anticipated Lenin in his belief that only by violence, terror, and a temporary dictatorship could power be seized and the rich dispossessed. George Lichtheim, *The Origins of Socialism* (New York: Frederick A. Praeger, 1969), p. 22.

The Utopian Socialists

A cluster of so-called Utopian socialists, writing from about 1815 to 1860, occupy the next stage in the intellectual development of socialism.[6] Some of these men were secular humanitarians, aggrieved by the sufferings of their fellowmen and eager to improve their wretched lot by educating Parliament and industry to recognize and act upon their responsibilities. Others found their humanitarian impulses reinforced and stimulated by Christian principles. Still others were social visionaries who believed the radical reconstruction of society along collectivist lines would bring about a wholesome, orderly, and harmonious environment conducive to the development of man's higher qualities. Their contemporary, Karl Marx, stood out as a searing critic of Utopian socialism, social reformism, and of capitalist society in general.

The French philosopher and social scientist Saint-Simon (1760–1825), although believing that great industrialists were the natural leaders of society, held a surprising number of ideas appropriated or stressed by later socialists. Like Marx, he saw economic change as the primary determinant of history, and viewed history in terms of class struggles. However, he described and anticipated the decline rather than the intensification of that struggle. Saint-Simon was perhaps the first social critic to recognize the need for large-scale economic planning in an industrial society.[7] He and his followers, according to George Lichtheim, did more "to shape our world than any other socialist school except the Marxian." [8] Their rejection of an agrarian ideal and the acceptance of modern industrialism as the source of unlimited abundance (if, that is, the public good was given preeminence over the "rights" of private property), their faith in science, their conviction that "the exploitation of man" must yield to the "exploitation of nature" —all made a deep imprint on socialist thought. Indeed, the eminent French sociologist Emile Durkheim regarded Saint-Simon as the true father of socialism.

Charles Fourier's revulsion against the workingman's lot in the French textile industry in the early nineteenth century prompted him to devise an elaborate system for the transformation of society. He advocated decentralizing society into "phalanxes" of about 1,600–1,800 persons, each being

---

[6] The term "socialism" was coined by a follower of Saint-Simon in 1822 and first appeared in print in 1826. The first article on socialism was published in 1835, written by Pierre Leroux.

[7] John Plamenatz, *Man and Society* (New York: McGraw-Hill, 1963), p. 53.

[8] George Lichtheim, *op. cit.* (above, n. 5), p. 40.

relatively self-sufficient on its 5,000 acres. Each phalanx would be just large enough so that men's diverse native inclinations and capacities would insure voluntary labor for the variety of jobs which society required. All members of the phalanx would live in one huge building or group of buildings (enjoying the delights of either "free love," or of normal family relations), from which they would sally forth each morning to work of their own choosing. To avoid monotony, they would change jobs every few hours (whenever possible). Efficiency would be promoted by competition between various groups. The less pleasant, the most essential, and the most dangerous jobs would receive higher remuneration; since children like to get dirty and naturally form gangs, they would be willing to do the "dirty work" so long as they worked together. Revenue from all labor would be divided as follows: 5/12 would go to the workers; 4/12 to the managers; 3/12 to those furnishing the capital. Fourier waited patiently but in vain for wealthy capitalists to finance his experiment.[9] In 1840 an attempt at least was made to incorporate some of Fourier's principles in a communal society at Brook Farm in Massachusetts. Numerous transcendentalists took part in this "system of brotherly cooperation," which survived for only a few years.

More realistically, Fourier also was responsible for sketching the outlines of a system of cooperatives for supplying credit to rural folk, for buying in mass quantities, and for storing and selling farm produce. In the words of Lichtheim, Fourier "was the founder of a tradition which increasingly made socialism synonymous with humanitarian sentiment." Because of his concern for the unfortunate, "sympathy with criminals, prostitutes and other outcasts of society became a standard theme of socialist writing." [10]

Among the precursors of socialism, the Welsh social reformer Robert Owen has won a prominent place. Like Fourier, he was appalled at working conditions in his country's textile mills, where children under the age of eight worked long hours, becoming "dwarfs in body and mind." A humanitarian and a moralist, but also a successful businessman, Owen managed his own cotton mills in New Lanark in accordance with his elevated principles. He cut the adult workday to ten and a half hours, improved the housing and working conditions of the workers, refused to hire children under the age of ten, and insisted that children below that age be given an education. Convinced that man is almost wholly the product of his environment, he believed a system of universal education would bring about the elimination

---

[9] Perhaps some of his wilder fancies raised doubts about him. E.g., Fourier believed the moon was once a lady named Phoebe whose death caused the Old Testament flood.

[10] Lichtheim, *op. cit.* (above, n. 5), p. 36.

of vice and social evils, preparing the way for man's steady ascent to ever higher planes of welfare and morality. Toward no concept was he more hostile than that which held the poor responsible for their own misery because of character defects which they could correct if only they would.

Brimming with optimism and enthusiasm, Owen tried to persuade other businessmen to follow his example. Assuring them that such behavior was good business, he argued that ". . . you devote years of intense application to understand the connection of the various parts of these lifeless machines, to improve their effective powers, and to calculate with mathematical precision all their minute and combined movements . . . will you not afford some of your attention to consider, whether a portion of your time would not be more advantageously applied to improve your living machines?" [11]

Since other manufacturers declined to follow his advice, Owen supported factory legislation to correct the worst abuses, and later urged workingmen to form one giant union to promote their common interests. At one point he called upon the building trade unions to take control of the construction industry by means of a Grand National Guild of Builders.[12]

Another important figure in the history of socialism has been singled out by G. D. H. Cole, one of the major historians of the socialist movement, who declares that "Louis Blanc, in many of his main ideas, can fairly be regarded as a forerunner of modern democratic Socialism." [13] Most of Blanc's ideas were described in *Organisation du Travail* (1839), in which he proposed that the state should supply capital enabling the establishment of a number of "national workshops." These workshops would be managed by democratically elected officials who would distribute the profits of the factories to the workers—after ample amounts had been set aside for reinvestment and subsidizing unprofitable but essential enterprises. The workshops—attracting competent and enthusiastic labor because of their high wages, good working conditions, and guaranteed employment—would operate so efficiently they would gradually displace private factories. Although wages would differ at first, eventually pay would equalize. Both politician and journalist, Blanc either originated or popularized the slogan, "From each according to his capacities; to each according to his needs." Cole summarizes: "He stood for a Socialism resting on public ownership, combined with worker's control of industry, and for a democratic parlia-

[11] Landauer, *op. cit.* (above, n. 1), p. 48.
[12] G. D. H. Cole, *A History of Socialist Thought* (New York: St. Martin's, 1953), I, 123.
[13] *Ibid.*, p. 176.

mentary system as the guardian of industrial democracy and of the sharing out of the social product in accordance with men's needs. . . ." [14]

The impact of Karl Marx upon the socialist movement was, of course, unparalleled (see Chapter 3). He towers, in fact, above all others as a contributor to socialist thought. During his lifetime and up to the 1920's, at least, most European socialists thought of themselves as Marxians. The fiercest arguments raged not between socialists who accepted and those who rejected Marx, but among various schools of Marxian thought, each maintaining that it alone represented the true interpretation of Marx's principles. Marx's influence was slightest in England; although he lived in England for thirty-four years, his impact on the nation was minimal.

Eduard Bernstein, a German socialist who came after Marx, was perhaps the most influential non-Marxian socialist of the late nineteenth and early twentieth centuries, and a major figure in the development of democratic socialist thought. Writing in the latter part of the nineteenth century, he took issue with Marx on the most basic questions—denying that capitalism was dying, that industry was being concentrated in ever fewer hands, that the working class lot was worsening, that the materialist interpretation of history was correct, and that the capitalist state was inevitably reactionary. Nor did he believe the proletariat could overthrow the state.

The "Christian socialists" made their initial appearance in England in the mid-nineteenth century. Advocates of factory reform and protective labor legislation, they were also critics of the capitalist system, insisting it was fundamentally incompatible with Christian principles. (The Christian spirit, they declared, was one of cooperation, helpfulness, and brotherly love. The capitalist spirit was one of avarice, covetousness, acquisitiveness, dog-eat-dog, the worship of materialism and the almighty dollar.) The capitalist system, the Christian socialists charged, stimulated the most selfish and predatory aspects of human nature, rather than muting these as the Christian faith required. Should Christians concern themselves only with individual salvation, not with the political and economic order? Most Christian leaders would have answered in the affirmative. Not so, said the Christian socialists, asserting that Christ's major deeds and words were concerned with the physical welfare of the common man rather than with theological creeds and rituals.

Christian socialism had its greatest vogue in England, where clergymen Charles Kingsley and Frederick Maurice wrote eloquently on behalf of its message. Kingsley's conception of Christian democracy was summed up in the following:

[14] *Ibid.,* p. 176.

I assert that the business for which God sends a Christian priest into a Christian nation is to preach and practice liberty, equality and brotherhood, in the fullest, deepest, widest, simplest meaning of those great words; that in so far as he does, he is a true priest, doing his Lord's will and with his Lord's blessing on him. All systems of society which favor the accumulation of capital in a few hands, which oust the masses from the soil which their forefathers possessed of old, which reduce them to the level of serfs and day-laborers, living on wages and on alms, which crush them down with debt, or in any way degrade or enslave them, or deny them a permanent stake in the Commonwealth, are contrary to the kingdom of God which Jesus proclaimed.[15]

The influential English philosopher John Stuart Mill, whose *Principles of Political Economy* dominated the universities in the latter part of the nineteenth century, was another contributor to socialism, steadily moving towards the left throughout his lifetime. His increasing willingness to restrict private enterprise, to support social services, and to redistribute income by public action was, self-confessedly, verging toward socialism. At one point, he wrote that

if the choice were to be made between communism with all its chances, and the present state of society with all its sufferings and injustices, if the institution of private property necessarily carried with it as a consequence that the produce of labor should be apportioned as we now see it almost in inverse proportion to labour, the largest portions to those who have never worked at all, the next largest to those whose work is almost nominal, and so in descending scale, the remuneration dwindling as the work grows harder and more disagreeable until the most fatiguing and exhausting bodily labour cannot count with certainty on being able to earn even the necessities of life; if this or Communism were the alternative, all the difficulties, great or small, of Communism would be but as dust in the balance.[16]

(Note: Mill's use of "Communism" in the text may be misleading to the reader; it would more properly read "socialism" today.)

One of the landmark figures in the evolution of British socialism was another nonsocialist, Henry George. George Bernard Shaw wrote, "When I was swept into the great Socialist revival of 1883, I found that five-sixths of those who were swept in with me had been converted by Henry George." [17] Henry George believed that the individual possession of land resulted from historic blunders and that land ownership by a minority produced the gravest sort of social ills. Unwilling to socialize land at this stage of civiliza-

[15] Quoted from Walter P. Hall, Robert G. Albion, and Jennie B. Pope, *A History of England and the British Empire,* 2nd ed. (Boston: Ginn and Co., 1946), p. 778.

[16] *Political Economy,* Book II, Chap. I, Sec. 3.

[17] Quoted in Francis W. Coker, *Recent Political Thought* (New York: Appleton-Century, 1934), p. 98.

tion, however, he hit upon the notion of applying a tax upon land values—without regard for the value of improvements—which would replace all other taxes. This tax should equal the total value of the economic rent. His overall theory, in the words of E. R. Pease, "suggested a method by which wealth would correspond approximately with worth; by which the reward of labour would go to those that laboured; the idleness alike of rich and poor would cease; . . . wealth . . . would be distributed with something like fairness and even equality, amongst those who [produced]." [18]

George's *Progress and Poverty* (1886) not only made a notable impression on English intellectuals, but led to a number of tax reforms in England and in Commonwealth countries. Most important, George triggered an explosion of socialist thought, in the form of the Fabian Society, which was to drastically alter the complexion of English politics.

The Fabians: Practical Visionaries

Up to the early 1880's, socialism had made little progress in England. When the brilliant group of intellectuals who organized the Fabian Society in 1884 began their work, however, there was ". . . a mass of Socialist feeling not yet conscious of itself as Socialism." [19]

Sidney Webb, George Bernard Shaw, H. G. Wells, Graham Wallas, and the other figures who formed the nucleus of the Fabian Society believed they saw a steady historic progression toward both democracy and socialism. This was altogether desirable, since ". . . the competitive system assures the happiness and comfort of the few at the expense of the suffering of the many. . . ." To further the growth of socialism (and democracy) this handful of men began preparing the first of a long series of pamphlets designed to educate the upper and middle classes to the wisdom and justice of the socialist way.

The Fabians were socialists, but not Marxists. They rejected Marx's labor theory of value, holding that value is primarily the product of the development of civilization rather than the product of the workman's hands. The capitalist, they added, makes his money not so much because of his work and wisdom as because of the location of his business, the steady rise in population, and the increasing affluence of the people—all superimposed on the advances made by his forebears.

Logically, too, they saw the major social conflict existing between the community and capitalist investors, not between wage earners and capitalists.

[18] E. R. Pease, *The History of the Fabian Society* (Liverpool and London: Frank Cass and Company Ltd., 1918), p. 20.
[19] *Ibid.*, p. 53.

The latter profited exorbitantly, yet they no longer even managed their own business enterprises, which had fallen into the hands of corporation managers operating a system which might be called "private collectivism." Thus, "the bulk of the wealth annually produced goes to a small fraction of the community in return either for small services or for none at all, and . . . the poverty of the masses results, not . . . from deficiencies of individual character but . . . from the excessive share of the national dividend that falls to the owners of land and capital." [20]

The goal of an intelligent and ethically concerned society, then, is to win back for itself the values which it has largely created, but which the capitalist has arrogated to himself. This can be done by gradually restoring land and capital equipment to the community (rather than to the proletariat). Nationalization, the Fabians concluded, should come by stages, as society is prepared to effectively administer industrial enterprise. And the capitalists should be at least partially repaid for that which is wrested from them.

The Fabians had great faith in the power of reason. Reasonable men themselves, they had confidence that men's respect for justice and fair play would bring about the reform of society if only the facts were clearly and persuasively brought forth. They felt that men could argue endlessly and fruitlessly about abstract theories, but might agree more easily to policy reforms supported by hard factual data. They concentrated, therefore, not on stratospheric philosophizing, or revolutionary heroics, but upon detailed and critical analyses of the existing state of affairs—combined with practical, concrete, carefully devised plans for correcting society's ills. Their reforms involved more than nationalization, covering the tax system, urban planning, and social welfare legislation as well. While the Fabians argued fiercely among themselves on many points, they built upon a foundation of shared premises which made possible their remarkably effective pamphleteering job. High on the list of those premises were deep commitments to constitutional government, to reform within that framework, and to socialism resting squarely upon majority consent fairly won on the battleground of ideas. That consent, they knew, would not come overnight, but they were prepared to await the gradual conversion of public opinion to their goals. Their commitment was to democracy first, and socialism second.

The new order which the Fabians envisaged, then, was to be brought about by the democratic process; more than that, it was to extend and amplify democracy itself. The fusion of economic democracy with political democracy would consummate the democratic ideal, currently stunted by economic impediments to human progress.

[20] *Ibid.,* pp. 70–71.

It has been rare that a small group of intellectuals have had such a significant impact upon the history of their country—significant because they were a unique blend of the idealistic and the practical, men who had accurately taken the measure of developing trends within their country and devised workable proposals for dealing with the problems and needs of their time. It is easy to exaggerate the importance of ideas in determining the course of history, but it is no exaggeration to say that England would not have been the same without the Fabians. Indeed, the leaders of the British Labour (Socialist) party drew their intellectual sustenance largely from the Fabians, and found the latter's political moderation congenial to the practical necessities which confronted them. Although the government of socialist Prime Minister Ramsay MacDonald in 1924 lacked the parliamentary strength to push through a socialist policy, the Labour government of Clement Attlee in 1945 followed quite faithfully the prescription of the Fabians.

Socialism in Power

Democratic socialist parties in a number of European and Commonwealth states vaulted into power after World War II. For the first time, socialism was to be given its chance, fortified by the parliamentary majorities and public support needed for thoroughgoing socialist experiments. In states where they failed to obtain a majority of seats, they often won enough votes to oblige nonsocialist government to adopt portions of their program as a defensive measure.

Daniel Bell has observed that all Western European socialist parties shared five principles or policies after World War II.[21] First, they uniformly repudiated the use of violence and revolution to achieve their ends and abandoned the view that participation with nonsocialists in a coalition government was an unacceptable compromise of principle. Second, they sought to broaden their political base beyond the working class to include other segments of the population. Third, the lingering Marxist belief that democracy was a "bourgeois" concept which masked the realities of class rule was repudiated. Fourth, they supported national policies of military opposition to the Soviet government and its satellites. Fifth, by the late 1950's they favored public control of industry rather than continued nationalization of industry. (The German Social Democratic Party motto became "as much competition as possible—as much planning as necessary.") In this connection, it is instructive to observe the process by which nationalization faded as a socialist objective.

[21] *International Encyclopedia of the Social Sciences* (New York: Macmillan, 1968), XIV, 523–24.

Nationalization of heavy industry had long been high on the socialist agenda. The ownership and operation of certain key industries was primarily undertaken in order to promote full employment: whereas private operation might lead to the curtailment of full production if private demand were not sufficiently great to sustain such production, publicly owned industry would continue to produce at a reasonable price as long as public needs were unfulfilled. Synchronized with a master plan, nationalization would effectively rule out a recurrence of the depression phenomenon, when men and machines were idled for long years despite grave shortages of goods and services. Human welfare, not private profit, would become the decisive factor in directing the economy.

Nationalization would also, in certain cases, facilitate the modernizing of backward industries. In Britain, for example, the coal industry had long been languishing, partly because the coal-mine owners lacked the capital necessary to purchase and install the latest and most efficient machinery. Where an industry was of vital importance to the nation and lacked the powers of self-regeneration, the government would step in, supply the capital, and do the job.

Socialists also hoped to obviate some of the wastefulness of competition. Under capitalism, the economy lacked a central planning agency with an eagle's-nest view of the whole, an agency which could rationalize industrial development by taking the best possible advantage of sites, power resources, mineral deposits, transportation facilities, manpower resources, and markets. As a result, competition often led to a chaotic scramble, the wastage of natural resources, cutthroat competition, periodic overexpansion, waves of bankruptcies—or to clandestine private arrangements which reduced the chaos and promoted security, but gave little or no consideration to the public interest. Orderly planning of industrial development would change all of this.

Finally, worker morale and productivity would presumably improve if the workers knew the plant was *theirs,* not the possession of a capitalist whose exclusive (or at least principal) interest was in using their labor to maximize his own profits. The age-old antagonism between employer and employee would vanish. Labor relations would improve, workers would recognize their self-interest in plant economies and greater efficiency. Knowing that increased output would not jeopardize their jobs, traditional worker resistance to labor-saving machinery would also decline.

Considerable business enterprise had already been nationalized in Britain and on the Continent before the socialists gained power. In Britain, for example, the British Broadcasting Company had always been a public monopoly. The British Overseas Airways Corporation (BOAC), the central electricity grid, the London docks and passenger transport had also been established or nationalized by the Conservatives. On the Continent, broadcasting, banking, electric power, communications, and railroads had often been nationalized by nonsocialist governments.

When the Labour party took the reins of government in 1945, it nationalized banking, gas, electricity, railroads, part of the trucking industry, coal, communications, and steel. Other industries were studied to determine the need for and practicability of expanding public ownership.

Practical men that they were, the Fabians had foreseen the need to reconcile the public ownership of industry with efficient management. They had warned against choking a nationalized industry with a flood of directives and red tape emanating from politicians blessed with more zeal than judgment. In an effort to maintain adequate public control without losing operational efficiency, therefore, Clement Attlee's Labour government established the following system. Each socialized industry was to be run by a board of directors appointed by the government. Where the national interest was at stake, the minister in charge of the department most closely related to that industry was empowered to issue general instructions to the board. Day-to-day decisions were to be out of his jurisdiction. Parliament could hold the minister accountable through the "Question Hour" (at which questions could be raised pertaining to the operation of the industry), and through debates upon the annual report prepared by the board of directors. Finally, all decisions about new investment were reserved to the Cabinet and Parliament—to insure that money was spent where it was most needed, and that investment was timed to coincide with the need for either stimulating or restraining the economy.

In general, the historic experiment was neither a success nor a failure. If the workers felt any exhilaration over working for a factory which they "owned," their euphoria faded rapidly. The work was as hard as ever, the weather as hot, the machines as dangerous, the foreman as cranky, the pay the same. The impersonality and anonymity associated with a vast enterprise was still present. And the unions found the government every bit as difficult to deal with as their former employers had proved to be.

As for ministerial and parliamentary control—the supposed essence of democratized industry—snags developed here, also. A cabinet minister was properly hesitant to override industrial managers (usually the same ones who had managed the firms before) when they knew more than he about the practical problems involved. Parliament lacked both the expertise and the time to give much attention to the annual report, so that public control was more nominal than real. A leading socialist and cabinet member of the British government, C. A. R. Crosland, recently concluded that "the public corporation in Britain has not up to the present been in any real sense accountable to Parliament, whose function has been limited to fitful, fragmentary and largely ineffective ex post facto criticism." [22]

Most observers seem to believe that nationalized heavy industry in general operates neither more nor less efficiently than under private management. [23] But this outcome was not responsible for the virtual collapse of the nationalization movement in the 1950's. John Maynard Keynes, one of the few writers whose works have changed the shape of history, can be credited with this feat. As indicated in the preceding chapter, Keynes's monetary and fiscal theories provided the framework within which a capitalist system could provide both full employment and a high rate of economic growth. And once the experience of the 1950's and 1960's had demonstrated that Keynes's theories worked, nationalization became largely irrelevant. Not that all of socialism's goals were summed up in full employment and rapid growth (in fact, the latter had not concerned the socialists very much until the 1950's), but its goals could be effectively pursued by Keynesianism plus other forms of national planning. By 1960 Labour party members in Britain opposed further nationalization by a margin of 3 to 1.

Planning: The Socialist Rudder

National planning remains a central socialist tenet, despite the disillusionment with nationalized industry. Socialists believe that the systematic application of human intelligence will lead to a more sensible production pattern—one reflecting the considered judgment, the balanced needs, and the long-range interests of the people—than will the haphazard, helter-skelter impulses of the free market. Planning by responsible public servants, under the critical eye of the press and subject to the final authority of the electorate, will further human welfare more effectively than the mindless market.

One of the foremost American spokesmen for democratic socialism, Michael Harrington, argues that modern technology is transforming our world beyond "the wildest imaginings of the science and social fiction of the last century." [24] But this revolution, according to Harrington, is an "acci-

---

[22] John K. Galbraith, "Capitalism, Socialism and the Future of the Industrial State," *Atlantic Monthly*, CCXIX (June, 1967), 62.

[23] Gregory Grossman observes that ". . . the experience of nationalized enterprises in Western Europe suggests that under comparable circumstances, management is approximately equally effective and efficient in [either public or private] sectors," *Economic Systems* (Englewood Cliffs, N.J.: Prentice-Hall, 1967), p. 47.

[24] *The Accidential Century* (New York: Macmillan, 1965), p. 22.

dental revolution," in which the search for private profit directs the transformation. If technological change is "left within a context of private, often hit-or-miss, decision-making, that is not so much free enterprise as it is the rule of corporate bureaucracy in the public sphere. . . . The cause of change—a personal or corporate investment in gain, a private cost and profit—stands in little or no relation to the effect—a new order of human life." [25] This "gentle revolution" of recent decades, which carefully weighs dollar costs and ignores social ones, produces the chaos and ugliness of our cities, transportation snarls, housing shortages and housing discrimination, the rape of resources, the contamination of the environment, the continued existence of poverty, the revolt of the young. Man must learn to think politically on a scale to match the prodigious challenges of technology.

To Harrington, socialism *is* planning. He wants planning by democratic leaders of democratic parties who see the future with a clarity and breadth of vision denied those preoccupied with the ledger. "The hope for the survival and fulfillment of the Western concept of man demands that the accidental revolution be made conscious and democratic." [26] Furthermore, the hour is late.

Planning has many other uses than regulating the technological revolution, socialists add. It can help a nation solve its foreign exchange problems by concentrating more production on export goods, and improve the efficiency of industries serving the export market. Planning may also reduce inflationary pressures, help keep wages in line with production increases, direct new industry to depressed areas, and give greater attention to the ecological needs of an expanding urban population.

Socialists continue to be deeply concerned with equality of opportunity, believing with English philosopher T. H. Green that children from low-income and low-status homes can only achieve their highest potentialities if they have the best education, the best health care, adequate housing, and a culturally stimulating environment. These will not occur by chance; they can come about only if government plans to that end. Most socialists also want greater equality of living standards, both in terms of a better distribution of national income and through the institution of various welfare state programs. This, too, requires planning. The same goes for the reduction of class consciousness and class barriers, to be accomplished largely through reform of the educational system to root out ingredients which subtly favor children of the rich and well-born.

So much for current socialist theory; how has planning worked out? The description and analysis which follows is largely drawn from Britain and

[25] *Ibid.,* p. 28.
[26] *Ibid.,* p. 42.

the Scandinavian countries, since they have had prolonged experience with socialist party rule.

Democratic socialists do not draw up a highly detailed master plan, which they impose authoritatively on the economy. Instead they prefer to establish desirable goals for economic growth, investment, and private consumption, with rather specific production targets for industries whose output is regarded as particularly vital. Tax incentives may be established for industries where expansion is desired and cash subsidies offered to induce desired construction. Firms which delay investment until the government decides the time is ripe may (as in Scandinavia) have part of their taxes forgiven. Negatively, higher taxes may be imposed on the output of low priority industries, and construction permits used to help shape investment along lines and in areas believed most beneficial to the public. Socialist governments usually engage in close and continuing discussions with labor and industrial leaders, seeking to educate them about the needs of the economy and to persuade them of the desirability of adjusting to the broad outlines of the master plan. The government thus relies almost entirely upon persuasion rather than coercion in achieving its "planned economy."

Welfare state programs have been carried further under socialist governments than in the United States. National health insurance, often supplemented by cash benefits during prolonged periods of illness, covers all or most of the population. Family allowances are common. Sweden adds to these: free tuition in college plus allowances to help pay other college expenses; maternity leave pay for working mothers; housing subsidies for low-income couples; cash grants to families whose breadwinner has died; interest-free loans for newlyweds buying household furnishings; free prenatal care.

Although socialist governments are ideologically committed to high inheritance tax rates, in practice these are usually little if any higher than in the United States. Nor are income taxes much higher (although other levies tend to raise total tax levels to a somewhat higher level).[27] The percentage of national income received by employees does not vary greatly in Britain and Scandinavia from that received in the United States, and the distribution of income between upper and lower brackets is not strikingly different. Herman P. Miller, a foremost authority, declares that "The United States has about the same income distribution as Denmark, Sweden and Great Britain. . . . There is no evidence that incomes are more widely

[27] For example, in 1964 about 37% of Sweden's Gross National Product went for taxes, about 34% of Norway's, and about 29% of Great Britain's—compared to 27% in the United States. Nathaniel Stone Preston, *Politics, Economics and Power* (New York: Macmillan, 1967), p. 127.

distributed in any country than they are in the United States." [28] A more elaborate system of social services guarantees lower income groups in socialist countries comparatively greater economic security than in America, however. Finally, the wealthiest 1 percent of American adults own less than 25 percent of the nation's privately owned wealth, compared to over 40 percent for Britain's richest 1 percent.

Will Capitalism and Socialism Converge?

The most notable conclusion to be drawn from a comparison of European democratic socialist government policies with those of "capitalist" United States, is that there are remarkable parallels. Although prudence dictates that "planning" should not be labeled as such, Washington uses its massive budget to establish national priorities and insure that services of national importance are provided. And it uses the budget to help bring about more equality of opportunity (through aid to elementary and secondary education, library subsidies, college scholarships, public health measures, Operation Headstart, the Job Corps, etc.). Programs to provide more adequate minimum living standards for the poor are constantly being expanded. From $30 to $40 billion per year is redistributed from the more affluent to the less affluent groups through various programs. Town and country planning, while more ambitious under socialist governments than in the United States, has its counterpart in America's urban renewal and Demonstration Cities program. (A "New Cities" program will doubtless occupy much of Washington's attention in the decades ahead.) Washington has sought to stimulate investment through an investment credit tax plan, and provides a variety of critically important subsidies to the construction and other industries. It uses various pressures (releasing stockpile materials, establishing wage guidelines, applying presidential pressures) in an effort to control prices and wages. It manipulates tax, spending, and credit policies to foster a high rate of employment and national growth and to subdue inflation. Intermittently but persistently, it has expanded its own welfare state, with the extension of health insurance and the provision of a minimum annual family income probably on the way. Its incipient programs to control air and water pollution, promote general beautification, and strengthen educational television are wholly consistent with long-stand-

---

[28] *Rich Man, Poor Man* (New York: Thomas Y. Crowell, 1964), pp. 11–13. Karl Deutsch, in *Politics and Government* (Boston: Houghton Mifflin, 1970), p. 31, notes that the top 10% of income receivers in the U.S. receive 31% of the national income, compared to 24% in Israel, 28% in Sweden, 30% in Britain, 35% in India, and 47% in Mexico.

ing socialist convictions that national planning is essential to creating a more harmonious, orderly, attractive environment. Indeed, John K. Galbraith's emphasis on the "need to subordinate economic to aesthetic goals—to sacrifice efficiency, including the efficiency of organization, to beauty" [29] prescribes a goal toward which America seems to be moving and one which socialists would warmly approve.

Socialists will tend to emphasize and exaggerate the differences between their policies and those of the United States, just as Americans tend to emphasize and exaggerate their differences from socialist governments. But the technological imperatives of an advanced industrial society, combined with the political imperatives of a mass suffrage society, seem to be bringing about a striking convergence of both ends and means in industrialized democratic socialist and capitalist countries.

Within West European countries (and Australia and New Zealand), moreover, it becomes ever more difficult to distinguish the policies and goals of socialist and nonsocialist parties. Dealing with common problems and appealing for majority support, both find it necessary to offer roughly similar programs. Even if the socialists were not restrained by political necessities, their compass dictates no markedly different course from the experimental, pragmatic, nondoctrinaire policies that their more successful opponents espouse. There is no socialist blueprint today, much as this distresses old-line socialists with a nostalgia for the past.

This is not to say that all differences between socialist and nonsocialist parties have disappeared. Residual ideological traces will continue to leave their mark on public policy. Socialist governments will continue to be less reluctant to interfere with business prerogatives, and more willing to plan on a bolder scale. They will probably go somewhat further in their efforts to realize greater equality of opportunity and of condition. But the differences will be of degree, not of kind; and they will probably be much less significant than the tendency of all industrial societies (Russia not excepted) to develop similar goals, problems, and methods of dealing with those problems.

Democratic socialism is an expression of man's search for justice, of his concern for the underdog, and of his optimism that reason and humanitarianism could and would lead to a better world. In the articulation of its indignation and its dreams, it has deepened and accelerated a political current that moves toward a future no man can foresee.

Robert Heilbroner, in a sentimental appraisal, finds that "Socialism is, at its root, the effort to find a remedy in social terms for the affront to reason

[29] Galbraith, *op. cit.* (above, n. 22), p. 67.

and morality in the status quo." He adds ". . . socialism is the expression of a collective hope for mankind, its idealization of what it conceives itself to be capable of. When the fires of socialism no longer burn, it will mean that mankind has extinguished that hope and abandoned that ideal." [30] To equate socialism with man's aspirations for equity, justice, and humanity may be to burden it with a heavier load of virtue (and imprecision) than it can bear. But the characterization would please nostalgic socialists.

Currently, democratic socialism has ceased to be a distinctive ideology for a number of reasons. First, the workingman is much less interested in economic equality than was once suspected. Both in America and Europe, the worker seems not to resent—or even to disapprove—large incomes for the industrial owners and managers, and for others who are able to succeed economically. Nor is he as interested as many socialists assumed he would be in democratic management of factories. The worker wants good wages, job security, insurance against major economic hazards, and personal dignity. While he also wants his views to be given respectful consideration, he seems quite willing for management to make most of the major decisions without consulting him. He'll do his job; let management do its. Economic democracy (except in areas clearly pertinent to his welfare) is not a particularly appealing idea to the average worker.

Second, the humanitarian ideals of democratic socialism, long shared by many nonsocialists, have now become so widely accepted that they no longer form the basis for a distinctive ideology. Success has exacted its price of democratic socialism, a price seriously destructive of its ideological appeal. Raymond Aron put it well: "Socialism has ceased in the West to be a myth because it has become a party of reality." [31]

The attainment of political power by any crusading group inevitably brings disillusionment. The problems of society are always more intractable than they appear to the opposition. Responsibility and power ineluctably bring with them an awareness that losses accompany gains, that democratic politics is the politics of half a loaf (or less), that compromises must be made and made again despite the sense of betrayal which this brings to "true believers"—above all, a recognition of how little can be accomplished compared to the high hopes which attend the ascension to power. No ideology can emerge unscathed from the opportunity to realize its promises. Even if it is able to succeed in some respects, the reality is never so gratifying as the anticipation.

Finally, democratic socialism's most seminal spokesmen have yet to think

[30] "Socialism and the Future," *Commentary*, XLVIII (December, 1969), 45.
[31] C. A. R. Crosland, *The Future of Socialism* (London: Jonathan Cape, 1963), p. 99.

through the implications of abundance and to evolve new policies uniquely representative of socialist thought. In the developed countries, the job of socialists and nonsocialists alike is to create a society in which a vital sense of purpose is present, a sense of purpose sufficiently compelling to reverse the centrifugal and disintegrative forces in today's unsettled world. Man has never faced a harder task.

Bibliography

Cole, G. D. H. *A History of Socialist Thought.* 5 vols. New York: St. Martin's, 1953–60.

Cole, Margaret. *The Story of Fabian Socialism.* New York: John Wiley, 1964.

Crosland, C. A. R. *The Future of Socialism.* Abridged and rev. ed. New York: Schocken Books, 1963.

Crossman, R. H. S. *The Politics of Socialism.* New York: Atheneum, 1965.

Friedland, William H., and Carl G. Rosberg, Jr., eds. *African Socialism.* Stanford, Calif.: Stanford University Press, 1964.

Heilbroner, Robert L. *The Great Ascent: The Struggle for Economic Development in Our Time.* New York: Harper & Row, 1963.

Laidler, Harry. *History of Socialism.* New York: Thomas Y. Crowell, 1968.

Landauer, Carl. *European Socialism: A History of Ideas and Movements from the Industrial Revolution to Hitler's Seizure of Power.* 2 vols. Berkeley: University of Berkeley Press, 1959.

Lichtheim, George. *The Origins of Socialism.* New York: Frederick A. Praeger, 1969.

Morgan, H. Wayne, ed. *American Socialism: 1900–1960.* Englewood Cliffs, N.J.: Prentice-Hall, 1964.

Robson, William A. *Nationalized Industry and Public Ownership.* Toronto: University of Toronto Press, 1960.

Schumpeter, Joseph A. *Capitalism, Socialism, and Democracy.* 3rd ed. New York: Harper & Row, 1950.

Sweezy, Paul W. *Socialism.* New York: McGraw-Hill, 1949.

Thomas, Norman. *Socialism Re-examined.* New York: W. W. Norton, 1963.

Wilson, Edmund. *To the Finland Station: A Study in the Writing and Acting of History.* Garden City, N.Y.: Doubleday, 1940.

Wilson, Harold. *Purpose in Politics.* Boston: Houghton Mifflin, 1964.

Chapter 9

Extremism on the Right and Left

On the Right

For one brief period, it seemed to many, the world had freed itself of the totalitarian mentality. Naziism had gone to the grave with Adolf Hitler, and fascism, with Mussolini. Never again would such discredited notions as those in *Mein Kampf* be taken seriously. Democracy and moderation triumphing over the fanatic, mankind had at last learned the folly of political extremism.

Of course such optimism was misplaced. True, many would argue the extreme improbability of a Fourth Reich, or its fascist equivalent (even so, others would insist that so long as the basic causative factors occur, the same result could recur). Our major preoccupation in the United States, since 1945, has been largely with the left, rather than with some budding form of neo-Naziism or neofascism. Nonetheless, the fact remains: the stuff from which extremist politics comes is still with us.

Political extremism is a force to be reckoned with. The aim of this chapter, therefore, is to explore such extremism more fully—first as it reveals itself on the political right, and then on the political left. Both of these extremes are an important part of the ideological landscape, and particularly so in the context of the American political system. In making our inquiry, then, the key questions to raise are these: What are the identifying characteristics of these ideological formations? What caused them to develop as they have? Of what moment are they, or are they likely to be? Finally, beneath the rhetoric, are extremists of left and right really cut out of the same cloth?

It would be well to start by putting the matter of the right in proper perspective. What exactly is meant by what is variously called the "extreme right," or "radical right," or "ultraright," or similar sounding labels? All of these refer to a syndrome which goes well beyond "mainstream" or "conservative" in its position on the right side of the political spectrum. Since ideologies have a way of scattering themselves along a continuum, it would be arguable that there should be some fixed point at which one ceases to be a conservative and suddenly graduates to the fringe. Of course extremism is a matter of *degree*. Still, just as it is possible to paint a representative picture of other ideologies, it ought to be possible to construct a composite model of radical right attitudes. What follows, therefore, is an effort to do just that—and thereby to provide some insight into the distinctive and identifying characteristics of right-wing extremism.

Reduced to its simplest components, the ideology of the radical right seems to revolve around three conveniently alliterative images: the crisis, the conspiracy, and the crusade. Where these concepts invariably lead, where they converge into one, is in an impassioned form of anticommunism. But that is perhaps better understood as the analysis proceeds.

To begin with, it is almost axiomatic that a new ideological entry premises its very being on some catastrophic turn of events. If the standard brands of politics produce only modest cause for complaint, there would be little reason to cast about for new alternatives. So it is desperate times which call for desperate responses; and crisis becomes the *sine qua non* of right extremism. It is not necessary that the crisis represent some real state of affairs, or that others perceive it in quite the same way—it is sufficient for the purposes of extremism that a crisis is premised to exist. Typical would be the following, a composite of ultraright views regarding crisis:

America is losing its way at home and losing its nerve abroad. A steady succession of "socialistic" measures gnaw away at the free enterprise structure which was once the glory and strength of America—the guarantor of a free and virile people. The domestic policies of the New Deal, the Fair Deal, and of Presidents Kennedy and Johnson were all of a piece—leading us step by step from our heritage of freedom to the bleak tundras of collectivism. Meanwhile, the nation seems incapable of manifesting its historic role abroad. It stands aside helplessly as China falls into communist hands; its will falters in the Korean War, as the advice of the authentic American hero—General Douglas MacArthur—is discarded in favor of an inglorious stalemate; Cuba goes Red—at our very doorstep—while Washington wrings its hands but will not act; America abandons the lovers of freedom in the satellite countries; finally, the "no-win" policy is confirmed when America refuses to give the military the authority it needs to crush the communist aggressors in Vietnam. Everywhere, it seems, the communists advance; everywhere the Americans retreat. This is hardly in the tradition of our brave and illustrious forefathers, who had both the courage to fight for their principles and the resolution to carry through to victory. At home there is a critical weakening of the moral fibre in America. The old commitment to self-reliance, individual initiative, and enterprise; the respect for hard work and work well done; the scorning of governmental paternalism; the insistence on maintaining a broad sphere of personal freedom against the encroachments of the state—these wholesome qualities seem to be withering away. Meanwhile, church attendance declines, and prominent church leaders advance liberal theological views which seem to cut the heart out of traditional religious doctrines. Everywhere the intellectuals seem to be challenging values and institutions which are held dear, and these insidious forces seem to command the eager cooperation of the mass media. The entertainment world and the universities join the challenge, exerting subtle or brazen pressures against the standards and restraints which marked the accepted pattern of belief and behavior a few short years ago. Patriotism is no longer encouraged and cherished; rather, it is the object of sneers and derision. People do not display the flag with the pride of bygone years; soldiers are not proud of their uniform; the pledge of allegiance is spoken less frequently and with less conviction. Something precious has departed from the soul of the nation.[1]

Of course these concerns are not the exclusive property of the ultraright, nor, for that matter, do they exhaust the list. They are intended simply to give some substance to the generalization that the radical right is a group deeply alienated by its assessment of its world. Crisis is indeed its stock in trade, precisely along the lines described, though not uncommonly sounding a much heavier note of doom and disaster. The message of the far right is thus more than just peril—it is a message of panic and alarm. Perhaps that is best conveyed by the language of its own leadership:

. . . this may be the most important letter I have ever written. On its results may well depend the freedom and the lives of those to whom it is addressed, as well as the future of our country and even the survival of your civilization. And the time has truly come for some realistic bluntness.

[1] This is but a mild imitation of radical right perspectives. A much more vivid sampler of attitudes, with direct quotes to match, has been assembled by Robert A. Rosenstone, *Protest from the Right* (Beverly Hills, Calif.: Glencoe Press, 1968), Chaps. 1 and 2.

THIS IS NEITHER EXAGGERATION NOR FANTASY——. These terribly—
and reluctantly—melodramatic phrases are based on the following considerations, which I honestly believe to be the stark and simple truth: (1) The Communist conspiratorial apparatus is now closing in, with every conceivable pressure and deception, on all remaining resistance to the establishment of its police state over our own country.[2]

Still more explicit is this view: "The hour of their final conquest draws near.
I think my prediction of world conquest for the Communists for 1973 was
too conservative. They are running ahead of schedule."[3] But for sheer,
unadulterated fear and desperation, it would be hard to surpass the very
militant Robert DePugh, leader and spokesman for the gun-toting Minutemen: "ALL PATRIOTIC AMERICANS WHO HAVE BEEN ACTIVE
IN THE ANTI–COMMUNIST MOVEMENT ARE NOW FACING A
PERIOD OF EXTREME DANGER," his organization's publication, *On
Target* warns. "If you are EVER going to buy a gun BUY IT NOW!"[4]

Crisis, then, is an important underpinning for the belief system of the
radical right. But crisis alone is hardly enough to satisfy the ideological
needs of ultraright-wing politics. What is needed further is an unmasking of
the culprit, the perceptiveness and simple honesty to identify the source of
this evil. In other words, blame must be fixed. We must know who or what
the enemy really is. For the radical right, it should be understood, this is no
innocent invitation to social science research. What the right seeks is not
some complicated academic theory to explain change in terms of technology, population, or other such variables: it is a conspiratorial explanation for
the national state of crisis. Nothing short of a conspiracy, in its view, could
possibly account for the enormity of evil which is sweeping over the community. Surely some devil or demonic force is at work, behind the scenes,
working its evil powers against the good and the innocent. The fixing of
blame is a typical and recurrent theme, as the following indicates:

> How can we account for our present situation unless we believe that men
> high in this government are concerting to deliver us to disaster? This must be
> the product of a great conspiracy, a conspiracy on a scale so immense as to
> dwarf any previous such venture in the history of man. A conspiracy of infamy

[2] Robert Welch, "A Stick of Dynamite," *Bulletin* (of the John Birch Society),
July, 1965, p. 4, as reprinted in Fred W. Grupp, Jr., "The Political Perspectives of
Birch Society Members," *The American Right Wing,* ed. Robert A. Schoenberger
(New York: Holt, Rinehart & Winston, 1969), p. 116.

[3] Dr. Frederick C. Schwarz, of the Christian Anti-Communism Crusade, as quoted
in Arnold Forster and Benjamin R. Epstein, *Danger on the Right* (New York: Random House, 1964), p. 56.

[4] As quoted in George Thayer, *The Farther Shores of Politics* (New York: Simon & Schuster, 1967), pp. 130 f.

so black that, when it is finally exposed, its principals shall be forever deserving of the maledictions of all honest men. . . .[5]

And again: "There is developing within our nation and the world a clear story of treason, that men in high places, not only here, but abroad, are being manipulated by powerful forces to do things that smack of cowardice and genuine betrayal. . . ." [6]

As the ultraright sees it, therefore, there are dark and sinister forces at work—a conspiracy of evil, if ever there was one. But just who are the conspirators that lurk within the shadows? In many quarters of the radical right there is very little doubt that the chief conspirator is seen as Jewish, or black, or of similar minority extraction. Groups such as the American Nazi Party, the National States Rights Party, and the Ku Klux Klan, make that abundantly clear.[7] Indeed, it has frequently been observed that the fringe right has been widely tainted by such bigotry, and that it is a rare rightest group indeed which can long resist the temptation to travel that road. But the most popular conception of the Grand Conspiracy, by far, is one which clearly centers on communism as the devil incarnate. To many observers, in fact, it is the true common denominator among all far right groups and is what many would argue is the defining characteristic of radical rightism.

Certainly this fixation with a communist conspiracy is of unparalleled importance in understanding the far right movement and its ideology. Furthermore, the intensity and the exaggeration which attach to this belief reveal still greater insight into the nature of the far right. Thus, a pattern emerges in which the ultrarightist first sees the crisis as wholly attributable to the conspiracy, and then sees the conspiracy as potentially capable of spreading to all corners of the community. Nothing is safe from the conspirators. Not our institutions—our government, our schools, our churches, our media, our unions, even our major corporations—all are vulnerable to infiltration and undermining by the out-and-out conspirators, or by their unwitting tools (dupes and sympathizers). All of the old solid, authentic American values—including the Constitution itself—are now vulnerable. We are warned: "Water containing Fluorine (rat poison—no antidote) is already the only water in many of our army camps, making it very easy for saboteurs to wipe out an entire camp personal (sic). If this happens, every

[5] Senator Joseph McCarthy as quoted in the *Congressional Record*, 82d Congress, 1st Session (June 14, 1951), p. 6602, and cited in Richard Hofstadter, *The Paranoid Style in American Politics* (New York: Alfred A. Knopf, 1964), Chap. 1.

[6] Billy James Hargis, *Communist America: Must It Be?* (Christian Crusade, 1960), p. 7, as cited in Rosenstone, *op. cit.* (above, n. 1), p. 5.

[7] See Thayer, *op. cit.* (above, n. 4), Part 1.

citizen will be at the mercy of the enemy—already within our gates." [8]

Worse yet:

> . . . The music designed for high school students is extremely effective in aiding and abetting demoralization among teenagers, effective in producing degrees of artificial neurosis and preparing them for riot and ultimately revolution to destroy our American form of government and the basic Christian principles governing our way of life.
> The music has been called a number of things, but today it is best known as rock 'n' roll. [9]

Obviously there are no limits to the reach of the conspiracy, such examples clearly suggest. In fact, the real seriousness of the situation is indicated not only by what is prey to the conspiracy, but by who can fall victim—even the most trusted of national leaders:

> . . . to put it bluntly, I personally think that he (Eisenhower) has been sympathetic to ultimate Communist aims . . . and consciously serving the Communist conspiracy, for all his adult life. . . .
> But my firm belief that Dwight Eisenhower is a dedicated, conscious agent of the Communist conspiracy is based on an accumulation of detailed evidence so extensive and so palpable that it seems to me to put this conviction beyond any reasonable doubt. [10]

That there was no way of combating the conspiracy was, of course, an unlikely ideological belief. That fact brings us directly to the third and final component of radical right ideology: the "crusade." Although by his last estimate Robert Welch, leader of the John Birch Society, calculated that the United States had already gone 60 to 80 percent communist, [11] there is apparently still time to save the ship. The only possible defense which the right extreme sees as viable here is to rally around its own flag, and to close

---

[8] Quoted in Rosenstone, *op. cit.* (above, n. 1), p. 10.

[9] Rev. David A. Noebel, *Rhythm, Riots and Revolution* (Christian Crusade, 1966), p. 17; quoted in *ibid.*, p. 8.

[10] This now notorious quote is from Robert Welch, leader of the John Birch Society. In the original it appeared as a part of *The Politician*, a manuscript which had only limited circulation, and which was later revised to soften its language. The stronger version is quoted in the *Congressional Record*, 87th Congress, 1st Session (April 12, 1961), pp. 5609–5611, and cited in Rosenstone, *op. cit.* (above, n. 1), p. 3. Among other things, Welch accused Milton Eisenhower of being the President's boss within the Communist party; and he associated both John Foster Dulles and Allen Dulles with the communist cause.

[11] Welch's figure dates to 1965. Based on its previous rate of increase, the United States should have been totally communist by 1969. See Thayer, *op. cit.* (above, n. 4), p. 189.

ranks behind its leaders. As Robert Welch puts it: "I want to convince you, as I am convinced that only dynamic *personal* leadership offers any chance for us to save either our material or our spiritual inheritance. . . . I intend to offer that leadership to all who are willing to help me." [12]

What is the nature of this crusade, as the radical right sees it? Perhaps its single most characteristic feature is its evangelistic and fundamentalist overtone. That shows through most clearly in its association with groups such as the Christian Anti-Communism Crusade, the Christian Crusade, the Twentieth Century Reformation Hour, and the Church League of America. They epitomize, in many ways, the tendency for the far right crusade to blur the lines between religion and politics. Somehow, Christ and country and anticommunism and capitalism are all inseparably linked in what has become a holy war—a veritable crusade—against Satan and the forces of evil.

> The ideological conflict is between the East and the West—slavery versus freedom. Communism versus capitalism, socialism versus Christianity, Satan versus God! In whichever realm one considers the conflict it is irreconcilable. The Bible says that we cannot walk together except they be agreed. The cold war makes a 'United Nations' impossible. [13]

In still another sense, the crusading syndrome also seems evident enough. That is suggested, at least, by the kind of disciplined faith and unquestioning allegiance which the cause commands. A good crusader does not make waves; he puts his trust in the good of the cause, and he obeys. Hence it is not uncommon to find that the radical right models itself after the most authoritarian of religious sects, and that it demands an uncompromising loyalty from its following. The John Birch Society wraps the subject up rather well:

> The John Birch Society is to be a monolithic body . . . democracy is merely a deceptive phrase, a weapon of demagoguery, and a perennial fraud.
> . . . The John Birch Society will operate under completely authoritative control at all levels . . . no collection of debating societies is ever going to stop the Communist conspiracy. . . .
> . . . The men who join the John Birch Society during the next few months or few years are going to be doing so primarily because they believe in me and what I am doing and are willing to accept my leadership anyway. . . . Whenever and wherever, either through infiltration by the enemy or honest differences of opinion, that loyalty ceases to be sufficient to keep some fragment in line, we are not going to be in the position of having the Society's work weakened by

[12] Quoted in Forster and Epstein, *op. cit.* (above, n. 3), p. 11.
[13] Carl McIntire, leader of the Twentieth Century Reformation Hour, as quoted in Rosenstone, *op. cit.* (above, n. 1), p. 6.

raging debates. We are not going to have factions developing on the two-sides-to-every-question theme.

Those members who cease to feel the necessary degree of loyalty can either resign or will be put out. . . .[14]

To sum up, then, the ideology of the radical right appears to revolve around three vital factors: crisis, conspiracy, and crusade. But there are unanswered questions about this phenomenon: How are we to account for its presence, and what is likely to be its future?

In a sense our first task is to explain why the far right exists in its present form. The purely historical answer to that question is easy enough to trace. In a very general sense, no doubt, political extremism is as old as the nation itself. But the modern version of radical rightism, with which we have concerned ourselves here, is most likely a by-product of currents which hearken back to the roaring twenties and depression thirties.

In retrospect, we can now see glimpses of the modern radical right movement in the intense isolationism which came in the wake of World War I, and in such other symptoms as an extreme nativism that expressed itself in a restrictive immigration policy and a revitalization of the Ku Klux Klan. Equally if not more important was the passionate concern over the Red Menace—a widespread obsession which left a deep imprint on the twenties.

For those who feasted on such causes, the advent of Franklin D. Roosevelt's New Deal provided all the more ammunition for fear and frenzy. As the more extreme opponents saw it, the social welfare measures of the 1930's signaled the beginnings of a collectivist-to-socialist-to-communist-to-hell course of events. Besides raising up the spectre of conspiracy, the extremists of those years called forth the same kind of virulent antisemitism and racism as had surfaced in the 1920's. But with a slight difference. This time there were better organized groups, with highly vocal leaders, to carry the torch. Thus, organizations like the Liberty League, the American Firsters, and Father Coughlin's Christian Front and National Union for Social Justice spread their messages of isolation, anticommunism, and antisemitism. In some cases it went further still: William Dudley Pelley's Silver Shirts, like Fuehrer Fritz Kuhn's Bund, paid open fealty to the Nazis and fascists. In the latter extreme, of course, lay the eventual undoing of all such organizations when war finally came.

What gave the radical right a new lease on life was the crusading spirit —during the early 1950's—of the late junior Senator from Wisconsin, Joseph R. McCarthy. McCarthy used his position of influence and authority to develop an even more elaborate image of communist conspiracy than had

[14] Speech of Robert Welch as quoted in Forster and Epstein, *op. cit.* (above, n. 3), pp. 21 f.

ever been developed before. Using a combination of wide-sweeping legislative investigations, shotgun charges of subversion in high places, and a good deal of publicity, McCarthy succeeded in creating a new climate of fear and suspicion. Most important of all, he obviously legitimized the whole radical right belief pattern of a gigantic, treason-tainted, doom-impending, conspiracy of communists.

That McCarthy was subsequently discredited by the Senate has obviously mattered little to the cause of right-wing extremism. Indeed, it is hard to see the 1960's as having brought anything like a relaxation of an ultraright crusade in the United States. Quite the contrary, it has been all within the last dozen or so years that groups like the John Birch Society have been launched, and that the far right appears to have become a political force to be reckoned with. If at one time there was an inclination to laugh away the followers of the extreme right as a group of political "loonies"—that time is no more. The far right obviously surfaced in the Presidential election of 1964 as an important element in Barry Goldwater's nomination, campaign, and ultimate defeat. And more recently still, it would be hard to discount the presence of a right extremism in the political threat of George Wallace and his following within the American Independent Party.

To sum up, then, one way of accounting for the latter-day radical right movement is to see it in its historical perspective—as a force which has been building over the past half century, and which has now matured into some sizable proportions. Just how sizable, no one seems to know for sure, since the far right tends to prefer the veil of secrecy and is somewhat sensitive about having its census taken. Nonetheless, ". . . a conservative estimate would put the hard-core activists at 300,000 with an additional three to four million part-time to casual supporters." [15] And to serve this group, there are apparently some 2,598 right-wing organizations available.[16] But perhaps the most impressive statistic of all is the one which estimates the spending of the extreme right to total some $14,000,000 a year.[17] If even roughly true, that would suggest that the far right carries a financial clout which makes up for anything it may lack in numbers of members. Indeed, that is precisely one of the factors about such fringe groups which gives real cause for concern: that is, the potential of the extremist organization to influence and disrupt far beyond the real weight of their numbers.

It would be difficult to truly understand the phenomenon of right-wing extremism without looking at it from still another perspective, the sociopsychological. The social scientist's view of the phenomenon has revolved

[15] Thayer, *op. cit.* (above, n. 4), p. 147.
[16] *Ibid.*
[17] See Forster and Epstein, *op. cit.* (above, n. 3), p. 8.

around two concepts—personality and situational crisis—neither of which should be unfamiliar after our explorations into the causes and characteristics of totalitarianism (see pp. 37–58). Here, as there, it has been theorized that one very likely explanation takes the form of a personality malfunction, a basic predisposition to see life in hostile and rigid terms. Such persons may have deep and acute anxieties, unshakable fears of their powerlessness and impotence, and a great deal of what pathologists would diagnose as the paranoid syndrome. In short, we are brought once again to the very intriguing possibility of the existence of an authoritarian personality, a psychological complex which might explain the attitudes and behavior of the political extremist. That theory, to be sure, is a hotly debated one, and for the moment it appears to remain an unsettled question within the research literature.[18]

About the second socio-psychological component of right-wing extremism, however, there seems much greater agreement among social scientists. That is the theory that various forms of stresses and strains have created severe shock waves within certain quarters of the political community. Those most deeply affected by such changes are the ones most likely to respond with intensity—to vent their frustrations in extreme political behavior. Thus, one variant of the theory has it that those persons who fall victim to anxiety about their status would be particularly susceptible to the appeal of extremist protests. Although there is some dispute here too about the exact nature of the crisis which may precipitate the turn to the far right, there is general agreement that some form of change or upheaval is the stimulus to most such movements and their followers. Where the extreme right is most successful, our research indicates, is where society is in its greatest state of flux (especially where the changes are social and political),[19] where the usual constraints and inhibiting controls are absent, and where the old order is changing most rapidly. Thus, there is some evidence to indicate that a strong two-party system works to the disadvantage of the far right, as does a Republican in the White House!

[18] Support for the personality theory is to be found in Daniel Bell, *The Radical Right* (New York: Doubleday, 1963), and in Richard Hofstadter, *The Paranoid Style in American Politics and Other Essays* (New York: Vintage Books, 1967). More recent research has been added by Ira Rohter, "Social and Psychological Determinants of Radical Rightism," in the *American Right Wing*, ed. Robert A. Schoenberger (New York: Holt, Rinehart & Winston, 1969), pp. 193 ff. But cf. Raymond E. Wolfinger *et al.*, "America's Radical Right: Politics and Ideology," in the *American Right Wing, ibid.*, p. 43: ". . . on the basis both of our data and our contacts with the [Christian Anti-Communism] Crusaders, we do not believe that they are social or psychological cripples."

[19] Ironically, times of prosperity seem more likely to bring on the right-wing extremists because it is easier to concentrate on questions of status once the economic issues are out of the way.

We arrive, therefore, at a theory of the radical right not unlike the totalitarian—though there are important differences to be sure. Both may well be the concomitant costs we must pay for an age of dramatic change, overwhelming problems, and highly complex societies. Indeed, these currents—which disorient, and bewilder, and alienate—and which extremism thrives on—are all an important and unavoidable part of the twentieth century.

The extremists will not carry the day, because, to borrow a phrase once applied to the other side, "they are miserable merchants of unwanted ideas." But neither will they depart the American political scene, because, as Richard Hofstadter observes, "the things upon which it [rightism] feeds are also permanent." We shall have to understand that the world changes, and that the extreme right panics with it. We will continue to meet the ultrarightists in some assault on the local schools or local library, in some new tirade against sex education or a communist takeover of the funnies. The battleground will no doubt change, but the battle will not.

On the Left

When Raymond Aron, Daniel Bell, Seymour Martin Lipset, Edward Shils, and others described the "decline" of ideology in the 1950's,[20] they wrote in the context of a value orientation which included faith in progress, industrialization, and rationality—mainstays of Western civilization for a century and a half. But within less than a decade, the values which these writers took for granted were challenged by a comparatively small, but vocal and influential part of the population in those very countries which had followed the progress-industrialization-rationality pattern most closely and, according to its own criteria, profited from it most. Those who questioned the existing system were, in fact, primarily university students who lived in the most "advanced" nations of the world—namely, the United States, France, and West Germany.

Bell held, in effect, that contemporary society had reached the point where its future well-being required, not ideological revolutionaries, but "tinkerers" who would adjust an economic rheostat here and a social gauge there in order to keep the entire mechanism running smoothly. Those dissenters who appeared in the early 1960's argued, however, that "the system"—as the status quo was designated—instead of moving forward, was sinking more and more deeply into putrefaction. The members of the New Left—as the emerging social critics had come to be known—having at least

[20] See Chap. 10, Bibliography.

initially little knowledge of the ideologues and ideologies of the past, reserved their chief scorn for the tinkerers who were running society.

The latter were accused in terms analogous to those reserved by Marx
for the bourgeoisie. The underpinnings of the entire capitalist society were
questioned. What was so great about mere material success? What was so
sacred about hard work? As the critics saw it, the prevailing standards of
capitalist society forced man into the stockades of the war-bent industrial-
military complex, where he labored for long hours—partly because he was
compulsive and partly to win the meaningless baubles of material success
offered by a consumer-oriented and value-corrupted society. But the harder
man worked and the more he accumulated, the less of real substance was
his. There were fewer opportunities to enjoy personal relationships, art,
leisure, the beauties of nature—in brief, to be truly human. To the contrary,
contemporary man was becoming numb to such values: he was becoming
trivialized, mechanized, even brutalized. Individuals as individuals lost their
worth; they were important principally as means to others' ends. Leisure was
not for rest, contemplation, and creativity; but increasingly it too yielded to
the forthright or subtle onslaughts of organization. As for nature, not only
did man fail to enjoy it, he was actively involved in its destruction.

The critique of the New Left was made from a position of idealism. Man
is "infinitely precious and possessed of unfulfilled capacities for reason, freedom and love . . . self-cultivation, self-direction, self-understanding, and
creativity." [21] He needs and thrives on personal relationships. Brotherhood
represents his deep yearning, but instead he experiences the "loneliness,
estrangement, isolation" of contemporary society. The New Left thus longed
for the true community of men, joined together in peace and fraternity and
dedicated to giving themselves to one another; yet it also gave the highest
regard to individualism, whose decline as a creative force was deeply la-
mented.

According to the New Left, whatever worthwhile individual values remained in society were rapidly being eroded by the electronic age. Automation, computers, television, wiretaps, IBM dating—all were seen as depriving man of the last vestiges of his individuality and driving him into the
confines of á universal mold, prepared by an impersonal bureaucracy which
regarded man not as an individual being, but as a number. As such, he was
at the mercy of the faceless and relentless manipulators of the electronic
keyboards.

[21] One of the earliest, and perhaps the best, statements indicating the idealism of the
New Left is to be found in Thomas Hayden's *Port Huron Statement* (1962), from
which this quote was drawn; in Mitchell Cohen and Dennis Hale, eds., *The New
Student Left* (Boston: Beacon, 1967), p. 12.

Man had thus succeeded in engineering his own slavery; and like all slaveries it was characterized by corruption and hypocrisy. "The system" prided itself on its celebrated values, but in practice these were violated whenever and wherever the occasion arose. "The system" preached sexual chastity, but practiced promiscuity. "The system" proclaimed equality for all, but practiced the rankest discrimination. It lauded the principle of self-determination, but practiced imperialism. It described itself as a force for universal peace, but practiced war. It declared itself the defender of freedom, but treated harshly those who challenged its assumptions.

The New Left thus criticized the power structure not only because of the nature of its values but also because it failed to live up to those values. "The system," the New Left held, was always prepared to compromise. It persisted in asking the wrong question: Can our policy prevail? It shied away from the question: Is it right?

What was to be done with such an incredibly hypocritical and dehumanizing system? At least three major voices were heard: one from those who would drop out of the system; one from those who would radically revise it; a third, from those who would totally destroy it. Of these three, the second, which was democratically oriented, belonged to the New Left only peripherally; the first moved increasingly in the direction of the drug-oriented world, becoming less and less politically significant. The third voice, by nature the most strident, grew until it came to be regarded as *the* dominant voice of the New Left.

This voice, embodied in a number of groups, is best known to the public in the Students for a Democratic Society (SDS) (and in a few of its loosely connected auxiliaries, such as the "Up Against the Wall Mother Fuckers," the Crazies, and the Yippies); but it is the SDS which will receive the major consideration here.

Holding forth against the evils, hypocrisies, and brutalities of existing society, the New Left concluded that there was hope for the future only if the institutions that society had thus far produced were largely demolished. How this was to be done was not specifically spelled out. Some members of the New Left were content just to sit and smoke pot—hoping the revolution would come simply because the system was so corrupt that it could not survive. But others, seeking personal involvement and recognizing that the system was not yet ready to collapse, developed means they hoped would speed its demise—in particular, the technique of direct confrontation.[22]

---

[22] To some degree the operational tactics of the New Left grew out of the experience of the black liberation movement as manifested in sit-ins, boycotts, demonstrations, and other more radical tactics.

The amount and nature of cooperation between the black liberation movement

The locus of operation was the university campus, because it was there that the most receptive audience was to be found. It was from the student body—their own peers—that the radicals expected to draw their support. It was the university that maximized the radicals' chance to become effective—because, at least initially, administrators and faculty were reluctant to admit that they could not handle their own students, that at times they could only teach with the assistance of the police. Moreover, the university represented a microcosm of the world and its evils: each student had a number, schedules were determined by computers, administrators and trustees were often absentee and unapproachable, professors were remote—more interested in research than in teaching, or in the student and his problems— and what was taught seemed outdated and irrelevant for the postindustrial age into which the students felt they and society had already been pushed. Thus, large numbers of students and faculty, far beyond the numbers that could be described as New Leftist, saw merit in much of the radical indictment of the university and society at large. And while they were not sympathetic to violence or to the destruction of existing society, they were not deaf to the New Left's critique of the status quo.

From the SDS point of view, confrontation with the power structure had a number of advantages. When the police charged into student ranks, the New Left's perception of the inherent brutality of the system was confirmed. Confrontation therefore could lead to the radicalizing of the "uncommitted" middle. The sight of uniformed policemen outfitted with helmets and gas masks and equipped with billy clubs, mace, and, upon occasion, with guns drawn, charging into unarmed students and drawing blood became a major factor not so much in putting down the student radicals, as in increasing their numbers.

One of the most persistent questions about the New Left is why it appeared on the scene at this time in history.[23] Certainly the war in Vietnam and the unfulfilled promises that the United States had made to its black minority were factors. But it seemed unlikely that, once American troops were withdrawn from Vietnam, the New Left movement would be stilled.

---

and the New Left varied. By the end of the 1960's two opposing trends were observable: on the one hand, the realization by increasing numbers of blacks that they were less interested in destroying the system than in gaining entrance to it; on the other, the growing awareness of radical black groups such as the Black Panthers that they could not stand alone, but required allies, the chief source for which was the New Left. Cf., Theodore Draper, "The Fantasy of Black Nationalism," *Commentary* (September, 1969, vol. 48, no. 3), 43–44.

[23] A comprehensive discussion of the causes of the student revolution is to be found in Reo M. Christenson, *Challenge and Decision,* 3rd ed. (New York: Harper & Row, 1970), Chap. I.

The military-industrial complex, which in the eyes of the New Left sought to oppress the revolutionary impulses of the nonwhite, developing peoples of the world, would continue to operate. The plight of the black would still require redress.

There are two main theories explaining the origin of the New Left. One theory revolves around the so-called Oedipal nexus [24]—the concept of the generation gap—which holds that youth is always poised for rebellion and that the decline in legitimacy of the contemporary generation in the eyes of the young due to the Vietnam war, as well as to the widening gap between profession and practice, has rendered it vulnerable to the natural propensities of the young. The other theory, belonging to the so-called Brzezinski-Bell school, is that of "historic irrelevance." The latter maintains that we have passed beyond the industrial age to the postindustrial age, and that the student is now rebelling against the changes forced upon him. The difficulty with both of these theories, say many social psychologists, is that they misinterpret or ignore the substantive complaints of the New Left. If the disaffection of the New Left is merely youth rebelling against age, or a recalcitrant element refusing to adapt to progress, then the specific charges against the war in Vietnam, racial discrimination, official and unofficial hypocrisy, the oppressiveness of society and its faceless bureaucrats need not be taken seriously. Nothing need be done to improve the quality and fulfill the promises of existing society.

Kenneth Keniston offers still another theory [25] to account for the emergence of the New Left, to the degree that it represents a new development in society: industrial progress has produced such affluence that the middle-class young find it pointless to strive for material satisfactions they take for granted. They now have the leisure, the perspective, and the inclination to criticize the existing social structure and to contemplate a culture appropriate to the nascent age. The New Left, says Keniston, seeks to universalize the liberal-democratic revolution and to find new values for society at large.

In the early days of the New Left, its partisans were hostile to "organization." They opposed not only the authority of the existing system but all authority. Spontaneity was a highly prized value. Consequently, the meetings of New Left units rambled on with everyone free to speak as long as he

[24] This theory is often associated with Lewis S. Feuer, *The Character and Significance of Student Movements* (New York: Basic Books, 1969).

[25] Kenneth Keniston, "You Have to Grow Up in Scarsdale to Know How Bad Things Really Are," *New York Times Magazine*, April 27, 1969. Also see his *Young Radicals: Notes on Committed Youth* (New York: Harcourt, Brace & World, 1968). The observation that two principal theories explain the origins of the New Left is drawn from Keniston.

wished and say whatever he wished with little interference from the chair or disapproval from the audience. And the resultant quality of "looseness" was highly valued.[26]

But it quickly became evident that such unorganized, individualistic, and amorphous discussion periods were not going to bring the revolution. There must be organization—leaders, the led, short-range and long-range goals, tactics and strategy. It was this development that produced a crisis in the ranks of the New Left.

The act of organizing involved the establishment of authority, a basic concept against which the New Left had originally mobilized. That the new authority was theirs made it acceptable to some, but to others the mere existence of authority—any authority—was intolerable. Then, too, the creation of authority involved a competition for it; ambition—as well as other lesser qualities of men—became no less evident in revolutionary circles than in establishment ones. As it became apparent that spontaneity alone would not bring the revolution, disputes arose as to what would. The battle was thus joined between those advocating rival revolutionary strategies.

In the early 1960's, the SDS—seeking support beyond its original student and occasional faculty member base—went "to the people," unconsciously repeating the steps taken by the Russian revolutionaries of the 1870's. In Chicago, Berkeley, and Newark, leaders like Tom Hayden of the SDS,[27] went to the poor and ghetto blacks and attempted to organize their support for the revolutionary movement. While in some cases the lot of the ghetto-dweller was ameliorated and some support for radical causes was gained, it soon became apparent that the slum dwellers of America were unlikely soon to provide the foundation upon which to build a new society. The young radicals neither offered them new significant symbols of identification, or realistic expectations concerning early achievement of the life style they were seeking. The New Left, it seemed to many of its advocates, would have to look elsewhere for its foot soldiers.

Some SDS student radicals headed for America's factories, believing that a blue-collar class, chained to its mortgage payments and the boredom of the assembly line, would provide recruits for the revolutionary cause. The successes of this radical group too were minimal, for as one of their favorite ideologists, Herbert Marcuse,[28] had pointed out repeatedly, the American

---

[26] *The French Student Revolt: The Leaders Speak* (New York: Hill & Wang, 1968), p. 78.

[27] Thomas Hayden, *Rebellion in Newark* (New York: Random House, 1967).

[28] Those of Marcuse's positions which are most attractive to the New Left are found in *One Dimensional Man* (Boston: Beacon, 1964) and in *Essay on Liberation* (Boston: Beacon, 1969). In the former Marcuse argues that liberalism is repressive in that it convinces its adherents that they are free when they are not, thus reducing their

blue-collar worker—the "traditional" Marxist proletarian—had been bought off by the system. Capitalist-bourgeois society with its high standard of living, welfare statism, liberalism, tolerance, and sexual permissiveness had turned the erstwhile proletarian—and not just the proletarians—away from his true revolutionary interests. Contemporary Western society has succeeded in producing, according to Marcuse, a "one dimensional man," activated only by material interests, rendered "quiescent" by lack of repression, and drained of any remaining revolutionary propensities by the prevailing sexual license.

The experience of the SDS on the assembly line thus seemed to confirm the Marcuse thesis that the proletariat was not interested in revolution. Still the New Left continued to seek the "new proletariat" from among various groupings of workers, poor whites, blacks, students (including those from high schools), and faculty members. It repeatedly urged the need for "participatory democracy"—wherein people at the local level would play a greater role in making those decisions which affected their lives rather than have them determined by bureaucrats at a higher level. The appeal of participatory democracy for a populace that found itself in a more and more distant relationship with state authority seemed apparent, even though, to the more sophisticated, the limited possibilities of the concept were quickly visible.[29] As compared with their interest in material benefits, though, the "people" as a rule had little interest in the attractions of participatory democracy—particularly insofar as the latter was connected with revolution. Unfortunately for the New Left, it was not change that the majority wanted, but preservation of the status quo and their material gains and opportunities.

Thus, frustrated in its drive to revolution, the New Left turned against the people. The objective now became not to win over the masses but to *manipulate* them.[30] Following Herbert Marcuse, many New Leftists became contemptuous of the majority. The majority, they believed, is ignorant, diverted by the luxury of contemporary society. The people do not know what is best for them; therefore, others must act for the people, in the name of the people. The only thing that can change the corrupt nature of society and liberate the people from subservience to the materialistic culture which

inclination and capacity to free themselves. Marcuse prefers an "educational dictatorship," a position he elaborates upon in *An Essay on Liberation;* he indicates that the repressive aspects of the Maoist and Castroite models do not trouble him. What Marcuse seeks ultimately is the "new man," who will be "biologically" incapable of succumbing to the entrapments of affluence.

[29] Cf. Irving Kristol, "The Old Politics, the New Politics, The *New,* New Politics," *New York Times Magazine,* November 24, 1968.

[30] Nathan Glazer, "The New Left and Its Limits," *Commentary* (July, 1968), 37.

has developed is the destruction of society. While the majority opposes its own liberation, the minority acts "on behalf of" the majority.

In the last half of the 1960's, then, a significant part of the New Left movement came full circle—from being overwhelmingly opposed to what it regarded as the threatened destruction of democratic values, to becoming contemptuous of those same values. The New Left had become antipopulist and elitist.[31]

The foregoing description has presented some of the concepts of the New Left and the various stages of their development, but it can scarcely be regarded as having presented an ideology of the New Left. The simple fact is, as the New Left itself has frequently admitted and sometimes regretted [32] —it has at most only a very limited affirmative ideology. But while some members have regretted the lack of a developed, positive ideology and others have taken pride in its absence, the New Left in general has been indifferent towards all ideologies except those of "the system," to which the radicals are implacably hostile.

On the New Left there was a tendency at first to see communism as an existing system with serious flaws. On the other hand, the New Left felt little of the bitter hatred of the traditional democratic left towards communism. For the New Left, the crimes attributed to Stalin and the Soviet invasion of Hungary in 1956 were of only passing consequence for the contemporary scene. In its early history, however, the New Left kept communists out of its ranks. By the mid-1960's communists were permitted to join, the rationale being that *all* opposed to the system were welcome.[33] By the end of the 1960's there were two communist groups within SDS—one representing the traditional Moscow-oriented party apparatus in the United States and the other, larger and more strident, the Progressive Labor party representing a Maoist orientation. The latter, carefully organized and centrally-directed, threatened to take over SDS.[34]

The essential strategy of the New Left became direct action now.[35] The New Left was unwilling to wait for fifty or even ten years until revolutionary prospects were brighter. To be engaged, constantly engaged, against

[31] Jack Newfield, *A Prophetic Minority* (New York: New American Library, 1966), pp. 120–121.

[32] Paul Jacobs and Saul Landau, *The New Radicals* (New York: Random House, 1966), p. 74.

[33] *Ibid.,* p. 77. Also, Thomas R. Brooks, "The New Left is Showing Its Age," *New York Times Magazine,* June 15, 1969.

[34] Thomas R. Brooks, *ibid.*

[35] Expressed in strongest form by the "Weathermen," who were in most ways the most determinedly revolutionary spinoff of SDS and who were alleged to have been responsible for a series of bombings in the fall of 1970. Cf. John Kipner, "Vandals in the Mother Country," *New York Times Magazine,* January 4, 1970.

the system was the *summum bonum* for the New Leftist. Confrontation upon confrontation—as the French student revolutionaries held—would set off shock after shock,[36] ultimately destroying the established order and making way for its successor. In its romanticism, the New Left saw the corrupt system as ready for a coup de grace.

What would succeed the existing system? On this crucial question, the New Left has been even more reticent than Karl Marx was. Presumably the future would encompass values of individualism, creativity, and personal independence that the system had blocked out, but how these were to be realized has never been described. When the question is asked as to the future program of the New Left, the typical answer is that to establish known programs would inform the system of New Left intentions, inviting the formulation of a counterstrategy.[37]

Even more relevant for the New Left in the decade of the '70s than the future of society was the future of the New Left itself—and that of SDS in particular. Much of the New Left was caught in a maelstrom of conflicting ambitions, goals, tactics, and strategies. The resulting squabbling and splintering seriously hampered recruitment. Indeed, it brought a reduction of followers. As the characteristics of the movement came to be widely known, there was decreasing faith in its ability to make positive achievements. Numbers were further depleted by the disaffection of those who anticipated easy cost-free victories, only to discover that their goals could be reached, if at all, only through major exertions. Were they certain that they wanted them? And what exactly were they fighting for? A heightening of revolutionary activity would clearly elicit a strong coercive reaction from an American society unprepared to sit in on its own dissolution, and harboring deep resentments against students and other intellectuals. In the American context, the pursuit of revolution would require great determination and fortitude over a long period of time—and it was not clear that many were prepared to make the commitment.

At the beginning of the 1970's some observers believed the New Left was moribund. True, there remained a large residue of frustration and bitterness but short of another massive incitement such as the war in Vietnam, that residue was unlikely to ignite widespread involvement. Hyperactivism might yield to cynical apoliticality for some and apathy for others.

But whether the New Left lived or died as a movement, its major truths still stood—that the United States in particular, and the capitalist world in

[36] Patrick Seale and Maureen McConville, *Red Flag, Black Flag* (New York: Ballantine, 1968), p. 21.

[37] *The French Student Revolt: The Leaders Speak, op. cit.* (above, n. 26), pp. 78–79.

general, had failed to live up to many of its promises; and that in a new technological age, in which monumental changes are telescoped into brief periods of time, yesterday's goals and styles would not do. What the New Left had done was to tell the most highly developed part of the world that, like it or not, the future was here—and it had best be prepared to meet it.

Bibliography

Bell, Daniel. *The Radical Right*. New York: Doubleday, 1963.

Cohen, Mitchell, and Dennis Hale, eds. *The New Student Left: An Anthology*. Rev. ed. Boston: Beacon, 1967.

Cohn-Bendit, Daniel, and Gabriel Cohn-Bendit, *Obsolete Communism*. New York: McGraw-Hill, 1968.

Feuer, Lewis S. *The Conflict of Generations*. New York: Basic Books, 1969.

Forster, Arnold, and Benjamin R. Epstein. *Danger on the Right*. New York: Random House, 1964.

The French Student Revolt: The Leaders Speak. New York: Hill & Wang, 1968.

Hofstadter, Richard. *The Paranoid Style in American Politics and Other Essays*. New York: Knopf, 1965.

———. *Anti-Intellectualism in American Life*. New York: Knopf, 1963.

Jacobs, Paul, and Saul Landau. *The New Radicals: A Report with Documents*. New York: Vintage Books, 1966.

Keniston, Kenneth. *Young Radicals*. New York: Harcourt, Brace & World, 1968.

Lipset, Seymour M. *Student Politics*. New York: Basic Books, 1967.

Marcuse, Herbert. *An Essay on Liberation*. Boston: Beacon, 1969.

———. *One Dimensional Man*. Boston: Beacon, 1964.

Newfield, Jack. *A Prophetic Minority*. New York: New American Library, 1966.

Oppenheimer, Martin. *The Urban Guerrilla*. Chicago: Quadrangle, 1969.

Rosenstone, Robert A. *Protest from the Right*. Beverly Hills, Calif.: Glencoe Press, 1968.

Schoenberger, Robert A., ed. *The American Right Wing*. New York: Holt, Rinehart & Winston, 1969.

Seale, Patrick, and Maureen McConville. *Red Flag, Black Flag*. New York: Ballantine Books, 1968.

Thayer, George. *The Farthest Shores of Politics*. New York: Simon & Schuster, 1967.

Chapter 10

A Postscript on Ideology:
Two Views

Ideology in Decline [1]

Since the early 1950's, an increasing number of scholars have been concerned with the apparent waning of ideological politics in advanced, industrial societies—a concern which has resulted in a significant body of literature on the "decline of ideology." Briefly, the decline hypothesis refers to one or both of two propositions: (1) that there has been a relative tempering over the last two decades of the extremism with which ideological goals are stated; or (2) that there has been a relative attenuation of the emotive intensity with which ideological goals are pursued.

One of the earliest writers on the decline of ideology was H. Stuart Hughes. In a 1951 article Hughes identified a "process of ideological dissolution" and a "wreckage of political faiths" in which radical ideologies have lost their force. He suggested that disagreements over ideological principles have been largely replaced by disagreements over methods. [2]

Raymond Aron has also elaborated upon the theme of ideological decline. In 1955, he emphasized the passing of fanaticism in political belief and the erosion of ideologies that were once sharp, distinct, and explicit. [3] He wrote, also in 1955, of an increasing awareness that "the political cate-

---

[1] For a more elaborate treatment of the themes touched upon in this section, see Mostafa Rejai, ed., *Decline of Ideology?* (New York: Atherton, 1971).

[2] H. Stuart Hughes, "The End of Political Ideology," *Measure,* II (Spring, 1951), 146–58.

[3] *The Opium of the Intellectuals* (New York: W. W. Norton, 1962), especially the concluding chapter. (The original French edition was published in 1955.)

gories of the last century—Left and Right, liberal and socialist, traditionalist and revolutionary—have lost their relevance." Having surveyed the ideological scene in Western and non-Western countries, he concluded that "In most Western societies, ideological controversy is dying down because experience has shown that divergent demands can be reconciled." [4]

The most significant impetus to the spread and acceptance of the decline thesis, however, was provided by a conference on "The Future of Freedom" sponsored by the Congress of Cultural Freedom in September, 1955.[5] Held in Milan, the conference was attended by some one hundred and fifty intellectuals, scholars, politicians, and journalists from numerous countries. After five days of discussion and debate there emerged among the Western representatives a clear consensus along the following lines: (1) extremist ideologies appeared to be in a state of decline; (2) this decline was due largely to the increasing economic affluence in Western countries; and (3) the decline was crystallized in the fact that traditionally antagonistic ideologies were moving closer together. By contrast, representatives from the non-Western countries insisted on the continued relevance of radical ideologies.

Since the Milan conference, a number of scholars have become centrally involved in further exploration and elaboration of the decline hypothesis. Addressing himself to the "exhaustion" of total ideologies, Daniel Bell wrote in 1960: "Few serious minds believe any longer that one can set down 'blueprints' and through 'social engineering' bring about a new utopia of social harmony. . . . In the Western world . . . there is today a rough consensus among intellectuals on political issues: the acceptance of a welfare state; the desirability of decentralized power, a system of mixed economy and of political pluralism." [6]

Seymour Martin Lipset specifically relates the theme of ideological decline to economic development (among other variables) and constructs a hypothesis capable of empirical verification. Having noted the general phenomenon of decline in ideological polarization in Western societies, he writes: "This change in political life reflects the fact that the fundamental political problems of industrial revolution have been solved; the workers have achieved industrial and political citizenship; the conservatives have accepted the welfare state; and the democratic left has recognized that an

<hr />

[4] Aron, "Nations and Ideologies," *Encounter,* IV (January, 1955), 24–32.

[5] See Edward Shils, "The End of Ideology?" *Encounter,* V (November, 1955), 52–58.

[6] Daniel Bell, *The End of Ideology* (New York: Collier Books, reprinted 1961), p. 397.

increase in overall state power carries with it more dangers to freedom than solutions for economic problems." [7]

Elaborating on this theme a few years later, Lipset notes a deintensification of class conflicts and the emergence of "the politics of collective bargaining." The causal relationships are stated in the following terms:

Greater economic productivity is associated with a more equitable distribution of consumption goods and education—factors contributing to a reduction of intra-societal tension. As the wealth of a nation increases, the status gap inherent in poor countries is reduced. As differences in style of life are reduced, so are the tensions of stratification. And increased education enhances the propensity of different groups to "tolerate" each other, to accept the complex idea that truth and error are not necessarily on one side. [8]

In general, then, the decline-of-ideology hypothesis seeks to establish a negative correlation between the degree of economic development and the intensity of ideological politics in modern societies. The hypothesis has been tested and verified in whole or in part in a number of advanced, industrial countries, both Western and non-Western. These include Finland, Germany, Great Britain, Japan, the Netherlands, Norway, Sweden, the United States, and the Soviet Union. [9]

The decline-of-ideology hypothesis has generated an array of criticisms, of which the most important are these: [10] First, say the critics, the decline hypothesis is unrealistic and farfetched. Ideologies have not ended in the affluent West, as witness the race and poverty issues, the emergence of the New Left and the radical right, and so on. Nor are ideologies about to disappear in the developing countries, where—if anything—they are on the rise.

Second, the decline hypothesis embraces a value judgment based on vested interest and a commitment to the status quo, the welfare state, "scientism," etc. It represents "a slogan of complacency," since it assumes that there are no longer any issues of great political consequence. It assumes, moreover, that history is moving toward an ultimate static equilibrium in

[7] Political Man: The Social Bases of Politics (New York: Doubleday, Anchor Books, reprinted 1963), pp. 442–43.

[8] Seymour Martin Lipset, "The Changing Class Structure and Contemporary European Politics," Daedalus, XCIII (Winter, 1964), 271–72.

[9] Consult the collection of papers in Rejai, op. cit. (above, n. 1), and the bibliography cited at the end of this chapter.

[10] See Chaim I. Waxman, ed., The End of Ideology Debate (New York: Funk & Wagnalls, 1968), especially the papers by C. Wright Mills, Henry D. Aiken, William Delany, Robert A. Haber, Donald Clark Hodges, and Irving Louis Horowitz.

which, given economic growth, the developing countries will join the sterile ranks of Western societies. As such, the decline of ideology is itself an ideology.

Third, the decline hypothesis stands for "a fetishism of empiricism" and a denial of the continued relevance of moral and human ideals.

Finally, the decline hypothesis confuses a shift in the arena of ideological conflict with a decline in ideology. While there has been a reduction of ideological cleavage surrounding old political issues, there has been a sharp increase of ideological dispute in new areas.

These and similar criticisms stem from either misunderstandings or disagreements about the meaning of ideology and the hypothesis of decline. The first criticism confuses a relative *decline* in ideology with a literal *ending* of all ideology. The decline hypothesis does not suggest the total disappearance of ideologies; what it does convey is an ending of "apocalyptic," "total," or "extremist" ideologies—that is to say, a decline of ideology. This is one of the key sources of confusion in the literature, and it must be attributed in large measure to the decline writers themselves, who have stated their hypothesis in two different ways: (1) a "decline of ideology," and (2) an "end of [extremist] ideology." There is no question that the decline writers consider ideology a permanent factor in human affairs. The criticism that ideologies continue to be important in the developing countries is particularly ill-founded, since the decline hypothesis refers to advanced industrial societies only.

The second criticism of the decline hypothesis involves a misunderstanding closely related to the first. The notion of an ultimate movement toward a static equilibrium is a logical implication of an *end* of ideology hypothesis, not of the decline proposition. Such an implication has not been contemplated by the decline writers because there is nothing inevitable about the direction of historical development. The decline hypothesis simply describes a particular state of affairs at a given point in time. While it may even express a preference for nonideological politics, it does not suggest that nonideological politics is the epitome of human achievement. The decline hypothesis, in other words, permits fluidity and dynamism; it is not closed to change.

Viewed in this light, the criticism that the decline hypothesis is itself ideological loses force and persuasiveness. The significant question is whether the hypothesis has any social-scientific value. If it does, then it is by definition empirical not ideological. The decline hypothesis, as Aron has aptly put it, "is first and foremost a diagnosis of the historical situation. For this reason, considered as a statement of fact, it requires either confirmation or refutation on that level. In short, the first question concerns the truth or falsity of the analysis, or if you like, its degree of truthfulness or falsehood." [11]

The third criticism—that the decline hypothesis stands for a fetishism of empiricism—is in part valid. The decline hypothesis does hope and intend to be empirical; there is, however, no evidence to suggest that the decline writers are indifferent to human values. It seems unwarranted to confuse an objective, neutral style of analysis with moral indifference.

The final criticism—suggesting that the decline hypothesis confuses a shift in the arena of ideological conflict with a decline in ideology—is an important one, though one must recall the relativistic character of decline hypothesis and its inapplicability to all situations. The point that there has been an emergence of ideology in certain new areas is well taken, to be sure; but it does not contradict the decline hypothesis, for it is addressed to another question.

So far as the new ideological movements are concerned (e.g., the worldwide student movement, the peace and civil rights movements, the New Left, the radical right), several points need to be borne in mind. First, just as the particular conditions of the eighteenth-nineteenth centuries gave rise to a distinct set of ideologies, new conditions logically generate corresponding ideological movements. Second, the new movements—whether left or right—have embraced relatively small numbers of people. Third, these movements—whether left or right—have been too seriously fragmented to be able to present a convincing and unified ideological front.

Finally, some observers have suggested that these movements are not even "ideological" in the conventional sense of that term, since they lack an explicit belief pattern, a statement of goals and aspirations, and an appropriate strategy for realizing them. Thus Richard Goodwin, a foremost spokesman for the new politics, has stated in an interview that, although there is widespread discontent among the new groups, "except for the young, this is a very non-ideological discontent, because people don't have a very clear idea of the direction of the change that they want, except that they know that it [the system] isn't working." [12] In this sense, one may say that there has been a resurgence of negative protest movements but not of ideological politics.

Indeed, with the exception of such fringe groups as the Maoists and the Birchers, the new politics are the politics of *de*-ideologization. There has been a call, in effect, for the abandonment of all ideologies. There is a de-

[11] Raymond Aron, *The Industrial Society: Three Essays on Ideology and Development* (New York: Frederick A. Praeger, 1967), p. 146.
[12] David Gelman and Beverly Kempton, "New Issues for the New Politics: An Interview with Richard N. Goodwin," *The Washington Monthly,* I (August, 1969), 18.

mand that men live together harmoniously and cooperatively, with no distinctions, no gradations, and no ideologies (cf. the notion of "commune"). The new politics, in short, are anti-ideological politics.

The new politics, however anti-ideological, have generated an intensification of feelings among the vast masses of the people (the "silent majorities") on a range of issues—including race, foreign policy, the youth, and the economy. With particular reference to the United States, the politics of polarization practiced by both the extreme left and the extreme right have forced the general population to choose sides—which means, more often than not, strengthening the right-wing groups. Whether this polarization is "ideological" is yet to be determined.

An End or a New Beginning?

The 1950's and 1960's witnessed much excitement about the decline, perhaps the end, of ideology. These Marxian-like diagnoses viewed ideology as a dependent phenomenon which emerges and recedes contingent upon societal, and primarily economic, conditions. Where there are great disparities of wealth, and resulting inequalities of social status and political power, the sharp contrasts in life conditions create intense class conflict and sharply contrasting ideologies. If, therefore, marked class differences are reduced by redistributing wealth, status, and power in society, ideology will wane.

This, it is argued, is what has happened in the advanced and industrialized societies of the West, where the "fundamental problems of the Industrial Revolution have been solved." [13] The working class has been admitted to "full citizenship," and given at least a mollifying share of prosperity, prestige, and power. The slogans and symbols of the recognized political orthodoxies may still be mouthed and revered, but they are more honorifics than convictions. The class struggle in these advanced and affluent societies has been replaced by collective bargaining. Political leaders no longer rally the classes around the flags of ideologies and reciprocal class hatred, but act as "brokers" to negotiate the slicing of an enlarging and enriched economic pie. Capitalists look after the health and declining years of their workers, accept government regulation and welfare programs with perfunctory protests, and pocket government subsidies with equanimity. Socialists no longer nationalize when they come to power. They accept welfare capitalism as an alternative to the class struggle, and cooperate with the capitalists in economic planning. Communists employ market incentives to spur productivity at home, export goods and ballets to capitalist countries, and sometimes

[13] Lipset, *Political Man, op. cit.,* (above, n. 7), p. 442.

even cooperate with the "imperialists" to protect international stability and spheres of influence. It is all very confusing—but it is at the same time increasingly clear that ideology has lost its relevance and appeal.

Some observers, following in the steps of Karl Mannheim (see p. 22), see the decline of ideology as freeing man to engage in political thinking that is rational, objective, and congruent with reality.[14] Others view the waning of ideology as supine acceptance of the status quo and warn that "as we reduce economic inequalities and privileges, we may also eliminate the sources of contrast and discontent that put drive into genuine political alternatives."[15] Still others who have reflected on the decline of ideology explain it as a product of modern man's loss of faith in himself. They see man as having lost his belief in his own humane and rational powers, and in his ability to achieve a just order. Man, they argue, has become disillusioned by economic inequalities and instability, political oppression, frequent and barbaric wars, the threat of thermonuclear annihilation in the quantum of "megamorts," and by the sight of men fleeing from democracy to totalitarianism. In the face of all this, modern man has lost much of his faith in progress, utopia, and himself. He no longer has confidence that human reason and humane spirit are capable of effective expression through the grand designs of political ideology.[16]

It is a bit of wishful, if not ideological, thinking to assume that the decline of raw want eliminates significant class conflict. The class system is relative: even in the most affluent society rewards remain unequal and class conflict persists, even if less intensely. In Western countries, with high levels of political and socioeconomic development, significant numbers of people have yet to attain "full citizenship," and ideology neither is irrelevant to their aspirations nor do its appeals fall on deaf ears. Even if for some the fundamental problems of the Industrial Revolution have been solved in the West, the fundamental problems of the Technological Revolution have moved from the horizon to our midst. Moreover, while ideology may have declined in advanced Western societies, the fundamental problems of the Industrial Revolution have not been solved in most of the world, where ideology remains a significant component in the struggle for national inde-

---

[14] Gustav Bergmann, "Ideology," *The Metaphysics of Logical Positivism* (New York: Longmans, Green, 1954). Aron, Bell, and Lipset also make this point.

[15] Barrington Moore, Jr., *Political Power and Social Theory* (Cambridge, Mass.: Harvard University Press, 1958), p. 183.

[16] Alfred Cobban, "The Decline of Political Theory," *Political Science Quarterly,* LXVIII (September, 1953), 321–337; and Judith Shklar, *After Utopia: The Decline of Political Faith* (Princeton, N.J.: Princeton University Press, 1957). Cf. Neal Riemer, *The Revival of Democratic Theory* (New York: Appleton-Century-Crofts, 1962).

pendence and development. Indeed, the problems of the underdeveloped
world are complicated further by international conflict in which ideology remains a force. Finally, as an instrument through which men define and establish their goals and the means to achieve them, ideology remains an
important component of politics. In *The Revolt of the Masses,* Ortega y
Gasset wrote of the purposelessness resulting from the absence of ideology:

we live at a time when man believes himself fabulously capable of creation, but
he does not know what to create. Lord of all things, he is not lord of himself.
He feels lost amid his own abundance. With more means at his disposal, more
knowledge, more techniques than ever, it turns out that the world today goes the
same way as the worst of worlds that have been; it simply drifts.[17]

With increased means at man's disposal—economic, political, organizational, military, medical, scientific, etc.—questions of the goals or ends to
which these means will be committed assume greater importance than ever
and open the way for a renaissance of ideology. The vast powers man
possesses are double-edged. Whether men beat swords into plowshares or
plowshares into swords, whether supersonic transport brings more men together faster for common survival or destruction, whether nuclear energy
is used to heat or incinerate the cities of man—all depend to a significant
degree upon the values and purposes men create for themselves. Ideology,
like oceans, can both separate and join men and societies, bring them to
conflict as well as cooperation. By his unique capacities and needs man has
transformed mankind into humanity and the earth into a human habitation,
but the process can be reversed. Always at the edge, nature lies in wait
ready to claim the splendid ruins and repossess the earth in an ultimate judgment. Our ideologies may well help determine the outcome.

Bibliography

Aiden, Henry D. "The Revolt Against Ideology." *Commentary,* XXXVII (April,
1964), 29–39.
Allardt, E., and Y. Littunen, eds. *Cleavages, Ideologies, and Party Systems.* Hel-
sinki: The Westmarck Society, 1964.
Aron, Raymond. *The Industrial Society: Three Essays on Ideology and Devel-
opment.* New York: Frederick A. Praeger, 1967.
Aron, Raymond. *The Opium of the Intellectuals.* New York: W. W. Norton,
1962.
Bell, Daniel. *The End of Ideology.* New York: Free Press, 1960.
Bell, Daniel, and Henry D. Aiken. "Ideology—A Debate." *Commentary,*
XXXVII (October, 1964), 69–76.

[17] Ortega y Gasset (New York: W. W. Norton, 1932), p. 47.

Dahl, Robert A., ed. *Political Oppositions in Western Democracies.* New Haven: Yale University Press, 1966.

Lane, Robert E. "The Politics of Consensus in an Age of Affluence," *American Political Science Review,* LIX (December, 1965), 874–95.

LaPalombara, Joseph. "Decline of Ideology: A Dissent and an Interpretation," *American Political Science Review,* LX (March, 1966), 5–16.

Lipset, Seymour Martin. "The Changing Class Structure and Contemporary European Politics." *Daedalus,* XCIII (Winter, 1964), 271–303.

Lipset, Seymour Martin. *Political Man: The Social Bases of Politics.* Garden City, N.Y.: Doubleday, 1960.

Rejai, Mostafa, ed. *Decline of Ideology?* New York: Atherton, 1971.

Shils, Edward. "The End of Ideology?" *Encounter,* V (November, 1955), 52–58.

Tarrow, Sidney. "Economic Development and the Transformation of the Italian Party System," *Comparative Politics,* I (January, 1969), 161–83.

Tucker, Robert C. "The Deradicalization of Marxist Movements," *American Political Science Review,* LXI (June, 1967), 343–58.

Waxman, Chaim I., ed. *The End of Ideology Debate.* New York: Funk & Wagnalls, 1968.

Young, James P. *The Politics of Affluence: Ideology in the United States Since World War II.* San Francisco: Chandler, 1968.

Index

Capitalism (*Cont.*)
  as Marx's chief interest, 101
  myth and reality, 230–232
  political creed of, 220–222
  and socialism, converging of, 273–276
  in United States, 247
  weakest link, Russia as, 108
"Capitalism" (term), definitions of, 219
Capitalist system, central features of, 219
Carriers, ideological, defined, 10–11
Castro, Fidel
  early activities of, 166ff.
  as leader in search of a movement, 167
  theories of Cuban revolution, 169
  "true democracy" of, 179
CCP. *See* Chinese Communist Party
Censorship. *See* Communications, control of
Centralization, and Soviet industry, 127
Chiang Kai-shek, 146
  coup in Shanghai (1927), 148
  establishing national government, 150
  five campaigns to wipe out communists, 150
  purge in Kuomintang, 148
China
  communism in, 144–157
    doctrine formalized, 152–157
    reasons for success of, 152
    strategy, evolution of, 146–152
    and totalitarianism, 50
  Western penetration of, 145
  "White" (KMT) regime, and Mao, 149
Chinese Communist Party (CCP), 147
  Central Committee at Tsunyi, and Mao Tse-tung, 150
  destruction of proletarian base, 148
  and Sun Yat-sen's stand against imperialism and feudalism, 148
"Christian socialists" in 19th-century England, 263–264
Christianity, and democracy, 191, 207
Citizens, in Athenian democracy, 189, 190
Civil war
  China, 151–152
  Russian, of 1918–21, 113
Cochinchina. *See* Vietnam, South
Coexistence, peaceful, 138
Collectivization
  opposition to, by small Russian farmers, 118–119
  feeling against Stalin, 126
  victims of, 119

Collectivization-industrialization, 123
  of Russian communism, 115
  "survivors" of, 125
Colonialism
  French, in Indochina, 157, 159
  and guerrilla warfare, 156
  19th-century, cheap raw materials and labor, 106–107
  Russian, 111n
Comintern, and communist party in China, 147
Communal society, 261
Communications
  control of, by Hitler, 88
  in fascism, 71
  monopoly of, as totalitarian concept, 46–48
  See also Media; Propaganda
Communism
  Chinese, 144–157
  Cuban, 164–172
  Guerrilla, 142–174
  North Vietnamese, 157–164
  Soviet, 95–140
Communist ideologies
  changing models, 125–127
  Leninist actualization, 106–112
  Stalinist reality, 112–117
  varieties of, 95
Communist Manifesto, 104, 247
Communist Party, 43
  controlled by Lenin, 113
  as mass organization (Marx), 108
  Marxism as justification of power, 24
  Russian, fear of Stalin, 126
    relations with Nazis and fascists, 133
    role of, 132–136
Communist state, specific details of, 102
Competition
  in capitalist system, 235
  substitute products and services, 234
  and German Social Democrat Party, 267
  political, and democratic popular control, 200–201
  under socialism, vs. capitalism, 268–269
Conflict(s)
  higher law vs. civil law, 187
  of ideologies, 13
    and intragenerational relations, 13
    control as function of, 16–17
  intranational, communist view of, 40
  political, in democracy, 185
    and unanimity, 186

in *Mein Kampf,* 81, 82
as scapegoat, 40
in Soviet Union, as national group, 111
John Birch Society, 92
as radical right model, 283, 285

Keynes, John Maynard, economic prophecy of, 228–229
American Keynesians, 229
and practical socialism, 270
KGB (Soviet Union). See Police, in totalitarian state
Khan, Ayub (Pakistan), scheme of basic democracies, 178–179
Khrushchev, Nikita S., 132
and class lines, 136
and freedom, 131
and goal of communism, 123–124
and Great Purge of Stalin, 119
opposing Stalinism, 126
and "peaceful coexistence," 138
and Russian masses, 124
"Secret Speech" (1956), 126, 133
Kingsley, Charles, conception of Christian democracy, 263–264
KMT. See Kuomintang
Komsomal (Soviet). *See* Youth, in totalitarian state
Kuomintang, 146, 148
adopting the Three People's Principles, 151
isolation of the masses, 155

Labor
and creation of values, 97
nazification of, 89
and "surplus value," 104
Labour Party, British, and 1945 nationalization, 269
Laissez-faire, theory vs. practice, 220
Laski, Harold, 251
Lasswell, Harold D., on ideology and utopia, 24, 25
Latin America, and Cuban revolution, 169–170, 173
Leaders
future, Soviet, 135
of ideology, 1-2
totalitarian, access to power, 43
crucial role of, 60
qualities of, 93
Leadership
democratic, and representation concept, 198–199

military and political, combined in Fidel Castro, 171–172
personalized, in Italian politics, 61
Soviet, post-Stalin, 126
Lebensraum. See Living space
Left
extremism, 287–296
term, origin of, 2
totalitarianism of, 36
See also New Left
Lenin, Vladimir Ilyich, 13
actualization of Marxism, 106–112
arrival upon political scene (1890's), 106
death of (1924), and departure from Marxist model, 113
on guerrilla warfare, 143
maintaining revolution in Russia, 109
and masses, 116, 118
and national differences, 110
and new concept of state, 37
and "peaceful coexistence," 130n
pragmatic influence, 133n
and the Revolution of 1917, 107
and role of peasantry, 153
Leninism, 106–112
Leninist-Stalinist theory, and role of peasantry, 153
Liberals
origin of term, 2
in social crisis, 9
Liberty. *See* Freedom
Lindsay, A. D.
on democracy, ideal, 185
revisionism of, 197
Lipset, Seymour Martin
on ideological decline, 298
popular control model of, 201, 203
on socioeconomic conditions, in democracy, 208–209
in totalitarianism, 54–55
Literary life
soviet, during Stalin period, 128–129
pre-Stalinist, 129
Living space
Folkish State concept, 84
Russia, 124
Locke, John
and democratic revolution, 193
on political power, 181
and principle of consent, 183

McCarthy, Joseph R., 284–285
McClosky, Herbert, on consensus in democracy, 210–211